WOMEN AND THE FUTURE

Women and the Future

Changing Sex Roles in Modern America

Janet Zollinger Giele

THE FREE PRESS
A Division of Macmillan Publishing Co., Inc.
NEW YORK

Collier Macmillan Publishers
LONDON

The Free Press
A Division of Macmillan Publishing Co., Inc.
866 Third Avenue, New York, N.Y. 10022

Collier Macmillan Canada, Ltd.

First Free Press Paperback Edition 1979

Library of Congress Catalog Card Number: 77-2472

Printed in the United States of America

printing number

HC   3   4   5   6   7   8   9   10

SC   1   2   3   4   5   6   7   8   9   10

Library of Congress Cataloging in Publication Data

Giele, Janet Zollinger.
  Women and the future.

  Bibliography: p.
  Includes index.
  1. Women's rights—United States.
2. Women—Employment—United States. 3. Education
of women—United States. 4. Sex role. I. Title.
HQ1426.G44   301.41'2'0973   77-2472
ISBN 0-02-911700-3
ISBN 0-02-911690-2 pbk.

Parts of Chapter 7 have appeared originally in "Centuries of Womanhood: An Evolutionary Perspective on the Feminine Role," by Janet Z. Giele in *Women's Studies*, vol. 1, no. 1, and appear here with the permission of the publisher, Gordon and Breach, London.

The diagram on page 314 originally appeared in "New Developments in Research on Women," by Janet Z. Giele as an introductory essay to *The Feminine Character* by Viola Klein, © 1972 by the Board of Trustees of the University of Illinois.

CONTENTS

FOREWORD

The Women's Movement of today is a world-wide phenomenon strongly tied to past efforts to promote equal rights for human beings, regardless of sex. In the United States, this movement gained new momentum in the 1960s and carried forward into the 1970s with vigor. It has had no single organization and no single leadership, and it is characterized by a broad spectrum of opinion and attitude and by equally diverse activities that have affected all segments of society.

In 1972, President McGeorge Bundy of the Ford Foundation appointed a special staff Task Force to study the origins and growth of the Women's Movement and to consider how the Foundation might be useful in assisting the effort to reduce discrimination based on sex. That group wrote a report recommending increased commitments by the Foundation to the cause of women's rights along lines that were subsequently followed.

In the course of its work the Task Force sought advice and help from numerous persons outside the Foundation. Dr. Janet Z. Giele, the author of this book, served as a special consultant to the Task Force, preparing papers for its consideration on a variety of topics and meeting with it to discuss such broad subjects as the changing role of women in the family, women and education, and the economic position of women.

Dr. Giele was encouraged by the Foundation staff to expand the scope of her analysis to include selected countries other than the United States. Several papers by selected authors were commissioned and became the basis for another book published in 1977 and co-edited by Dr. Giele and Dr. Audrey C. Smock. That volume, *Women: Roles and Status in Eight Countries*, John Wiley and Sons, offers insights into women's needs and problems in countries as diverse as Poland and Bangladesh.

Dr. Giele also decided to extend her research and analysis beyond what had been possible in preparing papers for the Foundation's Task Force on Women. What now appears in *Women and the Future* is the result of several years of scholarly work beyond her consultancy at the Foundation and the papers growing from it. This book represents an attempt to understand today's fundamental changes in women's roles and their effects on American society.

We are delighted to have played a role in starting the preparation of this book. While Dr. Giele has been working on it, we have moved into a larger grant-making program in the interest of equality for women. Our publication of 1975 entitled *That 51 Percent* is a record of the first few years of that program. We hope that Dr. Giele or someone carrying her torch will write in the year 2000 a follow-up volume to this one. In my view the present volume provides a new plateau for discussion of the nature and effects of the Women's Movement in the latter half of the twentieth century.

Harold Howe II
Vice President for Education and Research
The Ford Foundation

PREFACE

When in the 1950s I began my dissertation on the nineteenth-century suffrage and temperance women, there was no active women's movement. The word "feminist" had a somewhat pejorative ring to it. But in a few short years women's consciousness of themselves and their roles has revived to such an extent that the fervor of the nineteenth-century women no longer seems a thing of the past. It is here again, a groundswell that will not be short-lived, for the current changes in women's status are merely the tip of an iceberg. Ultimately these changes will touch men's roles and eventually they will reach into the very institutional fabric of the whole society creating a movement that may endure for decades.

This book is the culmination of an intellectual odyssey that I began in the spring of 1972 with a controversial paper entitled "Women's Strengths: An Affirmation" delivered to a conference at Radcliffe College. In that paper I was concerned to present some of the distinctive qualities and values of women that need to be given higher priority in society's current value hierarchy. The qualities that I mentioned were women's interest in facilitating growth rather than mastering nature, in cooperation rather than domination, in making peace rather than war, and in maintaining openness to mystery and intuition rather than relying exclusively on technical data and known facts. Some of my friends and colleagues were embarrassed if not outraged by my suggestion that women had anything special or different to offer society, especially since the qualities that I mentioned are frequently judged weaknesses.* But I have persisted in my view. This book is my attempt to present the nature of what the world would be if the values for which women have traditionally stood were given larger place.

Each chapter rests on the same underlying paradigm that points to the ultimate need for change in the institutions and values of the

* Jean Baker Miller in her book *Toward a New Psychology of Women* (Boston: Beacon Press, 1976, p. 27) provides corroboration that women have distinctive strengths. But as she says, these "strengths" (vulnerability, weakness, helplessness) have been called "weakness" and even women themselves have so interpreted them.

larger society. I grant that men and women, as all other major social categories of people, are different in important ways. But this does not negate the possibility of social justice and equality between the sexes. To realize that end a reconfiguration of roles, rewards, and cultural values is required. Otherwise, given our present system, women, the disadvantaged group, are consistently aligned with a lower rung on the social ladder, and men, the advantaged group, garner unequal privilege. This analysis is just as relevant to rich and poor, white and black, or young and old. In each case society has ranked functional positions according to a stratified hierarchy rather than on a plane that recognizes the equality of functional interdependence based on differences.

At present women are disproportionately found in peripheral positions that society has undervalued; men, on the other hand, are more frequently found in core positions that draw attention and command greater social rewards. Two major strategies for change follow from this analysis. Society can make a greater effort to redistribute *persons* (women and men) between the core and the periphery; our term for this strategy is *affirmative action*. A more radical approach is for society to redistribute the *rewards* between the core and periphery, replacing the present hierarchical relation between them with an equalitarian perspective that recognizes functional interdependence. This strategy is commonly called *changing the whole system*. Historically, Americans have come to affirmative action first, probably because it requires less fundamental change. Ultimately, however, I believe that present changes already set in motion will force a more far-reaching critique of all kinds of hierarchy and stratification.

In connection with these two types of change, I see the future challenge to society as one of learning how to engage in both affirmative action and institutional change. First, we have to learn how to promote *crossover between men's and women's roles*, and ultimately between all of the core and all of the periphery. Second, these changes will only be accomplished if there is a *reconfiguration of transcendent values to express complementarity and interdependence* rather than priority and social hierarchy.

Each of the following chapters on population, government, economy, family, and education proceeds by first describing current changes in men's and women's roles. Then each examines the environment in which these roles are imbedded—the social organization, laws and institutional regulations, and finally the most abstract political, economic, and social values. The last chapter works in the opposite direction. It begins at the most abstract cultural level—new images of women and men—spells out their specification, and finally rests with current changes in the individual personalities of males and females. This final chapter completes the future equalitarian society that I envision because it says something about the human being, the "modal personality," who will help to create and maintain social justice and equality. Taken in their entirety, these chapters represent not merely a utopian vision. They are a projection of changes already in progress.

This book is a direct outgrowth of my work from 1972 to 1974 with the Ford Foundation's Task Force on Equal Rights and Responsibilities for Women. I wish to thank Harold Howe, the chairman, and all the members of the Task Force for the education that they gave me in policy analysis. Particular mention is due Mariam Chamberlain who throughout the project showed remarkable faith that such a large undertaking was worth the effort. In her role as chairman of a successor committee to the Task Force she continued to facilitate my work until the book could appear.

Without generous help from a variety of colleagues and friends the interdisciplinary efforts required could not have been successful. To Alice S. Rossi and Joseph Pleck I owe particular debt for the complete and critical reading that each gave to a number of chapters. Joseph Pleck read the entire book and brought many new references to my attention. Alice Rossi read an early version of the manuscript and gave judicious yet supportive comment on later versions of the introductory and family chapters. Lorraine Klerman read parts of chapter one for accuracy. Irene Murphy, Eileen McDonagh, and Kay Lehman Schlotzman helped me in chapter two to integrate some of the major concepts of political science with a sociological analysis of changing sex roles in politics. Eli Ginzburg commented on an early version of the chapter on women in the economy; my long-time friend and colleague Hilda Kahne helped to correct and update a much later version. Both family chapters had the benefit of comments by Mary Ann Glendon, Isabel V. Sawhill, and Joan Waring. The education chapter was read by Patricia Albjerg Graham, Marion Kilson, Talcott Parsons, and Pamela Roby; Bernice Sandler and Shirley McCune commented on a much earlier version. Catharine Stimpson raised penetrating questions on the final chapter from the perspective of literature and the arts; Miriam Johnson alerted me to the several meanings of androgyny; and Eleanor McLaughlin shared her insights from the history of religion. It was, of course, impossible to make all the changes that some readers desired. For that reason I, rather than they, must be held responsible for what here finally appears.

To several institutions I am grateful for the support given me during completion of the research and writing: the Radcliffe Institute where the major part of the work was carried out, the Harvard Department of Sociology where in 1974-75 I held a Ford Faculty Fellowship for Research on the Role of Women in Society, and the Heller School of Brandeis University where the work was completed. In addition Sheryl Larsen provided intelligent research assistance during the first years of the project and Christie Olson gave a cheerful and competent hand with technical and clerical tasks at the end. As early as 1972 Gladys Topkis showed an interest in this book. It is a pleasure now to acknowledge her strong editorial support, which has culminated with publication by the Free Press.

Finally, however, it is with a small private company that the tension and joy of creative endeavor ultimately rest. I thank Hilda Dewsnap and June Blanchette for helping me at home and making this work possible. David Giele and our children Elizabeth and Benjamin praised and supported me as well as spurred me on with their impatience for the end. My parents Albert and Ellen Zollinger, along with my husband, have given me the hopeful alternative vision of reality imbedded in this book. I strongly believe that such a positive image of future possibilities is necessary to guide our efforts toward realization of equality, not only for women, but for other disadvantaged and undervalued groups as well.

Janet Zollinger Giele
Heller School for Studies in Social Welfare
Brandeis University

WOMEN AND THE FUTURE

1

REVOLUTION IN SEX ROLES

It was the bourgeoisie which embodied the expansive forces that ended the limitations laid on society by the feudal structure of the Middle Ages. . . . So perhaps it is time for a new force to venture out. A female revolution? Not exclusively by any means. But because women are the repository of the largest store of unused abilities they will surely be a primary source and resource of ideas and energy

—Elizabeth Janeway, *Between Myth and Morning*, 1974.

I view the current restructuring of sex roles as no less epochal than the restructuring of the class system which was one of the first consequences of the industrial revolution

—Jessie Bernard, *Women, Wives, Mothers*, 1975.

The future of women in the United States today is not simply a "woman's problem," nor is it an issue only for highly educated or professional women. Instead, changes in sex roles are a blow to all the established institutions of society and affect men and women alike—ordinary workers as well as the educated and professional elite.

The "woman problem" of the last decade has been viewed primarily from the perspective of what wrongs have been done to women, what discrimination they have borne, and how the system should be changed to treat them more fairly. Some people who are sympathetic to these themes, however, now believe that it is time to ask a much larger question: Can American society survive in its present form, and if it cannot and must change, what roles will women and men take in the future? Consider the changes said to be needed in limiting energy use, discouraging childbearing, and redistributing income and power. The consequences add up to a revolution in the structure of the larger society. A revolution in sex roles could be a concomitant of this larger system change—a central and crucial part of the dynamic that will help the larger revolution to occur.

1

A thoroughgoing change in sex roles implies altering the structure of family and work, plus a far more radical reordering of social priorities than is usually suggested by efforts to uproot discrimination against women or to give women equal protection under the law. Nothing less than a new social contract is at issue. It can use elements of our past heritage, but it must also take into account present population pressures, the shortage of resources, and the fact that we now live in a human social system of global proportions.

If the sex-role revolution has a crucial survival value, a general theory is needed to show what its effects will be. How will the technology and social structure of the future have to change if we are to survive? How will political representation need to be altered? How must cultural goals and values be reordered? And, in particular, how do these new requirements mesh with a revolution in the roles of individual women and men? When we try to answer these questions, it becomes obvious that revolution need not be merely the instrument of a special-interest group, as some have contended, but may act on behalf of the public interest as well.

Only when the questions are posed in this way does it seem likely that men will join with women on other than purely chivalrous grounds to realize the survival stakes that all humanity have in the women's revolution.

A THEORY OF SOCIETY AND SEX ROLES

Before considering the challenges that future Americans will face and their implications for women, we must deal with the striking claims presented at the outset of this chapter. Those predictions, independently made by two of the most influential feminist writers of our day, augur a revolution in sex roles that is comparable in significance to the French Revolution of 1789 or the Industrial Revolution of the early nineteenth century. The first revolution set the bourgeoisie against the feudal order and gave rise to the modern state. The second revolution set the working class against the bourgeoisie and established the basis for the modern economy. How can a twentieth-century revolution in sex roles be comparable to these in scope and significance?

The survival of a society in large part rests on the roles of individuals who are linked to the economic and distributive structure of the whole system. At present these individual roles are powerfully shaped by sex. Yet many women are now in a situation where they no longer simply accept the duties and obligations traditionally assigned to them. They press for piecemeal changes within their families or at their jobs. Some try to strike new individual role bargains within particular family and work settings and to get corporations and government agencies to pay greater attention to their needs. Over time, their individual solutions promise to affect larger economic, social, and educational institutions.

At the same time, environmental challenges coincide with women's rebellion from within. Some changes required for survival, such as population control, are congruent with change in sex roles that diminish traditional stereotypes. Other changes, such as energy conservation, adequate food production, or redistribution of income between rich and poor, may require even more fundamental reorganization of social institutions, as well as change in sex roles. How to change sex roles in the light of a dawning global age is still an unanswered question. If a new order does arise that balances world needs against world resources and simultaneously accomplishes fundamental change in sex roles, the results will indeed be revolutionary.

WHICH PARADIGM?

What form of analysis is appropriate to a discussion of whether women's roles are changing and whether society should also change?

Thomas Kuhn (1962) employed the term "paradigm" to describe the major changes in outlook that accompany scientific revolutions. "Paradigm" refers to the kind of general intellectual outlook that scholars consider appropriate for studying a particular phenomenon. The Copernican Revolution, for example, made it acceptable for scholars to think of the sun, rather than the earth, as the center of the universe. The Copernican paradigm overturned the earth-centered paradigm of the ancients because it could account for many more of the facts.

In studying women's changing roles, one paradigm may be better than another for describing changes in individuals and the larger society. We consider here the Marxist and functionalist explanations of the past and propose an evolutionary theory as being more illuminating.

Class struggle.

A classic paradigm for explaining social change is the Marxist model of class struggle. Both Jessie Bernard and Elizabeth Janeway describe the current sex-role change as a "revolution." Each calls to mind a class struggle of the kind that Marx saw in both the revolution of the bourgeoisie and that of the workers. For Marx the dynamic of revolution was a conflict of interests. When the oppressed saw that it was truly in their interest to throw over their oppressors, their consciousness was raised; they acted on behalf of their own class and mounted a revolution, after which they established their own alternative values as the legitimate order. One sociologist, Randall Collins (1971), has recently used this paradigm to describe the case of employment discrimination against women. Male employers discriminate against women employees because it is in their interest to do so; women have not resisted effectively because they are neither fully aware nor sufficiently organized to change the system. Thus, in this instance, sexual stratification appears to be another form of class stratification, and sexual struggle a form of class struggle (cf. Mitchell, 1971; Rowbatham, 1973).

But other references to class oppression and class revolution are not equally persuasive when applied to questions of women's disadvantage. For one thing, women frequently live with men, their "oppressors," and vicariously or directly share with them the benefits of the males' privileged position. Another difficulty is that the female social category is itself so crosscut by significant class interests, caused by differences of wealth, education, occupation, and family position, that a revolution of women against men in a Marxist vision of class war does not seem plausible. Furthermore, the nature of women's "oppression" is ironic. It is in many cases that of conspicuous leisure or conspicuous consumption, as Veblen (1899) described it. So the Marxist paradigm presents difficulties for envisioning what a sex-role revolution should be like, at least at the present moment.

Functionalism.

The major recent paradigm in the social sciences competing with the Marxist theory has been functionalism. The functionalist framework explains a particular social pattern by showing how it contributes to survival. If a pattern leads to maladaptive behavior, it will presumably be dropped. All societies have some division of labor that assures food production, defense, settlement of disputes, reproduction, and the handling of fear and anxiety. Sociologists and anthropologists, from Durkheim (1893) to modern functionalists (Aberle et al., 1950), have shown that all societies have an economy, a government, a family system, and a religious system that divide and perform these necessary functions.

It is a reasonable extension of functionalist theories to assume that there is some survival value in the division of tasks between the sexes. Most social scientists until 1960 used functionalist theories to explain why women achieved less prominence than men. Scientists espousing these explanations included anthropologists, psychologists,

and sociologists. Thus anthropologist Margaret Mead observed in
Male and Female (1949) that sex roles and temperament share
certain similarities across societies because only girls can be mothers
whereas boys have to learn compensatory forms of achievement. The
sociologist Talcott Parsons (1942) suggested that competing demands
of family and work are best handled by separating the instrumental
roles of men at work from the expressive roles of women in the
family. Psychologists were heavily influenced by Freud's emphasis on
the psychic consequences of the differences between male and female anatomies.

Betty Friedan (1963) found that these theories had a stultifying
effect on women in the postwar era. She lumped them all together in
an intellectual outlook that she termed the "functionalist freeze."
Friedan, like many social scientists, criticized the built-in conserva-
tism of functionalist theory. By looking for the adaptive features of
present and past structures, functionalists were in danger of over-
looking signs of dysfunction and conflict; their interest was heavier
on the side of analyzing sources of stability than sources of change.
Functional analysis of sex roles, while accounting fairly well for
social conditions during the 1950s under the prevailing "feminine
mystique," failed to measure the extent of discomfort and malaise
under that system and utterly missed prediction of the new feminist
movement that dawned in the 1960s.

Like all paradigms, the Marxist and functionalist modes of analysis still explain some phenomena fairly well under certain conditions.
But they provoke considerable intellectual strain when applied to
current feminist activity, and they do not seem particularly helpful
when it comes to making future predictions about a sex-role
revolution.

Continuous adaptation and selection.
Ernst Mayr (1976:3), a theorist of biological evolution, has said
that all evolutionary change is a two-step process: The first step is
the production of genetic variation through mutation and the like;
and the second step is the sorting and selection of successful individual variants. Evolutionary models of social change combine the best
features of both Marxist and functionalist theories. As a theory of
social evolution, Marxist theory helps explain the production of
cultural variations through its concept of special class interests.
Functionalist theory helps explain the selection of adaptive behaviors. However, the evolutionary paradigm goes beyond either of the
two earlier theories by emphasizing the importance of changing
environmental imperatives. New environmental challenges elicit a
variety of human responses which are, in the Darwinian sense, "se-

lected" over time if they contribute to survival (Alland, 1972: 150-151).

Social scientists have recently demonstrated considerable agreement that the evolutionary paradigm is helpful to an understanding of human social behavior. Psychologist B. F. Skinner (1953) says that adaptive behavior is "reinforced" over the long run. Robert LeVine (1969, 1973) suggests that the personality types associated with different cultures are in part a result of the selective process:

[C]ould it be that the greater potential for self-reliance and achievement of children raised in small families helped give small families a selective advantage in hunting and gathering groups? Or perhaps more reasonably, could it be that the greater potential for obedience and responsibility of children raised in large families contributed to the selective advantage of large domestic groups once the food-producing revolution had occurred? These are difficult problems to research, but they raise the possibility that the structure of the primary group in which children are raised might be more tightly adapted to ecological pressures than is readily apparent, with the personality outcome of early primary group experience being a factor in the evolution of more adaptive forms. [LeVine, 1969: 536-537]

Anthropologists and sociologists have recently extended the evolutionary mode of analysis to explain how different technologies and forms of social organization are selected under different environmental conditions. They find that whether a society hunts and gathers, fishes, or cultivates fields is related to local environmental conditions and the available technology. Ultimately, the societies that survive are the ones most able to compete successfully with others that are less well adapted (Lenski, 1966, 1970, 1975; Parsons, 1966, 1971; Linares et al., 1975).

Efforts to apply this modern evolutionary paradigm to the phenomenon of sex roles have only begun. One of the most stimulating examples is provided by the Danish economist Ester Boserup in her study of *Woman's Role in Economic Development* (1970). Boserup relates the roles of women to the system of economic production and ultimately to population pressure on the land. Where the environment is lush and the population sparse, men can hunt and women gather in fairly leisurely fashion. Where population rises to dense proportions and the environment is favorable, intensive systems of agriculture and irrigation are developed, as they are in parts of Southeast Asia, requiring heavy productive effort by both women and men. Under conditions of intermediate population pressure and favorable environmental conditions, agrarian systems develop that put men behind a plow and keep women close to home and courtyard, confined to family activities.

Boserup's work is limited, however, in that it analyzes primarily farming systems and the roles of women under rural conditions or migration to the city. No comparable analysis exists yet for understanding the sexual division of labor in primarily industrial and urban societies, although a rough outline is beginning to emerge (Giele, 1977: 3-31). Nor has anyone yet made a systematic prediction about what future sex roles will be like in the developed world. The clearest suggestions are found in the writings of demographers, population theorists, ecologists, and economists, all scholars who happen to be concerned with the limits of growth. Before turning to their work, however, it should be noted that a conservative analysis is possible using the Darwinian paradigm. Some examples follow.

CONSERVATIVE POSSIBILITIES

Evolutionary thinking and the logic of natural selection have socially conservative implications if they are confined to the natural order and exclude the cultural. Darwin himself, in *The Descent of Man and Natural Selection in Relation to Sex* (1890), gave extended consideration to sex differences—why the male bird is more brightly colored than the female bird, why the human male is larger and heavier than the human female, and so on. But Darwin limited himself to concern with *biologically* heritable characteristics and behaviors. He did not consider *culturally* heritable characteristics (except insofar as he believed in the heritability of acquired characteristics), nor was it in his realm to wonder why some human cultures select one kind of sex-role constellation to pass on from generation to generation while other societies have quite different patterns. In addition, he assumed that the environment itself changes only very slowly; he gave no special attention to man's ability to change the environment, although he gave a number of examples from the breeding of domestic animals to illustrate "artificial selection."

Natural selection, as it operates in relation to sex, determines what secondary sex characteristics a male must have to predominate over rival males. The successful male leaves more offspring; the traits that enable him to win the female or be chosen by her are thus subject to sexual selection over time. The process explains not so much those adaptations which foster survival of the whole species as the "advantage which certain individuals have over others of the same sex and species solely in respect of reproduction" (Darwin, 1890: 209). Secondary sex differences, according to Darwin, arise because the female exercises choice among males. Her choice is based probably not solely on appearance but also on ability to defend and support her. It is here that the process of selection of sexual characteristics operates, for "such well-endowed pairs would commonly rear a larger number of offspring than the less favored" (Darwin, 1890:599).

Despite the fact that Darwin was working without knowledge of modern genetics, his logic in explaining sexual selection among the lower orders of animals generally stands today, but elaborated now by modern mathematical and observational methods (Trivers, 1972). Darwin's assumption about the importance of female choice has been confirmed; a number of male ornaments and attractants seem to be due to sexual selection rather than to natural selection. However, Darwin was wrong in assuming that most aspects of sexual differences are to be explained by their contribution to differential reproductive success. Instead, natural selection rather than sexual selection explains a number of differences in animals that appear to contribute to their natural protection and long-term survival (Mayr, 1972).

When applied to human beings, both sexual selection and natural selection can be used to justify a conservative position. It can be reasoned that sexual selection will favor the female who finds a strong and provident husband and does not delay or inhibit her childbearing or reduce maternal behavior on account of conflicting goals. She will leave many healthy offspring who reproduce her characteristics. Such popular works as that of Lionel Tiger (1969) on natural male competitiveness in groups rely on this conservative application of the evolutionary model.

Natural selection can also be used to justify the present division of labor between males and females. George Gilder in *Sexual Suicide* (1973: 263–264) reasons as follows:

> Nonetheless, woman's place *is* in the home, and she does her best when she can get the man there too. That she cannot easily do alone. The society has to provide a role for him, usually as provider, that connects him to the family in a masculine way. . . . The fact is that there is no way that women can escape their supreme responsibilities in civilized societies without endangering civilization itself.

The foregoing examples focus primarily on the biological advantage in present-day sex roles. Furthermore, they assume an ahistorical world in which cultural difference and social change are ignored. When we take the wider vantage point, however, looking at survival of the whole species, and include natural selection of *cultural* arrangements as well as *biological* traits, contemporary application of the Darwinian model suddenly becomes revolutionary, for it holds forth a radical perspective on present-day sex roles.

REVOLUTIONARY POTENTIAL IN THE EVOLUTIONARY
MODEL

The contemporary human predicament has been described as the "closing circle" (Commoner, 1971). World population is multiplying at a phenomenal rate. The developed countries are drawing heavily on natural resources to produce the energy and goods required for enlargement of their gross national product (G.N.P.). The earth is rapidly being depleted of nonrenewable resources. Even as supplies are running out, economic systems require more growth to sustain employment and provide a rising standard of living. A common measure of well-being has been GNP per capita. The GNP of both rich and poor countries grows at about the same rate, but populations grow at vastly different rates in the two types of nations. Poor countries with more rapid population growth will have much lower standards of living than those with a slower rate of growth. Furthermore, each unit added to GNP in the rich countries will buy less-needed goods, while each unit in the poor countries must be used for essentials. As a result, the rich countries are using limited resources at a rapid rate to produce many goods and services that are not necessities, while the scarcity of fertilizer and gasoline in the poor countries threatens to produce crop failures and starvation and helps to perpetuate the pattern of overpopulation that goes with poverty.

The threat of undifferentiated growth.
Among an expanding number of economists, a new paradigm of the economic system has begun to emerge. In an effort sponsored by the Club of Rome, these theorists have begun to spell out a vision of a "no-growth" or steady-state economy, where human societies could live within limits of the resources available (Meadows et al., 1972). As early as 1966, Kenneth Boulding wrote of the "Coming Spaceship Earth." A spaceship cannot take the atmosphere or any number of other "free" natural resources for granted. A "spaceship economy" has to pace its consumption of land and limited resources so that they will not run out. The estimate of how much is left depends on whether the GNP remains henceforth stationary—that is, if the same amount of resources are used per year a decade from now as were used this year; or whether the GNP grows somewhat each year, as is considered desirable by orthodox economists. If economic growth continues at its present rate, coal resources will run out in a matter of hundreds of years, and oil in a matter of decades (Hardesty, 1974; Daly, 1973).

In its most recent statement, the Club of Rome pictures the threat to the world economy as one of "undifferentiated" or cancerous growth. What is called for instead is differentiated or organic growth that will enable development to continue but at a rate that does not pollute the atmosphere irreparably, deplete resources, over-populate the earth, or fail to provide enough food (Mesarovic and Pestel, 1974: 3-4).

It should be recognized that most people, while they concede energy shortages, do not yet see the problem in crisis proportions. Some—like Daniel Bell (1976:207), who has intensively studied the postindustrial society and does see increased global interconnected-ness—still do not anticipate a shortage of energy or resources (Wade, 1975:35). Others concede that the physical resources of the earth are finite but believe that governments can intervene in the marketplace to set prices and regulate the market so that growth continues without endangering the finite supply of natural resources (Hueckel, 1975). However, even if the Club of Rome's rather grim global view is not fully accepted, it has articulated issues that seem increasingly familiar and less likely to go away. Several environmental problems seem to be rapidly approaching crisis proportions—population pressure, resource depletion, pollution, food scarcity, and the gap between rich and poor nations. Each of these problems is no longer capable of being solved by any one country alone. Each society or region has to draw on its particular cultural and material resources to find an appropriate differentiated role in the world system. More-over, the authors of *Mankind at the Turning Point* contend that each individual must eventually develop a sense of world consciousness, a new ethic in use of material resources, and a new sense of identifica-tion with future generations. Unless these developments occur, the future will be "deadly" (Mesarovic and Pestel, 1974: 55, 147).

Implications for sex roles.

The most obvious link between sex roles and new environmental conditions is in matters of sexual reproduction and population con-trol. But there are links with every other major global problem as well. In connection with food production, for example, one group of futurists recently argued that sex roles are of immense significance because women are the major food producers in many parts of the world; universally they are primarily responsible for food prepara-tion; and in poverty situations their needs are frequently served last. Moreover, women's education and their general status have an impact on their ability to work, to have other outlets for self-realization than childrearing, and thus ultimately affect population growth and the disparity in economic development between rich and poor coun-tries (Cordell et al., 1975: 371-372). Within our own country it is also apparent that the structure of sex roles has an impact not only on the biological activity of men and women as expressed through reproduction and population growth but also on economic production and consumption, family behavior, and the different educational, political, and cultural activities of men and women.

So far one of the most extended economic arguments for changing sex roles has been made by John Kenneth Galbraith (1973), who points to the past luxury and future dysfunctionality of having men concentrate on production while women specialize in consumption. The ability of the industrial economy to continue growth has in part rested on the achievement of creating a group of consumers and "crypto-servants" (i.e., women) who help to absorb a rising number of goods. Yet this achievement by men has been costly to women:

> The conversion of women into a crypto-servant class was an economic accomplishment of the first importance. Menially employed servants were available only to a minority of the preindustrial population; the servant-wife is available, democratically, to almost the entire present male population. Were the workers so employed subject to pecuniary compensation, they would be by far the largest single category in the labor force. The value of the services of housewives has been calculated, somewhat impressionistically, at roughly one fourth of total Gross National Product. The average housewife has been estimated (at 1970 wage rates for equivalent employments) to do about $257 worth of work a week or some $13,364 a year. If it were not for this service, all forms of household consumption would be limited by the time required to manage such consumption—to select, transport, prepare, repair, maintain, clean, service, store, protect, and otherwise perform the tasks that are associated with the consumption of goods. The servant role of women is critical for the expansion of consumption in the modern economy. That it is so generally approved, some recent modern dissent excepted, is a formidable tribute to the power of the convenient social virtue. [Galbraith, 1973: 33]

But if our society is to switch from a growth economy to one that recycles materials rather than just purchasing and then discarding them, women's and men's roles in production, consumption, and reproduction must be reorganized. Galbraith (1973: 235- 238) suggests some of the major steps to be taken:

> Without denying that the family retains other purposes, including those of love, sex, and child-rearing, it is no longer an economic necessity. With higher living standards it becomes, increasingly, a facilitating instrument for increased consumption. . . .
>
>   Marriage should no longer be a comprehensive trap. A tolerant society should not think ill of a woman who finds contentment in sexual intercourse, child-bearing, child-rearing, physical adornment, and administration of consumption. But it certainly should think ill of a society that offers no alternative—and which ascribes virtue to what is really the convenience of the producers of goods. . . .

Four things are of particular importance:

(1) Provision for professional care of children. . . .
(2) Greater individual choice in the work week and work year. . . .
(3) An end to the present monopoly of the better jobs in the techno-structure by males. . . .
(4) Provision of the requisite educational opportunity for women. . . .

What women's and men's roles in family and job will be like in the future system has not yet been worked out. The women's liberation movement is an important force in the current situation, for it has shaped not only laws and current social practice but also the attitudes of a whole generation. Implicit in the movement is a belief that more crossover should be possible between men's worlds and women's worlds and between work and leisure.

If women and men could each have some work and some leisure, some time outside the home and a comfortable amount of time in it, the tasks of reproduction, production, and consumption would still get done, but each sex would have a chance to share in the best of both worlds. In his essay "In Praise of Idleness," written in the 1930s, Bertrand Russell imagined a pin factory that improved production to the point where it could make more pins than the world needed. One solution was to lay off half the workers, making them completely idle, while having the others work a full eight-hour day. Yet, Russell observed: "In a sensible world, everybody concerned in the manufacture of pins would take to working four hours instead of eight, and everything else would go on as before" (quoted in Daly, 1973: 71). This latter solution is perhaps analogous to family-job crossover.

With each sex allowed to "cross over" to take on some of the duties of the other sex, the crisis of overproduction and overpopulation might possibly be averted. The next question is how such far-reaching change can be brought to pass.

SEX ROLES AND SOCIAL EVOLUTION

During prehistoric times, human beings had an advantage over other species in the struggle for survival because they were able to think ahead. They could also create a culture and impart it to succeeding generations. Their culture carried not only language, symbols, and tools but also values and moral ideas. Just as in the past, our current efforts to meet new environmental imperatives require that we use both our moral and our scientific capacities to help us survive.

It is perilous to the scientific enterprise to exclude moral and political considerations from discussions of current changes in sex role. This lesson had to be learned through experience with such scientific studies as the Coleman report on racial integration of schools. After reporting a number of complex and ambiguous findings, the report concluded:

> Policy with respect to racial integration should be made on the basis of *moral*, *legal*, and *political* considerations, not on the basis of integration's alleged effect on the short-term careers of either black or white students. Such effects are at best problematic, certainly modest, and probably non-existent. [Quoted in Grant, 1972: 118; italics added]

The social scientists who wrote the report spent more time on methodological issues than on moral dilemmas. Perhaps for that reason their findings are moot. Unlike the physicists and mathematicians who developed the atomic bomb, the engineers who put a man on the moon, or the doctors who helped stamp out polio, Coleman and his colleagues worked in an arena of competing social interests. Their studies thus failed to implement a single-minded social purpose. Not until that social purpose is agreed upon through a moral and political process can related scientific endeavors be more fruitful.

It is equally perilous to the moral and political process to ignore scientific knowledge. More than two decades ago, B. F. Skinner described the value of experimental work in psychology for evaluating cultural practices such as bringing up children.

> Perhaps the greatest contribution which a science may make to the evaluation of cultural practices is an insistence upon experimentation. We have no reason to suppose that any cultural practice is always right or wrong according to some principle or value regardless of the circumstances or that anyone can at any given time make an absolute evaluation of its survival value. As long as this is recognized, we are less likely to seize upon the hard and pat answer as an escape from indecision, and we are more likely to continue to modify cultural design in order to test the consequences. . . .
>
> Punishment gives quick results, and casual observation recommends its use, but we may be dissuaded from taking this momentary advantage if we know that progress towards a better solution is being made in some alternative course of action. It is difficult to resist punishing a child for conduct which it will eventually outgrow without punishment until we have adequate evidence of the process of growth. Only when developmental schedules have been carefully established by scientific investigation are we likely to put up with the inconvenience of forgoing punishment. The process of extinction also requires a good deal of time and is not clear to casual inspection. We are not likely to use the process effectively until the scientific study of simpler instances has assured us that a given end state will be reached. It is the business of science to make clear the consequences of various operations performed upon a system. [Skinner, 1953: 436, 435]

In matters of changing sex roles and societal evolution, scientific knowledge thus nurtures the process just as political and moral considerations do. Each of these influences develops through certain stages. Only when policy is fairly clear is the scientist able to advise effectively. And only when scientific knowledge has established a good descriptive and theoretical base can it aid the implementation of policy. The two processes must go hand in hand to facilitate any fundamental social change.

Both moral and scientific change appear to occur by upward movement through a social-control hierarchy that gradually encompasses wider domains and more general organizing principles of the society. The women's movement contributes actual experience and a will to foster change. Other segments of popular feeling either resist the movement or become sympathetic. The result is a moral change or a shift in the norms that eventually influences public policy. At the same time the scientific understanding of sex roles also changes. New descriptions and explanations of sex differences result in theories that suggest steps to accomplish particular goals. The link between political consciousness and scientific endeavor is forged in the domain of what Kenneth Boulding (1976) has called "normative science." Normative science relates fact to value and suggests ways to accomplish specific goals such as equality. "Normative science studies what should be instead of what can be," but it also takes into account the constraints defined by "what cannot be."

A NORMATIVE SCIENCE OF SEX ROLES

To construct a normative science of sex roles one has to look for the relationship among our evolving consciousness of sex inequality, our scientific understanding of sex differences, and our emerging political concerns, of which one is global survival. To map the ways in which these realms are intertwined, I have drawn heavily for a theoretical model on the work of sociologist Neil Smelser, who in his *Theory of Collective Behavior* (1963: 32) describes a hierarchy of social controls that both govern the spread of moral and scientific innovations in society and at the same time determine the order in which such innovations will be selected and institutionalized. Smelser posits four levels of the social order graduated from specific and limited to general and inclusive. I have adapted the four levels as follows: (1) At the most specific level of the social structure are *personality and role characteristics of individuals.* (2) At the next most general level are to be found the *organizational characteristics of collectivities* (families, firms, schools, and so forth) in which people live and work. More general still are (3) the *institutional principles* governing the major functional complexes of the society (the government, the economy, the educational system, and the like). Finally, at the "highest" or most general and abstract level of the social structure are (4) the *values* and other major cultural themes on which the whole society is patterned.

In recent efforts to change sex roles, something like Smelser's control hierarchy appears to affect the selection of what topics become important at a certain point in time. Generally speaking, the earliest conscious efforts to question traditional moral or scientific views about the sexes are directed to change of personalities and only later move "upward" to question more general aspects of the social structure. This sequence of efforts for moral reform and scientific studies appears to be related as well to the actual social changes in sex roles that become institutionalized. If inequitable treatment of women appears to result primarily from personality differences between women and men and can be handled adequately through resocialization or education, the discontent is "contained" at this level, and scientific and political activity need go no farther. If, however, efforts to improve the situation by, for example, training little girls like little boys, meet with repeated failure or resistance, the diagnosis of the problem changes, implicating more general levels of the moral order and calling for scientific investigation that takes a larger set of environmental variables into account.

If inequalities in sex roles appear to implicate the most general organizing principles of the society—namely, its values—the situation is ripe for a confluence of both external and internal forces to reshape the society's overall structure. In matters of sex differences in occupational attainment, Galbraith might have argued that only a shift away from an affluent consumption-oriented society would help the lot of women. (As it was he proposed more moderate solutions requiring the restructuring of working hours, and other policies.) An attack on the ultimate economic purposes of the society would coincide with other critiques derived from an entirely different initial concern, namely, such groups as the futurists who are concerned with global interdependence.

Thus internal change moving up the control hierarchy to the topmost level—the value level—eventually joins external forces affecting the long-term survival possibilities of the society. This coincidence can in fact be explained. The culture of the society is tested by its ability to withstand dissatisfaction internal to the society as well as by its ability to provide a purpose that promotes long-term survival for the society as a member of the larger world community. If the structure withstands criticism from either external or internal forces alone, it can persist for some time; but if buffeted from both within and without, and faced by a double attack on its most basic assumptions, it is likely to change in order to adapt. The pressure to change social norms from within thus can provide the raw material from which an adaptation may be selected that will promote the long-term survival of the society. By this particular logic the patterning of men's and women's roles in America can affect the future well-being of the entire society.

If this formulation is correct, contemporary efforts to restructure women's and men's roles are important as an addition to the repertoire of available alternatives that society can use for adaptation to future challenge. In addition a standard emerges by which both the women's movement and the usefulness of research on women can be evaluated. The control hierarchy defines important categories and suggests the order in which issues occur. The evolutionary model directs our attention to the optimum fit between the needs and desires of the women's movement and the future social order of which it is only a part.

NATURE OF THE EVIDENCE

It appears that reform of the sexual division of labor follows a sequential pattern that moves from emphasis on the individual person to emphasis on the structure of the larger society. Evidence comes from the ideology and actions of the women's movement, the pattern of public policy issues, and the shifting focus of scientific research. It is too soon to confirm whether the time-order hypothesis is relevant in a precise way (using specific dates, quantitative measures of content, and the like). For the present, however, this hypothesis provides a meaningful set of categories for grouping feminist ideologies, public policies, and research findings. In this book it will be evident that the following four types of content appear in every major institution:

1. *Content centered at personality level.*
Signs of strain in the feelings of women are expressed in the popular press or channeled through the women's movement. Ideological statements reveal women's indignation, frustration, humiliation, and desire to withdraw or rebel. Applied research and political efforts are largely confined to changing the motives or behavior of the individual woman. The possibilities include retraining, resocialization, or improved opportunities for education, counseling, or other access to information.

2. *Content centered at the collectivity level.*

At the next more general level women's complaints and the related objective evidence focus on job inequities. There are signs of segregation in work performed by women and men. Related reform efforts are directed toward getting more women into high status roles. The possibilities include affirmative action (an active effort to recruit women for high-status positions) and raising the titles and salaries of jobs that women currently hold (making a secretary an "administrative assistant") but not substantially changing job definitions.

3. *Content centered on institutional regulations.*

More general than role differences in the organization are the standards governing institutions. They tend to assign the male-typed functions higher value and the female-typed functions lower value. Descriptive accounts reveal inequity in the choices available to males and females; the roles they occupy typically carry different privileges, with males performing functions that allow more opportunity for mobility, security, and promotion. Attempts are made to reform the basic institutional fabric so that the psychological orientation and occupational skills of women and other minorities are restored to proper balance with those of the dominant group. The possibilities in the economy include "flexitime" and work restructuring. In government, greater emphasis on citizen participation helps to restore balance.

4. *Content centered on language, image, and values.*

Dissatisfaction with the most general and abstract patterns of culture appears in protests against invidious distinctions between male and female images, symbols, and values. Evidence to support these protests reveals that male role models are almost everywhere predominant over female role models. Relevant reforms are of the sort that attempt to reorder cultural symbols, images, and values to achieve better balance of "female" and "male" elements. Examples include (1) modification of language (for example, by substitution of other words than "he," "him," "his," and "men" to mean "everybody"); (2) loosening of stereotypes to permit recognition that "female" virtues (like nurturance) may be found in males and "male" virtues (like courage) in females; (3) departure from past cultural goals (mastery and domination over nature) associated with male values, and new emphasis on alternative cultural goals (cooperation, sympathy, and vulnerability) that are associated with the female.

In sum, it is expected that in any reform movement personality and role issues historically will appear before institutional and value questions. The reason is that the former are less threatening to the established social order than the latter. Efforts to enhance educational opportunities and training, for example, emphasize *equality of opportunity*, but they do so largely by trying to reshape the *personality* to fit the available social slots. Some of these efforts pay off, and more women, as a result of better education and training, are able to hold jobs from which they were formerly barred by lack of qualifications.

However, if problems remain, reform efforts, scientific analysis, and popular political response move higher up the ladder of social control to achieve what Daniel Bell (1973: 431- 433) terms *equality of result*. Here programs of "affirmative action" reshuffle the races or sexes at the *role-status level* so that not all the inferior caste are found in the lower-status functions and all the superior caste in the high-status jobs. If affirmative action has disappointing results, reform thinking spreads to a still more abstract level of social structure where the rationality of *institutional goals and rules* is called into question. For example, radical feminists seek economic structures that overcome the present two-caste system of marginal, low-status jobs for women and core, high-status jobs for men. In the final analysis, however, when institutional structures are questioned, the reform process begins to touch the most general organizing principles of the *culture* and the *symbol system*—the basic assumptions and values on which the entire society is built. Proponents of cultural redirection argue that to accomplish all the changes in personality, roles, and institutions that are required to realize equality, there must be greater value accorded the heretofore downgraded qualities and capacities that are possessed by the lower caste. If marginal service jobs with low pay and low status are where women are found, the strategy for change, they contend, should be not only to get women out of those jobs and into management positions held by men but also, more important, to develop greater appreciation for functions performed by women that were formerly taken for granted and received less reward.

In fact there does appear to be a rough sequential pattern in the reform issues that become prominent. It is evident in the topics of scholarship, in the passage of antidiscrimination laws, and in feminist ideology. This is not to say, however, that all such communications are confined to any one level at a particular period in history. On the contrary, basic research that does not touch the relevant policy issues of the moment may be conducted at other levels; laws that are ahead of their time are passed and go unheeded. In particular, members of a social movement are likely to see need for change and propose reform at all levels of the social order simultaneously.

Such spillover is rather to be welcomed than discouraged, for suggestions made out of sequence do point the way to changes that must be made eventually. It is particularly characteristic of a social movement like feminism that it is far ahead of the general population in proposing certain changes that later seem natural. Members of the movement feel the problems and strains of the women's role more acutely than members of the larger society. Their anger prompts them to feed awareness of the strains to the outside society ahead of others' perception that there is a problem. To use Smelser's phrase (1963: 79-130), they "short circuit" the established channels for expressing grievance at each level. Rather than wait for a response at

Figure 1. A Model of Change in Sex Roles

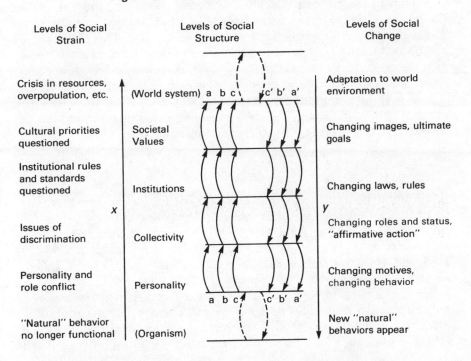

a, a' elements of reform ideology, and institutionalization of that ideology
b, b' research and scientific study, and application of that research
c, c' political interests, and new political consensus

X The reform process moves up the hierarchy of control
Y The institutionalization of change moves down the hierarchy of control

Strain may be contained at any one level or it may pass further up the hierarchy before causing change at a higher level which in turn trickles down to lower ones.

lower levels, the movement quickly extends its critique up the hierarchy of social control, at times risking the appearance of dangerous irrationality. Similarly, in its perception of reform possibilities, it jumps ahead of legal change or changes in practice. It would change the whole system in one sweep. But the suggested reforms are not accepted as legitimate by the larger society until others similarly perceive the problem and discover means for alleviating it.

By comparison with the women's movement, policy makers and policy scientists more often proceed in step-by-step fashion to roll back layers of habitual practice and discover possible alternatives. Only when they discover that not all desired change can be accomplished at one level do they move on to the next. Yet the movement members, the policy makers, and policy scientists need each other to facilitate the actual process of change. In the division of labor, feminists point the way to change at all levels, scientists provide information in a form usable for formulating and implementing policy, and policy makers develop rules that express consensus on social purpose and permit change to be instituted. The efforts of all are coordinated by the fact that the society is fundamentally resistant to change, allowing change at first only at the less threatening levels and not permitting change to widen until each major group shares certain common perceptions of environmental problems and certain common values. Figure 1 presents a model summarizing the interconnected processes by which sex roles change.

World Trends

Beyond differences within any one society or culture there are, of course, other societies that make up the global system. Ultimately there is feedback to each society that communicates whether its social structure (including its sex role structure) is adequate. This feedback from outside the society is, however, indirect and takes a very long time to be interpreted. Nevertheless an extra-systemic judgment is the final *sociological* test by which a given society's structure and values may be tried. For this reason, where established priorities and feminist values are opposed, it is possible to turn to global well-being as an ultimate criterion by which the relative merits of either may be judged.*

Since the Club of Rome has not worked out a picture of the optimum sex-role constellations for the ten regions of the world economy that it has defined, it is for each society and region to grope toward its own best adaptation in the world system. On their

---

* It would, of course, also be possible to turn to nonsociological criteria such as philosophical principles or religious standards, as, for example, in the work of John Rawls (1971) or Ernest Wallwork (1972).

way there Americans should perhaps turn to that part of their history and tradition that gave them an identity as leaders in democratic government and technological progress. A comparison of the status of women in the United States with those of other societies reveals that, as in most industrialized countries, they lead considerably less restricted lives than women in societies with peasant agriculture. However, their position does not allow so much latitude as in the Scandinavian socialist countries or in an East European country such as Poland (Giele and Smock, 1977). Nevertheless, the trend in America as well as in other modern countries appears to be in essentially the same direction—toward a more differentiated society where traditional tasks of women and men are broken down into components that become more easily exchanged across sex boundaries. Whether in France, Poland, Scandinavia, or the United States, more women are getting higher education and entering the labor force. And more men are helping in family activity; or the government is aiding family functions such as child care. Such crossover between male and female roles and the accompanying enlargement of the public sector to carry out traditional feminine responsibilities appear to be the direct outcome of a high degree of complexity and specialization in modern society (Giele, 1977: 3- 31; Giele, 1971).

When carried to the global level, the crossover principle appears to have adaptive advantage for meeting many of the key future problems of energy, population, and poverty that are by now familiar. The crossover principle represents a formula for achieving equity among unlike persons. It provides a mechanism by which to balance the repetitious tasks of recycling and saving with the excitement of growth and investment. It legitimates caring for children as well as engaging in exciting careers. By this principle the pioneering and innovative tasks need not be allocated to one sex or one class alone, and the maintenance and repetitive tasks to another. Instead further differentiation of tasks and the resulting crossover make it possible for almost everyone to do something of both.

Here at last the movement for change in sex roles and the evolutionary challenge to modern society are joined. Equity between men and women in our society is seen to foster global well-being through the ideal of a *balance* among all types of necessary human activity.

A CASE STUDY:
SEX ROLES AND FERTILITY DECISIONS

No issue links sex roles with current world crisis more dramatically than the rapid growth of world population. Nor in any other field is it so clear that both scientific knowledge and moral considerations are involved. The costs of unbridled population growth have only gradually become apparent to the contemporary world, although Malthus raised the specter of overpopulation, starvation, and death more than a century ago. But where Malthus pictured only a natural process of adjustment between numbers of people and food, the contemporary observer must consider additional artificial food production factors, chemical fertilizers and pollution, hybridization and loss of genetic variety, and modern medical advances that threaten overpopulation and starvation on an even larger scale. Fortunately the contemporary world also has artificial means to limit conception.

Yet population control is not merely a technological or scientific problem. In addition to the biological organism, it involves emotions, values, and social sanctions. One key element is the redefinition of women's proper roles. As early as the nineteenth-century women's movement, feminists realized that expansion of women's opportunities was tied to birth control (Banks and Banks, 1964). Lately, members of the larger society—demographers and policy makers— have begun to see that redefinition of sex roles is a crucial element in population control. Linda Gordon (1976:392), a feminist historian of the birth-control movement, sees a potential threat that women's interest in control of their own bodies may be subverted by people primarily interested in economic development. Nevertheless, the women's movement and the larger society share an interest not only in population balance but also in role changes that will help to achieve it.

THE NEW DEMOGRAPHIC CRISIS

The term *demographic transition* summarizes the changed relation between fertility and mortality that has occurred in the developed world in the last century. The death rate, particularly infant mortality, has dropped sharply to half of what it was at the turn of the century. Life expectancy has increased dramatically from forty-seven years in 1900 to seventy years in 1970. Many fewer conceptions are needed to attain a desired family size, and consequently fertility has, after some lag, eventually dropped to adjust to these changed conditions. In the United States, the drop has been dramatic, from a birthrate of 32 per 1,000 population around 1900 to 18 per 1,000 in 1970. The average number of children per woman went from 3.5 in 1900 to an average of 2.4 in 1970, and then 1.8 in 1975 (U.S. Commission on Population, 1972: 11-13; Reinhold, 1977: 46).

Despite the fact that the U.S. birthrate is currently at an all-time low, concern to maintain this rate persists, because there is an enormous difference in economic and social consequences depending on whether the American family averages three children or two children. A rapid rise to the three- or four-child average is entirely possible since much of the drop in fertility is due to postponement of marriage and childbearing among the young (Sklar and Berkov, 1975).

Interest on the part of the women's movement.

The need to establish a new population equilibrium is evident not only in demographic indicators but in the emotional consequences of the demographic transition for women as well. Women's age span has lengthened, while the period of childbearing has contracted (Ridley, 1972). In societies where women participate in productive work, this is clearly a positive step forward. But in the United States women have traditionally been encouraged to be full-time housewives. Some feminists suggest that more child-free years may now result in higher rates of illness and depression among middle-aged women who have no alternative activities to engage in (Bernard, 1972; Chesler, 1972; Bart, 1971).

In addition, many unwanted pregnancies still occur. Presser (1973: 134) reports a conservative estimate that 2.65 million births between 1965 and 1970 took place that would not have occurred if couples who did not want additional children had been successful in contraception. Furthermore, teenage pregnancy and illegitimacy have risen markedly since the Second World War. It is births given by mothers in this age group that contribute a disproportionate number of premature births and deformities. Moreover, early pregnancy appears to limit severely a young woman's chances of finishing high school or gaining further work experience (Presser, 1975; Furstenberg, 1976:96). Much of the rise in teenage pregnancy appears due to improvements in nutrition that have lowered the age of menarche and made it less likely that a girl's menstrual cycle will be anovulatory (Frisch and Revelle, 1970). Improvement in antibiotic treatment of venereal disease has reduced involuntary sterility (Cutright, 1973). In addition, increased sexual permissiveness combined with failures in contraception probably account for some of the rise.

The primary response of the women's movement to these events has been an effort to remove restrictions against contraception and abortion and provide instruction and self-help in gynecological procedures. Such women's groups as WEAL and NOW have counseled their members to mobilize opposition to any legislation that would restrict a woman's constitutional right to abortion as upheld by

Supreme Court decision in 1973. In Chicago, a women's health collective reputedly performed thousands of abortions before the operation was legalized. Other women's health collectives in Boston and Montreal and in areas of California have advocated self-examination and self-treatment in gynecological matters (Boston Women's Health Collective, 1971). A central tenet of the women's movement is that women should be sufficiently knowledgeable and free to determine the best ways to control their bodies.

Scientific and popular interest.

It is not only women or unwanted children who bear the costs of imperfect population control. The U.S. Commission on Population and the American Future, composed of scientists and citizens, concluded on the basis of expert testimony in the early 1970s that, even with families limited to two children, by the year 2000 there will be 50 million more people added to the American population. Such growth will strain the capacity of the environment to provide all the needed water and disposal of waste. Furthermore, much of the growth will occur in large metropolitan areas, putting additional strain on the fiscal and social resources of local governments to handle the growing population (U.S. Commission on Population, 1972: 55- 92). If growth occurs at a somewhat faster rate, income per capita will be lower, and the strain on existing resources and political institutions even greater.

To avert crisis, the commission recommended abandonment of the growth ethic and adoption of a different attitude toward nature. It called for change in basic institutions and attention to such features as sex roles. In the words of the commission,

> There is scarcely a facet of American life that is not involved with the rise and fall of our birth and death rates: the economy, environment, education, health, family life and *sexual practices*, urban and rural life, governmental effectiveness and political freedoms, religious norms, and secular life-styles. If this country is in a crisis of spirit—environmental deterioration, racial antagonisms, the plight of the cities, the international situation—then population is part of that crisis.
>
> Although population change touches all of these areas of our national life and intensifies our problems, such problems will not be solved by demographic means alone. Population policy is no substitute for social, economic, and environmental policy. Successfully addressing population requires that we also address our problems of poverty, of *minority and sex discrimination*, of careless exploitation of resources, of environmental deterioration, and of spreading suburbs, decaying cities, and wasted countrysides. By the same token, because population is so tightly interwoven with all of these concerns, whatever success we have in resolving these problems will contribute to easing the complex system of pressures that impel

population growth. [U.S. Commission on Population, 1972: 2, italics added]

Changes in the law.

As feminist, scientific, and popular interests in population control have evolved, so have legal and practical measures permitting contraception and abortion. In 1965 the Supreme Court in *Griswold* vs. *Connecticut* (381 U.S. 479) struck down a Connecticut law that made the use of contraceptives a legal offense. In 1972 the Supreme Court in *Eisenstadt* vs. *Baird* (405 U.S. 438) upheld a circuit court ruling that stated that the Massachusetts law restricting distribution of contraceptives to married persons violated the rights of single persons under the Equal Protection Clause of the Fourteenth Amendment. The 1973 Supreme Court decisions on abortion held Texan and Georgian abortion laws to be in violation of a woman's fundamental right to choose whether or not to end her pregnancy (*Roe* vs. *Wade*, 93 S. Ct. 705; *Doe* vs. *Bolton*, 93 S. Ct. 739).

Liberalization of the antiabortion laws clearly seems to have followed an important shift in popular opinion. As recently as 1968, a poll had shown that 85 percent of the general population opposed more liberal abortion rules. By 1971 in a poll conducted for the U.S. Commission on Population Growth and the American Future, the proportion had risen to 50 percent who said the decision should be left up to the persons involved and their doctor (Rosenthal, 1971: 1, 22).

While changes in the rules permit further important shifts in reproductive behavior, they do not initiate the efforts to change the birthrate, nor is it clear that they alone will suffice any more than will widespread dissemination of technological devices. If the available technology is to be used effectively, personal motivation and facilitating attitudes on the part of others are required.

POPULATION CONTROL STRATEGIES AND SEX ROLES

Personal, social, and cultural change are required to achieve population control. Our conceptual map shows four major levels at which the problems may be studied or strategies devised. Each of these is intimately tied to the sex-role revolution. The first is the individual level, at which related research and strategies attempt to increase women's *effectiveness* in contraception. Second is the role level, where research and action focus on rewards to the *mother role* and the provision of *alternative roles*. The third level addresses needed change in *institutional arrangements* such as health care, family, economy, and *changes in the law to eliminate hidden pronatalist bias*. The most abstract level concerns broadening *cultural purposes* to place more emphasis on living in harmony with nature and less on the growth ethic.

There seems to be a rough time order in which these different issues arise and hold greatest interest. Both scientists and policy makers appear to have attempted first to change individuals, then roles, then institutions, and finally cultural values toward population growth.

Personality change.

To enhance a woman's effectiveness in contraception, a logical first step is to understand her personality functions—moral, motivational, informational, and practical. For example, what are her moral and religious beliefs regarding birth control? Studies of contraceptive practice throughout the 1950s and 1960s showed that differences among Protestants, Catholics, and other religious groups were on the decline (Westoff, 1973: 24- 29). Is the woman motivated to achieve or to avoid pregnancy? Some recent evidence suggests that women with low achievement motivation are less effective in fertility control and that individuals lacking a sense of personal efficacy are also less likely to practice contraception (Miller and Inkeles, 1974). Does a woman have adequate knowledge of contraception, and are effective devices readily available to her? All our information suggests that low income is associated with low access to information and prescriptions for contraceptives and abortions.

As research questions focus on the individual's values, motivation, information, and access to contraception, so also policy can be similarly oriented to changing the person and the surrounding technology. Values and attitudes of the individual woman or man are the targets of such reform groups as Zero Population Growth, Inc., who periodically conduct sessions that teach viable alternatives to biological parenthood, such as adopting a child, living as a single person, or joining a special community.

The question of how to change the individual's motivation for contraception has led to discussion of direct incentives, but Americans have been loath to consider any approach that smacks of authoritarian control over individual choice. A more attractive possibility is to increase the individual's sense of personal efficacy through education and exposure to modernizing influences. Persons with a high sense of personal efficacy appear more likely to be effective contraceptive users (Inkeles and Smith, 1974; Miller and Inkeles, 1974).

Effective birth control is related to a woman's general level of education. This relation holds in populous countries such as India, where the state with highest overall educational levels, Kerala, has shown a recent decline in its birthrate (Weinraub, 1974). In the United States, a woman with less than a high school education is more than twice as likely to have an unwanted birth as is a woman with four or more years of post-grade school education (Ryder, 1973a: 63).

Sex education is an additional avenue for change. The Sex Information and Education Council of the United States (S.I.E.C.U.S.) for years has waged a difficult and sometimes discouraging battle to get more adequate information on sex presented as a part of school curricula. Ineffective contraception is strongly related to a lack of information about sex. Surprisingly, however, sex education has consistently met with considerable resistance.

In addition to these psychological and educational strategies for change, the possibility for improving the technology of contraception should not be overlooked. The birth control pill developed in the 1950s by Pincus, with the support of Margaret Sanger, resulted in an enormous leap forward. But women have recently become wary of its side effects (Seaman, 1972) and are increasingly resentful that the primary burden of contraception lies with them rather than with men. Experimentation with vasectomy, use of the intrauterine device (I.U.D.), and possibly refurbishing the condom may prove more advisable in the long run (Bengis, 1973).

All approaches aimed solely at improving technology or changing the woman, however, are not sufficient alone for dealing with population problems. Some change can be accomplished through improved sex education and access to effective methods, but the birthrate remains high in those parts of the population which can least afford more children; thus a broader approach may be needed. One possibility is that, if more alternatives to the mother role are available, women will of their own accord discover the ways to be more effective in controlling conception.

Alternatives to the mother role.

Much of the research on fertility rates by social scientists has pointed to the relation between women's employment and low fertility (Sweet, 1973; Cain, 1966). Whether it is having a smaller number of children that makes it easier for a woman to enter the labor force or whether it is employment that decreases her desire to have more children is not absolutely clear. Perhaps some additional underlying factor contributes both to lower fertility and to labor force participation.

Some observers suggest that where a woman has interesting and rewarding alternatives to childbearing, such as those provided by education and employment, she will voluntarily curtail her fertility

(U.S. Commission on Population, 1972: 152–156; Presser, 1973). By this logic, society should increase work opportunities for women so that the cost to a woman is greater if she forgoes these opportunities when she has more children. If child care is provided for those children she already has so that she is free to take employment, her desire to have more children may thereby be limited.

Following this line of reasoning, one of the major problematic areas for research and policy development in the future lies in the direction of improving women's chances for promotion and good pay in the job market. At present, women are concentrated in a few overcrowded occupations. An important question is how women's economic opportunities can be broadened.

Another major line of inquiry and policy development is how family structure, child-care arrangements, and community living patterns can be altered to foster the growth of children without requiring that the mother stay home full time lest her children be neglected and their growth and development suffer. Communal family arrangements suggest some of the experimental possibilities. The number of day-care facilities multiplied dramatically in the 1960s. However, a reliable system of household helpers or homemakers and the professionalization of household service have been slow to develop in the United States, slower than in Canada and several European countries.

Research and experimentation are needed both to change the sex-segregated nature of the occupational system and to provide satisfactory alternatives to women's full-time service in housework and child care. If there is to be progress in finding new alternatives, however, the examination must eventually proceed beyond piecemeal expansion of job opportunities and household help offered to a few individual women. Instead, the major organizing principles governing the division of labor among family, economy, and government must come under scrutiny. Some demographers find pronatalist forces deeply imbedded in these structures.

Changing pronatalist institutions.

In 1973 the current U.S. fertility was only 10 to 20 percent above the level of replacement. But the question of how to bring it down to a no-growth level plagued demographers. Norman Ryder (1973b: 59) described the situation as follows:

> Consider the possibility that demographic equilibrium is achievable. . . . We have no relevant experience. Our fertility has always occurred in the context of massive collective intervention of a pronatalist type; at the level of means, we have inhibited individual access to the knowledge, agents, and services required for effective fertility regulation, and at the level of ends we

have encouraged parenthood and discouraged nonparenthood using virtually the entire spectrum of available pressures. . . .

One of the most obvious avenues for change has been through the laws governing contraception, abortion, sterilization, adoption, and illegitimacy. The feminist movement and court decisions have combined to argue that equal protection of the law for women and men and the constitutional guarantee of right of privacy require that women be allowed to govern their own bodies and be permitted access to contraceptive materials and abortion (Babcock et al., 1975: 943–990; Ross, 1973: 192–207; Kanowitz, 1973: 118–162). For this reason, some demographers have advocated passage of the Equal Rights Amendment (U.S. Commission on Population, 1972: 156).

Study of government policy toward population is also relevant. But as Ryder says, there are no models on how to devise antinatalist policy. Some of the clearest models for governmental intervention in population matters were developed by European countries during the pronatalist spirit of the 1930s (Myrdal, 1941).

Ryder's own suggestions point the way and in fact are almost certainly closer to realization now than when he presented them. Ryder says that little additional effort is needed to obtain zero population growth beyond individuals' own determination of their reproduction, if the country abandons pronatalist policies:

> In other words, the elimination of population growth is a likely consequence of policies which enlarge the scope of individual freedom—policies eminently worthy of adoption whatever their demographic side effects. In particular, the government should encourage completely free and open access to the knowledge, supplies, and services requisite to contraception; abortion and sterilization without restriction by marital status or implicit restriction by economy; equality of opportunity for education and employment without restriction by sex; and openings to modern life for the depressed subcultures in the population. [Ryder, 1973b: 60]

In order to grant individuals more opportunity to act autonomously and without limitations imposed by marital status, sex, economic class, or ethnic group, change in the law will help. But other basic changes in social institutions must occur as well. Structural differentiation must proceed further so that sexual activity, child rearing, marriage, and employment can each occur without overdetermining the others. Thus, for example, while the traditional pronatalist pattern associates sexual intercourse, marriage, children, and housework all in one package, the new neuter-natalist or antinatalist pattern would break this package apart so that a woman could have some features of it without necessarily having to accept the whole. Love and sex would thus not necessarily be tied to the marital bond; the marital bond would not necessarily be tied to having children; marriage or children would neither bar nor encourage a person's participation in the labor force. Such differentiation moves away from pronatalism because it weakens the ties among sexual activity, children, marriage, and work. It does not assume that women who are married or are mothers are somehow disabled for the labor force. In other words, differentiation of the sex-marriage-children-work package into smaller specialized packages permits greater flexibility in the combination of different roles and allows more crossover in the patterns chosen by women and men, parents and nonparents, married persons and unmarried ones. When substantial crossover is realized, we can assume that most of the pronatalist institutional pressures have been neutralized.

Efforts to change pronatalist institutional arrangements also extend into the economy. "Flexitime" in work, a greater opportunity for part-time work, and parental leaves make it easier for each parent to both work and have children. The likelihood that women will stay home full time and be tempted to have more children thus decreases.

Finally, pronatalist pressures may also be found in the socialization process and educational system. But as opportunities for continuing education expand, there will be more alternatives to the full-time career as mother. Educational patterns typical of women in the past may become more common among men, such as late career entry, part-time work, and redirection of vocation in mid-life.

Commitment to new values.

All research and practical strategy at the personality, role, or institutional level present the society with choices. Should it truly opt for giving more freedom of choice to individuals rather than subtly pressuring people to become parents by making any other course difficult? Is there not something to be said on the side of a mother's staying home with her children, or of people who have children being married rather than being casually involved? Is not life valuable, and should it not be protected through careful control of the use of such techniques as abortion? Probably most people would answer yes to all these questions, whether they oppose or support the no-growth policy measures that have been listed so far.

Yet disagreements over practical measures persist. To resolve them, people eventually must turn to the more general values and standards in which they all share belief. Concerning population policy and its consequences for women, it has been difficult to discover the common purpose that will unite opposing factions. The relevant values and standards are not altogether clear, but they appear to involve (1) a shift in attitude toward nature, (2) a change in attitude toward material goods, (3) a critical attitude toward the place of government, and (4) a new relativism in valuing growth and stability. Each of these emerging values must make its way against an older pattern. When each is clear, it will color and shape future research and action.

1. There appears to be an emerging consensus that we should live in harmony with nature, not merely dominate it (Heilbroner, 1974: 127). This standard has important implications for the technology of birth control. Contraceptive techniques have in the past emphasized technological control of women's reproductive systems and women's personal control over their own fertility. New research, however, shows that diet, food intake, ovulation, and lactation are part of a much larger social system that in some societies keeps reproduction low through natural rather than artificial means (Kolata, 1974). Adoption of this organizing principle could possibly result in future research that would enlarge the variables under consideration to include not just women's fertility but also that of men, and not just narrowly focused technologies of contraception but also wider systems involving work, diet, fatigue, taboos on sexual activity, seasons, and cycles of leisure activity.

2. There appears to be growing disaffection with endless consumption of material goods as an economic end in itself. Change in the consumption ethic has important implications for women's economic roles as consumers and keepers of the household. If there is less virtue in consumption, women and society need not allocate so much home time or work time to care of possessions and maintenance of the home. Without that need, women's motivation to stay at home to have more children will have to compete with their other desires for paid employment. Economic well-being might have to be measured in terms other than income level, employment, or unemployment. Evaluation of household wages, volunteer work, and contribution of women to the GNP would also have to be reassessed.

3. There is a growing sense that government should expand its support for services that promote domestic well-being. For women to have greater role autonomy, there must be more structural differentiation and flexibility in jobs so that family and work functions can be performed interchangeably by many types of people, regardless of their age, sex, or family position. Differentiation creates added complexity and a need for added support services provided at public expense. Just as the roads or the postal service are publicly supported for the public good, so there is increasing belief that adequate child

care, health care, or family income will also serve the public as well as the private interest (Kahn and Kamerman, 1975).

4. There appears to be increasing acceptance of a relativist ethic regarding growth and no growth. The form of history is perceived in cycles rather than in a unilinear upward trend. Increasingly, neither pronatalism nor antinatalism is thought good in itself; all depends on circumstance. If a population has been seriously depleted by war or plague, a high fertility rate is of enormous survival value. On the other hand, if food is plentiful and disease under control to the point that population leaps out of bounds, control of fertility is of the utmost value for survival (American Association for the Advancement of Science, 1974: 57-69).

Most recent population policy explicitly recognizes the need for adaptation to the conditions of the moment rather than rigid application of rules appropriate to another era. Such thinking precipitated discussion among Catholics during the 1960s, precisely because individual believers disagreed as to whether traditional beliefs of the church regarding contraception should be revised in the light of circumstance (Berelson, 1973). Socialist countries have been through similar internal struggles over belief and currently tend toward encouragement of natality for nationalist and other reasons.

Of course, no country operates in complete isolation from the rest. At least for the moment, demographers and other population experts still argue that, in the world interest as well as in the national interest, no growth is the ethical position in population policy.

The implications of the no-growth ethic for the roles of women are profound. No major institution of society is untouched by major change in sex roles. Government, work, family, education—all must consider the changes in structure that are in order if women are not to be limited to the family sphere but are to take active part in all the affairs of society.

WOMEN'S CONTRIBUTION TO THE FUTURE

Problems of survival and overpopulation are a natural beginning point for showing that change in women's roles is necessary to the larger good of society. Efforts to control population show clearly that changes are needed in all segments of society. But it is particularly the question of what special contribution women can make that concerns us here. There are two major aspects of the matter. The first issue is whether there are such important *differences* among women (by race, class, religion, ethnicity, and the rest) that no statements can be made about their *similarities*. The second issue follows from the first; it concerns whether women are in any way different from men in the principles they stand for.

SIMILARITIES AMONG WOMEN

Throughout this book I have tried to sketch changes in sex roles on the widest possible canvas in order to note their fundamental significance for the entire society. Similarities among women are therefore emphasized rather than their differences. While the differences most assuredly do exist, they do not override certain important structural conditions that all women face as a result of their sex.

It is to these powerful sex-related characteristics of women's roles *regardless of race or class* that my analysis is therefore directed. Sex segregation of jobs in the labor market affects black women as well as white. The lack of pay and public recognition for home work and child care is true for women of blue-collar families who do not want paid employment just as it is for women dissatisfied with the housewife role who wish to enter the labor force. Patriarchal themes pervade the imagery of all the major organized religions, whether Protestant, Catholic, or Jewish. This is not to say that subcultural differences in the status of women should not be recognized or be explained. Rather this study concentrates on similarities among women in order to spotlight the consequences of basic sex differentiation.

WOMEN'S VIEWPOINT

A second vital issue is whether women represent any distinctive point of view that is different from men's. This is a controversial question; it even divides feminists. It can be honestly answered in entirely opposite ways depending on which particular subgroups of men and women one chooses to compare.

Several authors have observed that the views of men and women are strongly associated with the amount of power that they hold. Rosabeth Kanter (1977: 164-205) demonstrates that women in the corporation, if they are in positions that provide opportunity for advancement, are assertive, flexible, and innovative, just as men. If, however, their mobility is blocked, they act defensively, hide behind bureaucratic rules, and resist change. And so do men in a similar situation. Kate Millett (1970: 336-361) in analyzing the literary works of Jean Genet shows that males at the bottom of a homosexual hierarchy such as found in prisons adopt a passive "feminine" sexual attitude that includes loyalty and tenderness whereas those at the top are the "masculine" aggressors who are expected to be promiscuous.

Both Kanter's and Millett's characterizations associate the admired and stimulating aspects of power with the top of the hierarchy and they find a disproportionate number of men there. The characteristics of people at the bottom, the women and the powerless males, are implicitly judged to be low in value. This is natural enough. After all, power pyramids reflect the type of people and the type of standards that have gained ascendence and become institutionalized.

But it is not always necessary for us as onlookers to accept the established system of priorities as the best one. For example, we might question whether innovative, flexible, and change-oriented behavior is everywhere and at all times the most appropriate style to adopt; perhaps stability, loyalty, and maintenance of structure should not always have to take second place. Only if one maintains this critical stance toward established hierarchies does it seem possible to avoid "buying into" the present social structure and current "male" priorities. Only with such perspective can one perceive with Slater (1970) "American culture at the breaking point," victim of an overly "male" emphasis that teaches a relentless desire to dominate nature, repress feeling, and pursue "success" at all costs.

What if there are other alternative value systems that might be instituted instead? What if there are "outsider" values under which women might thrive, feel competent, and attain recognition and power? The distribution of men and women in the power hierarchy might then change.

Actual social change to bring more women into government, the economy, or the educational system requires both moderate and radical efforts. Acceptance of the standards underlying the present power pyramids leads to relatively moderate strategies such as affirmative action. Through provision of greater opportunity for training or promotion, women's *behavior* can be changed to make them more successful. Rejection of the underlying standards leads in contrast to more radical action. The remedy chosen then is not so much to change women's behavior as to reorder the priorities of the whole system and in the process create a more appreciative climate for the qualities and skills that women already have. Such reordering would level established hierarchies and bring the outsiders in by releasing their creative energy for a whole new set of concerns.

The process of radical change is not necessarily linked to a distinctively female viewpoint. Anthropologists and sociologists have long seen that innovative change frequently comes from the "marginal man" (Stonequist, 1937). However, within the Judaeo-Christian tradition that informs the American cultural heritage, the vision of social revolution has in fact been voiced by women as well as by prophets. The Magnificat sung by Mary when she was to bear Jesus envisions such revolutionary change—the leveling of hierarchies, the inclusion of those who had been dispossessed.

> My soul doth magnify the Lord,
> And my spirit hath rejoiced in God my Saviour.
> For he hath regarded the low estate of his handmaiden:
> for, behold, from henceforth all generations shall call me blessed.
> For he that is mighty hath done to me great things;
> and holy is his name.
> And his mercy is on them that fear him from generation to generation.
> He hath shewed strength with his arm; he hath scattered
> the proud in the imagination of their hearts.
> He hath put down the mighty from their seats, and exalted them of low degree.
> He hath filled the hungry with good things;
> and the rich he hath sent empty away.
> He hath holpen his servant Israel, in remembrance of his mercy;
> As he spake to our fathers, to Abraham, and to his seed for ever.
>
> (Luke 1: 46–55)

Mary's song shares common themes with the song of Hannah, who long before had sung praise to God when in her old age she bore Samuel. And Hannah prayed, and said,

> My heart rejoiceth in the Lord,
> Mine horn is exalted in the Lord:
> My mouth is enlarged over mine enemies;
> Because I rejoice in thy salvation.
> There is none holy as the Lord:
> For there is none beside thee:
> Neither is there any rock like our God.
> Talk no more so exceeding proudly;
> Let not arrogancy come out of your mouth:
> For the Lord is a God of knowledge,
> And by him actions are weighed.
> The bows of the mighty men are broken,
> And they that stumbled are girded with strength.
> They that were full have hired out themselves for bread;
> And they that were hungry ceased:
> So that the barren hath borne seven;
> And she that hath many children is waxed feeble.
> The Lord killeth, and maketh alive:
> He bringeth down to the grave, and bringeth up.
> The Lord maketh poor, and maketh rich:
> He bringeth low, and lifteth up.

He raiseth up the poor out of the dust,
And lifteth up the beggar from the dunghill,
To set them among princes,
And to make them inherit the throne of glory:
For the pillars of the earth are the Lord's,
And he hath set the world upon them.
He will keep the feet of his saints,
And the wicked shall be silent in darkness;
For by strength shall no man prevail.
The adversaries of the Lord shall be broken to pieces:
Out of heaven shall he thunder upon them:
The Lord shall judge the ends of the earth;
And he shall give strength unto his king,
And exalt the horn of his anointed.

(I Samuel 2: 1-10)

Both these songs by women are distinctively feminine, in the sense that they follow an event that no male experiences, giving physical birth to a child. Yet they are songs of power! And revolution! The mighty are thrown down from their seats; the poor and hungry are filled with good things. These humble women empowered by God, the good, the creative new life, envision a whole new social order unfolding. And theirs is a vision of power, not self-serving but godly.

The Song of Hannah and the Magnificat are in some sense poetic keys to the revolutionary potential of the modern women's movement. Some women envision possibilities for new life in themselves and their loved ones. But the creative changes now required in our social structure also entail a leveling of old power structures and a shift in basic priorities and values. Outsiders must be brought into the establishment and at the same time infuse the whole society with new life. Thus will the interests of women and the interests of all then be joined together. If sex role change does constitute a true revolution, it will reorder the whole society and its place in the world.

REFERENCES FOR CHAPTER ONE

Aberle, D. F.; Cohen, A. K.; Davis, A. K.; Levy, M. J., Jr.; and Sutton, F. X. 1950; 1967. "The Functional Prerequisites of Society." In *System, Change, and Conflict: A Reader on Contemporary Sociological Theory and the Debate over Functionalism.* Edited by N. J. Demerath III and R. A. Peterson. New York: The Free Press.

Alland, Alexander, Jr. 1972. *The Human Imperative.* New York: Columbia University Press.

American Association for the Advancement of Science. 1974. *Culture and Population Change.* Washington, D.C.: Office of International Science, AAAS.

Astin, Helen S.; Parelman, Allison; and Fisher, Anne. 1975. *Sex Roles: A Research Bibliography.* Rockville, Md.: National Institute of Mental Health.

Babcock, Barbara A.; Freedman, Ann E.; Norton, Eleanor H.; and Ross, Susan C. 1975. *Sex Discrimination and the Law: Cases and Remedies.* Boston: Little, Brown.

Banks, Joseph A., and Banks, Olive. 1964. *Feminism and Family Planning in Victorian England.* New York: Schocken.

Bart, Pauline B. 1971. "Depression in Middle-Aged Women." In *Woman in Sexist Society: Studies in Power and Powerlessness.* Edited by V. Gornick and B. K. Moran. New York: Basic Books.

Bell, Daniel. 1973. *The Coming of Post-Industrial Society.* New York: Basic Books.

———. 1976. *The Cultural Contradictions of Capitalism.* New York: Basic Books.

Bengis, Ingrid. 1973. *Combat in the Erogenous Zone.* New York: Bantam.

Berelson, Bernard. 1973. "Population Growth Policy in Developed Countries." In *Toward the End of Growth.* Edited by C. F. Westoff et al. Englewood Cliffs, N.J.: Prentice-Hall, Spectrum.

Bernard, Jessie. 1972. *The Future of Marriage.* New York: World.

———. 1975. *Women, Wives, Mothers.* Chicago: Aldine.

Boserup, Ester. 1970. *Woman's Role in Economic Development.* London: Allen and Unwin.

Boston Women's Health Book Collective. 1971; 1973. *Our Bodies, Ourselves: A Book by and for Women.* New York: Simon and Schuster.

Boulding, Kenneth E. 1966; 1973. "The Economics of Coming Spaceship Earth." In *Toward a Steady-State Economy.* Edited by H. E. Daly. San Francisco: Freeman.

———. 1976. "Comment I." *Signs* 1, no. 3, part 2 (Spring): 75–77.

Cain, Glen G. 1966. *Married Women in the Labor Force: An Economic Analysis.* Chicago: University of Chicago Press.

Chesler, Phyllis. 1972. *Women and Madness.* Garden City, N.Y.: Doubleday.

Collins, Randall. 1971. "A Conflict Theory of Sexual Stratification." *Social Problems* 19 (Summer): 3–21.

Commoner, Barry. 1971. *The Closing Circle.* New York: Knopf.

Cordell, Magda, and McHale, John, with G. Streatfield. 1975. "Women and World Change." *Future* 7 (October): 364–384.

Cutright, Phillips. 1973. "Illegitimacy and Income Supplements." In *Studies in Public Welfare.* Paper no. 12 (Part I). Joint Economic Committee, U.S. Congress. Washington, D.C.: U.S.G.P.O.

Daly, Herman E., ed. 1973. *Toward a Steady-State Economy.* San Francisco: Freeman.

Daniels, Arlene Kaplan. 1975. *A Survey of Research Concerns on Women's*

Issues. Washington, D.C.: Association of American Colleges.

Darwin, Charles. 1890. *The Descent of Man and Selection in Relation to Sex.* New York: Appleton.

Dumond, Don E. 1975. "The Limitation of Human Population: A Natural History." *Science,* 28 February, pp. 713-721.

Durkheim, Emile. 1893; 1933. *The Division of Labor in Society.* New York: Macmillan.

Friedan, Betty. 1963. *The Feminine Mystique.* New York: Norton.

Frisch, Rose E., and Revelle, Roger. 1970. "Height and Weight at Menarche and a Hypothesis of Critical Body Weights and Adolescent Events." *Science,* 24 July, pp. 397-399.

Furstenberg, Frank. 1976. *Unplanned Parenthood: The Social Consequences of Teenage Childbearing.* New York: The Free Press.

Galbraith, John K. 1973. *Economics and the Public Purpose.* Boston: Houghton Mifflin.

Giele, Janet Zollinger. 1971. "Changes in the Modern Family: Their Impact on Sex Roles." *American Journal of Orthopsychiatry* 41 (October): 757-766.

———. 1977. "Introduction: Comparative Perspectives on Women." In *Women: Roles and Status in Eight Countries.* Edited by J. Z. Giele and A. C. Smock. New York: Wiley.

Giele, Janet Zollinger, and Smock, Audrey Chapman, eds. 1977. *Women: Roles and Status in Eight Countries.* New York: Wiley.

Gilder, George. 1973. *Sexual Suicide.* New York: Bantam.

Gordon, Linda. 1976. *Woman's Body, Woman's Right: A Social History of Birth Control in America.* New York: Grossman.

Grant, Gerald. 1972. "Essay Review: On Equality of Educational Opportunity." *Harvard Educational Review* 42: 109-125.

Hardesty, John. 1974. "Economic Implications of Environmental Crisis." *Transaction/Society* 12 (November-December): 13ff.

Heilbroner, Robert L. 1974. *An Inquiry into the Human Prospect.* New York: Norton.

Hueckel, Glenn. 1975. "A Historical Approach to Future Economic Growth." *Science,* 14 March, pp. 925-931.

Inkeles, Alex, and Smith, David. 1974. *Becoming Modern: Individual Change in Six Developing Countries.* Cambridge, Ma.: Harvard University Press.

Janeway, Elizabeth. 1974. *Between Myth and Morning: Women Awakening.* New York: Morrow.

Kahn, Alfred, and Kamerman, Sheila. 1975. *Not for the Poor Alone.* Philadelphia: Temple University Press.

Kanowitz, Leo. 1973. *Sex Roles in Law and Society.* Albuquerque, N.M.: University of New Mexico Press.

Kanter, Rosabeth Moss. 1977. *Men and Women of the Corporation.* New York: Basic Books.

Kolata, Gina Bari. 1974. "!Kung Hunter-gatherers: Feminism, Diet, and Birth

Control." *Science*, 13 September, pp. 932–934.

Kuhn, Thomas S. 1962; 1970. *The Structure of Scientific Revolutions*. Chicago: University of Chicago Press.

Lenski, Gerhard. 1966. *Power and Privilege: A Theory of Social Stratification*. New York: McGraw-Hill.

——. 1970. *Human Societies*. New York: McGraw-Hill.

——. 1975. "Social Structure in Evolutionary Perspective." In *Approaches to the Study of Social Structure*. Edited by P. M. Blau. New York: The Free Press.

LeVine, Robert A. 1969. "Culture, Personality, and Socialization: An Evolutionary View." In *Handbook of Socialization Theory and Research*. Edited by D. A. Goslin. Chicago: Rand McNally.

——. 1973. *Culture, Behavior, and Personality*. Chicago: Aldine.

Linares, Olga F.; Sheets, Payson D.; and Rosenthal, E. Jane. 1975. "Prehistoric Agriculture in Tropical Highlands." *Science*, 17 January, pp. 137–146.

Mayr, Ernst. 1972. "Sexual Selection and Natural Selection." In *Sexual Selection and the Descent of Man 1871–1971*. Edited by B. Campbell. Chicago: Aldine.

——. 1976. *Evolution and the Diversity of Life*. Cambridge, Ma.: Harvard University Press.

Mead, Margaret. 1949. *Male and Female: A Study of the Sexes in a Changing World*. New York: Morrow.

Meadows, Donella H.; Meadows, Dennis L.; Randers, Jørgen; and Behrens, William W. 1972. *The Limits of Growth: A Report for the Club of Rome's Project on the Predicament of Mankind*. New York: Universe Books.

Mesarovic, Mihajlo, and Pestel, Eduard. 1974. *Mankind at the Turning Point: The Second Report to the Club of Rome*. New York: Dutton.

Miller, Karen A., and Inkeles, Alex. 1974. "Modernity and Acceptance of Family Limitation in Four Developing Countries." *Journal of Social Issues* 30, no. 4: 167–188.

Millett, Kate. 1970. *Sexual Politics*. Garden City, N.Y.: Doubleday.

Mitchell, Juliet. 1971. *Woman's Estate*. New York: Vintage.

Myrdal, Alva. 1941; 1968. *Nation and Family: The Swedish Experiment in Democratic Family and Population Policy*. Cambridge, Ma.: MIT Press.

Parsons, Talcott. 1942; 1949. "Age and Sex in the Social Structure of the United States." In *Essays in Sociological Theory, Pure and Applied*. Edited by T. Parsons. New York: The Free Press.

——. 1966. *Societies: Evolutionary and Comparative Perspectives*. Englewood Cliffs, N.J.: Prentice-Hall.

——. 1971. "Comparative Studies in Evolutionary Change." In *Comparative Methods in Sociology: Essays in Trends and Applications*. Edited by I. Vallier. Berkeley, Ca.: University of California Press.

Presser, Harriet B. 1973. "Perfect Fertility Control: Consequences for Women and the Family." In *Toward the End of Growth*. Edited by C. F. Westoff et al. Englewood Cliffs, N.J.: Prentice-Hall, Spectrum.

———. 1975. "Social Consequences of Teenage Childbearing." Paper presented at the Conference on the Consequences of Adolescent Pregnancy and Childbearing, Bethesda, Md., 29–30 October.

Rawls, John. 1971. *A Theory of Justice*. Cambridge, Ma.: Harvard University Press.

Reinhold, Robert. 1977. "New Population Trends Transforming U.S." *New York Times*, 6 February, pp. 1, 46.

Ridley, Jeanne Claire. 1972. "The Effects of Population Change on the Roles and Status of Women: Perspective and Speculation." In *Toward a Sociology of Women*. Edited by C. Safilios-Rothschild. Lexington, Ma.: Xerox.

Rosenthal, Jack. 1971. "Survey Finds 50 Percent Back Liberalization of Abortion Policy." *New York Times*, 28 October, pp. 1, 22.

Ross, Susan C. 1973. *The Rights of Women: The Basic ACLU Guide to Women's Rights*. New York: Avon.

Rowbatham, Sheila. 1973. *Women, Resistance, and Revolution: A History of Women and Revolution in the Modern World*. New York: Pantheon.

Ryder, Norman B. 1973*a*. "Recent Trends and Group Differences in Fertility." In *Toward the End of Growth*. Edited by C. F. Westoff et al. Englewood Cliffs, N.J.: Prentice-Hall, Spectrum.

———. 1973*b*. "Two Cheers for ZPG." *Daedalus* 102 (Fall): 45–62.

Sanday, Peggy R. 1974. "Female Status in the Public Domain." In *Woman, Culture, and Society*. Edited by M. Z. Rosaldo and L. Lamphere. Stanford, Ca.: Stanford University Press.

Seaman, Barbara. 1972. *Free and Female: The New Sexual Role of Women*. Greenwich, Ct.: Fawcett.

Skinner, B. F. 1953; 1965. *Science and Human Behavior*. New York: The Free Press.

Sklar, June, and Berkov, Beth. 1975. "The American Birthrate: Evidences of a Coming Rise." *Science*, 29 August, pp. 693–700.

Slater, Philip. 1970. *The Pursuit of Loneliness: American Culture at the Breaking Point*. Boston: Beacon Press.

Smelser, Neil J. 1963. *The Theory of Collective Behavior*. New York: The Free Press.

Stonequist, Everett. 1937. *The Marginal Man*. New York: Scribner's.

Sweet, James A. 1973. *Women in the Labor Force*. New York: Seminar Press.

Tiger, Lionel. 1969. *Men in Groups*. New York: Vintage.

Trivers, Robert. 1972. "Parental Investment and Sexual Selection." In *Sexual Selection and the Descent of Man 1871–1971*. Edited by B. Campbell. Chicago: Aldine.

U.S. Commission on Population Growth and the American Future. 1972. *Population and the American Future: Advance Copy of the Commission's Report*. New York: New American Library.

Veblen, Thorstein. 1899; 1924. *The Theory of the Leisure Class: An Economic Study of Institutions.* New York: Huebach.

Wade, Nicholas. 1975. "Daniel Bell: Science and the Image of the Future Society." *Science*, 4 April, pp. 35–37.

Wallwork, Ernest. 1972. *Durkheim: Morality and Milieu.* Cambridge, Ma.: Harvard University Press.

Weinraub, Bernard. 1974. "In Kerala, Smallest and Most Literate State in India, a Breakthrough in Birth Control Is Taking Place." *New York Times*, 20 October, p. 13.

Westoff, Charles F. 1973. "Changes in Contraceptive Practices among Married Couples." In *Toward the End of Growth.* Edited by C. F. Westoff et al. Englewood Cliffs, N.J.: Prentice-Hall, Spectrum.

2

SEX ROLES, POLITICS, AND LIBERATION

Women [in the 1930s] saw little relationship between their vote and conduct of public policy and hence felt no urgency to go to the polls

—William Chafe, *The American Woman*, 1972.

We are not going to change the way women live by "making it" in a man's world. It's not our objective to be a mayor of a city, or the president of a corporation or a bank the way a man is. Rather, our objective is to make a life more bearable for everybody, to eliminate racial and sexual caste systems, and to insure that we all share in the power

—Ronnie Eldridge, Executive Director
Ms. Foundation for Women
Statement to the 49th Congress of Cities, 1973.

American women today have a greater voice in politics than at any earlier point in history. Their voting participation has gradually risen so that sex differences in voting declined from 13 percent in the 1948 presidential election to 3 percent in 1964 and 1968. A new women's movement that emerged in the 1960s has created greater political awareness among women. It laid the foundation for wider participation by women in the Democratic and Republican National Conventions in 1972. It helped an unprecedented number of women to seek and win political office in 1974 and 1976. A drive for the Equal Rights Amendment (E.R.A.), which had languished since the 1920s, came to life again in the 1970s and by the spring of 1977 was only three states short of passage.

But signs of inequality in actual representation of women's interests are still all too evident. The number of women in political elites is still small; women account for less than 10 percent of all state legislators and less than 5 percent of Congress. Professor of law Ruth Bader Ginsburg, counsel for many cases on sex discrimination, recently said, "More pervasive than any other gender line in the law is the legislature's assumption of an adult population composed of two classes: breadwinning males and dependent females" (1977: 61). Such assumptions seem to underlie the success that organizations opposing ERA have had in getting some state legislatures to defeat the amendment. Even the recent Supreme Court decision in *General Electric* vs. *Gilbert,* by denying sick-leave benefits under a company insurance plan for pregnancy and maternity, seems to uphold an outmoded notion that males' interruption of work by disability should consistently be compensated (even for sporting injuries, cosmetic surgery, or other elective causes), whereas females' work interruption is subject to a different standard.

If women's participation is to continue to grow, and their interests to be effectively represented, it is necessary not only to identify those individual attitudes and aspects of the social and political structure that impede progress but also to note the conditions that facilitate their participation and power. We shall begin by trying to understand why the women's movement surfaced to such importance in the last few years. The first part of this chapter addresses the changing boundary between public and private life and documents the historical role of the women's movement in representing personal and family interests in the public arena. The next three sections of the chapter consider women's participation at each of three levels of contemporary political life—as citizens, as leaders among the political elite, and as lawmakers and lobbyists for their own interests—and how the new feminist movement has enhanced their effectiveness in each type of activity. Finally, the particular value positions identified with women are considered in the light of long-term trends in the welfare society and the world system.

THE GROWING INTERPENETRATION OF PUBLIC AND PRIVATE LIFE

It is a striking historical fact that the woman's movement that flourished in the nineteenth century virtually disappeared after its culmination in the suffrage amendment of 1920. Not until the 1960s was it to rise again transformed into a broad-gauge movement for equality that would question current definitions of sex roles in work, family, and public life. The remarkable growth of the new feminist movement is documented by Maren Carden (1974, 1977), who estimates that some 200,000 to 300,000 women and a few men are now members of independent feminist organizations such as Women's Equity Action League (W.E.A.L.), National Organization for Women (N.O.W.), National Women's Political Caucus (N.W.P.C.), and thousands of other nonestablishment groups. In addition, a second type of feminist group, establishment-related, emerged in the 1970s to oppose sexism and demand change in society's treatment of women. Organizations such as the YWCA, the League of Women Voters, and the National Federation of Business and Professional Women's Clubs revived or introduced feminist objectives. Other new organizations expressed the interests of women in business, professional, governmental, or religious organizations. Examples include the Coalition for Labor Union Women, the American Federation of Teachers' Women's Rights Committee, and Federally Employed Women. In addition to such organized groups, Carden estimates that there are several million unorganized sympathizers who subscribe to at least some feminist objectives.

SHIFTING DEFINITIONS OF THE PUBLIC INTEREST

How are we to explain this phenomenal rise of the new women's movement, its growth, and its complexity?

In a comparison done over time Lipman-Blumen (1973) found cyclical variations in women's employment and involvement in public life, which she explained as a system response to crisis. She argued that society de-differentiates sex roles in time of disasters such as wars and depressions to release needed untapped resources. In the case of the contemporary women's movement, however, this explanation is not entirely satisfying because it is difficult to pinpoint any one particular national crisis that is responsible for its upsurge.

Carden (1977) finds two themes in the modern feminist movement—"equity goals" and efforts for "role change." "Equity goals" are advocated by the great majority and appear to stem from post-1950 U.S. social-reform movements. These goals have been widely accepted in the larger society, at least in principle. "Role change," on the other hand, is advocated by more radical or utopian groups who see a need to restructure male and female roles in work life, living arrangements, child rearing, and leisure. It is less clear where these goals come from and what will become of them. Because role change seems to require significant restructuring of the entire society, Carden judges its future uncertain.

Several political scientists provide what may turn out to be the most fundamental explanation of contemporary feminism. They note a tendency toward the "politicization of personal life." In a recent review of literature on women's political roles, Kay Boals (1975: 171) argued for the need "to see as political substantive concerns that have conventionally been thought of as private and apolitical." Jane Jaquette (1976: 59) identifies as one of the critical political issues for women the problem of defining the *proper bound-ary* between the public and private sphere. The political problem for modern society that Eli Zaretsky (1976: 142) distills from an exami-nation of capitalism and the family is that its future goal will be personal development:

> If we think ahead, even hundreds of years, . . . What will society then be about? It seems to me that it will then be about some form of personal development, achieved by individuals both through social activity, and alone.

Perhaps the critical issue of the modern women's movement is then, in fact, the politicization of private life. Its counterpart in the public sector is a growing responsibility on the part of government to support human services. The total spent on health, education, and welfare is now much greater than the amount spent on defense (Blechman et al., 1975: 50). Analysis of this growing domestic budget shows that the money is going for human services that once either were not performed at all or were the responsibility of the family and the private sphere. Convergence between feminists' polit-icization of private issues and government's widening responsibility for once private functions (such as supporting aged parents under Social Security) suggests that a major change in the structure of society underlies both phenomena.

The nature of the underlying social change is toward greater social complexity based on increased specialization and differentia-tion of tasks. The shift affects all aspects of social life, but the particularly relevant shift is at the boundary between work and family life, or between public and private responsibility. In the past, *intermediate* levels of sex role differentiation resulted in segregation between men's and women's spheres. One sex was specialized to perform in the public realm, be it in paid employment, politics, or other recognized positions for community service. The other sex was prepared to perform in the private realm—caring for childen, nursing the sick, and engaging in private charity. Such a pattern was the ideal in the United States, Great Britain, and other modern Western countries during the nineteenth and early twentieth centuries.

But *advanced* levels of societal differentiation have a different consequence. Segregation is broken down; there is new opportunity for crossover between sex roles. At the same time the lines sur-rounding work and family become more permeable. Distinctions between the realms of public and private responsibility blur and change. I theorize (Giele, 1971: 759) that the differentiation process itself explains the crossovers:

> When a society becomes more complex, roles become more specialized or differentiated. That is, a job is broken down into several different opera-

tions, some of which may be performed by the person who originally did the whole job, some of which may be taken over by experts who perform newly specialized functions.

When a job is broken up like this (i.e., differentiated), two other things happen at the same time. First, parts of the job can now be performed by persons who under the old rule were not qualified. Second, the very fact of breaking up the job into component parts has an effect on the consciousness of all the people involved: they become aware that certain qualifications they once thought intrinsically necessary to the performance of the job are not in fact so, at least not for certain parts of the operation. As a result the original role, which was seen to be segmentally related to others around it, is now seen as an *integral* made up of several components, a number of which are like the components in other units. Thus is built the possibility of a *shared consciousness*—a sense of commonality or of universal qualities in persons and roles that were initially felt to be totally different from each other. . . . [S]uch a process of differentiation has been going on in men's and women's roles. . . . The upshot is that a *crossover* is possible in many aspects of role performance that were formerly linked to sex.

REPRESENTATION OF PRIVATE INTERESTS

The trend to differentiation and complexity did not spring up overnight. For well over a century the process of industrialization has been in motion. In the differentiation of factory work from cottage industry the activities of productive work and family life were literally pulled apart (Smelser, 1959: 180-224). This differentiation process became a paradigm for the separation of public life from the "woman's sphere." Because the separation in fact required more responsibility and independent action by women inside the home, the nineteenth-century women's movement struggled to achieve legal recognition for women's rights to represent home and family interests. At the same time because the public sphere was defined as the male's, women faced another order of disability as individuals in their own right. Suffragists therefore sought the right to represent themselves directly, not through a father or a husband.

Once suffrage was won it took further time to see that the political right to vote did not guarantee independence and equality in other activities such as work and education. Nor did the vote by itself ensure that women would have a positive role in shaping social policy. A review of the historical women's movement shows that it has taken a series of steps for women to attain full representation of their interests in the public sphere. Nor is the process yet complete.

The married women's property acts.

Beginning in the 1830s and continuing to the Civil War, several states revised laws concerning marital property and the custody of children. The reforms permitted a married woman to sue and be sued, to enter into contracts, to control her own earnings, to hold rights of guardianship over children, and to control property that she brought to the marriage. These acts, which mark the beginning of women's rights legislation in America, are especially interesting for the particular *level* of reform that they attain. Their provisions are centered on the home and on women's duties as parent, worker, and general partner in the family enterprise. It seems significant that these laws were enacted at the same time that industrialization brought young women into the mill as textile workers. The law could also safeguard to some extent a woman's individual rights as a worker or marriage partner (Warbasse, 1960). The earliest women's property acts, primarily not the result of feminist agitation, were enacted in seven Southern states between 1837 and 1848. By allowing women to hold property, these laws represented an effort to safeguard financial stability of a family even when a husband's business enterprise failed. Between 1848 and 1861, more liberal laws were enacted in the North, particularly in Massachusetts, Ohio, and New York.

Local and national suffrage.

When the first Women's Rights Convention was held at Seneca Falls, New York, in 1848, those attending called for not only equal marital rights but the ballot for women as well, Disappointed after the Civil War that their fight for the abolition of slavery had not also won the right to vote for women, the suffragists had to continue their efforts to gain the franchise for another half-century.

Their earliest successes were in winning limited forms of suffrage at the local level. By 1879 women in Massachusetts had gained school suffrage and tax and bond suffrage, and in 1881 they began a drive for municipal suffrage. Many people were not sympathetic with national women's suffrage, and yet they could understand the popular women's temperance movement's plea for the "Home Protection" ballot, a euphemism for the right to vote against the sale of liquor in a town (Flexner, 1959: 183-185; Giele, 1961: 92; Scott, 1970: 148; Paulson, 1973: 183). Most women did not have higher education or a direct sense of the powerful forces at work in the national economy. But they could see the effects of urbanization, the saloon, immigrants, expanding schools, and political bossism. To be included as responsible members in town affairs was clearly in women's interest.

Winning national suffrage was much more difficult. Though two Western states permitted women to vote as early as 1870, a long, drawn-out battle had to be waged state by state until a drive to adopt a federal suffrage amendment was mounted in 1914 and was finally passed in 1920. Growing support for suffrage coincided with women's greater participation in the labor force, their contribution to the war effort, and their association with the Progressive party. To be included as responsible participants in national affairs was consistent with women's efforts to get more education, employment opportunities, and power to effect humanitarian reforms.

Antidiscrimination laws.

The jump from having the right to vote to attaining full equality in all areas of life proved to be far more difficult than imagined. Barriers to women's full equality were subtle and resistant because they were woven into the very fabric of society.

The suffrage victory had several decades to bear its fruit before it was found wanting. Women turned out to vote, but in proportions that disappointed the early feminists. Congress was eager to please the new voters, and in the early 1920s passed the Sheppard-Towner Act, providing liberal benefits for maternal and child health, but later repealed the bill (Lemons, 1973: 153-180). Some outstanding women rose to power in the Roosevelt administration: Frances Perkins as Secretary of Labor, Grace Abbott as head of the Children's Bureau, Mary Dewson in the Women's Division of the Democratic Party, and of course Eleanor Roosevelt in the White House. The Second World War introduced massive numbers of women into the labor force, but just as quickly they were demobilized (Chafe, 1972: 39, 180). By the beginning of the 1960s the proportions of professionals who were women and the fraction of women holding doctorates had actually declined from the peak reached during the 1920s and 1930s.

Then in 1961 President Kennedy established the Commission on the Status of Women. The commission was formally charged with investigating relevant employment practices, federal social insurance and tax laws, labor laws, differences in legal treatment of men and women, and possible new and expanded services required by women such as education, counseling, home services, and day care. Margaret Mead best summarized one purpose of the commission when she wrote in the introduction to its report, "The great gains of American women in health, literacy, education, and opportunity have been compared with the relatively few positions held by American women in government and industry—a puzzling contrast between our claim to freedom of opportunity and our actual accomplishments" (Mead and Kaplan, 1965: 4).

The commission and its successor in 1963, the Citizen's Advisory Council on the Status of Women, discovered inequities woven into such basic American systems as employment, marriage and divorce, holding property, and serving on juries. They found for instance that women bank tellers were paid five to fifteen dollars less per week than men; that women in power laundries made nine to forty-nine cents less per hour than men (Mead and Kaplan, 1965: 57). In 1962 the commission recommended a policy of equal pay for equal work, embodied in the Equal Pay Act of 1963. Support for other antidiscrimination measures followed. The Civil Rights Act of 1964 and Executive Orders 11375 and -11478, together with significant court decisions of the 1960s, prohibited sex discrimination in hiring, promotion, and other benefits. The Educational Amendments of 1972 extended antidiscrimination rules to textbooks, athletic programs, and educational curricula. Supreme Court decisions in 1973 struck down state laws prohibiting abortion. Although the president's commission did not take a stand on the Equal Rights Amendment, the Citizen's Advisory Council has given the amendment vigorous support. With the help of a new, concerted feminist effort, the ERA was passed by Congress in 1972, and by the spring of 1978 had been ratified by all but three of the required number of states.

Like *Brown* vs. *Board of Education*, which in the civil-rights field attacked the concept of segregation and "separate but equal" treatment of blacks and whites, the new women's rights laws question the concept of "different but equal" treatment for men and women. The Equal Rights Amendment goes beyond the Fourteenth Amendment, which guarantees "equal protection of the law" and specifies that "equality of rights under the law" cannot be denied on account of sex. Sex, then, becomes "a prohibited classification" (except in laws dealing with unique physical characteristics) (Brown et al., 1971: 939). Thus any differences in access, duties, or privileges, if assigned purely on the basis of sexual classification and not on the basis of some inherent ability, become suspect.

Transition to this kind of "sex-blind" thinking was not accomplished easily, even by feminists. Although the Women's party and the Business and Professional Women had in 1923 endorsed the ERA, their efforts were opposed by moderate feminists and the labor movement who feared a threat to protective labor laws. During the 1930s, however, the principle was established that protection could extend to both men and women. The AFL-CIO and moderate women's groups such as the League of Women Voters are now numbered among the supporters of the ERA.

Social policy formation.

If there is a transition under way in current feminist programs, it is evident in an increased effort to reach beyond the gains of antidiscrimination laws to the policy-making functions of government.

Feminists first gained an intimate knowledge of the workings of government when they tried to pursue remedies to discrimination.

Perhaps the most dramatic example was the discovery of federal contract compliance as a tool against educational institutions. In this process of implementing antidiscrimination laws, women developed a network of information, expertise, financial backing, and moral support. They generated so much congressional mail to the Office for Civil Rights at HEW that at one point a full-time person had to be hired to handle the correspondence (Sandler, 1973: 443). They also learned how to put their case in a form that was useful to such federal agencies as the Office of Federal Contract Compliance or the Equal Employment Opportunities Commission. Furthermore, they learned what new laws were needed. The Educational Amendments Act of 1972, for example, in part grew out of women's extensive experience with bringing suit against institutions of higher learning. Where only a patchwork existed before, the act provided one consolidated legal instrument against discrimination in education and in addition covered such other issues as curricula, textbooks, and athletic programs.

The contemporary women's movement also takes an active interest in positive social policy for matters that once were considered private, such as birth control, day care, and adequate income for female-headed households. Antidiscriminatory legislation promises some help on these issues, but other policies are needed to subsidize day care, restructure work schedules, and otherwise establish alternative acceptable supports for functions traditionally assigned to women.

Feminists have acted as lobbyists and as a pressure group in connection with all these issues. A threatened cut in day-care funds under Social Security Regulation 14A resulted in a deluge of congressional mail in the spring of 1973 from all across the country. Litigation against a Connecticut antiabortion law was paid for by small contributions from women all over the state. National social policies relevant to women continue to be reviewed in periodic newsletters. *Women's Lobby Quarterly* and *Do It Now*, published by the National Organization for Women, review such matters as legislative and judicial rulings on abortion, the rise in female-headed families, and available training and employment opportunities for mothers of children enrolled in the Aid to Families with Dependent Children (A.F.D.C.) program. The *WEAL Washington Report* gives systematic and up-to-date coverage of bills before Congress and lists supporters, opponents, and other relevant legislative data.

The forces that will bring the efforts of the women's movement to fruition are many and complex. The paradigm of the hierarchy of control suggests an order in which to review the changes in women's political roles that have already been realized and those that are still pending. At the most concrete and specific level can be documented changes in *individual political behavior* (voting, campaign activity). At the next level, *participation in elite roles*, women have made noticeable gains in winning office, but their still small numbers indicate that significant barriers remain. Still more general and far-reaching are efforts to express women's interests through *change in the laws and formulation of social policy*. Finally, *alternative values* held by some women invite comparison with the actual needs of the society. Now we consider each of these levels in turn.

SEX DIFFERENCES IN POLITICAL BEHAVIOR

Haunting the efforts of the new movement to mobilize women are numerous studies by political scientists showing that females are less well informed and less active in politics than men. Many of these scholarly studies have recently come under criticism for their methods, logic, and interpretation of findings. The times are changing, so that the findings of the mid-seventies are different from those of the fifties and sixties. The facts fall into three broad groups: (1) opinion polls that indicated *general attitudes* toward women's political role; (2) reports of sex differences in actual *political behavior*, such as campaign activity and voting; and (3) studies of children's political awareness, generally referred to as *political socialization*. We add to this list a topic made important by the new feminism: (4) the mobilization of women's political interests and their *resocialization* to become politically involved.

POPULAR ATTITUDES

General views on women's and men's roles are indicated by a number of public opinion polls taken throughout the country at periodic intervals. In a review of the major 1970 poll questions that touched the sex-role division of labor, Mason and Bumpass (1975) found that the modal sex-role outlook in 1970 was neither strictly traditional nor equalitarian. People believe women deserve equal pay for equal work, but they also support the idea of sex-role segregation between women and men because they believe maternal employment will harm preschool children. The Virginia Slims American Women Opinion Poll of 1972 showed that a majority (56 percent) of the 3,000 women interviewed were happy to be supported by a husband (Harris, 1972). But a poll conducted by the University of Michigan Survey Research Center in 1972 found that a sizable majority of both men and women took a position favoring equality in response to a question whether "women should have an equal role with men in running business, industry, and government," or whether women's place is in the home. Seventy percent of both sexes registered an opinion closer to the equality end of the scale (Bozeman et al., 1977: 47).

Political involvement of women has everywhere appeared to be lower than that of men. However, Almond and Verba (1965: 333) in a cross-cultural comparison of five countries found that women in the United States (70 percent) were more likely to discuss politics than women in the other countries studied—Mexico (29 percent), Germany (18 percent), Great Britain (63 percent), and Italy (29 percent). They explained the findings by noting that the American family is more often a forum for political discussion and that volunteer humanitarian activities have a greater part in the American civic culture than is the case in the other societies. American women fall less far behind men in their political participation because they are heavily involved in both these spheres. More recent data reported by Kim, Nie, and Verba (1974) show less difference in participation rates of men and women in the United States than in India, Japan, Nigeria, or Austria. The Virginia Slims polls report that women in 1972 expressed a desire to become more involved politically. More women than men were against the war in Vietnam, and more women than men expressed an interest in humanitarian programs (Harris, 1972; cf. Verba and Nie, 1972).

Over the last several years a gradual rise in the number of women supporting women's equality is evident. A Harris poll in the spring of 1975 showed 59 percent in favor of the aims of the women's movement compared with only 40 percent four years earlier (*Women Today*, 1975a: 72).

There was also a rise in numbers of men and women supporting the Equal Rights Amendment. Nationwide, 51 percent were in favor and 36 percent opposed, with the strongest support in the East and West, among the young, and among men. Of men 56 percent were in favor and 31 percent opposed as compared with 48 percent of women in favor and 40 percent opposed (*Women Today*, 1975a: 72).

But the really striking contrasts come from comparisons over a longer period of time. A 1938 Gallup poll asked whether a married woman should be working if she had a husband to support her; 82 percent of the men and 75 percent of the women answered "no." In 1946 a Roper survey for *Fortune* magazine asked whether an efficient, married, woman worker should be subject to layoff before a less efficient family man; 72 percent of the respondents would lay off the woman (but 68 percent would also lay off a single efficient man before the family man). The 1972 Survey Research Center poll asked a similar question, whether the first workers to be laid off should be women whose husbands have jobs or whether male and female employees should be treated the same. Among respondents over fifty-five, a majority (58 percent) said the women should lose their jobs first. But among the younger women the opposite was true; of women under thirty with a college degree, only 29 percent said the women should lose their jobs first (Bozeman et al., 1977: 51-53).

It is an interesting question why it is the young who particularly favor equality, or, in the case of the 1975 Harris poll on ERA, the men who were more favorable than the women. In light of structural differentiation theory, these findings are quite plausible. If equality for women signifies crossover as contrasted with segregation ("women's place is in the home"), it would be logical if persons who had already lived in both worlds (men and the younger generation) would most easily accept the equality principle. The fact that many sex differences in political behavior have recently been declining is understandable in light of this theory.

SEX DIFFERENCES IN POLITICAL ACTIVITY

Actual differences in political behavior between adult women and men have consistently declined over the last decade. Political scientists have implicitly pictured participation as forming a scale of difficulty. Such common activities as discussing politics and voting or making a political contribution are relatively easy. The less common and more difficult activities such as serving as a delegate to a convention or running for office require particular interest and commitment (Milbrath, 1965). Common to studies of the 1960s was the theme that women participate less at all levels; their interest was characterized as personal, parochial, moralistic, and idealistic, while men were more issue-oriented, cosmopolitan, pragmatic, and realistic. The difference was presumed to result from women's expressive role in the family and men's rational and instrumental role in the outside world. Studies of the 1970s, however, show declining sex differences in political participation and call for new explanations. The most plausible new interpretation appears to be that sex roles themselves are changing, and with them the distinctive character of female and male participation.

General political involvement.
In 1965 Milbrath, reviewing the literature on membership and activity in voluntary organization, summarized a major theme when he noted that, with modernization of a country, sex differences

decline (cf. Almond and Verba, 1965). However, the Virginia Slims Poll of 1972 still found that American men were more likely to have participated in political discussion, helped in a campaign, or otherwise become involved than had American women. Verba and Nie (1972: 181) added an important dimension of understanding, however, when they noted that more men are likely to be members of a voluntary organization than are women (65 percent of the men studied as compared with 57 percent of the women studied), but of all those who are members, women are much more likely to be active than are men.

Voting.

The number of men voting has traditionally been higher than the number of women voting (Campbell et al., 1954; Lane, 1959). The differences are greatest in rural areas and in the South, where presumably the roles of men and women differ the most. But Lansing's recent analysis of election data collected by the Survey Research Center at the University of Michigan shows that differences in the percentage of men and women voting declined throughout the 1950s and 1960s, even to the point where highly educated women voting in the 1952, 1960, and 1964 elections equaled the number of men of their class who voted. In the population as a whole, sex differences in voting for president declined from 13 percent in 1948 to 3 percent in 1964 and 1968, and to 6 percent in 1972 (Lansing, 1974).

Employment appears to be one of the most powerful factors influencing a woman's political participation. Levitt (1967) showed that a woman with considerable employment experience was more likely to vote than one without. Recently Kristi Andersen (1975: 442) found that the narrowing difference between men's and women's political participation over the last twenty years is largely due to the increased numbers of women employed outside the home who now vote at a rate equal to men's. Her explanation of the relationship is consistent with the concept of role differentiation and crossover:

> It seems reasonable to expect that the dual processes of increased contact with a wider environment and a growth in feelings of independence and political competence would be occurring primarily among those women who have jobs outside the home. Indeed ... it is the group of employed women which has made the biggest gain in participation between 1952 and 1972.

These findings suggest that a woman's social position or a change in her role has more effect on her political involvement than does some innate sex-related propensity. But even with the small sex differences that do exist and that are declining even further, it should not be forgotten that, of all the major background characteristics, sex contributes the *least* weight in determining who will and who will not vote (Verba and Nie, 1972: 359).

POLITICAL SOCIALIZATION

Just as popular attitudes toward the women's movement have changed dramatically since the 1960s, so has the scholarly literature on sex differences in political attitude and behavior. Research on the political socialization of children has recently come under strong feminist criticism for the sloppiness of its method, logic, and conclusions. The critics charge that American political scientists have been biased in interpreting the attitudes or behavior of boys as politically more sophisticated than that of girls. Overall, they have played down the fact that sex differences are weak and in some cases not statistically significant. In fact, differences in education, social-class differences, or race are far more powerful as determinants of political knowledge and interest.

Past interpretations of sex difference in political socialization can be roughly divided into an earlier group, which found results congruent with adult sex-role stereotypes, and a later group, which pointed to the influence of other strong situational factors. The first group of studies discovered that girls personalized politics while boys were interested in public figures, took a more abstract interest, and were issue oriented (Hyman, 1959: 30- 31; Hess and Torney, 1967: 173- 194; Easton and Dennis, 1969: 335- 343). Boys were not only better informed on political matters; Greenstein (1961) found in a study of fourth graders in New Haven that boys were also more oriented to political news as a source of pleasure and to political figures as objects for admiration. Given a list of occupations, more girls would identify a milkman as a government official than would boys of the same age (Easton and Dennis, 1969). Girls were also judged to be more passive than boys. Girls chose war pictures less frequently than boys, suggesting to Greenstein a less aggressive, less active, and more passive political orientation among females (Bourque and Grossholtz, 1974: 244). Two of the most recent studies of children's political attitudes found only weak or nonsignificant sex differences (Hess and Torney, 1967; Easton and Dennis, 1969). Yet the authors of those studies concluded that girls' lesser sophistication is congruent with women's private roles in the household, and boys' "superior" interest and knowledge are consistent with male involvement in the public realm.

Susan Bourque and Jean Grossholtz (1974) sharply question the validity of these interpretations. To them it seems a bit farfetched to infer that choosing war pictures in the newspaper is a sign of active political orientation while not choosing them is a sign of passivity. A number of studies such as Greenstein's were based on small samples. A later study by Hess and Torney, based on 5,000 schoolchildren, found no strong sex differences even though the authors emphasized them.

A new body of research has uncovered differences in political knowledge and interest that are more strongly related to other social factors than to sex. Dowse and Hughes (1971) in Great Britain and Heiskanen (1971) in Finland both found greater differences among children according to the type of secondary school they were attending than they did between the sexes (though at each level boys were more knowledgeable). In the United States Orum et al. (1974) found situational factors such as social class and race to be strong determinants of political knowledge and participation. Sex differences were stronger among blacks than among whites, but on the whole the differences found were small and not significant.

Several recent studies perhaps provide a way of reconciling small but persistent sex differences in political knowledge and orientation with scholars' increasing skepticism about their meaning. Iglitzin (1972) suggests that women have been socialized to be interested in the private sphere and men in the public sphere. As women's political emancipation proceeds, it seems likely that sex differences in political socialization will also decline. Jennings and Langton (1969) found that mothers influenced middle-class children's political attitudes more than fathers and that the effect of each parent was equal among working-class children. The authors explain their findings by a generational hypothesis: that women have now enjoyed the franchise for some years, are better educated and are imparting a new set of political attitudes to their children. As Andersen's findings show, a rising level of employment outside the home is also giving women more interest in political participation (Andersen, 1975). In addition, there is the women's movement, which has, along with education and unemployment, proved a powerful force for resocialization.

RESOCIALIZATION

A 1974 flyer sent out by the National Women's Political Caucus begins,

Dear Friend,

Does politics turn you off? If so, that might be because you feel excluded from it, especially if you are a woman.

If being a political wife, having a law career, or standing as candidate for the school board were some of the few traditional avenues by which women entered professional political life in the past, activity in the women's movement appears likely to provide another. To its great credit, the movement has made politics *relevant* to women. It indicates political channels by which women can redress some private injustice. A particular woman's problem may be with the divorce law, employment opportunity, educational programs, or personal financial credit. Where once she might have accepted these difficulties as inevitable, a woman may now glimpse the possibility of change. Tasks of influencing legislation, lobbying, or electing feminist candidates have suddenly taken on a new interest.

Furthermore, the movement educates women in the effective use of such channels. The *WEAL Washington Report* periodically lists legislation before Congress that is of interest to women and encourages readers to write their congressional representatives. Local chapters of NOW, WEAL, and NWPC mobilize women to express their views to state legislators. In the process, women learn the political ropes and thereby are likely to increase their involvement.

Eventually women's actual increase in political activity should result in a wealth of new materials, changed images, and role models. Then the effect of the increase will be visible to future generations.

WOMEN AND MEN IN POLITICAL ELITES

For a long time the statistics on women in political office indicated that politics would be a rather unpromising vocational choice for a woman. Although more than 50 percent of the electorate were women, before the 1974 elections less than 5 percent of state legislators were women. Less than 2 percent of the jobs in the highest ranks of the federal civil service (GS ratings of 16 to 18) were held by females (Lepper, 1974: 112). Among all government jobs a familiar pyramid that Duverger (1955: 123) found in a Unesco study of several countries was evident: women were concentrated at the lowest and worst-paid ranks; only very small numbers could be found at the top. A number of political scientists explained the pattern as due to women's weak political party ties, lack of interest, and primarily parochial or moralistic involvement.

The 1974 and 1976 elections, however, challenged the validity of all these explanations for the small representation of women in politics. In 1969, 305 women held seats in the state legislatures; by 1975–76 the number had increased to 610, double the number represented five years earlier and constituting approximately 9 percent of the total (Edmiston, 1975; *NWPC Newsletter*, 1974; Citizens Advisory Council, 1976: 44). Ella Grasso in 1974 became the first woman governor to win an election in her own right (without succeeding a husband); Mary Ann Krupsak won the second-highest state office in New York, lieutenant governor. Women hold the position of secretary of state in eleven states. A total of fifty-one women in 1975 were in such high state offices as governor, lieutenant governor, and secretary of state, a gain of 36 percent over 1972. Three women ran for the Senate in 1974, and two of them (Judith Petty, Democrat of Arkansas, and Barbara Mikulski, Democrat of Maryland) won more than 40 percent of the vote against established senators. In all there were, after the 1976 elections, eighteen women in the House of Representatives, not yet equaling, however, the peak year of 1962, when there were twenty.

To explain the recent rise in women's political activity, one must review earlier findings critically as well as identify the changed circumstances that contributed to women's political success. In general, it appears that women's local involvement, political independence, interest in social welfare, and moral integrity were assets rather than liabilities in recent elections.

THE TRADITIONAL PYRAMID

Women are present in large numbers at the base of the political pyramid, and they are active in volunteer work. But as one proceeds up the levels of government to municipal and county office, state legislatures, and finally high federal positions, their proportions decline. Current statistics from the Civil Service exhibit the familiar pattern. Women comprise 72 percent of the GS-1 to GS-6 positions, 27 percent of the GS-7 to GS-12 positions, and only 5 percent of the positions with a GS rating of 13 or higher. In the "supergrade" category, GS-16 to GS-18, there were in 1977 only 192 women compared with 6,840 men, less than 3 percent women (*Women's Political Times*, 1977: 2).

Local political elites.
Several exploratory studies show different patterns to be typical of men and women in local political activity. In a study of forty-six women state legislators, Jeane Kirkpatrick (1974:68- 69) found that many of them began their political careers in volunteer activities, such as the Parent-Teachers Association (P.T.A.) or the League of Women Voters, that are different from, though comparable with, the Moose or Elks or Knights of Columbus and ethnic groups in which

their male counterparts participated. Volunteerism thus provided the potential for propelling both women and men to run for the library board or the school committee.

Marcia Manning Lee (1977), who studied women's political participation in four communities of Westchester County, New York, discovered quite different styles of participation according to sex. She defined as a political participant a person who held an elective or appointive public office or who was a board member of an ongoing, organized group with a primary objective of influencing local government. The people who met these criteria were about equally divided between men (53 percent) and women (47 percent). The women tended to spend more time in local political activities than the men, but the nature of their activity tended to be more limited, ladylike, and bound by their family responsibilities. "In contrast to men, their political participation was confined primarily to women's organizations or to party work at the lowest level of the party hierarchy." Few were in leadership positions or held elected or appointive public office.

A considerably larger proportion of school-board members are women (about 12 percent) than of state legislators (8 percent) or members of Congress (4 percent). Apparently, the experience of motherhood increases a woman's interest in the school board and other local political functions because she is concerned for the education of her children and the community facilities available to them (Flora and Lynn, 1974). However, a study of school superintendents' attitudes toward women on school boards shows that about one-third would like no women members at all, one-third have positive views about women as members, and the other third are indifferent. The negative reports emphasize women's talkativeness and myopia; the positive reports note their industry, interest, and conscientious attention to the issues (National School Boards Association, 1974).

When two scholars examined the role of women in Chicago's political machine headed by Mayor Richard Daley, they found that only those women succeeded who conformed to a particular feminine stereotype. Such individuals limited their political ambitions to family matters, volunteer activities for good causes, and precinct-level work (Porter and Matasar, 1974). The new feminist criticism suggests that women generally get few opportunities of any kind, however, from the political establishment. Women who in the past felt low political efficacy were therefore, in fact, realists (Bourque and Grossholtz, 1974: 231).

Past explanations for women's low representation in political leadership have hung heavily on the concept of political efficacy.

Men are "more likely to feel that they can cope with the complexities of politics and to believe that their participation carries some weight in the political process" (Campbell et al., 1960: 490). Furthermore, women's past decision-making experience appears to approximate men's more in family and school affairs than at the job or in politics. Almond and Verba (1965) show the percentages of males and females from a U.S. sample of voters who reported high participation in decision making. The number of women reporting high participation falls sharply in relation to men in both the job sphere and the political sphere. High participation in decision making is reported by 27 percent of both men and women in family matters and by 33 percent in school affairs. But in political participation and job-related matters, women report less than half the amount of involvement of men. Thus where political questions move beyond the family and the school spheres, women are more likely to withdraw. The same reasoning would suggest that, as women's labor force participation rises, their political interest and sense of efficacy will also rise, as well as their participation (Krauss, 1974; Andersen, 1975).

State office.

The women whom Kirkpatrick (1974: 53) studied who actually decided to run for state office, particularly the state legislature, had a very high sense of political efficacy. Still, women state legislators are less than 10 percent of the total, and recent studies suggest that they are somewhat different from the men in comparable positions. The women are older than the men. For men the job is a stepping stone; for women it is more likely to be the culmination of a long career in local politics. The education and socioeconomic status of the women are somewhat lower than the men's. Perhaps most striking is that the women define their style of politics as different from that of the men. They see themselves as more honest and more open with their constituents, better informed, more thoroughgoing in fulfilling their obligations, and more independent of party dictates (Constantini and Craik, 1972; Jennings and Thomas, 1968: 492; Eagleton Institute of Politics, 1972: 8).

Elites at the federal level.

Public opinion questionnaires have shown that, while over 80 percent of voters would vote for a woman for Congress, only 60 percent would vote for a woman for president (Kirkpatrick, 1974: 248). The electorate apparently feels that women will not be able to fulfill the demands of higher office as well as as men.

Yet women made some recent important gains at the national level, particularly as delegates to the Democratic and Republican conventions in 1972. At that time women constituted 40 percent of the delegates to the Democratic National Convention, and in 1976, 35 percent, as compared with only 13 percent in 1968. Their greater representation there was the result of reforms within the Democratic party to ensure greater representativeness of the delegates by age, race, and sex. At the 1972 Republican national convention women were 30 percent of the delegates as compared with 17 percent in 1968 (Kirkpatrick, 1975: 280–281).

Whether women delegates were any different from men in their political attitudes is, however, a matter of debate. Soule and Mc-Grath (1977: 187–191) through interviews of 326 delegates at Miami Beach (a 10 percent sample of the total number of Democratic delegates) concluded that women delegates were consistently more liberal than men, even when differences in background were taken into consideration: ". . . black women were more liberal than black men, Southern women were more liberal than Southern men, rural women more liberal than rural men, etc." Kirkpatrick (1975: 315), however, came to the opposite conclusion that there was little difference between women and men delegates. (Differences that she found were instead between the more liberal convention delegates and the rank-and-file within the party.) Using data from mail questionnaires completed by 51 percent of the Democratic delegates and 63 percent of the Republican delegates and data from face-to-face interviews with 1,336 delegates in the 1972 postconvention period, Kirkpatrick found no correlation between persons' sex and their attitudes on busing, crime, welfare, inflation, Vietnam, and the like.

Some observers have attempted to explain women's underrepresentation in federal elective office as due to their relatively limited mobility compared with that of men. One undisputed difference is that women start their political careers later than men. But political scientists have especially emphasized women's lack of ties to the party, their moralism, their inability to engage in horse trading, and their limited ability to get backing from the establishment and to amass campaign funds (Bourque and Grossholtz, 1974: 262–263; Jaquette, 1974: xxviii).

In light of such handicaps, how could women register any political gains, such as those in 1974?

Going to the people.

In the climate of reaction to Watergate, an open manner with constituents had new appeal. Before, women had been disadvantaged because they lacked political cronies and stood somewhat rigidly on the side of right rather than surrender to political realism. These same characteristics gave them an advantage in an atmosphere of political disaffection with established leaders.

In the past women often had to wage tough primary battles or regular election campaigns against an opponent whose victory seemed assured. In order to win they had to develop an open and direct style with their constituents—a style perhaps less characteristic of the men who had won by going the regular party route.

The careers of a number of congresswomen reveal the pattern. Martha Griffiths (Democrat, Michigan) stood for election in 1954 in a Democratic district of Michigan that no one had expected her to be able to win, and yet she was returned to Congress consistently for a period of twenty years, during which she was a remarkable proponent of equal rights for women. Margaret Heckler (Republican, Massachusetts) first served on the Governor's Council in Massachusetts, but in 1966 stood against the redoubtable Joseph P. Martin, who had been for many years Speaker of the House, and she won a seat to the House of Representatives. Ella Grasso was nominated for governor of Connecticut only after she entered a key local primary. One of Barbara Mikulski's earliest political accomplishments was to mobilize resistance to an expressway in her Baltimore neighborhood. She won a seat to the Baltimore City Council, then was appointed to the Democratic National Committee, in 1974 took up a senatorial race against a very hard-to-beat incumbent, and in 1976 won a seat in the House. Her strong showing in each contest seems to have been the result of a vast neighborhood campaign by feminists, ethnic groups, and her relatives. Barbara Jordan (Democrat, Texas) was the first black ever elected to the Texas State Legislature. Put on a committee to redraw congressional districts, she helped create a central city district in Houston, which later sent her to Congress. Like Elizabeth Holtzman (who had surprisingly won a primary against powerful incumbent Emmanuel Celler in New York City), Jordan spoke effectively to the nation on the moral issues during the televised House Judiciary Committee hearings on Watergate.

The experience of these women campaigners and officeholders has now been recently distilled to shape the advice that campaign consultants and the National Women's Education Fund give to women candidates. Because women lack recognition, campaign funds, and strong party ties, they need to take their case to the people, enter primaries, and mobilize volunteers. Nikki Beare, a political consultant in Miami, advises that women need at least a year more lead time than men (Tolchin and Tolchin, 1974: 158–189). But once having won at the local or state level, women need no longer accept those positions as their final destinations.

Help from the women's movement.

Mikulski's 1974 senatorial campaign treasury had one-sixth the amount spent by her opponent, Charles Matthias. Even candidates like Pat Schroeder (Democrat, Colorado), who in her initial 1974 campaign received help from organizations like the National Committee for an Effective Congress, got less than their male counterparts. In the face of such difficulty, the National Women's Political Caucus and the National Women's Education Fund have been particularly helpful in organizing women's support behind a candidate and teaching campaign organizing skills to the people involved. Because women have learned to gather a volunteer army of people to ring doorbells and get out the vote, they have been able to save money that could be used for television ads or printed materials. At the same time, the volunteer armies have probably also mobilized a bloc of women constituents who help to vote their candidates into office.

A new kind of political issue: social policy.
Many of the women candidates also seemed to speak to the people through a new kind of issue that was immediate and personal yet heavily influenced by government action. These were social policy questions that involved government support for domestic needs rather than defense, and for a range of human services from care of the elderly to day care.

Bella Abzug initially won nationwide support for her early opposition to the Vietnam War. Mary Ann Krupsak campaigned in upstate New York in 1974 and spoke of the need for more nursing homes. Ella Grasso in the same year talked about care for the elderly, retirement problems, and overcharges from the electric company. Barbara Mikulski in 1974 worried about inflation and its effects on health care, social security, and a college education for the young. She asked for the chance to develop alternatives to the "Republican economics" of her opponent.

Not too long ago social scientists and women officials themselves considered it a disparagement of women's ability for them to be assigned to "women's issues"—consumerism, education, health, and welfare (Bourque and Grossholtz, 1974: 259). But in a peacetime, affluent society it is no longer so clear what are "women's issues." Adequate income for the consumer and the distribution of health care, retirement insurance, and educational resources are issues for all the people. They appear to have captured a new place of importance among national priorities (Schultze et al., 1972). Women, who may be especially interested and knowledgeable about these matters, are likely to win votes as a result. Mikulski reports,

> In one breath, I informed everybody, "I announce my candidacy for City Council." Then I reminded everybody how my great-grandmother came to this country with sixteen dollars and a bed and a mattress looking for the American dream. And through efforts of women like her, that American dream could come true for people like me, her great-granddaughter. . . .

> We never played to the [racial] fears of people. We always played to the hearts of people. Everybody is concerned about drugs. Everybody is concerned about school. Everybody is concerned about health care. We tried to come up with constructive solutions. [Quoted in Tolchin and Tolchin, 1974: 185]

Aside from these general issues for all the people, there is also touching evidence that the electorate voted for women as a sign of identification and support for them as women. "Go get 'em, Barb," conveys the affection communicated by the cheers Mikulski heard through her campaign van as she went through the ethnic communities. As Elizabeth Holtzman recalled,

> There was no hostility to the fact that I was a woman. I remember truck drivers leaning out of their trucks and saying, "I think it's great . . . it's fantastic that a woman is running." . . . I found mothers taking their daughters up to meet me. . . . They wanted their daughters to have a different conception of the possibilities for them. [Quoted in Tolchin and Tolchin, 1974: 223]

Women candidates' support for day care, more liberal abortion legislation, and the Equal Rights Amendment apparently won votes and helped to defeat opponents of these measures (*NWPC Newsletter*, 1974). Since a majority of the general population now support the aims of the women's movement, it seems that some candidates have won in part because of their support for what were once labeled "women's issues" but are now becoming some of the central social policy questions of our time.

WOMEN AND SOCIAL POLICY

Women's growing involvement in the political world is the result of two complementary processes. Each is an answer to Nancy McWilliams's (1974: 158) query, "How do matters previously defined as belonging to the private sphere become recognized as political questions?"

On the one hand, the techniques of consciousness-raising groups have taught women to personalize the political. By drawing attention to minor sexist conventions, they helped to create what McWilliams (1974: 163) describes as a "revolution in public consciousness that has resulted from gestures like affixing the label 'This ad oppresses women,' sitting-in at all-male bars, insisting on the use of Ms., pointing out the hostility inherent in the catcall, or referring to God as She." *

---

* This chapter will not consider the consciousness-raising aspect of the movement in any detail. The reader is instead referred to Jo Freeman's (1973) classic article "The Tyranny of Structurelessness" and other work by Freeman (1975) and Carden (1974, 1977).

On the other hand, women have also learned to politicize the personal. McWilliams (1974: 160) notes:

> The relation of the new feminism to the 1960s civil-rights movement is interesting in this context. The "We Shall Overcome" era saw the most striking conversion of private to political issues: where one sat on a bus, whom one married, in whose company one ate, where one swam, slept, and urinated, became questions of public policy.

These observations raise a question about how the political is in fact defined and how the modern differentiation and crossover in sex roles is related to it.

The political is variously defined by political theorists and ordinary citizens. One major definition focuses on power, the ability to coerce compliance. Another emphasizes the capacity of a social group or collectivity to act in concert on the basis of shared values and interdependent interests. Changing sex roles become political in both senses of the word. First, diverse women's interest groups must organize, lobby, and win legislative contests in order to get their programs adopted. But when their aims become law and their programs public policy, their power is no longer dependent merely on the strength of their group but is institutionalized in a pattern of action for the whole society. They then engage in a third type of political activity that combines the coercive and institutional aspects of power: they form a policy system concerned with the implementation and enforcement of the laws and policies that have been accepted.

DIFFERENTIATION OF WOMEN'S INTEREST GROUPS

Descriptions of the contemporary women's movement suggest that it is extraordinarily differentiated. In a recent account Carden (1977) lists as many as 170 organizations out of a much larger number that she estimates to be in the thousands. The differentiation is both horizontal (in the sense that different groups concentrate on special interests such as education, employment, religion, the media) and vertical (in the sense that some organizations work at a local consciousness-raising level, others at a state or regional level, and still others at the federal level). Some organizations such as NOW form a wide umbrella that encompasses both local groups and a central national office.

This complexity I take not only to indicate the internal complexity in the women's movement, but also to reflect the range and variety of sex roles in the larger population where certain themes of the movement have greater relative salience than others.

It is convenient to depict the women's groups and members of the larger population as ranging along a continuum. At one end are those committed to maximum separation and distinction between men's and women's roles (such as Stop-ERA and groups that oppose public support of child care). At the other end are persons who are committed to maximum flexibility and interchangeability between male and female roles (feminists, pro-ERA groups). Persons who inhabit each point along the continuum are probably sociologically as well as ideologically different; that is, they are likely to occupy quite different social roles in the larger society. Their personal concerns thus vary considerably by their social location. Surveys have already shown that women with higher education and those employed outside the home are likely to vote at a rate equal to men's (Lansing, 1974; Levitt, 1967; Andersen, 1975). A person's age also makes a difference: younger women more often subscribe to an egalitarian viewpoint than older women (Bozeman et al., 1977). As a general rule, it appears that women will support sexual equality if their experience has encouraged them to live public and private roles simultaneously rather than to confine themselves to the woman's sphere.

The variety of women's groups from which women can choose provides a mechanism for articulating a range of interests, ideologies, and programs. In the spring of 1977 typical newsletters of the major women's rights organizations reported on such widely diverging topics as the following: a plan by the Coalition of Labor Union Women for some of their members to study child-care programs in several European countries; a statement of support for ERA from the Catholic group Call to Action; efforts by anti-ERA forces; the threat that a woman's legal right to abortion might soon be severely limited.

Yet across this array of publications there were also themes in common. The major newsletters of NOW, WEAL, NWPC, and the Women's Lobby all show certain recurring issues. During the first half of 1977 the following topics surfaced in more than one publication: concern that Title IX of the Higher Education Act of 1972 was not being enforced; concern that cost of abortion might no longer be covered by Medicaid unless a mother's life is in danger; anger and frustration at the U.S. Supreme Court decision (*General Electric* vs. *Gilbert*) that denied payment of disability insurance to pregnant employees.

In addition, more than one group expressed support for particular items of new legislation such as raising the minimum wage (many women would be affected) and providing benefits, jobs, and training to displaced homemakers. Not only are these groups converging on common themes that are presented somewhat differently to each constituent audience. Evidently a foundation is also being laid for later concerted action, when power of numbers will be needed to change law and the direction of social policy.

The broad range of subjects covered—from health, work, education, and family to religion and the media—is symptomatic of where the present sex-role system is confining and destructive for a sizable number of women. The range of legal remedies that women envision is just as broad.

CHANGES IN THE LAW

As a combined result of the equal rights movements for blacks and for women, a body of law has built up piecemeal over the last decade and a half that has provided an armamentarium for women seeking recourse against unequal treatment in work, education, family, and health care. Until the 1970s the key pieces in the arsenal were the Equal Pay Act of 1963, Title VII of the Civil Rights Act prohibiting sex discrimination, and Executive Orders 11375 and 11478, which prohibited sex discrimination and enjoined affirmative action in organizations holding federal contracts. Because the Executive Orders called for withholding federal contracts from offending institutions, they were for a time one of the few instruments that women in higher education could use to bring suits against universities for sex discrimination in hiring, promotion, or pay.*

After 1970 the range of remedies broadened. The Educational Amendments Act of 1972 gave a unified base from which to protest all forms of sex discrimination in education; but enforcement continues to be a problem. The two Supreme Court Decisions on abortion, *Roe* vs. *Wade* (1973) and *Doe* vs. *Bolton* (1973), constituted strong support for equality between the sexes even in biological matters (but continuing efforts by antiabortion groups to nullify the decision through legislation show that there are still significant pockets of citizen disagreement with the principle that a woman has the right to control her own body).

Other new areas for policy development have been opened by the recent Supreme Court decision on disability payments for pregnancy

* Title VI of the 1964 Civil Rights Act forbade discrimination in federally assisted programs but not on the basis of sex, and Title VII, which forbade discrimination in employment, excluded faculty. The Equal Pay Act of 1963 did not include administrative, executive, or professional employees. Thus the contract compliance strategy developed by Bernice Sandler of WEAL, using Executive Order 11246, which prohibits all federal contractors from discrimination in employment, was the *only* remedy available to academic women (Sandler, 1973: 441).

TABLE 1. Major Rulings Against Sex Discrimination, 1960-1974

	LEGISLATIVE ACTS		EXECUTIVE ORDERS AND REGULATORY ACTIONS		COURT DECISIONS
1963	Equal Pay Act. Requires equal pay for jobs requiring same skills under similar working conditions. Enforced by Wage and Hour, Public Contracts Division, Department of Labor.	1968	Executive Order 11375 (issued in 1967). Prohibits sex discrimination by federal contractors. Administered by Office of Federal Contract Compliance (OFCC).	1965	*Griswold* vs. *Conn.* Supreme Court (S. Ct.) struck down state law making use of contraceptives a criminal offense.
1964	Civil Rights Act, Title VII. Forbids discrimination in terms, conditions, or privileges of employment on basis of sex, except where sex is a bona fide occupational qualification. Enforced by Equal Employment Opportunities Commission (EEOC).	1969	Executive Order 11478. Enjoins affirmative action in federal agencies. Administered by U.S. Civil Services Commission.	1969-1971	For major lower court decisions on employment, see Chapter 3.
				1971	*Reed* vs. *Reed.* S. Ct. ruled unconstitutional an Idaho law giving males preference as executors.
1971	Comprehensive Health Manpower Training Act. Prohibits discrimination in all training aspects of health programs.	1971	Revised Order 4. Sets out guidelines for enforcing EO11375 with respect to sex. How to establish goals and timetables.	1971	*Phillips* vs. *Martin Marietta.* S. Ct. struck down practice of excluding mothers of preschool children from important jobs.

Table 1. (Continued)

	Legislative Acts		Executive Orders and Regulatory Actions		Court Decisions
1972	Equal Rights Amendment passed by Congress and sent to states.	1973	Major out-of-court settlement between EEOC, OFCC, and American Telegraph & Telephone Company, awarding $15 million in back pay to women employees who had suffered job discrimination.	1973	*Pittsburgh Press vs. Pittsburgh Commission on Human Relations.* S. Ct. barred press from referring to sex in want ads unless jobs not subject to prohibition against sex discrimination.
1972	Educational Amendments Act. Extends coverage of Equal Pay Act to executive, administrative, and professional employees.			1973	*Frontiero vs. Richardson.* S. Ct. struck down armed forces regulation denying dependents of women members the same benefits as dependents of male members.
1974	Women's Educational Equity Act. Supports improved training and counseling for women.				
1974	Equal Credit Opportunity Act. Prohibits creditors to discriminate on the basis of sex or marital status.			1973	*Roe vs. Wade; Doe vs. Bolton.* S. Ct. upheld women's constitutional right to abortion.
1974	U.S. Commission on Civil Rights given jurisdiction on sex discrimination.				

SOURCES: Freeman (1975: 191-204), Purcell (1974: 136-137); Citizens Advisory Council on the Status of Women (1974: 12; 1975: 6-14).

(*General Electric* vs. *Gilbert*) and by a decision in *Goldfarb* vs. *Califano* upholding a widower's right to collect survivor's benefits automatically under his deceased wife's Social Security coverage (without passing a dependency test). A summary of the principal legislative, executive, and judicial rulings related to sex discrimination between 1960 and 1974 appears in Table 1.

The Equal Rights Amendment.

Because the legal sanctions upholding sex equality constitute a patchwork rather than a single integrated system, supporters of the Equal Rights Amendment have held that a unified approach such as that provided by the amendment is necessary to consistent and efficient establishment of sex equality.

Up to now the only constitutional guarantees of equal civil rights for women have been in the Fifth and Fourteenth Amendments, which guarantee due process and equal protection of the laws. But these provisions have not been so interpreted as to protect women's equal rights. The ERA states, "Equality of rights under the law shall not be denied or abridged by the United States or by any State on account of sex."

The California Commission on the Status of Women (1976: 6- 7) in a study of the possible future impact of ERA concluded that it will serve as a necessary clarification of the equal protection clause of the Fourteenth Amendment:

> While the Fourteenth Amendment has been interpreted to define race as a "suspect" (i.e., illegal) classification, the same has not been done for sex. Sex is, in fact, the only "class" not covered explicitly by the Constitution as illegal; "equal protection" has been explicitly extended to all other groups, to blacks, aliens, even corporations, but sexual equality remains implicit, and therefore, debatable. What this means is that a law or practice involving race discrimination is "suspect" and must be subjected to "strict scrutiny" by the Court in order to be upheld. Since the burden is on the discriminator to prove a serious necessity for the classification, this has generally meant that it is almost never upheld. On the other hand, when a classification (e.g., sex) is not "suspect," the standards of review under the Fourteenth Amendment are far more lenient . . . the significance of ERA is that it provides a universal legal definition of female equality, outlawing distinctions between people on the basis of sex as a violation of constitutional rights. And this is the most serious sanction in our legal system.

Typical opposing arguments to the ERA suggest either that a constitutional amendment is not the best means by which to attain sex equality, or that the ERA will undermine established institutions by depriving homemakers of the right to support, nullifying protective labor laws, or making women subject to the draft.

With regard to family obligations, proponents of the amendment respond by listing injustices under the present system. An exámple is child support and custody. The Common Cause handbook containing arguments on behalf of ERA notes that present support laws do not work, that one year after a divorce decree only 38 percent of the fathers are meeting their support payments. After ten years, only 13 percent are in full compliance with the support order. The ERA would make obligation to support children an equal responsibility of husband and wife. To quote Common Cause (1973: 83), the ERA "might therefore be used to require that spouses in divided families contribute equally to the support of the children within their means. Therefore, the spouse with the children would not be bearing a larger share of the responsibility for support as is now often the case."

Protective labor laws that apply only to women in most cases deprive them of jobs that they can easily perform and bar them from jobs with higher pay. Women who serve in the Armed Forces are not entitled to the same veteran's benefits as men. The ERA would give consistent and swift recourse against these injustices. It also allows women to continue to choose the homemaker role and recognizes their contributions as homemakers. It extends to men the protective labor laws that provide optimal working conditions. And it allows women to decide their position in relation to the draft, just as men now do (Common Cause, 1973: 81-85).

Implicit in these projected outcomes is a principle of equality that reflects maximum opportunity for role flexibility and inter-changeability. In the words of the California Commission on the Status of Women (1976: 7):

> The issue here is whether biological difference between the sexes is responsible for their present social roles and functions or whether these roles are socially learned, are culture-bound, and have little relevance to physiology. In a broad philosophical sense, any law or principle promulgating equal rights for both sexes assumes, if not a minimum of biological differentiation, then certainly a maximum of social malleability despite the differences.

National organizations listed by the Citizen's Advisory Council on the Status of Women (1974: 34-36; 1975: 29-31) as officially supporting the ERA in 1973 and 1974 numbered between 75 and 80; those opposed numbered between 10 and 15. Only a fifth of the pro-ERA organizations listed are women's rights groups. Fully one-half of the groups supporting ERA are ordinarily considered apolitical—Church Women United, B'Nai B'rith Women, the National Association of Railway Business Women, and so on. The remainder are a mixture of general political and federated organizations such as the Republican and Democratic parties, the AFL-CIO, the American

Bar Association, Common Cause, and the like. The new women's organizations thus seem to represent merely the tip of the iceberg of widespread popular support for the ERA. Yet their sustained pressure together with the help of such general purpose reform groups as ACLU, Common Cause, organized labor, church groups, and professional associations has been necessary to undertake the difficult state-by-state battle that is necessary for ratification. Although in early 1978 only three more states were needed before 1979, there have been some puzzling setbacks, such as rejection of the state equal rights amendments in New York and New Jersey. Nevertheless, there does now appear to be an effective women's rights lobby, not only in support of the ERA, but for all sorts of other pending legislation on sex discrimination (Murphy, 1973: 65-69).

IMPLEMENTATION AND ENFORCEMENT

The Equal Pay Act of 1963 charged the Labor Department with enforcement. The Civil Rights Act of 1964 prohibited sex discrimination in certain covered occupations and set up the Equal Employment Opportunities Commission (E.E.O.C.) to handle complaints. Executive Order (E.O.) 11375 of 1968 prohibited sex discrimination in organizations with federal contracts. It charged the EEOC with enforcement in educational institutions and the Office of Federal Contract Compliance in the Labor Department with enforcement in certain other areas. But enforcement is in difficulty. Enormous backlogs of cases have mounted up. More than 130,000 cases are said to be waiting for action by the EEOC. In addition three-year delays occurred in issuing guidelines for enforcement of EO 11375 and the Educational Amendments Act of 1972. Yet despite understaffing and heavy work load in enforcement agencies, some landmark rulings have been issued. The most famous was the decision in 1973 that American Telephone and Telegraph would have to restore some $15 million in back pay to women employees who had suffered sex discrimination in jobs and wages.

Not only are some of the same legal principles, court rulings, and legislative acts applicable to several major types of discrimination. Women's strategies for proof of complaint, and the remedies they invent, because they have wider applicability, benefit both the enforcement agencies and the movement. Various agencies of government must ferret out examples of discrimination, develop cases for prosecution, or use other means to negotiate change. In this process the official agencies have to be prodded and in the end be aided by interested women's organizations. One observer of the movement, Jo Freeman (1975: 230), terms the relationship between government and the women's movement *symbiotic*. The movement uncovers facts and cases, and develops statistics on a pattern of discrimination. Then a federal agency such as the Equal Employment Opportunities Commission, with sanctions and resources of government, is able to bring enforcement proceedings. Government also disseminates the results and helps the movement in so doing.

To get desired legislation passed, and to enforce it, the women's movement has had to maintain itself in a mobilized state. Freeman (1975: 227-229) describes the resulting relationship of the movement with government as a policy system in which whirlpools or centers of equal-rights activity have developed that involve lobbyists, members of Congress, civil servants, and some unofficial research authorities. Over the years these people meet, have lunch together, discuss common human problems, and gradually develop strategies and programs. In the women's movement the equal-rights policy system was principally created by the campaign for the Equal Rights Amendment and the WEAL effort in higher education to enforce sex equality through threat of withdrawing federal contracts from discriminating universities. Changes have resulted as quickly as they have (the passage of the 1972 Educational Amendments, the drive for ERA, and so on) in large part because of the incipient structure that the movement created and because the changes were part of a larger equal-rights revolution.

There is, however, considerable distance yet to go when the new equal-rights rules are applied. In the interim other signs of greater interest in women's issues have appeared in various corners of government. There are now more than fifty commissions on the Status of Women in various states and territories and more than thirty municipal and county commissions in or around major cities. In 1971 and again in 1973, as a result of pressure from women's groups, President Nixon appointed a special assistant in the White House to recruit women into the administration. Also in 1973 Representative Martha Griffiths chaired Hearings on the Economic Problems of Women before the Joint Economic Committee of Congress. The 1973 Economic Report of the president contained a chapter on women. President Ford named a woman to a cabinet position. President Carter has named two women to cabinet posts, Juanita Kreps as Secretary of Commerce and Patricia Roberts Harris as Secretary of Housing and Urban Development. In addition the president and Mrs. Carter, like their predecessors in the White House, have actively supported the Equal Rights Amendment.

DO WOMEN STAND FOR A NEW VALUE PERSPECTIVE?

Whether women have any distinctive outlook is a question that makes most feminists uncomfortable. Others thrive on it. Some argue that women are no different from men in politics—they are just as corruptible, just as hardheaded and power hungry, and potentially just as warlike. Others like Wilma Scott Heide, former president of NOW, contend that women will bring humanity back into government when they reach positions of power (Heide, 1973). Gloria Steinem, cofounder of *Ms.* magazine, likewise points to women's traditional loving and peacemaking attributes, their concern for the quality of life and the individual person rather than for mere success and domination (Steinem, 1972).

It is difficult to produce solid evidence of sex differences in these attitudes. Psychologists and anthropologists find more aggression in boys than girls (Edwards and Whiting, 1974), but other observers also note that parents and teachers have expectations that girls will be more gentle and boys more tough. There is no study that I know of that compares the political actions of men and women in office. Even if there were and no difference was found, one might argue that the women who made it into politics had to be more like men to get there.

About all we can do at the moment is ask whether the *ideology* of the women's movement focuses on any distinctive values that are different in emphasis from the ones of the established order. First, we find that there is considerable discussion about whether different kinds of women have any common outlook. It is frequently asserted that feminism is primarily a middle-class manifestation. Yet a National Black Feminist Organization was founded in 1974, and anecdotal evidence showing working-class women's interest in liberation continues to mount. Next, we find certain recurring themes in feminist thought. One theme is nonhierarchical. It emphasizes mutual participation in decision making. Another theme is pacifist or, in time of war, emphasizing the moral and humanitarian purpose of the conflict rather than the power objectives.

DIFFERENCE OR UNITY AMONG WOMEN

The charge is frequently made that the women's movement is predominantly white and middle class, catering to the needs of women with educational and professional qualifications who want to make it in a man's world.

Working-class women have other goals. Their men do not work in such attractive jobs, and therefore having what men have is not so desirable for them. In Barbara Mikulski's words,

> If your husband is a factory worker or a tugboat operator, you don't want his job. We're not after the jobs that our men have because we know how our men feel. We know that when they come home from work every day they feel they've been treated like the machines they operate. [Seifer, 1973: 59]

Black women are concerned with ridding their local communities of rats and debris, improving housing, and giving moral support to their children and husbands in the struggle against racism. Audrey Colom, a black feminist from Washington, D.C., found that neighborhood clean-up campaigns could mobilize tremendous support from uneducated black women. But these same women were turned off by white feminists' talk of abortion reforms or their worries about how to attain success in top positions (Colom, 1973). A special issue of *Transaction/Society* magazine reveals the contradictory feelings that blacks feel over these issues. On the one hand, Linda La Rue (1970) argues that women's liberation invites blacks to examine critically their own goals and question a feminine mystique for black women that white women are already abandoning. In contrast, Nathan and Julia Hare (1970) repeat the standard black arguments that racism is more important than sexism, that "the black women still longs to escape the labor force and get into the home."

In a sensitive description of *Working Class Women in America*, Nancy Seifer (1973) distinguishes some of the major differences between middle-class and working-class feminists. The working-class women are largely of immigrant origins from Eastern and Southern Europe. Their families are Catholic and fervently anticommunist, and they generally supported the Vietnam War. Typically, they stand against "liberal" reforms like busing and legislation permitting abortion.

How then, with all these differences, can there be any common meeting ground? Perhaps the key answers are to be found in politics and employment where the *means* to achieve greater representation and employment are a focus that interests all.

With respect to work, the middle-class feminist organizations and working-class women may be about to come together in an effort to organize clerical workers and other white-collar occupations. Feminists also see the value of leadership in union positions as a stepping stone to wider political responsibilities. The fact that the AFL-CIO now supports the Equal Rights Amendment is an additional sign of mutual support. Throughout society at each class level there appears to be overwhelming consensus that women should be able to work at meaningful, well-paid jobs.

With respect to politics, a coalition also seems likely. Working-class and black women have strong interests in their neighborhoods and social communities. Women who have been successful in running for office have also been particularly open and responsive to social needs and community sentiment. Thus political convergence on human services and local issues may be the funnel that will unite interests of women from different racial and class origins.

PARTICIPATION: THE NONHIERARCHICAL OUTLOOK

The basic value that unites feminists is the belief that all persons are created equal. This belief is a value that applies just as much to slaves or other oppressed minorities as it does to women. In the 1830s and 1840s the Grimké sisters of South Carolina and other early feminists like Lucretia Mott made their first public protests in opposition to slavery.

In the 1890s and early 1900s another group of female reformers became prominent for their work on behalf of the urban and immigrant poor. Jane Addams, Florence Kelley, Edith and Grace Abbott, and Lillian Wald established the settlement-house movement and worked for enlightened city government, labor laws, and consumer legislation that would protect the average person against the big established powers of political bossism and large corporations.

In the 1920s the League of Women Voters carried these major crusades forward. They worked for an honest civil service system. Despite opposition from the private power interests, they supported projects for government dams such as TVA. They sought establishment of a central department of education and social welfare, a goal that was realized only in 1953 in a unified Department of Health, Education, and Welfare (Lemons, 1973: 124-147).

Throughout the history of feminism, women have worked for a different model of social action that would enlarge opportunity for everyone, men included, not just promote upward mobility for themselves. Shortly before the suffrage victory, Emma Goldman, the anarchist feminist, expressed this ideal: "A true conception of the relation of the sexes will not admit of conqueror or conquered: it knows of but one great thing: to give of one's self boundlessly, in order to find one's self richer, deeper, better" (in Rossi, 1973: 516). Susan La Follette in 1926 wrote also that men would share in the benefits of the equality that women sought, saying, "There is no reason to expect that women, emerging from tutelage, will be wiser than men. . . . It is impossible for a sex or a class to have economic freedom until everybody has it, and until economic freedom is

attained for everybody, there can be no real freedom for anybody"
(Rossi, 1973: 563).

In 1971, at the founding of the National Women's Political
Caucus, Betty Friedan put this continuing ideal of liberation for all
in contemporary terms:

> Women do not seek power over men or to use power as men have used it. I
> believe that women's voice in political decisions will help change our whole
> politics away from war and toward the critical human problems of our
> society—not because women are purer or better than men, but because our
> lives have not permitted us to evade human reality as men have, or to encase
> ourselves in the dehumanizing prison of machismo, the masculine mystique.
> Shana Alexander suggested that our slogan should be "Women's Participa-
> tion—Human Liberation." [Quoted in Carden, 1974: 169]

In an examination of women's organizations throughout the
world, Elise Boulding recently observed that a nonhierarchical theme
runs through them all. She derives an explanation from the nature of
women's past experience in the household:

> [I]n general the small scale of the household meant a minimum of hier-
> archy. . . . Community redistribution systems, whether in terms of sharing
> food, nursing the sick, or caring for children, became the business of women
> anchored to the households. For one thing, they were the only ones who
> knew about neighborhood needs. The female role in redistribution operated
> at every level of society from the poorest to the richest. [Boulding, 1977:
> 212–213]

Women have also been outsiders. To be included in the system on
equal terms, they have to argue that *a different standard of excellence* must be brought to bear—whether it be the quality of life, and
health and education, or the benefit for the consumer and little guy
rather than those already rich and in power. *Because they are
outsiders, women's standard of excellence cuts across the standards
by which achievement is judged in the established system.* Therefore,
when women argue equality, they do not first argue bringing women
up to men's level, or men down to their level (Janeway, 1973).
Instead, they really mean that the whole society will benefit under a
changed list of priorities—that all people will be liberated, not just
themselves.

WOMEN, WAR, AND PEACE

Perhaps it is a combination of women's egalitarian outlook and
their household experience that explains their interest in making
peace, not war. Feminists believe in inclusion rather than exclusion.

They emphasize unity rather than differentiation and competition. Through the ages it has been predominantly women who have had to move into the strange and sometime hostile surroundings of their husband's family. Boulding (1977: 213) argues that this is one reason why women become peacemakers.

> Historically, women have been the mediators in every society, largely through the marriage alliance systems. It is usually the woman who leaves her home village, not the man. A woman's skills in developing networks for communication and cooperation in an alien setting, not only in terms of making friends with hostile relatives of her new husband in her new home, but also in terms of linking them in positive ways with her own family back in her old home, is one of the major unstudied sets of social organization skills to be found in the human record.

Two of America's most admired women leaders, Jane Addams and Eleanor Roosevelt, took special interest in work for peace and international cooperation. Before the First World War Jane Addams was a leader both of the U.S. Woman's Peace Party and the International Congress of Women at The Hague. Later as prominent members of the Women's International League of Peace and Freedom, both Addams and Emily Balch won a Nobel Peace Prize. Eleanor Roosevelt took important part in founding the United Nations and in service to the U.S. mission there.

Women have also been able to undertake military roles effectively, particularly in underground warfare and guerrilla fighting. Even in a purdah society such as Algeria, women contributed heavily to the liberation struggle against the French. Boulding says that "while women are usually a small minority in permanent national armies, in guerrilla and other types of underground warfare, they may reach as high as 40 percent participation levels, as in the P.L.A.F. (People's Liberation Armed Forces) in Vietnam" (Boulding, 1977: 177). Accounts of Algerian women in the liberation movement show that they participated out of a driving sense of patriotism, loyalty, and cultural identification.

American women's experience in war has never been of the guerrilla or underground variety. But particularly noble accounts remain of the Southern women who managed plantations and supported the Confederate Army during the Civil War (Scott, 1970). Accounts from the First World War show women selflessly serving as nurses and ambulance drivers. During the Second World War, women served in the armed forces, but the great majority contributed in support services, keeping the factories running.

Contemporary American feminists have recently expanded their political activity to encompass worldwide concerns. In 1973 the first meeting of an International Feminist Planning Conference was held at Lesley College in Cambridge, Massachusetts, with delegates from many foreign nations and some of America's leading feminists, particularly the top leadership of the National Organization for Women. In 1975, International Women's Year, American feminists turned more of their attention to their international sisters and the possible adverse effects of war and economic development on women of the Third World. More American women now recognize their responsibility to face the effects of U.S. action on the women of other countries (*Women Today*, 1975b: 87-89).

Carden (1974: 170) reports that American feminists look for a time when structural changes in men's and women's lives will make people "more concerned with the rewards of friendship rather than the rewards of achievement." Boulding (1977: 189-192) notes the tremendous revolutionary potential in the worldwide communities of Catholic sisters. They live like Saint Francis, dedicated to simplicity, poverty, and humility. Their example proves that a nonhierarchical and peaceful style can marshal enormous resources for health, education, and welfare, concerns that transcend national boundaries.

On occasion women may find violence necessary to resist dehumanization or defend their selfhood or liberty. The Algerian and the Vietnamese women showed bravery and courage in their wars for liberation. American women supported the Second World War at the same level as American men (Ellsberg, 1972). Ordinarily, however, women engage in cooperation; they build networks, doing so without much money or other resources. They use their social skills to achieve positive effects, and they are less concerned about machismo and possible defeat than are men.

When Daniel Ellsberg began to change his views toward American involvement in Vietnam, he discovered a cultural difference between men and women in their attitudes to the war. Early in 1971, speaking to a League of Women Voters meeting, he asked how many of the women present were opposed to the war. Almost every woman raised her hand. Then he asked how many of them had reached this position before their husbands had. Again, almost every woman raised her hand. Ellsberg had earlier found that even the wives of top Pentagon officials were known to oppose the war. While the men's policy discussions used "phrases indicating toughness, guts, and mastery," the women, Ellsberg concluded, had a different set of values that made them more sensitive to atrocities committed against another people and more ready to admit the senselessness and defeat of the war (Ellsberg, 1972).

Perhaps contemporary women believe with Emma Goldman that women and men—all people—must learn to relate to each other, not as conqueror and conquered, but as persons engaged in a common human enterprise of growth and self-realization.

SUMMARY

American women's quest for political rights in the long run coincides with the larger society's need to develop more equal opportunities for all. At the same time the women's movement has helped to raise once private issues to public attention where they are important in the shaping of future social policy. If women are to use their full capacity, however, for helping society to meet its future challenges, their energies must be mobilized at the citizen level, at the level of elective and appointive office, and at the legislative and policy-making level.

We have seen how barriers to women's involvement at each of these levels of participation are slowly being eroded, though many obstacles yet remain. At the level of *individual political behavior* (voting and so forth) the century-old women's movement has won an irreversible right for women to participate. Recently women have been socialized by a new political consciousness, stemming in part from the women's movement. Their voting rates and political partici- pation have greatly increased in the last two decades, now just about equaling that of men. At the level of *participation in elite roles*, women are still grossly underrepresented in top positions; however, women have recently become more visible and successful in running for political office and winning. At the *institutional level of working for change in laws and social policy*, their efforts have been particu- larly successful on behalf of equal rights. Their broadening interests in health and child care, minimum-wage laws, and the like, promises that they will make an important future contribution to public policy for human services. At the *value level* women have stood for restoration of peaceful, localized, and nonhierarchical forms of par- ticipation. Their international interest, rather than dealing with the military or economic balance of power among nations, has focused on social conditions in each country. By setting up a network through an emerging international sisterhood of feminists they have been able to exchange information on the world food supply, popu- lation measures, and social arrangements such as working conditions and day care.

Having found their way a little deeper into the political establish- ment, women now promise farther advancement in coming years that will truly carry them beyond the goal of the presuffrage era when their chief hope was to change the course of events by winning the vote. Now no longer either so naive or hopeful, women understand that they must join with men not only in voting but also in seeking the burdens of office, engaging in the debates over public policy, and participating in the military, even if it means risking their lives for the country.

Eventually, women even look for a time when one of them might be president. Such an event does not, however, seem likely until America is part of a world order where military might is no longer the central theme of national power, and the male leader the ultimate protective figure in national defense. Only mutual respect and shared prosperity between nations will bring such a time. Much work is yet to be done before women attain this final symbolic position that demonstrates the highest capacity for national leadership. To suggest otherwise would be to expect too much from the present era of change, an error of which we have so well been warned by the example of our suffragist forebears.

REFERENCES FOR CHAPTER TWO

Almond, Gabriel, and Verba, Sidney. 1965. *The Civic Culture: Political Attitudes and Democracy in Five Nations.* Boston: Little, Brown.

American Bar Association. 1972. *Review of Legal Education: Law Schools and Bar Admissions Requirements in the United States 1967-1971.* Chicago: A.B.A.

Andersen, Kristi. 1975. "Working Women and Political Participation." *American Journal of Political Science* 19 (August): 439-453.

Blechman, Barry M.; Gramlich, Edward M.; and Hartman, Robert W. 1975. *Setting National Priorities: The 1976 Budget.* Washington, D.C.: Brookings Institution.

Boals, Kay. 1975. "Review Essay: Political Science." *Signs* 1, no. 1 (Autumn): 161-174.

Boulding, Elise. 1977. *Women in the Twentieth-Century World.* New York: Halsted Press.

Bourque, Susan C., and Grossholtz, Jean. 1974. "Politics an Unnatural Practice: Political Science Looks at Female Participation." *Politics and Society* 4 (Winter): 225-266.

Bozeman, Barry; Thornton, Sandra; and McKinney, Michael. 1977. "Continuity and Change in Opinions about Sex Roles." In *A Portrait of Marginality.* Edited by M. Githens and J. L. Prestage. New York: McKay.

Brown, Barbara; Emerson, Thomas I.; Falk, Gail; and Freedman, Ann E. 1971. "The Equal Rights Amendment: A Constitutional Basis for Equal Rights for Women." *Yale Law Journal* 80 (April): 872-985.

California Commission on the Status of Women. 1976. *Impact ERA: Limitations and Possibilities.* Millbrae, Ca.: Les Femmes Publishing.

Campbell, Angus; Gurin, Gerald; and Miller, Warren. 1954. *The Voter Decides.* Evanston, Il.: Row, Peterson.

Campbell, Angus; Converse, Philip; Miller, Warren; and Stokes, Donald. 1960. *The American Voter.* New York: Wiley.

Carden, Maren Lockwood. 1974. *The New Feminist Movement.* New York: Russell Sage Foundation.

———. 1977. *Feminism in the Mid-1970s: The Nonestablishment, the Establishment, and the Future.* New York: Ford Foundation.

Chafe, William Henry. 1972. *The American Woman: Her Changing Social, Economic, and Political Roles, 1920-1970.* New York: Oxford University Press.

Chamberlin, Hope. 1973. *A Minority of Members.* New York: Praeger.

Citizens Advisory Council on the Status of Women. U.S. Department of Labor, Employment Standards Administration. 1973. *Women in 1972.* Washington, D.C.: U.S.G.P.O.

———. 1974. *Women in 1973.* Washington, D.C.: U.S.G.P.O.

———. 1975. *Women in 1974.* Washington, D.C.: U.S.G.P.O.

———. 1976. *Women in 1975.* Washington, D.C.: U.S.G.P.O.

Colom, Audrey. 1973. Interview with Janet Zollinger Giele, Washington, D.C.

Common Cause. 1973. *Action Program for Ratification of the Equal Rights Amendment.* Washington, D.C.: Common Cause.

Constantini, Edmond, and Craik, Kenneth H. 1972. "Women as Politicians: The Social Background, Personality, and Political Careers of Females." *Journal of Social Issues* 28, no. 2: 217-236.

Derthick, Martha. 1975. *Uncontrollable Spending for Social Service Grants.* Washington, D.C.: Brookings Institution.

Dowse, Robert E., and Hughes, John A. 1971. "Girls, Boys, and Politics." *British Journal of Politics* 22 (March): 53-82.

Duverger, Maurice. 1955. *The Political Role of Women.* Paris: Unesco.

Eagleton Institute of Politics. 1972. *Women State Legislators: Report from a Conference Sponsored by the Center for the American Woman and Politics, 18-21 May, Rutgers-The State University.* New Brunswick, N.J.: Eagleton Institute of Politics.

Easton, David, and Dennis, Jack. 1969. *Children in the Political System.* New York: McGraw-Hill.

Edmiston, Susan. 1975. "Out from Under! A Major Report on Women Today." *Redbook*, May.

Edwards, Carolyn P., and Whiting, Beatrice B. 1974. "Women and Dependency." *Politics and Society* 4, no. 3: 343-356.

Eldridge, Ronnie. 1973. "Statement: Current Attitudes of Women toward the Political Process." In *Women in Municipal Government.* Based on a workshop held at the 49th Annual Congress of Cities, San Juan, Puerto Rico, 5 December. Washington, D.C.: National League of Cities.

Ellsberg, Daniel. 1972. "Daniel Ellsberg Talks about Women and War." *Ms.*, Spring, pp. 36-39.

Flexner, Eleanor. 1959. *Century of Struggle: The Woman's Rights Movement in the United States.* Cambridge, Ma.: Harvard University Press.

Flora, Cornelia B., and Lynn, Naomi B. 1974. "Women and Political Socialization: Considerations of the Impact of Motherhood." In *Women in Politics.* Edited by J. S. Jaquette. New York: Wiley.

Freeman, Jo. 1973; 1974. "The Tyranny of Structurelessness." *Berkeley Journal of Sociology* 17: 151-164. Reprinted in *Women in Politics.* Edited by J. S. Jaquette. New York: Wiley.

——. 1975. *The Politics of Women's Liberation.* New York: McKay.

Giele, Janet Zollinger. 1961. "Social Change in the Feminine Role: A Comparison of Woman's Suffrage and Woman's Temperance, 1870-1920." Ph.D. dissertation, Radcliffe College.

——. 1971. "Changes in the Modern Family: Their Impact on Sex Roles." *American Journal of Orthopsychiatry* 41 (October): 757-766.

Ginsburg, see *Women Today* 1977.

Greenstein, Fred. 1961. "Sex-related Political Differences in Childhood." *Journal of Politics* 23: 353-372.

Hare, Nathan, and Hare, Julia. 1970. "Black Women 1970." *Transaction/Society* 8 (November-December): 65-68ff.

Harris, Louis, and Associates. 1972. *The 1972 Virginia Slims American Women's Opinion Poll.* New York: Louis Harris Associates.

Heide, Wilma Scott. 1973. "Revolution: Tomorrow Is Now!" Speech delivered at Sixth National Conference of National Organization for Women, 17-19 February, Washington, D.C.

Heiskanen, Veronica Stolte. 1971. "Sex Roles, Social Class, and Political Consciousness." *Acta Sociologica* 14, nos. 1-2: 83-95.

Hess, Robert D., and Torney, Judith V. 1967. *The Development of Political Attitudes in Children.* Chicago: Aldine.

Hole, Judith, and Levine, Ellen. 1971. *Rebirth of Feminism.* New York: Quadrangle.

Hyman, Herbert H. 1959. *Political Socialization: A Study in the Psychology of Political Behavior.* New York: The Free Press.

Iglitzin, Lynne B. 1972. "Political Education and Sexual Liberation." *Politics and Society* 2, no. 2: 241-254.

Janeway, Elizabeth. 1973. "The Weak Are the Second Sex." *Atlantic Monthly* 232 (December): 91-104.

Jaquette, Jane S. 1974. "Introduction: Women in American Politics." In *Women in Politics.* Edited by J. S. Jaquette. New York: Wiley.

——. 1976. "Review Essay: Political Science." *Signs* 2, no. 1 (Autumn): 147-164.

Jennings, M. Kent, and Thomas, Norman. 1968. "Men and Women in Party Elites: Social Roles and Political Resources." *Midwest Journal of Political Science* 12 (November): 469-492.

Jennings, M. Kent, and Langton, Kenneth P. 1969. "Mothers vs. Fathers: The Formation of Political Orientations among Young Americans." *Journal of Politics* 31: 329-357.

Kim, Jae-on; Nie, Norman H.; and Verba, Sidney. 1974. "The Amount and Concentration of Democratic Participation." *Political Methodology*, Spring, pp. 105-132.

Kirkpatrick, Jeane. 1974. *Political Woman.* New York: Basic Books.

————. 1975. "Representation in the American National Conventions: The Case of 1972." *British Journal of Political Science* 5 (July): 265–322.

Kraditor, Aileen S. 1965. *The Ideas of the Woman Suffrage Movement, 1890–1920.* New York: Columbia University Press.

Krauss, Wilma Rule. 1974. "Political Implications of Gender Roles: A Review of the Literature." *American Political Science Review* 68 (December): 1706–1723.

Lane, Robert E. 1959. *Political Life.* New York: The Free Press.

Lansing, Marjorie. 1974. "The American Woman: Voter and Activist." In *Women in Politics.* Edited by J. S. Jaquette. New York: Wiley.

La Rue, Linda J. M. 1970. "Black Liberation and Women's Lib." *Transaction/ Society* 8 (November-December): 59–64.

Lee, Marcia Manning. 1977. "Toward Understanding Why Few Women Hold Public Office: Factors Affecting the Participation of Women in Local Politics." In *A Portrait of Marginality.* Edited by M. Githens and J. L. Prestage. New York: McKay.

Lemons, J. Stanley. 1973. *The Woman Citizen: Social Feminism in the 1920s.* Urbana, Il.: University of Illinois Press.

Lenski, Gerhard. 1966. *Power and Privilege: A Theory of Social Stratification.* New York: McGraw-Hill.

Lepper, Mary M. 1974. "A Study of Career Structures of Federal Executives: A Focus on Women." In *Women in Politics.* Edited by J. S. Jaquette. New York: Wiley.

Levitt, Morris. 1967. "The Political Role of American Women." *Journal of Human Relations* 15: 23–35.

Lipman-Blumen, Jean. 1973. "Role De-differentiation as a System Response to Crisis: Occupational and Political Roles of Women." *Sociological Inquiry* 43, no. 2: 105–129.

McWilliams, Nancy. 1974. "Contemporary Feminism, Consciousness-raising, and Changing Views of the Political." In *Women in Politics.* Edited by J. S. Jaquette. New York: Wiley.

Marshall, T. H. 1963. *Class, Citizenship, and Social Development.* Garden City, N.Y.: Doubleday.

Mason, Karen Oppenheim, and Bumpass, Larry L. 1975. "U.S. Women's Sex-role Ideology, 1970." *American Sociological Review* 40 (March): 1212–1219.

Mead, Margaret, and Kaplan, Frances Balgley, eds. 1965. *American Women: The Report of the President's Commission on the Status of Women and Other Publications of the Commission, 1963.* New York: Scribners.

Milbrath, Lester W. 1965. *Political Participation.* Chicago: Rand McNally.

Mill, John Stuart. 1869; 1970. "The Subjection of Women." In *Essays on Sex Equality.* Edited by A. S. Rossi. Chicago: University of Chicago Press.

Murphy, Irene. 1973. *Public Policy on the Status of Women.* Lexington, Ma.: Heath.

National Organization for Women (N.O.W.). 1971–1977. *Do It NOW.* Monthly newsletter. Chicago: NOW.

——. 1977–. *National NOW Times*. Monthly newspaper, official journal of NOW. Title changes from *Do It NOW* with Vol. 10, no. 12 (December).

National School Boards Association. 1974. *Women on School Boards: Report of Research Conducted for the National School Boards Association Commission on the Role of Women in Educational Governance*. Evanston, Il.: National School Boards Association.

National Women's Education Fund. 1975. "Facts: Women and Public Life." Washington, D.C.: N.W.E.F.

NWPC Newsletter. 1974. "Win with Women." Newsletter 3, no. 8 (November-December). Washington, D.C.: National Women's Political Caucus.

Orum, Anthony M.; Cohen, Roberta S.; Grasmuck, Sherri; and Orum, Amy W. 1974. "Sex, Socialization, and Politics." *American Sociological Review* 39 (April): 197–209.

Paulson, Ross Evans. 1973. *Women's Suffrage and Prohibition: A Comparative Study of Equality and Social Control*. Glenview, Il.: Scott, Foresman.

Porter, Mary C., and Matasar, Ann B. 1974. "The Role and Status of Women in the Daley Organization." In *Women in Politics*. Edited by J. S. Jaquette. New York: Wiley.

Purcell, Susan Kaufman. 1974. "Ideology and the Law: Sexism and Supreme Court Decisions." In *Women in Politics*. Edited by J. S. Jaquette. New York: Wiley.

Rossi, Alice S., ed. 1973. *The Feminist Papers: From Adams to De Beauvoir*. New York: Columbia University Press.

Sandler, Bernice. 1973. "A Little Help from Our Government: WEAL and Contract Compliance." In *Academic Women on the Move*. Edited by A. S. Rossi and A. Calderwood. New York: Russell Sage Foundation.

Schlesinger, Arthur, Jr. 1973. "The Runaway Presidency." *Atlantic Monthly* 232 (November): 43–55.

Schultze, Charles L.; Fried, Edward R.; Rivlin, Alice M.; and Teeters, Nancy H. 1972. *Setting National Priorities: The 1973 Budget*. Washington, D.C.: Brookings Institution.

Scott, Anne Firor. 1970. *The Southern Lady: From Pedestal to Politics, 1830–1930*. Chicago: University of Chicago Press.

Seifer, Nancy. 1973. *Absent from the Majority: Working Class Women in America*. New York: American Jewish Committee.

Smelser, Neil J. 1959. *Social Change in the Industrial Revolution*. Chicago: University of Chicago Press.

Soule, John W., and McGrath, Wilma E. 1977. "A Comparative Study of Male-Female Political Attitudes at Citizen and Elite Levels." In *A Portrait of Marginality*. Edited by M. Githens and J. L. Prestage. New York: McKay.

Steinem, Gloria. 1972. "Women Voters Can't Be Trusted." *Ms.*, July, pp. 47–51ff.

Tolchin, Susan, and Tolchin, Martin. 1974. *Clout: Womanpower and Politics*. New York: Coward, McCann, and Geoghegan.

Verba, Sidney, and Nie, Norman H. 1972. *Participation in America*. New York: Harper and Row.

Warbasse, Elizabeth Bowles. 1960. "The Changing Legal Rights of Married Women, 1800–1861." Ph.D. dissertation, Radcliffe College.

WCVB-TV 5. 1974. *Report of Women's Opinion Survey.* Boston: mimeographed.

WEAL Washington Report. 1973–. Bimonthly publication. Washington, D.C.: Women's Equity Action League.

Women's Lobby Quarterly. 1974. "Congress versus Abortion." Vol. 1, no. 3 (November). Washington, D.C.: Women's Lobby, Inc.

Women's Political Times. 1977. "A NWPC Memorandum to President Carter." Vol. 2, no. 1 (Winter). Washington, D.C.: National Women's Political Caucus.

Women Today. 1971–. Biweekly publication. Washington, D.C.: Today Publications and News Service.

——. 1975a. "Lou Harris Polls Show Support for Women's Rights and Abortions Is Growing." Vol. 5, no. 12 (9 June): 72.

——. 1975b. "Ten-year World Plan of Action, 'Declaration of Mexico' and Resolutions Adopted." Vol. 5, no. 15 (21 July): 87–89.

——. 1977. "Ruth Bader Ginsburg Clarifies Recent Supreme Court Decisions for *Women Today*." Vol. 7, no. 10 (16 May): 61.

Zaretsky, Eli. 1976. *Capitalism, the Family, and Personal Life.* New York: Harper and Row.

3

WOMEN, MEN, AND WORK

The real truth is that 40 percent of the labor force is women. And they are being discriminated against. That is the reason why the welfare rolls have increased, almost exclusively. And the Department of Labor should forget about only taking care of men, and see to it that they take care of those who work. And all of us are working

—Representative Martha Griffiths before the Joint Economic Committee of Congress, 1973.

More women are now engaged in paid work in the United States than ever before. In 1900 about one-quarter of all women of working age were in the paid labor force. This figure had barely changed by 1940. But in the last thirty-five years, the figure has zoomed upward until 48 percent of all women now work for pay. Many women contribute the difference between poverty level and adequate incomes for their families (*Economic Report of the President*, 1973: 91).

But the news is not all good. Even in the absence of adequate provision for day care, a very sharp increase has appeared in the proportion of working women with very young children. Between 1948 and 1975, the percentage of working mothers with children under the age of six increased about fourfold from 10 to 37 percent (Nye, 1974: 13, 5). At the same time the unemployment rates of women have worsened faster than those of men. Yet the great majority of women do not work for "pin money" alone. Women are the sole support of 13 percent of all families, and yet their incomes are much less likely to keep the family out of poverty than those of a single male earner. In 1975, one out of three of all families headed by a woman were living below the poverty level (Hayghe, 1976; McEaddy, 1976). In general, the incomes of families with a single female earner were about one-half those with a husband as the sole earner. The difference is comparable with pay differentials between working men and women that have been noted in the United States for more than a century (Abbott, 1910: 85, 312).

87

These figures suggest the size of the intellectual and social task that Americans must undertake if they are to provide equal employment opportunity and adequate income for all citizens. First is the question of why the present challenge to women's economic roles has occurred at all, and whether it is to be met and accepted. The first part of this chapter presents both economic and historical answers to this question. Then if women working for pay is a fact of life to be faced and even encouraged, there is a second question of what factors influence an individual woman's motivation to participate in the labor force. These issues are taken up in the second part of the chapter. Once women are in the labor force, there is the fact or allegation of discrimination. The third part of the chapter summarizes various theories of why sex differences in pay and promotion occur and how they can be remedied. Next are raised the larger institutional questions of law, job design, social stratification, and family that surround workers and the workplace and shape their actions. Finally, the last part of the chapter suggests that alternative values implicit in the service economy perhaps hold promise for women's more equal economic participation in the future.

THE NEW CHALLENGE: EQUAL RIGHTS DESPITE INFLATION AND RECESSION

In 1973 the economist Sonia Gold surveyed the employment outlook for women and concluded that their future looked bright if there was continued growth in the economy. But it looked dismal if there was a combination of both zero population growth and a steady-state economy. The result would be tension in the work force so serious as to challenge current values and question the current institutional arrangements that govern work and leisure (Gold, 1973: 659).

In fact, Gold's pessimistic forecast proved more accurate than the optimistic one. With an inflation rate over 10 percent a year and an unemployment rate that rapidly climbed from 4.8 percent in 1973 to 8.9 percent in the spring of 1975, the employment situation became tight for women *and* men (Blechman et al., 1975: 23). But it was a particular challenge to women whose position in the labor force had not only changed rapidly, but whose benefits from recent antidiscrimination legislation had also seemed to be on the verge of major gains.

Scarcity of jobs, however, now puts women's recent economic progress in jeopardy unless the movement discovers a rhetoric and strategy appropriate to the current combined economic conditions of inflation and recession. Equal treatment of the sexes is in itself an important value position. Even if accepted, its implementation requires carefully developed supportive policy if it is not to have adverse economic consequences for individuals in the short run.

THE PROBLEM OF ADEQUATE INCOME

Inflation and unemployment have undoubtedly made it more important than ever that families be able to rely on more than one income to meet rising costs. A greater threat of unemployment or inadequate income makes the family who can rely on several earners much more likely to maintain an adequate level of living. One large study of 5,000 families conducted at the University of Michigan over the last several years shows that the most important variable explaining changes in the family's economic well-being was household composition. The family that could extend itself to include several earners and realize economies of scale was definitely better off (Morgan et al., 1974: 337-338). Such arrangements must be particularly important for the "working poor," the people working as dishwashers and pants pressers and making only 60 percent of what is enough for a decent standard of living (Spring et al., 1972). Most families do contain more than one earner. And surprisingly, of all married couples with an earned income, more than half consist of a working wife and a working husband (Bell, 1975: 114).

The size of a wife's contribution is larger than might be supposed. In 1970 half of the working wives were contributing between 20 and 50 percent of the family income. In 1974 the median income of families where the wife was not working was $12,360. If she worked part time, it was almost $13,500. If she worked full time, it was almost $17,500 (Hayghe, 1976).

From one perspective, it seems obvious that a two-earner family should be financially better off and that a working wife will raise family income. But traditional ideology has blinded most people to these facts. For over a century, it has generally been thought that women work until they get married and then stop work unless they "have to work." There is thus a lingering belief that families with working wives are less well off and that they are the exception rather than the rule. Indeed this ideology is so deeply ingrained that young women still seriously underestimate the proportion of their future lives that will be spent in the work force. Economists at Ohio State who asked women aged eighteen to twenty-four their work plans found that these women expected to spend a far smaller proportion of time in employment than is the actual case with older women in the work force (Jusenius and Sandell, 1974: 42).

To face and accept the reality that more women are working and will continue to work outside the home, we need to remember the facts that caused the change. Women's lives lengthened, and their childbearing shortened. More of them were divorced or separated. Perhaps most important was the change in the relation of the household to the workplace. People left the farms, and women were deprived of the combination of productive work and housework that they had once known. These changes hardly seem transitory or easily reversed; in short, they are here to stay. Women's entry to the paid labor force is a major adaptation to the change.

In 1890 nearly half of all families still lived on farms, and families were larger then. A woman's time was taken up with baking bread, tending a garden, sewing many of the members' clothes, and so on. One-fifth of all families took in boarders (Smuts, 1959: 14). By 1960 family size had declined, the great majority of the population lived in urban places, and a woman's household chores were lightened by electric appliances and store-bought goods. A new opportunity emerged for men to have their efforts at supporting a family supplemented by the paid work of other family members. The pattern was first evident at the turn of the century among poor immigrant laborers who needed every penny that women and children could earn (Chafe, 1972: 55). Their pattern foretold the emerging contemporary model of multiple-earner families with working wives.

Women's current involvement in the paid work force is the natural consequence of more than a century of change in women's roles. The first steps led into the mills or domestic service and then into teaching and the clerical occupations. Now blue-collar women are moving into training programs that give them access to well-paid craft jobs formerly given almost entirely to men. Women in staff supervisory positions seek recognition in the middle and top levels of management. Professional women are demanding equal access and promotional opportunities. Each of these steps resulted from large-scale institutional change in the country at large, as well as the efforts of women themselves. Now it is difficult to imagine any turning back, even though the destination of equality still lies far ahead.

STEPS TOWARD EQUITY IN EMPLOYMENT

To understand women's current employment needs, it is instructive to review gains already accomplished. The first major step was accomplished during the early days of the Industrial Revolution with the employment of thousands of mill girls and the passage of the Married Women's Property Acts. Next there was phenomenal growth in "female" occupations such as teaching and clerical work between the Civil War and the First World War, culminating in protective labor laws of the early 1900s. In the current era an unprecedented number of women are in the labor force for a longer segment of their lives; legislation against sex discrimination in hiring, promotion, and pay is characteristic of this period. The next stage, which we are about to enter, promises more crossover in the types of jobs held by women and men. At the same time, it will require effort to encourage women's employment through appropriate training and provision for flexible hours, parental leave, and child care so that both men and women can fulfill family functions without prejudice to their jobs.

The mill girls and the Married Women's Property Acts.

Throughout the Western world during the nineteenth century, women began entering the factories as workers. In England they were accompanied at first by children. Whole families entered wage work in the mills for a brief period before 1850 (Smelser, 1959: 198- 201). In France, young women were employed as seamstresses, as hat makers, and in many other segments of the needle trades. In the Northeastern United States, young women came from the farms of New Hampshire and Massachusetts to work in the mills at Manchester, Lowell, Waltham, and Fall River in the 1830s and 1840s. At the same time thousands of women took positions in domestic service.

Accompanying these changes were agitations for change in the laws to permit a married woman to work without her husband's permission and to have control over her own earnings. Single women did not face the same barriers to their right of contract as did married women, who were governed by the principle of coverture— their husbands had control. The laws passed governing these rights during the 1850s, known as Married Women's Property Acts, permitted a woman to stand as an independent economic entity—to work, to keep her earnings, to enter into a contract, and to sue and be sued.

Women's occupations and the protective labor laws.

Beginning shortly before the Civil War and in the several decades following, women won the right to enter various professions. One of the first woman ministers, Antoinette Brown Blackwell (1825-1921), completed the Oberlin College program in theology in

1850. But she was not allowed to graduate, and it was not until 1878 that she was granted an honorary A.M. Her sister-in-law, Dr. Elizabeth Blackwell (1821-1910), became the first American woman to receive a medical degree in 1849. One of the earliest lawyers was Belva Ann Lockwood, who was admitted to the bar in the District of Columbia in 1873 and was the first woman admitted to practice before the Supreme Court in 1879 (James et al., 1971: I, 158-163; II, 414). But by far the greatest number of women went into the teaching profession. Catherine Beecher had, in the 1840s, argued that women should be able to fill the vast need for teachers on the frontier. Quickly the teaching profession tipped from a predominantly male occupation to a predominantly female one. At higher levels of the academic profession, such as the Social Service faculty at the University of Chicago, women like Sophonisba Breckinridge and Edith Abbott reached high rank primarily through such "women's" departments as the Social Service Administration and Home Economics, or they were brought into a tenured position from an outside university (Freeman, 1969; 1971). Nursing and office jobs were also filled predominantly by women. In 1969, one-fourth of all women workers could be found in five occupations—elementary schoolteacher, secretary, bookkeeper, household worker, and waitress (Hedges, 1970).

Between the Civil War and the Second World War, women's labor force participation grew rapidly, but the biggest change occurred between 1900 and 1910, when the proportion of women doing paid work rose from 20 to 25 percent. Even as growth occurred, it channeled women into different kinds of work situations from those of men. Protective labor laws were upheld by the Supreme Court decision in *Muller* vs. *Oregon* (1908), and subsequent court decisions during the 1920s and early 1930s. Women could not work at night in some states, or overtime, or at certain prohibited occupations. But women failed to be hired for the high-paying jobs that were labeled men's jobs. They failed to receive on-the-job training that fitted them for promotion. And they were more subject to layoffs.

Despite these disadvantages, women's participation in the work force rose dramatically after the Second World War, from 36 percent in 1945 to 38 percent by 1960 and 43 percent by 1970. Yet even much of this growth apparently was due to increased demand in the white-collar women's occupations. Teaching jobs and office jobs were crying for workers. Because these were labeled female positions, they brought a significantly larger number of women into the labor force (Oppenheimer, 1970: 120).

Women's rising employment and laws against sex discrimination. As the proportion of women with jobs rose steadily to the halfway mark, expectations about women's place also changed. Probably no claim of the women's liberation movement after 1960 carried more weight than the argument that women had an equal right to jobs and an equal right to the pay that went with those jobs. The earliest piece of legislation in contemporary feminists' armamentorium for equality was the Equal Pay Act of 1963. One of their most significant victories was the settlement with the American Telephone and Telegraph Company to remedy the effects of its discriminating employment policies. Earlier cases had laid the foundation for questioning weightlifting requirements, state protection laws, and plain custom as a basis for the sex-labeling of jobs. Ida Weeks, who had been denied a job as switchman with Southern Bell, was granted that job when the Fifth Circuit Court ruled in her favor (*Weeks* vs. *Southern Bell*, 1969). A man who had been denied a job as airplane cabin attendant was granted that job when the court ruled that such a job could not be denied on the basis of sex (*Diaz* vs. *Pan Am World Airways*, Fifth Cir., 1971).

These and other decisions showed that past practice of segregating male and female jobs and giving them different treatment was no longer legally acceptable. There had to be a bona fide occupational qualification (B.F.O.Q.) to justify different treatment of the sexes.

Positive employment policy for both sexes.

Beginning in the late 1960s and still to reach full tempo is a phase of the women's movement that will extend beyond remedies against direct discrimination to a positive facilitation of women's full employment. This effort involves provision of appropriate social arrangements to support women's work. Counseling and training is needed to guide them to job opportunities. Continuing education is necessary to maintain and improve their skills. Parental leaves, child-care facilities, and flexible hours would help both women and men to carry their family roles as well as work roles. Job rotation and job redesign would permit movement across job functions so that flexible hours and part-time work would become more feasible.

So far, feminist organizations, such as NOW and WEAL, have put great emphasis on maternity leaves and child-care facilities. But, except for the efforts of such isolated experimental collectives as KNOW, Inc.—a feminist publisher based in Pittsburgh—little explicit attention has yet been given to innovations in the structure of work.

Clearly, to right segregated work structures, combat discrimination, and institute any positive measures for the full employment of women, a great deal of analysis and understanding of the forces at work and the levers that must be pressed to get any change are necessary. Again, as with the population problem or the problem of women's political participation, there appears to be a hierarchy of levels at which change occurs. It is first visible at the *personal* level in individual women's decisions whether or not to work. Then pressure for change appears in *firms and work roles* as a challenge to occupational segregation. Next the laws must be tested and enforced, and economic and familial *institutions* are subject to criticism and reform. Finally, the *values* underlying the economy itself come under scrutiny. Now we begin our journey up through each successive level of this hierarchy of changing economic relations.

PERSONAL CHARACTERISTICS OF WOMEN WORKERS

Much of the postwar inquiry into women's economic activity has posed the question of why women work. Psychologists asked what deep-seated motives and personality factors predisposed a woman to seek a career rather than raise a family. Economists asked how a woman's education, marital status, number and age of children, and husband's income affected her decision to enter the paid labor force. Each discipline has also been interested in the effect of a woman's age on her work decision. Psychologists asked how changing personality needs affected work at different points in the life cycle. Economists were interested in the way that a woman's past job experience affected her future job opportunities and earnings. Finally, as the effects of the women's movement have reverberated through the potential female labor force, new questions are being raised as to how women can better be trained for the work they will do in the future.

Psychological Factors in the Decision to Work

In her famous book *The Feminine Mystique* (1963), Betty Friedan put the scholarly reaction to women's postwar housewife syndrome in sharp focus. In general, social scientists found all sorts of functional reasons why women should stay at home. Parsons and Bales (1955) said that the division of labor which kept women in the home promoted harmony and minimized competition between husband and wife. From her vast cross-cultural experience, Margaret Mead (1949) documented women's attachment to children and their near-universal work in and around the home and local village with other women. Such popular guides as Dr. Benjamin Spock's *Baby and Child Care* (1946) cautioned the young mother about taking a paid job lest it hurt her child's development.

The upshot of this general outlook was that married women who took paid work were regarded as psychologically somewhat suspect, especially if their working was a matter of choice and not of dire economic necessity. Ravenna Helson (1972), who has reviewed this literature, shows that, beginning around the early 1960s, the major premise began to change. Where the Vassar studies on college student career plans for the 1950s had tended to interpret career striving as a sign of uncertain feminine identification and inner conflict, the studies of the next decade began to view women's employment in a more positive light. About the same time, Nye and Hoffman's landmark collection of studies in *The Employed Mother in America* (1963) showed no substantial harmful effects of maternal employment on children.

As expert opinion on women's working became more positive, the variables under study also changed. Inner conflict, poor relations with parents, and an uncertain identification with the feminine role that earlier explained women's work motivation were replaced by such factors as role ideology, achievement motivation, and the presence of positive role models. In a national survey of college graduates of the class of 1961, James Davis (1964) discovered that girls were more likely to give humanitarian and service-oriented reasons for choice of career while boys gave reasons relating to money and power. Both Hoffman (1963) and Lipman-Blumen (1972*a*) found that women with high work aspirations were more likely to have a nontraditional ideology about what constituted the feminine role. Ralph Turner (1964) and Lipman-Blumen (1970) further showed that women with high career aspirations were more likely to desire direct rather than vicarious achievement. Horner (1972) argued that conflict over femininity and achievement blocked women's performance in competitive situations. Having role models of feminine achievement or special encouragement from others could also strengthen a woman's interest in work and career (Tangri, 1972; Lipman-Blumen, 1972*b*).

By 1975, the interest in all these questions of motivation had been somewhat overshadowed by the strength of the feminist wave and a shift in attention to situational factors. The psychologists had reinterpreted the image of career woman from that of a conflict-ridden and less attractive one to one consistent with the healthy development of young women (Helson, 1972). Hoffman (1974: 62) went further to conclude that "at the present time, maternal employment is so common that it is not possible to characterize the working woman in terms of personality traits." And radical psychologists such as Naomi Weisstein and feminist sociologists like Jessie Bernard and Alice Rossi began to argue that social institutions were creating many of the problems that working women had, not just women's motivation. Interest was thus shifting from the psychological factors in employment to the social institutions that either facilitate or impede a particular woman's desire to work.

SITUATIONAL FACTORS IN THE DECISION TO WORK

Situational factors can be identified at several different levels of analysis. In succeeding sections, I shall treat factors more distant from the individual, such as the nature of the job setting or the availability of legal remedies to job discrimination. Here we treat social background characteristics of the individual woman such as age, race, education, marital status, and location that affect her likelihood of being employed.

The relevant work has been done largely by economists and demographers. The factors to be considered have to do with both supply and demand. On the supply side are such matters as a woman's marital status or income from other sources that influence her decision to work. On the demand side are factors such as the unemployment rate in the city where she is located, the industry mix with "female"-type jobs, and so on. The scholarly literature is voluminous, but there is general consensus on the overall picture in two important matters: the first explains the historical trend of women's rising employment, and the second, the factors in an individual woman's decision to work at a given time.

Explaining the historical phenomenon.
An important economic puzzle following the Second World War was the continuing rise in women's employment. It had been thought that women worked primarily out of economic need; either they were single and had no male support, or their husbands did not make much money. Yet, although fewer women were single and the incomes of married men were getting better, more women were taking paid work, especially the married women. Two answers to this puzzle were provided by Mincer and by Oppenheimer.

Mincer (1962a: 66) showed that over the long run rising pay for women's work outweighed the short-run effect that high family income usually had in keeping a woman out of the labor force. This was due to the changing value of a woman's time. The family made a rational decision to encourage her to work because her leisure and unpaid productive work in the home became more costly to them. In most cases money that she could earn in the labor force far surpassed the costs of buying additional home appliances or hiring household help.

Oppenheimer (1970) offered a demographic explanation for the phenomenon. She found that the demand for women workers increased at the same time that a smaller than usual group of eligible women was available. After the war, the baby boom created a great demand for teachers, and thousands of new clerical jobs opened up. These positions were sex-labeled as female jobs, creating a situation where women were not likely to be crowded out by a host of male competitors. On the supply side, there was a shortage of single women or older women with the requisite training and qualifications. As a result, the marriage barrier to employment began to soften. Women who had the needed qualifications were hired despite the fact that they were married or had children (Oppenheimer, 1970).

The cross-sectional explanation.

At the present time, women participate in the paid labor force at the highest rate in American history. Yet they constitute only about half of all the women in their age group. Slightly more than one-half of adult women are not in paid employment, as compared with about one-fifth of adult males. The question is why some women are employed and others are not.

Economists have generally answered this question by precise measurement of census statistics to discover the relative weight of such factors as the employment situation in the area where a woman lives and the individual characteristics that she would actually bring to a job. Mincer (1962a) worked out a theoretical formula that could be used to weigh each of these major factors. It was tested and refined by Cain (1966), who measured women's rate of employment in several major metropolitan sampling areas and related it to husband's income, wife's education, age of children, and so on. In 1973 James Sweet pursued the particular effect of age of children on the mother's employment. The work of Bowen and Finegan (1969) stands as perhaps the single most comprehensive empirical work on the subject.

Bowen and Finegan used data on individual women from the 1-in-1,000 sample of the 1960 census. They added to it a picture of the labor market in each of the major metropolitan areas where these women lived. As a result, they were able to come up with a picture of the relative weight that each background or situational factor contributes to a woman's employment.

Imagine that a married woman's score is 100 if she is employed and 0 if she is not. Bowen and Finegan's formula can explain only about 35 points of the score by using the statistics that they gathered. Labor market conditions appear to carry about twice the weight of a woman's own individual and family characteristics in determining whether she is employed or not. If the metropolitan area in which she lives contains industry with a good number of "female" jobs and if there are high female wages, married women in that area are more likely to work. But if the cost of household help is high and there is a high female ratio in the population, their chances are less favorable. The lower her husband's income and the more her own schooling, the greater the likelihood that a married woman will work. However, if she has preschool-age children, she is deterred from working. If she is black but all of her other characteristics are the same as a white woman's, she is also more likely to work (Finegan, 1975: 52–53).

Although the form of the theoretical analysis is likely to be the same, new figures from current census data may result in some change in the weights of a variable such as unemployment. Contemporary figures on unemployment show that the gap between rates for women and men has gradually widened over the last fifteen years (Ferber and Lowry, 1976). The rate in 1956 for men was 3.8 percent, and for women 4.9 percent. In 1972 the rate for men rose to 4.9 percent, for women to 6.6 percent. In 1975, as male rates approached 9 percent, some estimates put the female rate at 12 to 15 percent. The traditional positive effect of husbands' unemployment on women's decision to work may now be offset by the negative effect of the high female unemployment rate on women's own chances for jobs.

Life Cycle, Generation, and Secular Trends

There are now signs that the intellectual problems of explaining women's employment are moving to a new level. Having fairly well worked through some of the psychological factors and situational pressures behind women's employment, social scientists are ready to take a somewhat more relativistic perspective on the whole question.

The key variable in this new outlook is age. The age of a woman affects her likelihood of working in at least three ways. First, depending on the point in a woman's *life cycle*, she is more or less likely to work. The economists have shown that if she is in school or has young children, she is deterred; if she is older and her family is complete, she is more likely to be in the labor force. The psychologist Baruch (1966) suggests that women's achievement motivation may also undergo change over the life cycle—dipping in the late twenties and early thirties and then rising with age, possibly reflecting thereby increasing interest in the family in the earlier period and in paid work later on.

Second, if a woman was born in a certain period, she is part of a *generation* that is more or less likely to find working acceptable.

Before the women's liberation movement got started, Riley et al. (1963) found in a study of over 700 high-school girls that their expectations about working were more positive than the ones of earlier generations. Detroit-area surveys conducted over the past twenty-five years likewise show a change in the acceptance of women's work, and there is a greater acceptance among the younger generation (Duncan et al., 1973: 21–26). Mason and Bumpass (1975: 1219) compared attitudes toward women's roles that were measured in several major surveys between 1964 and 1974 and found consistently that "the proportion of women supporting the traditional familial division of labor has declined with time and the proportion supporting women's rights in the labor market and their options for a life without marriage or motherhood has increased."

Third, there are *secular variations* in demand at different times that affect women's work. If there is high demand, a woman is at the right age to make the most of the opportunity, and if her attitudes permit, she is likely to enter the work force and remain in it. Zellner (1975) examined data on women who took jobs in male-dominated occupations between 1942 and 1950. She was interested in whether entering the work force at a certain age and under certain economic conditions would affect chances of staying in the same job. She found that "of women employed in 1951, 46.8% of those who got their current job before January 1942 and 37% of those who got their jobs between January 1942 and September 1945 were still with their original employer in 1963, whereas of those who got their job after the end of the war (October 1945 to June 1950), only 17.5% were still with their original employer in 1963." Zellner explains this curious phenomenon by the average age of women in male-dominated occupations, which was fifty-two in 1950. She reasons that they were over thirty-two in 1942; therefore their family size was complete, and they could enter, get on-the-job training in, and remain in such jobs. Their opportunities were greater than for younger women, both because they were at the right age and because their labor was more in demand.

Collecting and analyzing the work histories of individual women may be one of the best ways to sort out each of these age effects and see how they interact. In its National Longitudinal Surveys, the Center for Human Resource Research at Ohio State University has gathered a large body of data on work patterns of men and women over the last decade (see Jusenius and Shortlidge, 1975). More qualitative accounts are just beginning, but they may be beneficial as guides to some of the strategies of vocational choice, education, retraining, and job mobility that will help other women in the future (Kahne et al., 1976).

Changing women's skills and interests.

As we shall see, the job situation affects women's work experience, but women's own attitudes and skills undoubtedly also have a bearing. The women's movement has brought change to women's work participation, just as it did to their political interest. Women's caucuses and women's interest groups have sprung up in business enterprises and academic settings. The Coalition of Labor Union Women has organized and become active. The feminist impulse has carried into the micropolitical context of informal women's groups, in which members have encouraged each other to return to school, reenter the labor market, change vocations, or try for a promotion.

In addition, programs in continuing education burgeon at the community colleges and local universities and are in large part populated by women. Pressure for vocational guidance and counseling accompanies women's massive reentry to the labor force (Campbell, 1973). The full agenda that such programs should carry is not entirely evident, however, from a look at the women who need help. The whole picture has to include awareness of the overcrowded fields that they should avoid and the job segregation and dead-end occupations that await them unless they are forewarned and forearmed (Johnstone, 1968). The pitfalls in the work situation itself are the next challenge, once the hurdle of employment itself has been cleared.

DISCRIMINATION AND JOB SEGREGATION

It is one thing to ask whether or why a woman works. What work she does and how she is treated once she is in the workplace is another question. Probably no single aspect of women's employment conditions has received more attention than the size of her pay. The findings are very clear and very consistent. Women receive about 60 percent of the wages that men receive, even when they are similar with respect to all important personal characteristics other than sex.

Puzzled by these findings, economists have tried to discover the cause. They have been especially interested that the lifetime earnings profile of women is flatter than that of men. Single women's earnings rise a little more steeply than those of married women, but even single women, who presumably spend just as much time in the labor force as males, earn much less than men over the life course. Sawhill calculated what all women would earn if they had as much work experience as single women. She came to the startling conclusion that women would still earn about 57 percent of what men earned. As she put it, "there remains a 43 per cent differential between men and women who are similar with respect to age, education, race, region, hours and weeks worked, *and* time spent in the labor force" (Sawhill, 1973; Suter and Miller, 1973).

Scholars who have probed the cause of this differential do not believe that failure to enforce equal pay laws is the main issue. The problem is rather associated with the segregation of women and men into different occupations. Only 2 percent of the 5.6 million managers and proprietors in the country are women. On the other hand, 38 percent of all employed women are found in clerical occupations (see Table 2).

It is not just the earnings profile or the type of occupation that distinguishes the experience of women and men in the workplace. Opportunities for promotion apparently also differ. Disproportionate numbers of women are found in subordinate ranks, and large numbers of men in the high ranks. This is true in virtually every occupation and industry. Women are the schoolteachers in the lower grades; men are the principals and the superintendents. Nurses and healthcare paraprofessionals are largely women; most doctors are men. The full professors at the large universities are men; many more women are in the nontenured or peripheral ranks or in the small liberal arts colleges. While women make up 20 percent of all labor union membership, they comprise only 4.7 percent of the union leadership (Wertheimer, 1972).

Some insight into the process by which such differences occur is provided by the case against the Bell Telephone System brought by the Equal Employment Opportunities Commission (E.E.O.C.) in 1972. American Telephone and Telegraph (A.T. and T.) is the largest private employer in the world, and 55 percent of its employees are women. Yet the proportion of females in management positions is minuscule (even counting secretaries as first-level "managers," which they did). The EEOC traced a pattern of discrimination in hiring, promotion, pay, and working conditions. Women were routinely channeled into the Traffic Department, where they entered jobs as operators. Working conditions for operators were so rigid, emphasis on punctuality and other aspects of discipline so strict, and the job

TABLE 2. Occupational Distribution of Men and Women Workers

Occupation	Men, %	Women, %
White collar above clerical	34.5	22.1
White collar clerical	6.2	38.0
Blue collar skilled	19.0	2.7
Blue collar semiskilled and unskilled	34.9	27.2
Service workers	5.3	10.0
Total	99.9	100.0

Source: Equal Employment Opportunities Commission (1972*b*: 47).

such an obvious dead end that turnover was extremely high, approximately 100 percent in nineteen of the metropolitan areas served by the system in 1969.

By contrast, entry-level jobs for men were through the Plant Department, where they had opportunity to work on equipment, do "outside" work, enjoy considerable freedom to come and go, and experience much more chance for promotion. Their turnover was much lower. Management came primarily from the departments with a disproportionate number of males. Whereas pay scales showed the entry-level female operator to be making a maximum of $5,000 to $6,000 in 1970, the typical entry-level male in a craft position was making a maximum of $7,500 to $8,500 per year. The jobs were equivalent in the amount of skill and training they presupposed: *neither required any prior experience.* The telephone company had the opportunity to use its "unique competence" in taking untrained persons and overcoming racial and sexual barriers to move them into rewarding jobs. Yet this is precisely what the EEOC held that the company had failed to do (EEOC, 1972a: E1244–E1245).

Few other examples so boldly reveal sex discrimination. The causes of women's inferior pay and status are usually much more elusive. Economists have tried to pinpoint the principal factors and have come up with several major types of explanation, which I here classify in three categories. The first puts emphasis on the competitive interests, predilections, and experience or human capital of the *workers* themselves, which make them more likely to choose or be more fitted for one type of occupation than another. The second explanation discovers segregation in the labor market that is attributable to *employers*—their power, tastes for discrimination, or some other pressure that limits women to a small number of occupations. The third explanation, based on *institutional factors*, promises a synthesis of the first two explanations. A major application of this analysis is the dual labor-market theory. It looks at the intersection of supply and demand factors and reasons both (1) that women are statistically less likely to remain attached to a job and (2) that employers use sex as an efficient source of information to discriminate among those employees in whom they will invest on-the-job training and those in whom they will not (Blau and Jusenius, 1976; Kahne and Kohen, 1975).

DIFFERENCES IN HUMAN CAPITAL INVESTMENT OF MALE AND FEMALE WORKERS

The theory of human capital looks to the age, background, training, and decisions that people themselves make rather than to discrimination as the source of different individual experience in the labor market (Fuchs, 1971). If persons have forgone long training for an immediate return, their earnings over a lifetime are likely to be considerably less than those of a person with more extended preparation. If they have chosen to enter a crowded field where pay is low, this is their own decision, though perhaps misguided. In 1965 and 1970, for example, nearly one-half of all women college graduates expressed preference for a teaching career, while only 2 percent selected nonclerical business careers (Kahne, 1974: 5). It is often argued that traditional female occupations such as teaching, nursing, or housework are an extension of the female role that women themselves seek to enter (Prather, 1971; Gitlow, 1972). Such plans are clearly individual, though influenced by the socialization process. They cannot be attributed only to the employer's discrimination.

The human capital perspective has been applied to women's earnings. The fact that women on the average drop out of the work force for approximately eight years seems to have crucial bearing on their later earnings. If they are academics, even if they begin at the same salaries as men, their earnings gradually fall behind those of their male peers (Johnson and Stafford, 1975). Over and beyond this difference in actual work experience, women tend to enter occupations requiring less training and to receive less training than men even in jobs that offer on-the-job training. Polachek (1975: 111) concludes, "As a result, we observe females being overrepresented in lower-paying occupations while also receiving lower pay in the higher-paying professions."

Furthermore, women make decisions about whether they will invest in their own human capital, or in that of their children. They can leave the labor force to spend time in the family, or they can build up their own capital by keeping themselves in the labor force. Mincer and Polachek (1974: S107) conclude that the causal factors associated with family responsibilities have more to do with women's modest earnings than does any discrimination. The "foregone market-oriented human capital of mothers is part of the price of acquiring human capital in children. . . ." just the way the specialization and longer hours of the father is part of the price that he also has to pay.

EMPLOYERS' TASTES FOR DISCRIMINATION AND OVERCROWDING

Gary Becker in 1957 put forward the idea that discrimination is a form of consumption by employers and workers. Employers are willing to pay the price of forgoing a cheap and plentiful labor supply in order to indulge their tastes or prejudices. For example, neither men nor women may like to work for a female supervisor, as has been found in some surveys (Baas et al., 1971). Failure to promote women to management could conceivably reflect such preference.

Cultural preference might explain segregation, but it does not really account for the fact that women are crowded into so few occupations. In 1969 one-half of all female workers could be found in twenty-one occupations, as compared with one-half of all male workers who were found in sixty-five occupations (Weisskopf, 1972). Even during periods of growth in female labor-force participation, the increase has been most evident in largely female occupations. As a result of such heavy concentration, some economists propose an overcrowding hypothesis.

Bergmann's (1971) theory of overcrowding suggests that male workers have something to lose if the floodgates of employment are opened to a plentiful labor pool. The drop in wages might be as much as 10 percent for the advantaged workers, and as many as one-fourth of the people in the overcrowded occupation might leave it. By this reasoning, advantaged workers press employers to engage in discriminating practices, not merely because they wish to indulge their noneconomic "tastes," but because it is also in their economic interest to do so.

Neither the Becker nor the Bergmann theory explains, however, the way that the original sorting took place—how certain occupations became the preserve of the discriminators, and others the over-crowded ghettos of the powerless. Nor do their theories explain why sex became such a salient variable in the process of discrimination. For a clue to these questions, we have to turn to the more comprehensive theory of the dual labor market.

THE DUAL LABOR MARKET

As Blau and Jusenius (1976) observe, an elementary principle of economics is that prices (wages) are determined by the intersection of supply and demand curves. Therefore, it behooves students of occupational segregation to show how it is a combination of both the different human capital of workers and the selective hiring by employers that results in sex-typed jobs with different levels of pay and security. The theory of the dual labor market promises a more comprehensive framework.

On the supply side, women and men have different statistical probabilities of being continuously in the work force and of being on any one job for a considerable length of time. While in 1972 the average work life of an adult male in the United States was thirty-eight years, the average for an adult female was thirty years (Sawhill, 1973). Days absent due to injury or illness were about five and one-half per annum for both men and women, and monthly quit rates were roughly the same, 2.2 percent for males and 2.6 percent for females. But *the length of service on the job* was typically twice as great for males, 4.8 years, as compared with 2.4 years for females (*Work in America,* 1973: 59).

On the demand side, unions and long-time employees press for seniority and more job security, and employers face a decision about who should receive an investment in on-the-job training. Gradually over time, an internal labor market develops within each firm. It has a primary sector and a secondary sector. Into the primary sector go persons who look as though they will give long-term service; they receive training, good pay, and benefits that bind them to the company. To the secondary sector are assigned persons who look as though they are less committed, persons like students or women. They are placed in jobs that require little training and promise no advancement and that may be fluctuating or temporary. In 1958, for example, employers spent $1.4 billion for on-the-job training of women as compared with $13.5 billion for men (Mincer, 1962*b*). Wages for the two types of jobs are related not so much to actual productivity of the individual workers as to the job label and the *expected* employment tenure in the particular job type (Doeringer and Piore, 1971: 77–78).

The intersection of the supply and demand factors occurs at the port of entry when employers assign jobs to new applicants. Employers make a statistical judgment about the likely tenure of the applicant by referring to crude indices such as race, sex, age, and so on. Accordingly, they channel most of the women into the secondary jobs, where they will receive less pay, less training, and less job security.

What happens next may be as much the outcome of "a self-fulfilling prophecy" as of any purely economic process. If women stay a shorter time in these secondary jobs, get less training from them, or are less productive, it is difficult to prove that their action is any more the result of their own choice than it is of the structural situation into which they were channeled. Having been put in less desirable jobs, where the pay is low, women have less incentive to stay. Denied on-the-job training, they have little opportunity to increase their human capital. Employed in less heavily capitalized sections of the plant, they have less opportunity to increase productivity. When they go to their next job, they will again bear the female sex marker that summarizes these statistical probabilities, and they will likely be put in situations which only reinforce them.

When applied to the individual woman, expectations based on these statistical tendencies result in gross injustice. Levitin and her colleagues (1971), using data from the Survey of Working Conditions at the University of Michigan, compared the salaries of women and men who had the same attitudes toward achievement, same tenure on the job, worked the same number of hours, had the same degree of supervisory responsibility, and so on. Still the salaries of women averaged about $3,500 a year less than those of men. Blau and Jusenius (1976: 197) are careful to note that not all such discrimination is explained by the dual labor-market theory. Additional sex discrimination goes on within the primary sector, even when women have cleared the hurdle of being assigned to it.

REMEDIES

How is the vicious circle to be broken? There are many possible answers. Suggestions that promise the most immediate result include better training, counseling, nondiscriminatory hiring practices, provision of maternity leave, and day care. Generally these short-term remedies do not attempt more fundamental change in legal and economic institutions, but they do represent logical extensions of the three major theories of occupational segregation.

Counseling and retraining.

The simplest extension of human capital theory is that women need longer and more diversified training if they are to get out of overcrowded occupations and into those in which there is a high demand for their work (Hedges, 1970). Another obvious suggestion is for women to shorten their childbearing period and have fewer children so that they will lose less time from the job market.

For other minorities as well as women, however, the solution is not quite that simple. Thurow (1969) finds that the marginal return for an added year of education is about one-half as much for a black as for a white. Or, as Bergmann and Adelman (1973) say, the average woman college graduate earns no more than the average male high-school dropout. Between 1962 and 1973, while the education of both men and women improved, resulting increases in occupational status went only to the men (Featherman and Hauser, 1976: 481). Thurow's explanation of such a discrepancy is that there is now job competition rather than wage competition in the American economy. Education essentially becomes a defensive strategy for joining the job queue in an advantageous position. The advantage is lost if one fails to get a job with security and good built-in opportunities for specialized training (Thurow, 1969; Thurow and Lucas, 1972).

Affirmative action.

Solutions thus cannot rest with having women improve their own human capital. Employers' traditional practices of assigning jobs according to sex must also be challenged. Here such remedies as not classifying help-wanted advertising according to sex are useful.

Deliberate experimentation is also in order and receives positive sanction from the law. EEOC guidelines for implementing nondiscriminatory hiring practices suggest that employers survey their area to measure the ratio of women in the population with the requisite skills. They should then make a deliberate positive effort to make the numbers of women in major occupational categories more representative of the sex ratio in the qualified population at large. In the process, employers should critically review the qualifications they require and the ones actually needed for the job, to be sure that irrelevant tests are not being set that have the effect of screening out women or other minorities (Women's Bureau, 1974).

Part of affirmative action may be a willingness to take as much risk on a woman as on a man. A British study of women who reached top jobs in the BBC showed that the company was less willing to take a risk on putting a woman into a managerial position than a man. Yet women have done well, and one of the major factors in success of the Second World War women managers was that the company had been willing to take a risk on them (Political and Economic Planning, 1971: 214-220). Perhaps women are generally most likely to be the beneficiaries of such trust in times of crisis or in fields where there is a labor shortage, as during the war.

Provision of positive supports.

Clearly the woman worker has certain things within her power; the employer has others. But the dual labor-market theory teaches that it is the combination of supply and demand factors that is crucial. What can both employee and employer do that will take into account the complexity of the matter? The answers are not yet completely clear, but a number of pieces of the puzzle have been identified.

For women, and increasingly for men, productive activities in both paid and unpaid work take a wide variety of forms over the life course. Kahne (with Kohen, 1975; et al., 1976) points out that a career is constructed from experiences both inside and outside the paid labor force. Consequently, the credentialing of all productive activities becomes increasingly important. From studies of longitudinal work histories Kahne (et al., 1976) hopes to construct a clearer picture of how the professional woman worker can most effectively build her investment in human capital and receive recognition for a broad range of training and experience.

Suggestions for how employers can improve their environments for women seem to fall into two groups (Doeringer and Piore, 1971). On the one hand, employers can try to develop in women the traits for primary employment by reducing the risk of unsteady work commitment. They can provide child-care services, maternity leave, or flexible hours, or give attention to welfare laws that may decrease work incentive. On the other hand, they can convert secondary jobs into primary employment by introducing career ladders, job training, and possibly job rotation that moves between primary and secondary jobs. From her study of large corporations, Rosabeth Kanter (1977: 267) concludes that the quality of work life for both men and women will be improved by "opportunity-enhancing, empowering, and number-balancing strategies."

Radical economists have thought that monopoly capitalists created the segmented labor market because it was in their interest to have a well-disciplined, homogeneous labor force and no competition from independent artisans, craftsmen, and other small competitors. In addition, the big firms were thought to let marginal firms who employed secondary workers take the risks on smaller jobs and the less profitable work (Edwards et al., 1975; Deckard and Sherman, 1975). According to this perspective, it would be surprising to see these same employers converting a secondary labor force into a primary one, unless there were some external pressure to do so, either political, legal, or economic. But indeed this change may be occurring: more women are joining unions, legal rules are changing, and the restructuring of work may prove to be economical as well as pleasant. Such changes, however, herald more basic structural transformations in the economic institutions themselves.

RESTRUCTURING ECONOMIC INSTITUTIONS

In his penetrating analysis of the American Negro problem, Gunnar Myrdal noted that the typical American tendency in the face of social difficulties is to inscribe their ideals in laws (Myrdal, 1944, 1962: 1, 14).

In matters of sex inequality, since 1963 there have been, in fact, laws that prohibit discrimination in hiring, promotion, and pay. But the problem is to get these laws to work. Enforcement is needed, but more basic changes are also required. Jobs must be designed so that part-time work is not a disability but an asset. Unpaid work in the home or community should somehow receive credit as a contribution to the nation's economy and should give women the right to retirement security and other benefits by virtue of their status as workers, not dependents.

Flaws in present economic institutions governing women's work virtually all come down to need for a change in expectations regarding the "typical woman" or "typical man." Most of the existing inequities in the law result from a time when men were the main breadwinners and women stayed at home with their children, dependent on their husbands for any cash income. This picture may never have fitted reality very well, but it fits even less well today.

By 1974, the *majority* (55 percent) *of middle-aged women* (ages forty-five to fifty-four) *were in the labor force*, as compared with 37 percent in 1950 (Klein, 1975: 12). In 1971 Juanita Kreps (1971: 64) estimated that more than one-half the women in the labor force did not have the luxury of choosing home work over paid work. More than a third of the women at work were single, divorced, separated, or widowed. Many of them were the sole support not only for their children but for their parents as well. An additional 15 percent were married to husbands who made very low incomes.

To keep women from being a massive burden on the welfare rolls, it is only realistic to search for ways by which they can both stay in the labor market and earn more money and at the same time have the work they do at home count for something. They take care of children; they do "consumer maintenance" in their homes; they serve their communities as unpaid volunteers. To accomplish the massive reorientation that is needed, not only the laws must be changed. We must also critically evaluate the way we structure and reward different jobs. We must examine the links we make between employment and income maintenance, such as Social Security and welfare. Finally, we must question the price we put on unpaid work and see how we can give it more credit.

CHANGES IN THE LAW

With respect to race prejudice, Gordon Allport (1954: 438- 440) long ago remarked that the great value of legislation against discrimination is that it helps break vicious circles. If the law actually changes behavior, it may in turn lessen prejudice and the limitations of the disadvantaged, which up to then have only reinforced the stereotypes.

In some respects, remarkable changes in the law have taken place since the passage of the Equal Pay Act in 1963 and the Civil Rights Act in 1964. The new laws were followed by decisions in the state and federal courts that challenged state protective labor laws that barred women from overtime or night shifts and denied them jobs on the basis of an irrelevant weightlifting requirement (*Rosenfeld* vs.

Southern Pacific, Ninth Cir., 1971; *Weeks* vs. *Southern Bell*, Fifth Cir., 1969; Women's Bureau, 1971).

Long-accepted sex labeling of jobs was questioned. A man could not be denied a job as cabin attendant on an airplane solely on the basis of his sex (*Diaz* vs. *Pan American World Airways*, Fifth Cir., 1971). A woman could not be prohibited from being a bartender solely on the basis of her sex (*Sail'er Inn* vs. *Kirby*, Calif. S. Ct., 1971). Merely by labeling a job as "male," an employer could not pay a man more if he was doing essentially the same work as a lower-paid female employee with a different job title (*Schultz* vs. *Wheaton Glass*, Third Cir., 1970).

Though the change in the law has been important, court decisions momentous, and considerable clout available through the Executive Orders, general employment conditions of women remain largely unchanged. The difficulty is in enforcement. There are just too many firms to check on, and the process of litigation is just too time consuming to touch more than a tiny fraction of the country.

Enforcement.

There are seventeen federal agencies coordinated by the Office of Federal Contract Compliance that oversee compliance in the firms doing business with the federal government. One of these operations is in the Department of Defense, which lets 75 percent of all federal contracts and does business with 30,000 establishments. Although the defense agency had 320 compliance officers in 1971, they were still too few to review even half of the contractors as is required by the law (Lyle and Ross, 1973: 100-104). By 1974 this number was to reach 570 people in the Department of Defense program for contract compliance (Joint Economic Committee, 1973, 1: 100).

When back pay is actually won after discrimination is proved, only about 50 percent of it is ever recovered, and eventually the statute of limitations may run out so that it is never paid the women to whom it is due (Joint Economic Committee, 1973, 1: 103-105). From September 1971 to the summer of 1973, only four contractors had ever been declared ineligible for award of a federal contract on the basis of sex discrimination, and *no university* had ever suffered termination of contract, though their funds were delayed in a few cases (Joint Economic Committee, 1973, 1: 110, 119).

In 1971 there were a total of 1,619 people in the Central Office of Federal Contract Compliance and its seventeen cooperating agencies with a potential for reaching one-third of the work force in the United States, in a total universe of some 250,000 firms. Together they had to work with a budget of only $23,500,000 (Moskow, 1973). Using present exhaustive techniques of investigation and litigation, adequate enforcement could entail enormous costs. But women and organized labor are potential allies of the compliance agencies. And so might be business itself if the proper incentives were derived.

JOB REDESIGN

We have already seen in chapter 2 how the women's rights groups and the equal rights agencies of government developed a symbiotic relationship or policy system in which they helped each other. At the base what may be necessary to equal employment opportunity is the development of such a policy whirlpool in which not only women and government but also organized labor and corporations are involved. At issue is the whole design of occupational slots, the schedules, locations, and organizational hierarchy that govern them. Women have got to identify changes in the structure of work that are in their own interest and then show management, unions, and government that these changes are in their common interest.

Women's interest: flexibility and participation.
The lesson of the dual labor market is that women pay for part-time hours and any discontinuity in their job history by receiving less commitment from their employers and less opportunity to advance in their occupation and earnings. They have two major alternatives: either they can try to approximate the male worker pattern by getting maternity leaves and day-care centers, or they can try to break the economic reward structure that devalues flexible hours, part-time work, and shorter job tenure. The first type of change involves transformation of the social benefits associated with work; the second type involves restructuring of the work itself. It is in women's interest to work for both types of change.

If maternity leaves are treated like any other temporary disability and day care is at least in part supported by the public or subsidized by business, women with young children can maintain their attachment to the work force and better repay their employers' investment in their training. However, a recent study by the Pennsylvania Commission on Women shows that America is among a handful of countries that have not adopted legislation to assist prospective mothers by protecting their jobs and offering them financial assistance at time of delivery (*Women Today*, 1977c: 47). In what constituted a significant setback to such protection, the U.S. Supreme Court in December 1976 ruled in *General Electric* vs. *Gilbert* that the employer had the right to exclude pregnant women from company sick-leave benefits. In response the Congressional Subcommittee on Employment Opportunities in March 1977 announced that it would draft legislation to require employers to treat pregnancy-related disabilities the same as they treat any other disability. Meanwhile experiments with maternity leave go forward. For example, under a new government contract with McNeil Laboratories, a pharmaceutical firm, employees are eligible for maternity leave for any reasons related to pregnancy and childbearing and are guaranteed return to a position with prior pay and status without loss of seniority (*Women Today*, 1977*b*: 32).

If permitted to do part-time work and follow flexible hours, women can devise innovative work patterns that allow their jobs to be covered adequately and well while still permitting them the freedom to attend to family matters. Such routines are already established for doctors covering each other's rounds or consultants working part-time on several jobs, but they have not been widely legitimized in the lower occupational ranks where most women and men work. Woman architects who have redesigned their own jobs have suggested the following alternative arrangements: (1) flexible-time contracts with an agreement to work a specific amount of time per year rather than follow a specific schedule; (2) work-related contracts that agree to complete a specific task by a specific date; (3) paired workers that assure consistent backup in case of emergencies; (4) expansion of the consultant approach to establish a retainer fee, not for full-time support, but to allow schedules to be set as needed (Berkeley, 1972).

In the last few years experiments with flexible hours have been instituted in such government agencies as the Social Security Administration's Bureau of Data Processing (where 80 percent of the employees are women) and the U.S. Geological Survey Center in Reston, Virginia. In the private sector insurance companies, such as Metropolitan Life and Northwestern Mutual, and a number of firms manufacturing electronics equipment have experimented with having employees arrive anywhere from 7 to 10 A.M. and work for a fixed number of hours. Reports of results are clearly positive: absenteeism, tardiness, and use of sick leave have been reduced. In some instances productivity and mutual trust have increased (Robison, 1976: 23; Hartley, 1975: 47; Committee on Alternative Work Patterns, 1976: 4–5).

Job sharing (having two or more persons work part-time to do a single job) is still relatively rare—on the order of 1 to 2 percent of all jobs. But other types of part-time work in 1974 accounted for 21 percent of all employed persons (Committee on Alternative Work Patterns, 1976: 7; Robison, 1976: 18). Recent innovations in part-time work have involved provision for leave time, health benefits, insurance, and pension contributions. Part-time schedules have been particularly useful in those industries with great fluctuations in peak demand such as retailing. In addition, plants like a Control Data Corporation bindery in St. Paul or Massachusetts Mutual Life who employ large numbers of working mothers have found the system to be very successful with their employees (Committee on Alternative Work Patterns, 1976: 10-11).

Where such routines are accepted, they can change women's own job expectations and employers' investment in part-time workers. It is optimistic to expect a rapid breakdown in the segmented labor market. But it is probable that men will also increasingly seek part-time or flexible hours. Then they too will bear family responsibility along with women, and the idea of dual roles will become more legitimate for all.

Management's interest: predictability and profit.

Management not only must meet government enforcement of affirmative action guidelines; it must also try to keep production costs low and maintain a profit margin. In the past, it has relied on a homogeneous labor force with certain skills and predictable tenure that it can count on once it has invested in on-the-job training for the worker. Other than to avoid penalties for discrimination, how could it possibly be in the employer's interests to adopt what it regards as expensive maternity, day-care, or pension plans for its women workers or institute flexible hours and part-time work that it regards as administratively cumbersome?

The answer lies in new trends in business and management that appear to reward precisely the type of job redesign that is in women's interest. Hierarchical, top-down modes of management now appear to be giving way to a new style that rewards high participation by workers, flexibility, and the opportunity for workers to set their own goals and hours, organize their own work, and cooperate on a total project rather than split it up in assembly-line tasks (*Time*, 1972: 96-97). A new young breed of managers has reached the top in major corporations by their ability to raise quality and lower production costs when they follow those methods (*Business Week*, 1975*b*: 56-68; Bennis and Schein, 1969; Davis and Taylor, 1972: 9-20; *Work in America*, 1973: 96-104).

If management wholeheartedly adopts this new flexible style in its relation to workers, the dual labor market will be threatened. Furthermore, managers may also adopt hiring, training, and retention policies that make women a much more attractive labor pool. The requirements of achieving affirmative action are burdensome unless the manager sees it as in his business interest to hire women. EEOC guidelines say that he must (1) analyze the size of female unemployment in the surrounding area, (2) look at the percentage of the total work force that is female, (3) assess the general availability of women with the required skills in the immediate surroundings, (4) ascertain whether any could be recruited from outside the area, and (5) ask whether any women can be promoted or transferred from *within* (Moskow, 1973). Furthermore, since the passage of the Age Discrimination in Employment Act that became effective in 1968, he must be careful not to discriminate against the older woman who is most likely to be seeking work and who may appear to him either "overqualified" or "lacking in experience" (Women's Bureau, 1969).

The only way affirmative action can escape being onerous is by a change in attitude on the part of the employer that makes him define women's employment characteristics as assets rather than liabilities. This is most likely when effort is made to redesign jobs and encourage a participatory rather than a hierarchical style of management.

The unions' interests: job security.

Even if it were in both women's and men's interests to redesign jobs, there would be obstacles raised by the unions. Louis Davis (1971: 445) describes some of the issues:

> The first concerns the existing job definitions and job boundaries that are cast in concrete in agreements between unions and managements, in state and federal civil service commissions, in personnel policies, and in a multitude of other ways. What will be required to break these molds? Simply to go to an employer with a proposal for job restructuring is, in many instances, to go to only half of the essential power. The union is the other half. Federal and state governments have contributed to the rigid stance of both halves by institutionalizing jobs and job descriptions. Jobs can be made infinitely better than they are. Jobs can be restructured for entry purposes and for advancement. But the issue must be made a matter of public and private policy, arrived at by open discussion.

In the few years since Davis wrote, there have been some remarkable examples of management and union cooperation to restructure the work environment. One such began in 1973 with the cooperation of the United Auto Workers local in Bolivar, Tennessee, in a plant making automotive mirrors. Workers who completed their production quota for the day were allowed to leave early or attend free classes provided by the company. Suggestions by workers for improving production were solicited. The role of the foreman shifted from that of policeman to that of adviser to a work team. The union participated in preparing bids for major contracts. At the same time workers were assured that there would be no speed-up and no loss of jobs. At the end of three years the company could report an increase in individual productivity (from $132 to $165 per day), an ability to maintain profit while reducing prices, and significant reductions in turnover and absences (*Business Week*, 1975a: pp. 52ff.; Committee on Alternative Work Patterns, 1976: 18-20). The key to such success was attributed by management to a belief that all workers should feel secure in their jobs, be treated fairly, be given a chance to develop their individual potential, and have a say in the decisions affecting them. In addition, all should have a respect for each other's differing roles. The experiment was apparently a success because the management and the union were able to work together in that spirit.

It is in women's as well as the unions' interest to form an alliance not only for job redesign but also for more general considerations of power and well-being. Women who are union members make 75 percent more salary than nonunion women. The differential is even more striking for them than for men, for whom the difference is 25 percent (Bureau of Labor Statistics, 1972a: 22).

It is, on the other hand, in the unions' interest to involve more women, for they populate the fields of teaching and white-collar work, in which unions have yet to make gains that equal their success in the blue-collar occupations. In fact, there has been a significant growth in the number of women union members since 1962. Between 1958 and 1970, 1 million women members were added, increasing their percentage among all women workers from 18.2 to 20.7 percent, though still far from the 30 percent of all male workers who are unionized.

While the 1960s saw little change in the proportion of women in union leadership (they hovered at 4.6 percent), beginning around 1970 the unions showed signs of interest in women's issues such as maternity leave, child care, and complaints to the EEOC. Major unions like the United Auto Workers and the American Federation of Teachers then began to take positive positions on women's issues such as maternity leave, child care, and the ERA (Bureau of Labor Statistics, 1972b; Dewey, 1971; *U.S. News and World Report*, 1972).

An important recent development has been the emergence of the Coalition of Labor Union Women (C.L.U.W.), which in March 1974 brought together 3,200 women unionists in an emotionally stirring founding convention. Such women are now particularly working to get increased union commitment to affirmative action, election of women to top posts (especially in the women's divisions), labor education, and attention to special needs of women such as paid maternity leave, parental-leave days for child care, experimental flexible hours, tuition refund, and released time for education (Wertheimer, 1976: 203-205).

Society's interest: employment for all.

In the short term, it is reasonable to suppose that both management and labor will resist the redesign of jobs and that, seeing this, women will give up any radical aims to restructure the work week and the work year. But in the long term, it seems clear that industries like the railroads or the printing trades will stagnate and decline if either management or unions are allowed to maintain their rigid practices of protecting seniority and monopolizing the market rather than improving their services. In the final analysis, incentives are needed to get any long-term change. Boudon (1973) has shown that people will choose short-term self-interested gain over long-term societal benefit whenever the pay-off matrix gives the slightest advantage to the former. Only a clear set of incentives or punishments will make people choose action on the behalf of society.

On the face of it, part-time work, flexible hours, job rotation, and team cooperation have many advantages. They have potential for breaking down the dual labor market that operates against minorities, and they thus spread the work around. Furthermore, they appear to result in greater productivity, less absenteeism, less turnover, fewer people needed to do some jobs, and higher-quality products (*Work in America*, 1973: 96–104). But to reward such practice, government will have to adopt not only tax incentives for innovation by unions and management but also stiffer penalties for past practices that result in discriminatory treatment of secondary workers. Otherwise, established practice will continue to be more rewarding both for the steady year-round workers who are lucky enough to be protected by seniority and tenure and the big established firms that have captured a large portion of the market and are therefore insensitive to consumer demand for flexibility and innovation.

The Civil Service Commission recently proposed a law to permit experiments with flexible work schedules and a three-year test of the consequences for efficiency of government operations, service to the public, mass transit use, and energy consumption. European firms have experimented with "sliding time" for a number of years. In January 1977 Senator Gaylord Nelson introduced a bill that would direct the federal government to use flexible and compressed work schedules. The legislation authorizes four flexible work schemes to be tried in a three-year voluntary experiment supervised by the U.S. Civil Service Commission. A second bill would increase part-time work opportunities throughout the entire Civil Service career ladder (*Women Today*, 1977a). In November 1975 the U.S. Congress established a National Center for Productivity and Quality of Working Life. Within the private sector experimentation is also growing. In

1975 the Business and Professional Women's Foundation was able to report the experience of fifty-nine organizations that have experimented with staggered hours and flexible time (Hartley, 1975). The Work in America Institute documents other experiments and monitors their results. All these innovations in the structure and schedule of work are likely to have positive effects for the future work roles of women.

EMPLOYMENT AND INCOME POLICY

Carolyn Shaw Bell (1975: 117) has said that "we should recognize that there are two distinct problems: creating jobs and maintaining incomes." If we think that every job should be able to support a family, we are in danger not only of failing to expand flexible and part-time employment. We may also contrive to give jobs mainly to "breadwinners," discourage multiple-earner families, and commit ourselves to support any family at a minimum income level regardless of its size or of its members' willingness to work. Committed to such a policy, we are in danger of forever breaking the tie between payment for a job and entitlement to income.

It seems more realistic to recognize that *fair earnings for a job* and *adequate family income* are two different concepts. Although tied together in the past by the male breadwinner and the independent farm economy, the two entities are no longer necessarily the same. Rather than try to devise a single policy that will provide adequate family income, it seems wiser to adopt a mixed system that puts together *earnings-related* income with *needs-related* income (cf. Wilensky, 1975: 40–41).

To maximize everyone's earnings, an employment policy is required that will channel persons into sectors of the economy where they are needed, impose income maximums on the most attractive jobs, and offer added rewards or incentives to fill the least attractive occupations (Ulman, 1972). Such changes in work structure as flexible hours, training programs, maternity leaves, or day care help women join the population of wage earners.

Need rather than earnings is the basis for awarding allowances to mothers with dependent children who receive public-welfare assistance. As now defined, these persons do not appear to have earned their keep, and there is great public resentment at their growing numbers on the welfare rolls. The number of women in the program of Aid to Families with Dependent Children (A.F.D.C.) rose from 650,000 in 1950 to 3 million in 1970. Several types of solutions have been offered, including training programs that would prepare such women to get jobs, day care that would free them from home duties, and other examples. In some ways, the simplest and most radical solution is to convert these women to earners not by sending them into the job market but by giving credit for the work that they do at present in the home without pay. Most such women, divorced or deserted and unable to obtain adequate child support from the absent or remarried father, are nevertheless cooking meals, caring for their children, and performing other important family services that would cost many times the same amount if they were to be handled by public institutions or done by paid workers.

Rather than ignore the contributions of all women who work in the home, tax credits have been suggested for those women who have another earner in the household. A cash allowance based on their household service is suggested for those without other means of support. Such a system would replace both the present devaluation of women's work in the home and the rationale of the present welfare system. Both the public and the recipients alike could interpret the subsidy as "earned," at least in part, and the work of all women in the home could gain dignity by virtue of having a value put on it.

If such changes were to occur, women would no longer be put in the anomalous position of being automatically considered "dependents" on their male breadwinner. All sorts of inconsistency in the way women are treated with respect to income tax, credit, insurance, Social Security, and public assistance would then be able to be resolved.

Taxes.

Inequities in taxes largely result from the assumption written into the law that a wife is a dependent and not an earner in her own right. As a consequence, married couples with both partners working are now subject to higher income taxes than if they remained single and merely shared a common household. The reason for this is that they file a joint return. The wife's income is treated as a kind of supplement and is therefore taxed at the husband's highest marginal rate. For this reason, many couples regard a wife's work as costing more than it is worth and the income tax system in effect operates as an incentive not to work (Joint Economic Committee, 1973, 2: 221-223).

Two types of remedies have been suggested. First, as in certain European countries, each earner could be taxed as an individual rather than as a member of a couple filing a joint return. Second, a tax deduction could be allowed for the cost of child care and household services, as is permitted with any other business expense. The present law, revised in 1976, gives a tax credit equal to 20 percent of the total amount spent on child care or household expenses, but not to exceed $400 for one child or $800 for more children. These expenses must, however, be employment-related, that is, necessary to allow a person or a spouse to be gainfully employed (Internal Revenue Service, 1976: 149- 151).

Credit and insurance.

While there is a myth that women control most of the wealth in the country, women over the last decade have documented a series of inequities in the opportunity to receive credit and to procure insurance that belies contentions that they are economically powerful. Instead, their position is contradictory, caught halfway between status as independent earners and status as dependents. A study by the New York Stock Exchange of women stockholders shows that men register their stocks in women's names largely to limit their own liabilities (Glazer-Malbin and Waehrer, 1972: 245- 247). Auto insurance companies frequently make it more difficult for women to be insured, and other types of insurers are likely to regard women as bad risks. The Federal Home Loan Bank Board found that 25 percent of banks who insure federal home mortgages would not count a woman's earnings in reckoning the capacity of the couple to take on the liability. And many women who are divorced or separated suddenly find that the credit cards in their husbands' names do not establish their own credit and that they will have to begin all over to establish their credit rating (Joint Economic Committee, 1973, 1: 152- 153).

Remedies to these problems are not altogether straightforward. On the one hand, a recent handbook for women undergoing divorce, separation, or marital difficulty (*Women in Transition*, 1975) advises women not to take on debt obligations with their husbands that they cannot meet entirely on their own. This approach suggests caution toward pooling resources, wife's *or* husband's, when counting assets and liabilities. On the other hand, considerable feminist effort has gone into establishing women's credit unions in Massachusetts, New York, Connecticut, and Pennsylvania, and raising awareness about discriminatory credit practices based on sex or marital status (Lotman, 1973; *Business Week*, 1974: 76- 78).

Social Security, unemployment compensation, and public assistance.

Various measures provide income support for persons if they are not working at paid jobs. Social Security and private pension plans provide for retirement. Unemployment compensation is supposed to carry persons on a temporary basis until they find work. And public assistance or welfare and disability insurance provide funds to those unable to work. But each type of measure entails inequities for women.

Drawbacks of present Social Security coverage for women largely result from treating wives as dependents whose coverage rests on their husband's earnings rather than on their own contribution as workers in the home. A man thus gets benefits for his "dependent" wife. But a lifetime homemaker cannot get benefits in her own right. If she is divorced from her husband, she can make no claim to benefits even if she was married for fifteen or eighteen years, because she has to have been married for at least twenty years before she can claim coverage. At the same time, the Social Security system taxes the working wife disproportionately. Unless a wife's earnings are over half that of her husband's, she gets no more at retirement than she would as a dependent of her husband. The system also discriminates against the two-earner family. Even if a husband and wife pay maximum Social Security taxes, they will at the end of their working life receive only one-third more than the benefits paid to a single-earner family (Joint Economic Committee, 1973, 2: 289–291).

Unemployment compensation for women is flawed by its uneven coverage of persons in part-time positions, many of whom are female. Many part-time workers pay into their state unemployment plan, but they cannot withdraw their benefits when they need them. Many state laws specify that only the full-time and wholly "available" workers are eligible for coverage. Because women frequently search for a part-time job, are limited to certain hours or schedules, or are subject to temporary conditions such as pregnancy, they are frequently categorically excluded from receiving unemployment compensation. The reason is that they are adjudged workers who are not fully "available." Thus women who are combining work with family responsibilities are at a particular disadvantage (Joint Economic Committee, 1973, 2: 341–345).

Welfare payments are largely made to *mothers* with dependent children. If fathers are present, it is difficult to get income supplements, even if the family is poor. The flaw in this system is a commonplace of both public and scholarly discourse: families may be forced to split up in order to qualify for assistance. A disproportionate number of poor families consist of a woman with her children of whom only 41 percent had paid jobs in 1971, as compared with 77 percent of the men who were heads of poor families. The main reason such women gave for not taking paid jobs was that they were "keeping house" (Bureau of Census, 1973). The present structure of public assistance thus seems to rely on an outmoded picture of women's and men's roles. It does not build on the potential contribution of the father as well as the earning capacity of the mother, but rather assumes that fathers are earners and mothers are housekeepers. Only if the father is retired, disabled, or absent does the mother get some support. And being alone, she is less likely to have some of the help with family responsibilities that would enable her to work. She is thus forced into the stereotyped dependent woman's role. No improvement seems likely in this system until the American people and public leaders are able to picture the male as both parent and earner and the female as both paid worker and mother. Only then can the system stop destroying families and build on their capacity to pool resources and survive.

One of the most fundamental questions about women's work is thus how paid, market work relates to unpaid, nonmarket work. Women's roles in family and volunteer activity are labeled nonmarket work. Nonmarket work is usually said to interfere with market work by standing in the way of women's mobility, promotion, and pay. For example, although lack of day care is not the primary reason women are out of the labor force or not looking for work, "it does prevent approximately one-half of the blacks and one-tenth of the white mothers of children under six from looking for work" (Jusenius and Shortlidge, 1975: 63). Remedies aimed at the institutional level usually suggest that women's nonmarket work be done by paid workers. The recent drive for publicly supported day-care services is an example (Schultze et al., 1972: 252- 290).

Other possibilities are to have men do as much unpaid work as women or to give credit for unpaid work to both men and women. However, these latter suggestions imply a more fundamental break with established practice. They take us into the value realm, because they question the fundamental market mechanism that assigns a higher value to paid activity.

VALUES AND OTHER NONECONOMIC CONSIDERATIONS

The moment we consider asking men to do as much unpaid work as women or consider giving credits for unpaid work, we question a fundamental institution of Western economics—the market and the price system. We imply that in their present state they may not be adequate mechanisms for guiding the economic destiny of human societies.

As E. F. Schumacher points out in *Small Is Beautiful* (1973: 24), Western economics has raised means above ends. According to the maxim of Lord Keynes, we must put up with foul means a little while longer until affluence is reached, and then we can concentrate on ends and the good society. The Western form of economic analysis results in a system where people act because of the profit motive; a price is put on every good and service; production and consumption are maximized to enlarge profit. But while the level of affluence continues to rise, there is enormous production of goods that are not needed, waste of resources that cannot be renewed, pollution and destruction of the environment, and boredom and alienation in the work of many, in addition to too much stimulation, tension, and work for the small minority who can continue to create. Schumacher's diagnosis is precisely that noneconomic considerations that affect the quality of life have by and large been ignored because they are not quantifiable. Such goods as beauty, meaning, or conservation are violated because they are literally priceless. The market mechanism is therefore not adequate to representing them in the equation of supply and demand.

SEX-ROLE IMPLICATIONS OF THE STEADY-STATE ECONOMY

Radical critics by and large advocate two remedies to the short-sighted materialism and corporate giantism of the modern economic order, which is blind to the real needs of people. On the one hand, the economic equation needs to be enlarged to take into account such important noneconomic considerations as health, beauty, and permanence. On the other hand, actual productive enterprises and governmental units need to decrease in size and be dispersed throughout the land so that they can be brought into more intimate relation with the neighborhoods and populations that depend on them.

Each of these remedies has profound implications for sex roles. To enlarge economic analysis by bringing in nonmarket considerations is to put a whole new complexion on human feelings, family considerations, and the quality of personal ties that have long been a concern of women. To disperse production and government is to bring outside-the-home activities once again into closer touch with the family, where women can more easily take active part. Certain other changes also follow: (1) market and price mechanisms must be altered to credit people for their nonmarket work *(institutional change)*, (2) firms and households must discover how to operate on a smaller scale, closer to each other so that less cost and energy are required for transportation and distribution of workers and materials *(corporate and role change)*, (3) the individual traits that are cultivated and the education that prepares women and men for adult roles must give a more balanced emphasis to achievement and cooperation *(personality change).* Such needed changes at each of these levels have already been described by pioneer legislators, reformers, and social scientists. By and large, their suggestions are consistent with the new critique of established economic practice and the radical vision of the steady-state economy.

AN ECONOMY TO SATISFY HUMAN WANTS

One of the principal criticisms of Western economic practice is that it emphasizes growth in production and consumption to the neglect of actual human wants. Among the products found on the supermarket shelves in 1970, 55 percent were not even in existence in 1960. Of the dollars that the consumer spends to satisfy real wants, such as having enough to eat, only a fraction goes to pay for the actual production cost of food itself; the other two-thirds has to pay for marketing and distribution costs (Morris and Hess, 1975: 119).

While consumers are paying for what they do not want or do not need, and the general level of affluence is rising, some other aspects of life that they treasure but cannot pay for are in scarcer supply— personal safety and a clean, open, and unpolluted environment. Delinquency, crime, crowding, and deterioration of beautiful places are instead on the rise.

What is needed is a new kind of "invisible hand" that better regulates the balance of production and consumption, a market that represents noneconomic as well as economic considerations. Many economists are now sure that economic growth is not the magic formula that it was once thought to be. Schumacher (1973) gives "Buddhist economics" as one example in which noneconomic principles such as religion, ethics, or art have put human activity in proper perspective. His message is that human societies should not run their economies as though they were the creators of the universe, for they are only its stewards.

What practical arrangements are needed to introduce such larger moral considerations into modern economies? No one has the answer yet. People who consider the question in relation to women's work point out that women do very valuable service for their families and their communities; yet, because their work goes unpaid and is regarded as no more challenging than that of "parking lot attendant" or "animal trainer" in the *Dictionary* of *Occupational Titles,* women act rationally according to the present economic system if they desert the homemaker occupation for a better-paid and more prestigious position. Nor is it surprising that men, who have traditionally been encouraged to get out of the home, should not be eager to return to it even though modern sex-role change suggests such crossover, when it promises no more satisfaction or opportunity than is now granted.

Yet all that we know about communities with low crime and delinquency, clean streets, and honest citizens is that persons who live there have a sense of personal involvement, identification, and belonging. Families are strong. Not only are mothers near by, combining family activity with productive work, but fathers probably are also close at hand, working yet available to their families. Children of a certain age have access to one or both parents and are expected to perform some useful work. Such a scene implies that economic considerations of work and production are in balance with noneconomic considerations of family and consumption. It also implies that . in such a balanced system the optimum ecological arrangement places work and family near each other in neighborhoods of manageable size, not exceeding a population of, say, 30,000 to 50,000.

Crediting nonmarket work.

Although we do not know how to give human care and attention economic credit without putting a price on it, we must discover ways of giving such noneconomic activity its proper weight in our total equation of human costs and benefits. Otherwise it will disappear and not be missed until the destruction has been done. Representative Donald Fraser and his wife, Arvonne Fraser of WEAL, suggest that housewives be allowed to build up their own Social Security credit through spouses working in covered employment, basing their coverage on the joint income tax return (*Women Today*, 1975*b*: 124). This solution does not of course help the woman without a spouse who may be performing work in the home that is entitled to equal credit. But the Fraser suggestion is a beginning opportunity to give credit without bringing nonmarket services into the pricing system.

Carolyn Shaw Bell (1972) has suggested that the occupation of "consumer maintenance," caring for a sick spouse or child, waiting for a delivery in the home, repair work, washing the clothes, and other valuable services to human beings that are usually performed in the home should be recognized as worthy activities in their own right and should receive credit. Juanita Kreps has calculated that the total volume of women's nonmarket work is worth approximately one-sixth to one-fourth of the Gross National Product. But nonmarket work is potentially devalued if there is no price attached to it.

Therefore Kreps (1971: 67-75) suggests that we count women's contributions by giving them entitlements, training opportunities, and rights to public assistance for taking care of children rather than make them accept what is commonly regarded as a dole. Along these lines, Alice Cook (1975: 67) suggests that we institute a Maternal Bill of Rights, modeled after the GI Bill of Rights. Such a bill would recognize interruption of work for maternity and child rearing as a service to the country, much as military service is recognized. It would acknowledge that such interruption results in some loss of skill and productivity, and yet it would provide compensation by giving means for a vocational or general education, counseling, and guidance, and also subsidies to employers for the cost of on-the-job training. Such a system could also be used as a basis for maintaining a woman's right to unemployment compensation, help with child care, and support during her training period. The authors of *Work in America* (1973: 65), in a special report to the Secretary of Health, Education, and Welfare, have noted that in some instances women may choose market work because their nonmarket work is under-valued and that in fact their contribution in taking care of their children may be greater than in a paid job. However, homemaking (for both women and men) must receive higher status before noneconomic family and community considerations can in many cases outweigh the economic rewards now offered by paid work.

Ecology as if people mattered.

Much of the current difficulty in women's roles is the result of the distance between home and work. In order to take care of their families, women must withdraw too much from productive work and outside activities. In order to achieve in their jobs, men must with-draw too much from the family and local community. A division of labor that once gave each sex a slight primacy in one or the other of these spheres has now been distorted by the modern economy into too much of an either-or proposition for each sex. But the solution is not a romantic return to the farm or cottage industry; rather, an ultramodern effort is called for to discover how to disperse small, local production and consumption units. The mechanics for such dispersion still seem largely utopian. They rely heavily on schemes to use solar power, wind power, and local sewerage systems to produce energy, fertilizer, and food grown locally. Electronic communication, knowledge-intensive industry, and occasional exchange of experts between communities are the means by which visionaries of this new system would link neighborhoods and combine creative work by inventors with rewarding everyday activity by all (Morris and Hess, 1975). In this environment, neither mother nor father would be very far from a child. Adults of both sexes would be involved in food production, distribution, and human services to the community, as well as in caring for their own families. Such a vision promises to answer both the need for a steady-state economy and the problem of lopsided sex roles. The workplace and the home may have greater physical or communicative proximity or, increasingly, be one and the same place.

OCCUPATIONAL DESIGN IN SPACESHIP EARTH

A number of social reformers and critics have warned of the dangers of industrialization as traditional workshops and farms have disappeared with its onslaught. The nineteenth-century Russian reformer Peter Kropotkin (1899, 1974: 169–187) advocated dispersion of production throughout the countryside in small farms and factories. He warned that formal education should not be separated from the play experiences of children or the work experiences of adults; science should not suppose that the development of formal principles can proceed separately from practical inventions. The modern French sociologist Jacques Ellul (1964) says that technological society has created an inhuman environment for men by forcing them to live in sunless and confined urban spaces and to have their time regulated by a clock and their motion paced by machines. The results are tension, irritability, and lack of satisfaction. The contemporary radical American economist Samuel Bowles (1971) has noted that more people are being trained for demanding jobs than the number of openings available. America's high level of affluence is built on an alienating social technology that replaces jobs with machines and results in waste and irrational production.

Common to all such criticism is the theme that industrial work may become so specialized—country separated from city, brain work from manual work—that human wants end up not being very well satisfied. Many jobs may become repetitious and boring, science may be split off from practical needs, and high rates of unemployment may develop and persist—all because industry becomes at once too highly organized and too distant from control by worker and consumer.

Kropotkin's (1899, 1974: 17) view was that the main subject of social economy should be the best use of energy to satisfy human needs. The industrial order, while eradicating terrible scourges and plagues and raising the standard of living in its corner of the world, has done so at disproportionate cost to the rest of the world. While containing only 31 percent of the world's population, the developed countries consume 87 percent of its irreplaceable fuels (Schumacher, 1973: 26).

How could things be different? First, a better fit could be established between economic motives, work, and satisfaction of basic needs. At present, many people in need have no work or are inadequately paid, while others have more work and income than they need. The advocates of local production see a large part of the solution in population redistribution. But more is needed: the creation of viable jobs and productive work that is accessible and satisfying not just to a few but to all.

Jobs are called for that allow flexibility in task and schedule, participation by workers, autonomy, and inventiveness. Small-scale technology is called for that permits workers to contribute their own ideas and control the machines that they tend. Self-help and self-reliance are once again the order of the day.

Job redesign was treated earlier as an institutional reform serving the interests of affirmative action. It undermines the dual labor market and provides opportunity for outsider groups such as women and other minorities. The point here is no different, but it goes deeper. Job redesign to reward autonomy and maximum participation will go farthest when it flows from a new world view. That world view acts to give people more say in their work, and not just because they want it or because egalitarian ideals so dictate. Rather, the new perspective on work emanates from a vision that all people want to work and that they are naturally industrious and inventive. Furthermore, industrial reorganization promises to bring human beings into a more balanced relationship with nature, their fellow inhabitants on earth, and their own ideals.

POSTINDUSTRIAL WOMEN AND MEN

Whether he was historically correct or not, Max Weber (1904-1905, 1958) in *The Protestant Ethic and the Spirit of Capitalism* made a very important theoretical contribution to our understanding of social change. He suggested that a radical alteration took place in the personalities of those people who were Puritans. Because they were concerned with whether they were among God's chosen, they developed a pattern of work that helped them cope with their uncertainty. The historical result was Puritan leadership, not only in capitalism but also in modern science (Merton, 1957: 574-606).

A modern-day analogy to Weber's question would go something like this: Today, which people carry within their own personalities the seeds of a new economic order? Who will help fashion a system that is at once more intimate and humane and yet adapted to survive within the natural limits of the earth's resources?

Undoubtedly, persons of each sex will be involved, but I suggest, as do a number of others, that the personality characteristics traditionally associated with women will become more important in shaping the future society than they have been in the industrial era. Judith Bardwick (1974: 60) summarizes the traits traditionally associated with men and women:

> As far as we know, throughout history and across cultures of very different characteristics, women have been expected to be the main caretakers of young children, and men have been expected to be able to assume the aggressive stance of defender. Two polarities of personality developed which represent the two milieus in which the sexes have had to function in our society and most other societies.
>
> Men have been characterized as having ego strength, a capacity for delaying action upon impulse, a future time orientation, an ability to be separate from others through the development of strong ego boundaries, and a general quality of objectivity. The emphasis for men has been upon the development of separation, mastery of the task, isolation, and repression of feelings and impulses.
>
> Women have been encouraged to become, and have been characterized as, forces of feelings, as sharing expectancies with others, as predictable, as concerned with others. The emphasis for women has been on communion, contact, union, cooperation, and openness to others and to one's own feelings and impulses.

Our scientific, rational, and technological order has by and large emphasized achievement and devalued the ability to care about others. Much criticism of the modern industrial order rests precisely on this point. The obvious need seems to be to right the imbalance. Our social order overemploys men and underemploys women. As Bardwick (1974: 55) asks, "Is it not possible that it is a more worthwhile goal for society, under the leadership of women, to truly honor the more interpersonal, intrapsychic, humanistic, personalized style of women?"

While all psychologists point out that *there is significant overlap in the traits shown by men and women*, a number of theoretical and descriptive works support the overall personality distinctions between women and men that Bardwick has drawn. Carlson (1972) notes the more *agentic* style of male research in the field of psychology, which relies heavily on controlled experiments and quantitative techniques. The feminine style is, by contrast, *communal* or complementary, leaning on naturalistic, qualitative, and open methods. Helson (1972: 43) characterizes creativity in men and women; she terms the male style phallocentric, purposive, analytic, forceful, and penetrating. The alternative female style is like that of a company of friends; it incorporates initiative, independence, intellect, and symbolic creativity as a variety of elements that work together in the feminine self. Hoffman (1972) reports very high affiliative needs in girls and a more diffuse achievement need than in boys. These characteristics may allow women greater flexibility over the life course; as Hoffman (1972: 150) states,

> A richer life may be available to women because they do not single-mindedly pursue academic and professional goals. And from a social standpoint, a preoccupation with achievement goals can blot out consideration of the effect of one's work on the welfare of others and its meaning in the larger social scheme.

Bearing out Hoffman's speculation, Lyle and Ross (1973: 107) found that only one-sixth of the women managers they studied had exploitive attitudes toward their position as compared with three-fourths of the men. Cartwright (1972) similarly discovered that women medical students cited economic and prestige factors in their desire to study medicine much less often than did men. More frequently, they stated that their motives were based on long-standing interest, a desire for self-development, or altruism.

As a vision of neighborhood cooperation, small industry, and closely integrated family and work setting emerges, it seems obvious that interpersonal style based on cooperation and flexibility is very much called for. If strict achievement orientation and *agentic* purposive styles have not in fact been dysfunctional in the past, they hardly seem sufficient for establishing a more humane order in the future.

If women and their traditional qualities are very much needed, however, there has to be a reward structure that will elicit their contribution and make it visible. These mechanisms are still far from being worked out. In the meantime, women will in their own groups have to act out the style of a *company of friends*, enabling individual creative women to make their contributions toward a better economic order.

SUMMARY

Inflation, unemployment, overproduction, and the rising cost of energy are some major challenges now facing the American economy. At the same time, women's work roles are undergoing profound changes in ways that suggest the shape of alternative economic arrangements in the future that will serve not only women's interest but that of the larger society as well.

The historic growth of industrialism during the past century had a paradoxical effect on women's and men's work. On the one hand, introduction of labor-saving devices and standardized production decreased the need for a sexual division of labor based on differences in strength or differences in men's and women's craft knowledge. On the other hand, distance between the industrial workplace and the home forced greater separation between the working worlds of men and women.

Women's rising frustration fed the new women's movement. In the nineteenth century they fought for the rights to work, to control their own earnings, and to enter into a variety of fields and professions. The contemporary women's movement takes these fundamental gains as a point of departure and tries to increase women's participation in the labor force and the amount of responsibility and benefits they receive.

As with women's political participation, the amount of change accomplished appears to be correlated with the level at which it falls in the hierarchy of social control. The most noticeable change has occurred at the bottom rung where *persons make individual decisions whether or not to participate in the work force.* Between the Second World War and the present, adult women's labor force participation nearly doubled.

Next, at *the job level,* there was growing awareness during the 1960s of sex differences in earnings, promotion, and pay. Suggested remedies range from giving better training and counseling to women to corporate programs for affirmative action.

At *a more general institutional level,* changes in the law prohibited job discrimination on the basis of sex, but enforcement has been weak. Flexible hours, maternity leaves, and child care are frequently suggested means by which women can more easily combine family and work responsibility. Such arrangements are gradually becoming more common.

Even among feminists, however, it is still rare to find articulation of *alternative economic values* to the ones at present enshrined in the American industrial order. Rather than think small or tailor wants to needs, the women's movement has thought primarily of "making it" in the established system. Yet localized production and dispersed communities pictured by missionaries of the steady-state economy may do more for women in the long run. In neighborhoods where production is close to consumption and work is close to family, both men and women may better partake in every function, bringing each sex at long last closer to a true state of equality. Egalitarian belief alone probably will never accomplish the necessary change. Only a new kind of social fabric based on human needs rather than corporate profit is likely to permit women the measure of responsibility and recognition for which they hope.

REFERENCES FOR CHAPTER THREE

Abbott, Edith. 1910. *Women in Industry.* New York: Appleton.

Allport, Gordon. 1954. *The Nature of Prejudice.* Garden City, N.Y.: Doubleday-Anchor.

Baas, Bernard M.; Krusell, Judith; and Alexander, Ralph A. 1971. "Male Managers' Attitudes toward Working Women." *American Behavioral Scientist* 15, no. 2 (November-December): 221-236.

Bardwick, Judith. 1974. "Androgyny and Humanistic Goals or Goodbye, Cardboard People." In *The American Woman: Who Will She Be?* Edited by M. L. McBee and K. A. Blake. Beverly Hills, Ca.: Glencoe Press.

Baruch, Rhoda. 1966. "The Achievement Motive in Women: A Study of the Implications for Career Development." Ph.D. dissertation, Harvard University.

Becker, Gary. 1957. *The Economics of Discrimination.* Chicago: University of Chicago Press.

Bell, Carolyn Shaw. 1972. "A Full Employment Policy for a Public Service Economy." *Social Policy* 3 (September-October): 12-19.

————. 1975. "Should Every Job Support a Family?" *Public Interest* 40 (Summer): 109-118.

Bennis, Warren G., and Schein, Edgar H., eds. 1969. *Leadership and Motivation: Essays of Douglas McGregor.* Cambridge, Ma.: MIT Press.

Bergmann, Barbara R. 1971. "The Effect on White Incomes of Discrimination in Employment." *Journal of Political Economy* 79, no. 2 (March-April): 294-313.

Bergmann, Barbara R., and Adelman, Irma. 1973. "The 1973 Report of the President's Council of Economic Advisors: The Economic Role of Women." *American Economic Review* 63 (September): 509-514.

Berkeley, Ellen. 1972. "Women in Architecture." *Architectural Forum* 137, no. 2 (September): 46ff.

Blau, Francine D., and Jusenius, Carol L. 1976. "Economists' Approaches to Sex Segregation in the Labor Market: An Appraisal." *Signs* 1, no. 3, part 2 (Spring): 181-199.

Blechman, Barry M.; Gramlich, Edward M.; and Hartman, Robert W. 1975. *Setting National Priorities: The 1976 Budget.* Washington, D.C.: Brookings Institution.

Boudon, Raymond. 1973. *Education, Opportunity, and Social Inequality: Changing Prospects in Western Society.* New York: Wiley.

Bowen, William G., and Finegan, T. Aldrich. 1969. *The Economics of Labor Force Participation.* Princeton, N.J.: Princeton University Press.

Bowles, Samuel. 1971; 1972. "Contradictions in U.S. Higher Education." In *The Capitalist System*. Edited by R. C. Edwards, M. Reich, and T. E. Weisskopf. Englewood Cliffs, N.J.: Prentice-Hall.

Bureau of the Census, U.S. Department of Commerce. 1970. *Current Population Reports, no. 77*. Washington, D.C.: U.S.G.P.O.

——. 1973. "We the American Women." Washington, D.C.: U.S.G.P.O.

Bureau of Labor Statistics, U.S. Department of Labor. 1972a. *Selected Earnings and Demographic Characteristics of Union Members, 1970, Report no. 417*. Washington, D.C.: U.S.G.P.O.

——. 1972b. *Directory of National Unions and Employer Associations, 1971*. Washington, D.C.: U.S.G.P.O., Publication no. 1750.

Business Week. 1974. "Women Win More Credit." 12 January, pp. 70-78.

——. 1975a. "How Workers Can Get Eight Hours' Pay for Five." 19 May, pp. 52ff.

——. 1975b. "Young Top Management: The New Goals, Rewards, Lifestyles" and "It Pays to Listen to Workers' Complaints." 6 October, pp. 56-67, 68a-68c.

Cain, Glen G. 1966. *Married Women in the Labor Force: An Economic Analysis*. Chicago: University of Chicago Press.

Campbell, Jean W. 1973. "Women Drop Back In: Educational Innovation in the Sixties." In *Academic Women on the Move*. Edited by A. S. Rossi and A. Calderwood. New York: Russell Sage Foundation.

Carlson, Rae. 1972. "Understanding Women: Implications for Personality Theory and Research." *Journal of Social Issues* 28, no. 2: 17-32.

Cartwright, Lillian Kaufman. 1972. "Common Factors Entering into Decisions of Women to Study Medicine." *Journal of Social Issues* 28, no. 2: 201-215.

Chafe, William. 1972. *The American Woman: Her Changing Social, Economic, and Political Roles, 1920-1970*. New York: Oxford University Press.

Committee on Alternative Work Patterns. 1976. *Alternatives in the World of Work*. Washington, D.C.: National Center for Productivity and Quality of Working Life.

Cook, Alice H. 1975. *The Working Mother: A Survey of Problems and Programs in Nine Countries*. Ithaca, N.Y.: New York State School of Industrial Relations, Cornell University.

Davis, James A. 1964. *Great Aspirations: The Graduate School Plans of America's College Seniors*. Chicago: Aldine.

Davis, Louis E. 1971; 1972. "Readying the Unready: Post-Industrial Jobs." In *Design of Jobs*. Edited by L. E. Davis and J. C. Taylor. Baltimore, Md.: Penguin.

Davis, Louis E., and Taylor, James C., eds. 1972. *Design of Jobs*. Baltimore, Md.: Penguin.

Deckard, Barbara, and Sherman, Howard. 1975. "Monopoly Power and Sex Discrimination." *Politics and Society* 4, no. 4: 478-482.

Dewey, Lucretia M. 1971. "Women in Labor Unions." *Monthly Labor Review* 94, no. 2 (February): 42-48.

Doeringer, Peter B., and Piore, Michael J. 1971. *Internal Labor Markets and Manpower Analysis.* Lexington, Ma.: Heath.

Duncan, Otis D.; Schuman, Howard; and Duncan, Beverly. 1973. *Social Change in a Metropolitan Community.* New York: Russell Sage Foundation.

East, Catherine. 1972. "The Current Status of the Employment of Women." In *Women in the Work Force.* Edited by M. E. Katzell and W. C. Byham. New York: Behavioral Publications.

Economic Report of the President, 1973. Washington, D.C.: U.S.G.P.O.

Edwards, Richard C.; Reich, Michael; and Gordon, David M. 1975. "Introduction." In *Labor Market Segmentation.* Edited by R. C. Edwards, M. Reich, and D. M. Gordon. Lexington, Ma.: Heath.

Ellul, Jacques. 1964; 1967. *The Technological Society.* New York: Knopf. Chapter 5 in *Analyses of Contemporary Society.* Edited by B. Rosenberg. New York: Crowell.

Equal Employment Opportunity Commission. 1972*a.* "A Unique Competence: A Study of Equal Employment Opportunity in the Bell System." *Congressional Record* 17 (February): E1243–E1268.

————. 1972*b. Sixth Annual Report, 1972.* Washington, D.C.: U.S.G.P.O.

Featherman, David L., and Hauser, Robert M. 1976. "Sexual Inequalities and Socioeconomic Achievement in the U.S., 1962–1973." *American Sociological Review* 41 (June): 462–483.

Ferber, Marianne, and Lowry, Helen. 1976. "Women—The New Reserve Army of the Unemployed." *Signs* 1, no. 3, part 2 (Spring): 213–232.

Finegan, T. Aldrich. 1975. "Participation of Married Women in the Labor Force." In *Sex, Discrimination, and the Division of Labor.* Edited by C. B. Lloyd. New York: Columbia University Press.

Freeman, Jo. 1969; 1971. "Women on the Social Science Faculties since 1892, University of Chicago." In *Hearing before the Special Subcommittee on Education of the Committee on Education and Labor, U.S. House of Representatives, Part 2* (1971). Washington, D.C.: U.S.G.P.O.

Friedan, Betty. 1963. *The Feminine Mystique.* New York: Norton.

Fuchs, Victor. 1971. "Differences in Hourly Earnings between Men and Women." *Monthly Labor Review* 94, no. 5 (May): 9–15.

Gitlow, Abraham. 1972. "Women in the American Economy: Today and Tomorrow." *Labor Law Journal* 23, no. 4 (April): 232–237.

Glazer-Malbin, Nona, and Waehrer, Helen Youngelson. 1972. *Woman in a Manmade World.* Chicago: Rand McNally.

Gold, Sonia. 1973. "Alternative National Goals and Women's Employment." *Science,* 16 February, pp. 656–660.

Hartley, Jo, ed. 1975. *Hours of Work When Workers Can Choose.* Washington, D.C.: Business and Professional Women's Foundation.

Hayghe, Howard. 1976. "Families and the Rise of Working Wives—An Overview." *Monthly Labor Review* 99 (May): 12–19.

Hedges, Janice Neipert. 1970. "Women at Work. Women Workers and Manpower Demands in the 1970s." *Monthly Labor Review* 93 (June): 19–29.

Helson, Ravenna. 1972. "Changing Image of the Career Woman." *Journal of Social Issues* 28: 33-46.

Hoffman, Lois W. 1963. "The Decision to Work." In *The Employed Mother in America*. Edited by F. I. Nye and L. W. Hoffman. Chicago: Rand McNally.

———. 1972. "Early Childhood Experiences and Women's Achievement Motives." *Journal of Social Issues* 28, no. 2: 129-155.

——— 1974. "Psychological Factors." In *Working Mothers*. Edited by L. W. Hoffman and F. I. Nye. San Francisco: Jossey-Bass.

Horner, Matina S. 1972. "Toward an Understanding of Achievement-Related Conflicts in Women." *Journal of Social Issues* 28: 157-175.

Internal Revenue Service, U.S. Department of the Treasury. 1976. *Your Federal Income Tax: 1977 Edition*. Washington, D.C.: U.S.G.P.O.

James, Edward T., and James, Janet Wilson, with P. S. Boyer. 1971. *Notable American Women, 1607-1950*, 3 vols. Cambridge, Ma.: Harvard University Press.

Johnson, George E., and Stafford, Frank P. 1975. "Women and the Academic Labor Market." In *Sex, Discrimination, and the Division of Labor*. Edited by C. B. Lloyd. New York: Columbia University Press.

Johnstone, Elizabeth. 1968. "Women in Economic Life: Rights and Opportunities." *Annals of the American Academy of Political and Social Science* 375 (January): 102-114.

Joint Economic Committee. U.S. Congress. 1973. *Economic Problems of Women: Hearings before the 93rd Congress of the United States*. Washington, D.C.: U.S.G.P.O.

Jusenius, Carol L., and Sandell, Steven. 1974. "Barriers to Entry and Reentry into the Labor Force." Columbus, Oh.: Center for Human Resource Research, Ohio State University.

Jusenius, Carol L., and Shortlidge, Richard L., Jr. 1975. *Dual Careers: A Longitudinal Study of Labor Market Experience of Women*, vol. 3. Columbus, Oh.: Center for Human Resource Research, Ohio State University.

Kahne, Hilda. 1974. "Women in Management: Strategy for Increase." Excerpt from Statement to Advisory Committee on the Economic Role of Women, Council of Economic Advisors. Washington, D.C.: Business and Professional Women's Foundation.

———. 1976. "Future Issues for and about Women." Paper presented to the Lilly Endowment, Indianapolis, In., December.

Kahne, Hilda, with A. Kohen. 1975. "Economic Perspectives on the Role of Women in the American Economy." *Journal of Economic Literature* 13 (December): 1249-1292.

Kahne, Hilda; Moore, Jonelle; and McDonagh, Eileen. 1976. "Career Patterns and Rewards: A Comparative Study of Professional Women." Washington, D.C.: Business and Professional Women's Foundation.

Kanter, Rosabeth Moss. 1977. *Men and Women of the Corporation*. New York: Basic Books.

Klein, Deborah P. 1975. "Women in the Labor Force: The Middle Years." *Monthly Labor Review* 98 (November): 10-16.

Kreps, Juanita M. 1971. *Sex in the Marketplace: American Women at Work.* Baltimore, Md.: Johns Hopkins University Press.

Kropotkin, Peter. 1899; 1974. *Fields, Factories, and Workshops Tomorrow.* Edited, introduced, and with additional material by Colin Ward. New York: Harper Torchbooks.

Levitin, Teresa; Quinn, Robert P.; and Staines, Graham L. 1971. "Sex Discrimination against the American Working Woman." *American Behavioral Scientist* 15: 237–254.

Lipman-Blumen, Jean. 1970. "Selected Dimensions of Self-concept and Educational Aspirations of Married Women College Graduates." Ph.D. dissertation, Harvard University.

——. 1972*a.* "How Ideology Shapes Women's Lives." *Scientific American*, 3 March, pp. 34–42.

——. 1972*b.* "Perspectives on the Development and Impact of Female Role Ideology." Presented at Women: Resource for a Changing World conference, 17–18 April, Radcliffe Institute.

Lotman, Arline. 1973. *Credit Report.* Harrisburg, Pa.: Pennsylvania Commission on the Status of Women.

Lyle, Jerolyn R., and Ross, Jane L. 1973. *Women in Industry.* Lexington, Ma.: Heath.

McEaddy, Beverly Johnson. 1976. "Women Who Head Families: A Socioeconomic Analysis." *Monthly Labor Review* 99 (June): 3–9.

Mason, Karen Oppenheim, and Bumpass, Larry L. 1975. "U.S. Women's Sex-role Ideology, 1970." *American Sociological Review* 40 (March): 1212–1219.

Mead, Margaret. 1949. *Male and Female: A Study of the Sexes in a Changing World.* New York: Morrow.

Merton, Robert K. 1957. *Social Theory and Social Structure,* Rev. and enlarged ed. New York: The Free Press.

Mincer, Jacob. 1962*a.* "Labor-Force Participation of Married Women: A Study of Labor Supply." In *Aspects of Labor Economics.* A Report of the National Bureau of Economic Research. Princeton, N.J.: Universities– National Bureau Committee of Economic Research.

——. 1962*b.* "On-the-job Training: Costs, Returns, and Some Implications." *Journal of Political Economy* 70, Supplement (October): 50–79.

Mincer, Jacob, and Polachek, Solomon W. 1974. "Family Investments in Human Capital: Earnings of Women." *Journal of Political Economy* 82 (March-April): S76–S108.

Morgan, James N.; Dickinson, Katherine; Dickinson, Jonathan; Benus, Jacob; and Duncan, Greg. 1974. *Five Thousand American Families—Patterns of Economic Progress. Vol. I: An Analysis of the First Five Years of the Panel Study of Income Dynamics.* Ann Arbor, Mi.: Institute for Social Research, University of Michigan.

Morris, David, and Hess, Karl. 1975. *Neighborhood Power: The New Localism.* Boston: Beacon Press.

Moskow, Michael H. 1973. "Government in the Lead." In *Corporate Lib: Women's Challenge to Management.* Edited by E. Ginzberg and A. M.

Yohalem. Baltimore, Md.: Johns Hopkins University Press.

Myrdal, Gunnar. 1944; 1962. *An American Dilemma: The Negro Problem and Modern Democracy*, 2 vols. New York: Harper Torchbooks.

Nye, F. Ivan. 1974. "Sociocultural Context." In *Working Mothers.* Edited by L. W. Hoffman and F. I. Nye. San Francisco: Jossey-Bass.

Nye, F. Ivan, and Hoffman, Lois W. 1963. *The Employed Mother in America.* Chicago: Rand McNally.

Oppenheimer, Valerie. 1970. *The Female Labor Force in the United States.* Berkeley, Ca.: University of California, Population Monograph Series no. 5.

Parsons, Talcott, and Bales, R. F. 1955. *Family, Socialization, and Interaction Process.* New York: The Free Press.

Polachek, Solomon W. 1975. "Discontinuous Labor-Force Participation and Its Effect on Women's Market Earnings." In *Sex, Discrimination, and the Division of Labor.* Edited by C. B. Lloyd. New York: Columbia University Press.

Political and Economic Planning. 1971. *Women in Top Jobs.* London: Allen and Unwin.

Prather, Jane. 1971. "Why Can't Women Be More Like Men?: A Summary of the Sociopsychological Factors Hindering Women's Advancement in the Professions." *American Behavioral Scientist* 15, no. 2 (November-December): 172-182.

Riley, Matilda White; Johnson, Marilyn E.; and Boocock, Sarane S. 1963. "Women's Changing Occupational Role—A Research Report." *American Behavioral Scientist* 6 (May): 33-37.

Robison, David. 1976. *Alternative Work Patterns: Changing Approaches to Work Scheduling.* Scarsdale, N.Y.: Work in America Institute.

Sawhill, Isabel V. 1973. "The Economics of Discrimination against Women: Some New Findings." *Journal of Human Resources* 8 (Summer): 383-395.

Schultze, Charles L.; Fried, Edward R.; Rivlin, Alice M.; and Teeters, Nancy H. 1972. *Setting National Priorities: The 1973 Budget.* Washington, D.C.: Brookings Institution.

Schumacher, E. F. 1973. *Small Is Beautiful: Economics as if People Mattered.* New York: Harper and Row.

Smelser, Neil J. 1959. *Social Change in the Industrial Revolution.* Chicago: University of Chicago Press.

Smuts, Robert W. 1959; 1971. *Women and Work in America.* New York: Schocken Books.

Spock, Benjamin M. 1946; 1968. *Baby and Child Care*, Rev. ed. New York: Hawthorn.

Spring, William; Harrison, Bennett; and Vietorisz, Thomas. 1972. "Crisis of the Underemployed." *New York Times Magazine*, 5 November, pp. 42ff.

Stein, Robert L. 1970. "The Economic Status of Families Headed by Women." *Monthly Labor Review* 93 (December): 3-10.

Suter, Larry E., and Miller, Herman P. 1973. "Income Differences between Men and Career Women." *American Journal of Sociology* 78 (January): 962-974.

Sweet, James A. 1973. *Women in the Labor Force.* New York: Seminar Press.

Tangri, Sandra Schwartz. 1972. "Determinants of Occupational Role Innovation among College Women." *Journal of Social Issues* 28, no. 2: 177-200.

Thurow, Lester C. 1969. *Poverty and Discrimination.* Washington, D.C.: Brookings Institution.

Thurow, Lester C., and Lucas, Robert E. B. 1972. "The American Distribution of Income: A Structural Problem." Prepared for the Joint Economic Committee, U.S. Congress, 17 March. Washington, D.C.: U.S.G.P.O.

Time. 1972. "Is the Work Ethic Going Out of Style?" 30 October, pp. 96-97.

Turner, Ralph. 1964. "Some Aspects of Women's Ambition." *American Journal of Sociology* 70 (November): 271-285.

Ulman, Lloyd. 1972. "Labor Markets and Manpower Policies in Perspective." *Monthly Labor Review* 95 (September): 22-28.

U.S. News and World Report. 1972. "Women Workers: Gaining Power, Seeking More." 13 November, pp. 104-107.

Waldman, E., and Gover, K. R. 1972. "Marital and Family Characteristics of the Labor Force." *Monthly Labor Review* 95 (April): 4-8.

Weber, Max. 1904-1905; 1958. *The Protestant Ethic and the Spirit of Capitalism.* Translated by T. Parsons, with a foreword by R. H. Tawney. New York: Scribner's.

Weisskopf, Francine Blau. 1972. " 'Women's Place' in the Labor Market." *American Economic Review* 62 (May): 161-176.

Wertheimer, Barbara. 1972. "Barriers to the Participation of Women in Unions." Ithaca, N.Y.: New York State School of Industrial Relations, Cornell University.

——. 1976. "Search for a Partnership Role: Women in Labor Unions Today." In *Economic Independence for Women.* Edited by J. R. Chapman. Beverly Hills, Ca.: Sage Publications.

Wilensky, Harold. 1975. *The Welfare State and Equality.* Berkeley, Ca.: University of California Press.

Women in Transition. 1975. *Women in Transition: A Feminist Handbook on Separation and Divorce.* New York: Scribner's.

Women Today. 1975a. "Business and Professional Women's Foundation Publishes Flexible Hours Study." Vol. 5, no. 17 (18 August): 99.

——. 1975b. "Hearings Focus on Problems of Older Women including Social Security Inequities." Vol. 5, no. 21 (13 October): 124.

——. 1977a. "Flexible and Part-time Work Bill Introduced in the Senate." Vol. 7, no. 4 (21 February): 19.

——. 1977b. "Labor Department Announces New Maternity-Leave Policy with Pharmaceutical Firm." Vol. 7, no. 6 (21 March): 32-33.

——. 1977c. "Pennsylvania Commission Study Shows U.S. Lagging in Maternity Protection." Vol. 7, no. 8 (18 April): 47-48.

Women's Bureau, U.S. Department of Labor, Wage and Standards Administration. 1969. "How You Can Help Reduce Barriers to the Employment of Mature Women." Washington, D.C.: U.S.G.P.O.

——. 1971. "Status of State Hours Laws for Women since Passage of Title VII of the Civil Rights Act of 1964." Washington, D.C.: U.S.G.P.O.

——. 1974. "Steps to Opening the Skilled Trades to Women." Washington, D.C.: U.S.G.P.O.

Work in America; Report of a Special Task Force to the Secretary of Health, Education, and Welfare. 1973. Cambridge, Ma.: MIT Press.

Zellner, Harriet. 1975. "The Determinants of Occupational Segregation." In *Sex, Discrimination, and the Division of Labor.* Edited by C. B. Lloyd. New York: Columbia University Press.

4

CHANGE IN THE FAMILY CONTEXT

The trouble was that while the educated middle-class girl of the twenties was eager for self-fulfillment, she had almost no idea how to get it. Public service was boring, if not actually discredited, the careerist myth had been deflated. . . . What remained, as it turned out, was marriage and motherhood

—William O'Neill, *Everyone Was Brave*, 1969.

The revolution in the status of women can most simply be summarized in the fact that 32 million working women won't go home again. . . . The task of the next revolution is to bring about a situation where the work performed at home is a responsibility for human beings instead of a burden for women

—Carolyn Shaw Bell, "The Next Revolution," 1975.

There is a close tie between the change in men's and women's roles and the change in family structure. But the relative status of women in family life is more difficult to measure than their status in public affairs. Political, economic, or educational activities operate in "markets" that assign the individual a formal status and pay a stated income. The family by contrast is "associational" (Weinstein and Platt, 1969: 1-19). The status of each member is enmeshed with facts of birth and death, marriage or divorce. Participation in the family hinges on the emotional life of others as well as on individual accomplishment. Laws and public policies directed at child care, the elderly, tax rates, or public welfare affect not only one member or one sex but also the whole family unit. Consequently, examination of the relative status of women and men in the family very quickly leads to considering the structure of the family unit and the situational realities that determine its form.

Women's and men's roles will not really change unless family institutions also change, but it is not at all clear in what order and in what direction family life will be transformed. Maybe, as some economists suggest, the next steps to be taken are public measures that will support a new occupation of consumer maintenance, or allow tax deductions for household costs such as heat, light, or child care, much as corporations are allowed tax deductions for their expenses (Bell, 1975; Lekachman, 1975). Or perhaps the next steps must be personal and ideological, through commitment to the idea that the family is the responsibility of both men and women.

No matter what change comes first, it is clear now that the traditional sex-typed division of labor between women's work at home and men's work at a job is under strain in every major industrial nation. Although 40 to 60 percent of women are employed in such countries as the United States, Russia, Poland, and Japan, they pay a penalty of being overburdened by both domestic *and* paid work (Blake, 1974). Employed American women who have families average a total of seventy hours of work a week (Gauger, 1973: 23). Each week they have a few hours less leisure time than men for sleep or relaxation (Szalai, 1973). Thus more women have entered employment without having secured the needed adjustments in family life.

The balance of work and leisure is only one issue raised by change in sex roles. Other issues are related to problems that emerge when individuals deviate from the preferred life cycle. The poverty of female-headed households is one example. If through divorce, widowhood, or desertion a woman is left alone to head a household with children, her children are about six times more likely to grow up in poverty than children living in male-headed families (Bane, 1976: 118).

Family issues become especially significant for changing sex roles as the boundary between public and private life becomes more permeable. Demographic shifts (lengthening of life, the changing life cycle of women and families) are behind current public-policy issues such as child care or homemaker allowances. However, current extension of government supports into various functions of private life such as health care and care of the elderly gives public policy potential power to influence the shape of family life and sex roles in the future.

Over the past century, family and sex roles changed to produce the ferment we experience today. This chapter begins with a historical review of the social process through which women's family responsibility increased. The rest of the chapter describes contemporary changes in sex roles and family behavior at two levels. First are changes in the life cycle of women as indicated by such demographic measures as age at marriage, length of the child-bearing period, and length of life. Second is the increasing variety of viable family forms exemplified by the dual-worker, single-parent, communal, and other types. The implications of these behavioral changes for family policy and family ideals are then treated in the following chapter.

AMERICAN FAMILIES IN HISTORICAL PERSPECTIVE

In 1884 Friedrich Engels projected a time when the single family would cease to be the primary economic unit of society, when private housekeeping would be transformed into an industry and the care and education of children would become a public affair. A sexual revolution would also ensue in which public opinion would tolerate women's interest in sexuality as well as men's. Engels's (1884; 1972: 138-139) predictions rested on his conclusion that private property and the monogamous marriage system that supported it would soon be outmoded, women benefitting from the change. In his words,

> We are now approaching a social revolution in which the economic foundations of monogamy as they have existed hitherto will disappear. . . . Monogamy arose from the concentration of considerable wealth in the hands of a single individual—a man—and from the need to bequeath this wealth to the children of that man and no other. . . . But by transforming by far the greater portion of permanent heritable wealth—the means of production—into social property, the coming social revolution will reduce to a minimum all this anxiety about bequeathing and inheriting . . . therefore, the position of men will be very much altered. But the position of women, of *all* women, also undergoes significant change.

It is surprising how many of Engels's predictions have very nearly been realized, although there are now other, more refined explanations for why these events occurred. Engels posited a state of early equality between the sexes in primitive tribes where the family was not the primary unit of production. Then in agrarian society the family became the basic unit of economic activity. Land and property were passed through it to sons, and males held superior rank over females. The breakdown of the patriarchal family began with the Industrial Revolution, when economic control moved out of the family. A final state of equality between the sexes was to come when the industrial process would have gone far enough to create social revolution.

Modern anthropological and sociological research suggests that Engels was not far wrong in depicting a drop in the status of women when landholding became important in agrarian peasant societies (Leacock, 1972; Sacks, 1974). But there is disagreement on whether later modernization improves the status of women. In nineteenth-century America, for example, the "cult of true womanhood" appeared to confine women to home and hearth much more drastically than in the seventeenth and eighteenth centuries (Welter, 1976). Some historians have argued therefore that the first moves beyond colonial "peasant" society brought a further drop in the status of women (Demos, 1974: 432). Women in the early 1800s appeared less active in business and professions than they had been in the colonial period. For example, professionalization of medicine kept them from being midwives (Lerner, 1969). Early dame schools were replaced by public institutions. Nor were such changes confined just to the United States. They also occurred in Britain, with the imposition of Blackstone's interpretation of women's inferior place in the common law (Beard, 1946), and in France, where patriarchal conceptions of family life were rationalized in the Napoleonic era and extended into the twentieth century (Silver, 1977).

On the other hand, there were opposing trends in the late colonial period and early republic that eventually led to improvement in women's status. In some ways the American family even in the colonial period had never been a truly peasant type. Rather than a long-term community based on generations of landholding, traditional agriculture, and patriarchal control, a small town like Andover or Dedham, Massachusetts, in the seventeenth century was new, containing hundreds of strangers. Furthermore, there was land beyond town boundaries if sons could not inherit and wished to move (Henretta, 1973). Thus in some respects the American family always bore within its frame the essential spirit of early modern society—individualism, risk taking, and innovation. These qualities worked in the long run to improve women's status.

Records of early pilgrim and Puritan families in Plymouth Colony and Salem, Massachusetts, suggest that mutual respect and equality were implicit in much of the relationship between husband and wife, although Demos (1974: 426) reports that women were definitely regarded as being inferior to men. Yet parents together decided on placement of a child in apprenticeship. Respect was due to each parent from both children and servants, though the husband was said to be the "Head of the Wife," and she the "Head of the Family" (Morgan, 1944: 45, 46). The Puritan family ideal expressed in Milton's writings on marriage and divorce must have been carried over into the American setting. Central to Milton's thought was a notion of *mutual* affection and *mutual* respect between husband and wife (Haller and Haller, 1941- 42).

A religious revival known as the Great Awakening, which took place throughout the colonies in the 1730s and 1740s, further enhanced the spirit of egalitarianism and reliance on individual conscience. The Puritan theocratic ideals that joined state and church were replaced by individualistic beliefs that each person's soul must be saved by the confession of faith and the personal decision to proceed in the direction of right. Such a religious position had profound liberating consequences for women.

Denominational groups like the Quakers, Methodists, Baptists, and Presbyterians were strengthened by the movement, and from their ranks were eventually drawn some of the most prominent women in nineteenth-century reform movements. Women leaders who stood for temperance, abolition, and women's rights could not have stood against the tide of popular sentiment about women's proper place without firm conviction that their inner thoughts should take precedence over outward convention (Giele, 1961).

At the same time, however, the changes in family induced by the Industrial Revolution were creating a process of structural differentiation between work outside and inside the home much as Smelser (1959) described in England from 1820 to 1850. Accompanying this change in America was the creation of a new, more responsible role for women in the home which the historian Daniel Scott Smith (1974: 121-123) has termed "domestic feminism." The ideology of domestic feminism promoted women's autonomy in the domestic sphere with respect to three major functions: management of the household and housekeeping, health of the family (including contraception and her own child-bearing role), and child rearing.

The spirit and practice of domestic feminism was embodied in Catherine Beecher's famous *Treatise on Domestic Economy* first published in 1841 and reprinted annually until 1857. The book dealt with practical domestic matters such as workable floor plans, how to care for the sick, and how to bring up children. In the words of Kathryn Kish Sklar (1973: 154), Beecher's biographer, the *Treatise* was "a badly needed compendium of the domestic arts relating to health, diet, hygiene, and general well-being." Beecher, though a spinster, probably shared with other women of the period an interest in the limitation of childbearing. However, while many women used a "contraceptive strategy" of invalidism, Beecher urged women to be active and conscious of their own worth. She seemed to believe in basic (though not outward) equality of wives with their husbands. A woman was not forced to take a husband; she could remain single. By preparing women for a domestic vocation, the *Treatise* "urged readers to approach the female life cycle as a work cycle and prepare for it as a man would prepare for a vocation" (Sklar, 1977: ix-xv).

Although the home and the outside world were viewed as two quite different spheres, the autonomy of women inside the home was soon extended to a wider plane. The contraceptive strategies employed in mid-nineteenth century had by 1900 resulted in a dramatic drop in total fertility rate of whites, from 7.04 in 1800, to 5.42 in 1850, and 3.56 in 1900. Nor could the drop be explained by women's increasing employment outside the home since only 2.5 percent of married women were so employed in 1890 (Smith, 1974: 123).

Engagement in productive work did, however, increase somewhat throughout the period. The productive work that women had done inside the home was gradually extended outside the home to domestic work and other paid employments. Tilley et al.'s (1976) description of women's transition to paid work in France and England is probably not too unlike what happened in America. Young people worked and sent their money home so that they would be less of a burden on the family. Artisan families sent wives and daughters to work to strengthen their tenuous economic position. In all of Great Britain in 1911, 4 percent of women were in the nonagricultural paid labor force of whom half were domestic servants; this compares with a total of 2 percent in the nonagricultural labor force in 1841. In the United States, 35 percent of the single women and 2.5 percent of the married women were in the labor force in 1890.

At the same time that some women were engaging in paid employment (particularly before marriage) and having fewer children, others were expanding their capacity and interest in mothering to the wider community. Even before the Civil War, women extended their benevolent interest outside the family through myriad Bible societies, missionary associations, and other voluntary groups to help the poor, the sick, and the orphaned (Melder, 1967). With the Civil War, large numbers of women volunteers served as nurses and organized medical and supply groups to offer support in the North and the South. After the war many volunteer women's groups sprung up and grew to significant size. Among them were the Women's Christian Temperance Union; the missionary societies of the Methodist, Baptist, and Presbyterian churches; the suffrage associations; and women's clubs of many varieties. Some were aimed at reform, others at supporting the arts and cultural life of the community. Whatever their specific purpose, it was not so much to change the traditional roles of men and women as to restore them to health and wholesome participation. The vote for women, designated the "Home Protection Ballot" by the large and popular Women's Christian Temperance Union in the 1880s, was to be a tool to restore men to their rightful place as chief providers for the household by banning alcohol and other vices from the community. Women in seeking to institute such protection were carrying out their roles as cultural guardians of children, the community, and the home (Giele, 1961).

By 1920, when the nineteenth-century women's movement had run its course, having extended the domestic interests of women outward into the larger community and the nation, several dramatic changes in women's life cycle had been registered that clearly changed the social definition of the feminine role. Women typically had fewer children, and since they lived longer they were free part of their lives for other activities. Moreover, a great many more of them were able to live long enough to complete the preferred life cycle.

MEN'S AND WOMEN'S PARTICIPATION IN FAMILY

The most concrete level at which changes in sex roles are apparent in the established family is the level of the *individual life cycle*, where demographic changes reveal that some marked shifts in behavior have occurred. Statistics show two major trends that suggest that traditional patterns are undergoing change: first, the *compression* of the child-bearing years coupled with the lengthening of life; and second, the increased *combination* of family responsibilities with paid market work. Besides these powerful underlying demographic and economic trends, there are also major social problems that arise for people who deviate from the preferred life course that these patterns imply. Two in particular are the rise in teenage pregnancy and an increasing divorce rate that brings a rise in the proportion of households headed by females.

These changes in pattern are summarized by Peter Uhlenberg (1969) in the accompanying graph (Figure 2). He defines the *typical* or preferred life cycle as the chance to survive to age twenty, marry, have children, and survive with husband alive to age fifty-five. Five major deviations from this pattern were (1) the *abbreviated* (where a woman dies before the age of twenty); (2) the *spinster*; (3) the *barren* woman; (4) the woman who *dies as a young mother*; and (5) the *widow* whose husband dies before the age of fifty-seven.

What is striking is that the number of persons in each birth cohort of 100,000 who were able to complete the "typical" or preferred life cycle nearly tripled between 1830 and 1920 (Uhlenberg, 1969: 415).

Cohort of:	1830	1850	1870	1890	1920
Number who lived typical life cycle	20,900	23,000	22,600	27,400	57,100

Given these powerful underlying demographic changes that have occurred in women's life cycle, sex roles and family styles are inevitably faced with a lag between the ideology of "woman's place"

Figure 2. Number of Women in Each Cohort Who Experience Various Life Cycles

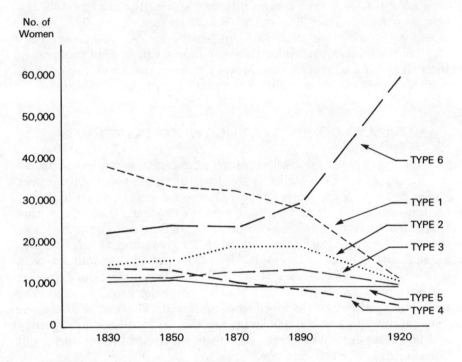

Type 1 life cycle: *Abbreviated;* woman dies before age 20.
Type 2 life cycle: *Spinster;* woman survives to 20, never marries.
Type 3 life cycle: *Barren;* woman marries, remains childless.
Type 4 life cycle: *Dying mother;* woman has children, dies before age 55.
Type 5 life cycle: *Widowed mother;* woman has children, survives to 55, husband dies before he is 57.
Type 6 life cycle: *Typical;* woman survives to 20, marries, has children, survives with husband alive to age 55.

SOURCE: Uhlenberg (1969:415).

in the home and modern-day realities. Where almost half of women's lives are now free from child-rearing responsibilities, and where technological progress has taken away the need to make bread or medicine or even lye and soap as in Catherine Beecher's day, there is a need to consider what plan for the life cycle is now appropriate and what forms of family life best take these changes into account.

Indeed there are even more recent changes in the life cycle of women with further implications for marriage, employment, and motherhood.

THE CONTEMPORARY LIFE CYCLE OF WOMEN

Two major demographic changes have taken place that affect the family life cycle and women's role within it. The child-bearing period has been compressed, and adult women's average length of life has increased. As a result the typical American woman in this century bears fewer children and has her last child at the age of thirty; that child leaves home when a woman is in her late forties, and she can still expect to live thirty more years. As recently as the turn of the century women were bearing their last child when they were thirty-three, seeing their last child married when they were fifty-six, and themselves living only ten or fifteen years more. Table 3 shows how the number of years between the time a youngest child would go to school (at age six) and the death of one of the parents has nearly quadrupled in the last 200 years.

TABLE 3. Ages at Which Women Experience Typical Life Events, Pre-1786 to the Present

STAGE IN LIFE CYCLE	WIVES BORN			
	before 1786	*1880-1889*	*1920-1929*	*1950-1959*
Age at:				
A. First Marriage	20.5	21.6	20.8	21.2
B. Birth of Last Child	37.9	32.9	30.5	29.6
C. Marriage of Last Child	60.2	56.2	52.0	52.3
D. Death of First Spouse to Die	50.9	57.0	64.4	65.2
Number of "Child free" Years*	7.0	18.1	27.9	29.6
Women's Life Expectancy (at birth)	35.1[†]	51.6	58.1	72.3

*Calculated by subtracting median age of woman at school entry of last child (B + 6 years) from median age at death of first spouse to die (D).

[†]Life expectancy for males and females.

SOURCE: Wells (1971:281); Taeuber and Taeuber (1971:480-499); *Statistical Abstract of the United States* (1973:57); Glick (1977:6); Bureau of the Census (Part 1, 1975:55). Part of this table reprinted from Robert V. Wells, "Demographic Changes and the Life Cycle of American Families,"*Journal of Interdisciplinary History* 2 (1971): 281, by permission of the *Journal of Interdisciplinary History* and the M.I.T. Press, Cambridge, Massachusetts. Copyright 1971, by the Massachusetts Institute of Technology and the editors of the *Journal of Interdisciplinary History*.

In addition to having a longer time to live, more women in each generation have been able to achieve the preferred life pattern of being married and having children. Of women born around 1890 approximately 9 percent never married, compared with only 4 percent of those born in the 1930s. The number who were childless declined from about 15 percent of those women married at the turn of the century to only about 4 percent of those married in the 1960s and 1970s (Glick, 1977: 8). These trends, coupled with the declining mortality of males and females between the ages of twenty and fifty, have resulted in a smaller amount of variability in the life-cycle experiences of females. Uhlenberg (1974) shows that among white females of the 1890 to 1894 birth cohort only 425 out of 1,000 who were alive at the age of fifteen were able to experience the preferred life cycle (marriage, childbearing, and living with spouse until at least the age of fifty). But almost two-thirds of the 1930 to 1934 birth cohort were able to achieve this preferred pattern, and if women who remarried after divorce are added to that group, more than three-fourths of women born between 1930 and 1934 were able to follow the preferred pattern.

Among nonwhites many more women deviate from the "preferred" life cycle. An important factor is the higher rate of deaths among nonwhites between the ages of twenty and fifty. Even considering only the people who survived to age fifty, less than 30 percent of the nonwhite females born between 1890 and 1894 were able to follow the preferred life cycle, and this proportion increased to only 39 percent for the nonwhite women born between 1930 and 1934.

Among the white population as well, Uhlenberg (1974) predicts that a growing number will deviate from the preferred path in future years. Indeed, even now, data on women born in the 1950s show that they have a higher proportion of women never married and childless than those born in the 1930s (Glick, 1977: 8).

Several significant types of deviation from the preferred pattern, such as early pregnancy or divorce, can be thought of as variations in *timing*, and each carries certain costs. Major costs of deviation in timing are shown by Glen Elder's longitudinal study of some seventy females born in the 1920s who were part of the Oakland Growth Study. Elder followed the careers of these women through data collected first in the 1930s and then updated with facts on their education, marriages, and adulthood during the 1940s, 1950s, and early 1960s. His findings show the crucial importance of the timing of marriage for a woman's subsequent life pattern. The women who married very early (before the age of twenty) thereby closed off options to more education. They tended to have more children than did the women who married at the average age (between twenty and twenty-two) or who married late (after the age of twenty-two). In addition more of the women who married early had by 1964 experienced divorce or other forms of marital disruption than the ones who married at the average age or later (Elder, 1974: 209; Elder and Rockwell, 1976).

Teenage pregnancy.

Two classic examples of deviation in timing are teenage pregnancy and unwed motherhood. Each can have costly effects for a woman's later life by foreshortening her education and work experience. Harriet Presser (1975) in a study of a representative sample of 400 mothers who had recently given birth in New York City found that, the younger a woman at the birth of her first child, the less likely she was to have achieved certain role accomplishments. Of the teenage mothers (age fifteen to nineteen) only 39 percent were married, 33 percent had graduated from high school, and 39 percent had worked—"suggesting that a first birth at a relatively young age has a restricting effect on women's role achievements."

Between 1920 and 1940 the illegitimacy rate stood nearly steady at around 4 per 1,000 births. But in 1940 the rate rose to 7.9, and by 1970 it had nearly tripled, having reached 22.9 per 1,000 live births (Cutright, 1972: 391, 413). In 1966 illegitimate births comprised 18.6 percent of all first births to white teenagers and 57.6 percent of all first births to black teenagers. By 1973 these proportions had risen in each group to 30.3 percent for white teenage girls and 76.5 percent for blacks aged fifteen to nineteen (Sklar and Berkov, 1974a: 88).

There appear to be medical and technological reasons, not just changes in sexual attitudes, that account for these shifts. Improved health and the use of antibiotics, for example, have probably lowered involuntary sterility that in the past was due to venereal disease. At the same time there is a strong secular trend in the direction of lower age at menarche (when girls begin to menstruate). Good nutrition has speeded growth and enabled girls to attain the ratio of height and weight (typically 106 pounds) that triggers onset of puberty at an earlier age. Thus more young girls are capable of pregnancy than was the case ever before (Cutright, 1972; Frisch and Revelle, 1970; Frisch and McArthur, 1974). It is in this young group that the likelihood of a first child's being illegitimate is particularly high. Finally, permissive attitudes have made sexual activity outside marriage more acceptable (Shorter, 1973: 49). Even if a pregnancy occurs there is a feeling that it should not force a marriage. The 1974 Virginia Slims Poll of 3,000 representative American women found, for example, that 73 percent disagreed with the statement that "a couple who are having a child out of wedlock should marry for the sake of the child even though they don't want to" (Roper Organization, 1974: 101).

But while the trend to unwed motherhood among teenagers continues to rise, the general trend of research has held that this usually unplanned event in the life of the young woman is deleterious to her future development, if not also to her child. While Furstenberg (1976) recently found no harmful effects on the social adjustment of children born of unwed teenage mothers—especially when families or the nonresident father helped the young mother—he did find that the woman's own education and employment chances were impaired. Particularly if a first pregnancy was followed closely by a second, the young woman who might have preferred employment to welfare was faced with child-care responsibilities as a single parent that created adverse circumstances for continued employment. Even among the couples who married after the pregnancy was initiated, more were subject to marital instability than marriages begun otherwise, perhaps as Furstenberg suggests, because the courtship process had been cut short by the unplanned event.

Recently there has been growing attention to the possibility of keeping young mothers in high school so that some of these decrements can be avoided. In addition, the legalization of abortion has apparently lowered the illegitimacy rate in states with liberal abortion laws (Sklar and Berkov, 1974b).

Marital disruption and the female-headed household.

Disruption of a family before children have grown can also be viewed as a deviation from the typical timing of the preferred life cycle. Divorce or widowhood can bring economic hardship and at the same time overburden a woman with simultaneous responsibilities for child care, housekeeping, and financial support of the family.

Marriages made at a very early age such as sixteen or seventeen are twice as likely to end in divorce as marriages made between persons in their late twenties. Nevertheless, though the age at marriage is now rising, divorce rates are still high. In 1972 there were twice as many divorces as in 1962 (Hornblower, 1973: 37). Analysis of present California divorce rates suggests that three out of seven first marriages now being made in that state will end in divorce within thirty-five years (Schoen, 1975). These rising rates of divorce have been given technical as well as social explanations.

Changes in the law provide a technical explanation of rising divorce rates. In a state such as California, which instituted a no-fault divorce law in 1970, the number of divorces has unquestionably increased. But observers of the change contend that the rate of "real" marital disruption or marital dissolution has held fairly constant. What has changed is merely the willingness to get outward legal sanction for what in fact was already a breakdown of the marriage (Schoen et al., 1975; Lerman, 1973: 8).

Changes in the larger society and in general social attitudes toward divorce constitute another important part of the explanation. Divorce as a solution for an unsuccessful marriage was favored by 52 percent of women in 1970 and 60 percent in 1974. Two-thirds opposed alimony for a divorced woman if she was herself able to earn a living (Roper Organization, 1974: 54, 58).

Changes in household and family functions seem to be the largest single underlying factor in divorce trends. As the number of persons living in a typical household has declined and the economic functions of the family have shrunk, interpersonal compatibility has taken on increasing importance, making an individual's dissatisfaction in the marriage all the more intolerable because it is less likely to be mitigated by other economic or social benefits.

Modern geographic and social mobility may further contribute to the fragility of marriage. Since colonial times in such settlements as Andover or Plymouth Colony, Massachusetts, the opportunity to move beyond the confines of the village diminished parental authority and the general hold of the kinship unit over the individual (Henretta, 1973). Today there is anecdotal evidence that mobility may be associated with a sense of rootlessness and rising marital instability and may be particularly hard on women whose ties to the community are broken by a move (Packard, 1972: 143). A husband may continue to have friends at his work, but the wife does not. Lack of shared experiences and friends may deprive the couple of needed external supports when internal disagreements erupt that threaten the marriage.

Five years after the disruption of a marriage, 65 percent of the divorced women and 21 percent of the widowed women have remarried (Heclo et al., 1973: 13, 8). In the interim, however, women typically form a household with their children and with themselves at the head.

Only about 40 percent of the separated, divorced, or single mothers formed their own households in 1940 and 1950, as compared with roughly 50 percent in 1970. Social scientists who have observed the change note that general social trends have made it less likely that people of *any. status* will live with relatives, whether they be the elderly, the young married, or single-parent families (Heclo et al., 1973: 6; Cutright, 1974). About twice as many women over sixty-five, for example, were likely to live alone in 1970 as in 1940

(Kobrin, 1976; Sweet, 1971). Among widows, the changes were even more striking. In 1950 about a fifth of all widows lived alone, as compared with one-half in 1970 (Chevan and Korson, 1975).

It is particularly the dramatic rise in numbers of single-parent families with young children that is alarming to some observers of the American family. The rise signifies to them a dangerous decline in the numbers of adults present in the home to care for children (Bronfenbrenner, 1975). Between 1950 and 1970 there was an increase of almost 1.75 million mothers between the ages of fifteen and forty-four who were heading families with at least one child (Cutright, 1974). The rate of increase was much more marked among nonwhites, where the rate rose from 17.6 percent of all families in 1950 to 30.1 percent in 1972, in large part because of social circumstances such as poverty, less education, and location in large cities. Among whites the proportion changed from 8.5 percent in 1950 to 9.4 percent in 1972 (Lerman, 1973: 9). But between 1960 and 1970 Bronfenbrenner (1975) notes that within each setting and income level the percentage of single parents is increasing about as fast for whites as for blacks.

Being a single head of household with children is disadvantageous for women in several respects. First of all, their income is likely to be low. In 1973 families headed by a male with a wife present and at least one child under six had an average income of $12,000. But the corresponding figure for a single-parent female-headed family was $3,600, less than a third of the income for the intact family and well below the poverty line (Bronfenbrenner, 1975: 11). In their longitudinal study of 5,000 families from 1967 to 1973 Duncan and Morgan (1976: 28) reported that the female-headed families in their sample, although only 16 percent of all families, accounted for 52 percent of all the families whose income was less than their needs. Moreover, a mother with young children is likely to be emotionally and physically overburdened without another adult present to share her responsibilities. If in addition she must be employed, the problems are worsened.

Other life-cycle alternatives.

Although two-thirds of women are able to achieve the "preferred" life cycle with its complement of marriage, childbearing, and a modicum of longevity, it is well to remember that still more than a fifth of any given cohort will follow a different pattern. An important variant is living alone as a primary individual. Kobrin (1976) reports that now one-third of all women aged sixty-five and over live alone as primary individuals as compared with only 16 percent of men of the same age.

In the last decade the single state and childlessness have also grown in favor. While a national survey by Campbell, Converse, and Rodgers (1976) that measured life satisfaction found married women to report greater satisfaction than single women, other studies have emphasized that the single or widowed state is relatively healthier and more satisfactory for women than it is for single, divorced, or widowed males (Gove, 1973).

Communal living arrangements are another alternative to conventional marriage and family living. Cogswell and Sussman (1972: 507) estimated that about 8 percent of the population were living in "experimental" marriages or families in 1970, 13 percent in single-parent families, and all the rest in some form of nuclear family or other traditional form (see Table 4).

In summing up changes in the life cycle of women over the last three decades, Van Dusen and Sheldon (1976) are inclined to note the *diminishing* importance of family in women's lives rather than the extent to which a large percentage follow one typical pattern. Education is now prolonged so that 80 percent of women complete four years of high school as compared with only 35 percent in 1940. Marriage now on the average occurs at least a year later than it did in 1950. The proportion of women aged twenty to twenty-four who are single has increased from 28 percent in 1960 to 39 percent in 1974. Childbearing is postponed so that 10 percent fewer women than in the 1960s now bear their first child in the two years immediately following marriage. More married women now also remain childless. Perhaps most important of all, labor-force participation of married women rose from 24 percent in 1950 to 44 percent in 1975. Van Dusen and Sheldon (1976: 115) concluded that "—one way of summarizing these various trends was in terms of the declining

T A B L E 4. Distribution of Family Types in the U.S. Population, 1970

FAMILY TYPE	DISTRIBUTION %
Nuclear Family (with children)	44
Nuclear Dyad (without children)	15
Single Parent	13
Reconstituted (remarried, nuclear) Presence of children unspecified	15
Other Traditional*	5
"Experimental" Marriages and Families	8

SOURCE: Cogswell and Sussman (1972: 507). Copyright © 1972 by the National Council on Family Relations. Reprinted by permission.

*E.g., middle-aged or elderly couple, three generation, nuclear dyad, bilateral or extended kin.

importance of the family life cycle in women's total life cycle—the diminishing social importance of the distinction between married women and those who are unmarried (never married, no longer married, not yet married). . . . The traditional family life cycle for women has been slowly disappearing for the past quarter century."

FAMILY CLOCKWORK AND THE TIMING OF MALE AND FEMALE CAREERS

Each major demographic trend affecting women points to the uncertainty of following any single prescribed route over the life course. Marriage may end in divorce; a woman may have to support herself and children; a man may have to work out complicated schedules and relationships with children by a former marriage. Rather than be confined to sex-stereotyped activities or try to meet rigid timetables of accomplishment, men and women may do best to adopt a flexible time perspective that permits them to negotiate twists and turns as they appear. By this perspective the family is not so much a distraction from work as the primary social system for synchronizing the achievement and affiliative needs of both sexes.

Using the life-cycle perspective, Elder (1975) shows that the problems of the dual-career family are frequently ones of timing—handling the decision on when and where to move and whose career should take precedence, or smoothing out the periods when both members are overloaded and neither can relieve the other (Elder and Rockwell, 1976). Early in her life a woman's time at home typically coincides with childbearing and care of young children. Later a woman's employment can help the family meet periods of slowdown or unemployment. Women's work can help raise family status by raising overall income; it frequently evens out income differences of families in the same occupational or social category. Most crucial, it tides families over periods of heavy financial obligation and helps pay for children's education during a period that Oppenheimer (1977) has termed the "life cycle" squeeze.

The interpenetration of family and work are perhaps best studied as a dynamic process going forward through time, carrying residues of each past decision. Many a husband's attitudes bear on wife's work. A married woman's work in turn affects the internal family division of labor. A husband may respond by helping more or less, depending on how the wife's work is perceived (Bahr, 1974: 185). Children are affected by the activities of each parent. A mother's employment appears to provide her daughter with a less restricted view of the female role and may involve the father more in child rearing. However, if the mother is guilt ridden for being employed and has less than adequate household arrangements, or is under emotional stress, her mothering may be less adequate than that of a nonemployed mother (Hoffman and Nye, 1974: 163-166; Hoffman, 1974). A couple's location in one city rather than another may offer opportunities for a wife's employment and wages that lower fertility by discouraging decisions to have more children (Havens, 1972).

Hareven (1975) has described the interplay of such diverse events as migration, employment, and births by analyzing family and employment records from Manchester, New Hampshire, which had some of the largest textile mills in the world in 1910. Families extended their influence into the factory workrooms, where they tried to obtain jobs for their relatives under a sympathetic foreman or with compatible co-workers. Family connections also extended into French Canada and had a direct effect on the timing of migration. Confluence of different members' fortunes determined the intervals at which marriage and conception and other important family events took place.

The life-cycle perspective focuses on the family decisions that synchronize events such as marriage, births, education, and employment. The way these decisions are timed has implications for all the family members, not just for the husband or the wife or the children. Timing regulates the interplay of one individual's needs with those of the others. It is too soon to describe all the principles of this "family clockwork." But some evidence is available to suggest that a new set of norms is emerging to govern the interaction of paid employment, parenthood, and household work. The new normative ideal appears to be one that encourages flexibility over the life span in the tasks that one takes up at each age and in the sex-typing of these tasks. In general it appears that greater crossover between age and sex roles may be more widely institutionalized as a result of two relatively new developments. On the one hand, there is wider recognition that work patterns of men and women are becoming more similar over the life span. On the other hand, there is increasing recognition that responsibilities for parenthood and household work fall unequally on the shoulders of men and women, and there are frequent suggestions as to how the tasks might be more evenly divided. These two themes signal an emerging norm of sex equality to be achieved by flexible role allocation over the lifetime of the individual.

Paid employment.

Between 1950 and 1975 the number of families with two workers or more increased from 36 to 49 percent. Most of the increase was due to increased participation by married women in the paid labor force. Slightly less than a quarter (23.8 percent) of all wives participated in the labor force in 1950 as compared with almost half (44.4 percent) in 1975. In 1974, of those women with children aged six to seventeen, one-half worked at some time during the year, and of those with children under six, one-third were employed. The median income of husband-wife families with a wife in the labor force was $14,885 as compared with $12,360 for the families where a husband only was employed and $8,225 where a wife only was employed (Hayghe, 1976). Gradual acceptance of married women's work and its positive contribution to the family now causes social scientists to examine more closely the internal dynamics of family decision making that either enable women to work or make such a decision difficult for them.

As household size has diminished, the family enterprise has become a more limited unit requiring less total input of time in its care and maintenance. Yet it is still a demanding unit because there is less help for household work or child care. In 1790 there was an average of 2.8 children under age sixteen in each household, and the average size of the private household was 5.7 persons. In 1950 there were likely to be only 1.0 persons under sixteen, and the average number of people living in the household had dropped to 3.4 (Grabill et al., 1958, 1973: 379; Laslett, 1973). Furthermore, among working-class families who were under economic pressure to support either young or adolescent children, as many as 20 to 35 percent once took in boarders (Modell and Hareven, 1973: 479). The practice of taking in lodgers and boarders declined markedly, however, from the nineteenth century to the present.

More married women entered the work force after 1900 as a result of the decline in the birth rate, the lengthening of women's lives, and the trend to smaller households that took place during the past century. The change is reflected in a steady rise in labor-force participation rates of women. Between 1940 and 1974 the proportion of married women in the labor force rose from 14 to 43 percent (Kreps and Clark, 1975: 8). Moreover, the shape of the curve representing their participation at various ages also changed. Whereas the pattern through 1940 showed women entering paid employment, then leaving it at the age of marriage and childbearing, the pattern after 1940 showed a dip in participation around the age of thirty, then a rise during the middle years (thirty-five to fifty-four) and then another fall after that as women approached the age of retirement. For men, by contrast, the years between 1953 and 1973 show falling labor-force participation rates, particularly in the later years. For married men between the ages of fifty-five and sixty-four, the participation rate has fallen ten points in the last twenty years. And since the late 1960s, there has been some decline in the participation rate of married men between the ages of forty-five and fifty-four (Taeuber and Sweet, 1976: 51-52; Kreps and Clark, 1975: 9, 14-15).

The gradual convergence of men's and women's labor-force participation rates and the greater concentration of work in the middle years (caused by longer education in the early years and retirement in the later years) prompts Kreps and Clark (1975: 57-58) to suggest that work should be more evenly distributed over the life span:

> The married woman's earnings have enabled families to finance additional years of schooling for their children. Similarly, the family with two salaries over an extended portion of worklife can afford earlier retirement than the one that must rely on a single worker's income, assuming the same wage scale. Thus, the capacity to purchase an increase in free time for the male is enhanced by woman's market work. Intrafamily support of the young adults still in school and of older men in retirement offers the male greater flexibility in scheduling his work; market activity during the woman's middle years substitutes for the male's labor-force activity at each end of worklife.

But Kreps and Clark (1975: 56, 3) argue that alternative allocations of working and nonworking time could have been made over the last several decades if, instead of accumulating leisure to be used at the beginning and end of adulthood, it had been used in more piecemeal fashion through the middle years as well. "It would have been possible," they say, "to reduce workweeks, add vacation time, or even provide worker sabbaticals for education and job retraining, as productivity improved and the size of the labor force grew." Furthermore, if nonworking time were more evenly apportioned over the work life, "it would greatly enhance the male's availability for home work at critical times in the family's life cycle." Instead, as it is now, much of males' use of time freed of market work cannot easily be applied to daily performance of household chores. Leisure comes in a form that causes it to be applied to other forms of activity or to work-related pressures such as commuting time.

Parenthood.

Corresponding to the growing similarity between the labor-force participation rates of men and women, there are important parallel themes in parenting trends. As families grow smaller and women's input of time to parenting diminishes, one possibility is that both parents' time with children declines. There are then smaller families as a result of the relatively higher value of both women's and men's time in the paid labor force. Economists reason that, as the price of our time increases, we substitute services we can buy, such as sending children to a day-care center or sitting them in front of a television set (Sawhill, 1977: 118). Alice Rossi (1977: 14-16, 22) finds alarming the type of similarity between men and women that de-emphasizes the child-bearing function and child rearing. Among the avant garde advocates of new marriage forms and among the more extreme feminists concerned with women's work achievement, she notes that it is adults' satisfaction rather than the needs of children that is central.

An alternative theme, however, is also finding greater promi-nence. It emphasizes the role of the father in child rearing and the greater need for more nearly equal sharing of parenthood responsibil-ities by mother and father. Beginning in the 1960s the Scandinavian countries, particularly Sweden, engaged in a great debate over sex roles that resulted in official policies supporting the right of fathers to take leave from work or work part-time during a child's early years. In the United States the Moynihan report focused attention on the positive role of the father in child development and argued for income support systems that would keep the father in the home rather than make him desert so his wife could qualify for welfare.

Now there is a positive interest in showing that fathers can be nurturant parents and adequate to the task if they need be single parents. David Lynn (1974) has marshaled an impressive array of research findings on the positive role of the father in child develop-ment and the potentially harmful effects of father absence. James Levine (1976) provides evidence from interviews with contemporary fathers that show child rearing should not be thought of so exclu-sively in terms of the mother-child relationship. Rather, men are capable of as much role flexibility in moving into the nurturant parent role as women are of engaging in the paid labor force. Rochelle Wortis (1971: 739), after reviewing the social-science litera-ture on mothering, concludes, "The acceptance of the concept of mothering by social scientists reflects their own satisfaction with the status quo. The inability of social scientists to explore and advocate alternatives to current child-rearing practices is due to their biased concepts of what should be studied and to their unwillingness to advocate social change."

Nonmarket work: housework, volunteer work.

It would seem reasonable, if more women are working, that men would be helping women more with the household work. In fact, however, as recently as 1972, men did an average of only about 1.6 hours a day of work in the home, whether their wives worked or not (Hedges and Barnett, 1972). In addition women also use their base in the home to perform many needed volunteer activities in the community. When it comes to taking care of elderly parents or other older members of the community, what evidence there is suggests that these tasks fall overwhelmingly on middle-aged women, usually daughters (Blenkner, 1963: 50–51).

Some historical and sociological studies have furthermore indicated that household work has not shrunk so fast as we might have thought. Survey data show that since the 1920s there has been no shortening of the housewife's work week, despite improvements in technology and compression of family functions. A study conducted by the Survey Research Center in Michigan in 1965–1966 showed that nonemployed women spend fifty-five hours a week in household work, as compared with an average of fifty-two hours a week reported by housewives in 1925–1926, before the widespread introduction of the refrigerator or automatic washing machine (Vanek, 1974). And standards were raised: not only were the clothes washed more often and the house kept cleaner, but more time also was spent on child care, because increasing importance was accorded to the maternal function (Cochran and Strasser, 1974; Cowan, 1973; Wortis, 1971). These changes were all particularly salient for the *nonemployed* housewife.

By contrast *employed* wives spent only about half as much time on housework—twenty-six hours. The difference could not be accounted for by their having more help either from husbands or from workers in their households (Vanek, 1974). The employed women probably had to "cut corners," accept messier houses, and perhaps eat out more.

Despite the overwhelming concentration of women in the household functions of housework, cooking, and care of clothing, and the tendency for men to take care of yard work and maintenance tasks, there is nevertheless some impressionistic and anecdotal evidence that men's involvement in female-type tasks is becoming more acceptable. Along with men taking care of children, stories on the family page of the newspaper sometimes feature men doing needlework or cooking. Retired men sometimes become involved in household tasks such as cooking and cleaning. Or they throw their energies into community volunteer activities that were once the preserve of women.

It may be in fact the possibility of experimentation with the allocation of work over the life span that will provide most leverage against the "buffers" that now prevent men from taking on household responsibilities. Joseph Pleck hypothesizes that housework within the family is like the secondary sector of the dual labor market. Men don't engage in it because their energies are preserved for their primary work outside the home. According to Pleck (1977:

420) the most significant feature of the relation between husband and wife family role performance is the apparent bottleneck in which husbands' family time does not respond to variations in wives' family time resulting from wives' paid employment. In addition the female work role is more vulnerable to family demands. For husbands the work-family boundary is permeable as well, but only in the other direction: to allow demands from work to impinge on family time. As I would also argue using the concept of crossover, Pleck believes that, to balance the new roles of husband and wife, each role must become symmetrically permeable to work and family demands. Within the family what will make this permeability or crossover occur?

Some norms have already developed to define how couples can carry dual careers in which both are involved in family and work. For example, there is an increasing belief that a wife should get as much education as possible so that her position in the job market will be advantageous. The more work experience she has before marriage and childbearing, it is believed, the more likely her ability to reenter that world later on. She may be wise to delay marriage or child-bearing until her mid- to late twenties. While she has heavy responsibilities at home, she can "keep a hand in" by taking continuing education courses, holding a part-time job, maintaining outside interests, or building up a list of credentials through volunteer work that will lead to a paid job (Loeser, 1974: 117–131).

Implied in the wife's maintenance of flexibility is that the husband will also remain open to his own inner development and perhaps after mid-career choose other directions of activity or choose more involvement in the family in order to develop his emotional side as much as his occupational side. Current interest in the male "mid-life crisis" in large part seems to reflect this emerging set of expressive concerns on the part of middle-aged males (Brim, 1976).

The new flexible life course for husband and wife is not yet fully institutionalized. Not all the public and private supports necessary in industry or education have yet been set in place. Before considering policy changes that are needed, it is useful to examine some of the major family forms that now exist. What support does each type give to flexibility and symmetry in the roles of men and women?

TRADITIONAL AND EMERGING FAMILY FORMS

Given the changing demographic realities for women's lives—they are through raising children sooner, live longer, and are more likely to combine paid work with family life—what will be the shape of family life that will allow them a more equitable share in leisure as well as in work and family? How are family forms even now changing to show us the outlines of a more egalitarian arrangement to come? The answers are important, for they suggest not only how younger generations should be prepared to select from the available alternatives, but also how practical legislation or voluntary efforts may be undertaken that will support the forms that seem most desirable to us now.

If recent books and articles on family life can be taken as any trustworthy guide, there is remarkable convergence on a new, more egalitarian family form, which Young and Willmott (1973) term "the Symmetrical Family." Changes in the industrial and ecological order as well as limited fertility and feminism have brought about this change. The phenomenon is observable not only in the managerial and professional class but also among shift workers in the manufacturing and service trades. Yet at the same time as marriages are becoming less hierarchical, husbands being asked to share more housework, and wives working more outside the home, another development is taking place alongside. Alternative family forms are springing up here and there: communes; female-headed families that result from separation, divorce, or unwed pregnancy; or households made up of unrelated individuals living together. These new forms challenge the assumption on which the traditional nuclear family is based. Alternative styles show, for example, how child-care or cooking arrangements can be modified. But they also illustrate that any social system lives with constraints of one kind or another.

EVOLUTION OF FAMILY FORMS

Changing patterns of participation in family life precipitate strains in the established patterns. As we have seen in the case of higher divorce rates, remarriage, and the increase in dual-worker families, new "scripts" for action are being tried out as each family experiments with its internal division of labor and timing of decisions.

There is now a repertoire of several types of family script that may be selected to fit various economic or cultural conditions. There is considerable consensus among historians and sociologists on what these types are, though there may be differences over terminology and more refined categories. Each broad type is associated with a particular rhythm of life and a characteristic ecological niche.

Young and Willmott (1973) used the terms *Stage 1, 2,* and *3* families to describe the types that they observed in a broad cross-sectional study of 2,600 London families in 1970. *Stage 1* roughly corresponds to what others have called the *peasant* or *preindustrial family*. The whole family participates in a family-related economic endeavor; family and occupational life are still undifferentiated, and the husband has primary authority. *Stage 2* families are similar in form to the Victorian ideal of the early industrial period. In them occupation and family life are no longer joined; husbands are ideally the sole breadwinners, and wives remain at home in charge of children and other domestic responsibilities. Yet the family is not patriarchal in the way it was in the preindustrial form. Instead the two sexes have different and complementary spheres of authority. *Stage 3* families have become common only recently. They differ from the Victorian ideal in that both husband and wife typically work outside the home, and ideally both share in family duties. Greater equality emerges between them because their duties are not just complementary but are nearly symmetrical.

Hayghe (1976: 16) estimates that families with both a husband and wife in the labor force now make up 41 percent of all U.S. husband-wife families, a larger single block than any other form; families with husbands only in the labor force account for 34 percent and families with wives only in the labor force account for 3 percent. Although it has been edged out of first place by the dual-worker form, the Victorian or early industrial type of family still constitutes a major alternative in America today, perhaps especially during that period in the family life cycle when children are young. Variant forms may occur among young adults who have not yet launched their childbearing, or among persons who have experienced marital disruption and are between families. The dual-worker family may be most common among people in the middle years when wives have reentered the labor force.

Although there now appears to be a greater range of family forms available from which people can choose depending on their point in life, the development of these alternatives seems to have been linked to the historical process of modernization. However, some sociologists and historians of family change have questioned whether any such connection exists. Rosabeth Kanter (1977) notes that the company town, the family store, and the two-person career of the clergyman or doctor have all traditionally blurred the boundary between family and work. Elizabeth Pleck (1976) points out that poor agricultural workers frequently had to hire themselves out as laborers and the work of men and women was separate even in preindustrial times. Tamara Hareven (1975) shows the connections between family time and the actual flow of work in the factory. Nevertheless, in my opinion, the overall process of differentiation between family life and productive work that Smelser (1959) described in the cotton-manufacturing towns of early industrial England still largely describes the main trends in change of family life over the last century. The preindustrial family was both a family unit and a unit of production. The early industrial family separated child rearing and consumption tasks from the productive and instrumental tasks performed in the paid labor force. The modern symmetrical family is open to greater permeability between work and family as a result of further differentiation of tasks, which makes much of the work of males and females potentially interchangeable. We review each of these major types to consider their consequences for the relative position of men and women in the family.

TRADITIONAL FAMILY FORMS:
PREINDUSTRIAL AND EARLY INDUSTRIAL

Distinctive characteristics of the symmetrical family stand out most clearly when they are contrasted with family types in the preindustrial and Victorian eras. Most Americans never really experienced the preindustrial family of the kind that flourished in peasant society. But there were two major exceptions to this rule. People who lived in stable villages such as Plymouth Colony or Andover, Massachusetts, in the 1600s brought with them the traditional European expectation that there was limited land, and that as a result their sons would have to inherit from their fathers or find other work roles in the town. But by the end of the seventeenth century, the young people had discovered vast reaches of land outside these towns and had begun to break out from under the economic and social restraints of their parents and families (Demos, 1974; Henretta, 1973).

The other major exception was the immigrant generations that left Europe beginning with Germans in the late 1700s, the Irish in the 1840s, and Scandinavians, Italians, and East Europeans in the late 1800s and early 1900s. O. E. Rölvaag's *Giants in the Earth* (1927) shows the continuing patriarchy of the Scandinavian immigrant farmers eking out their existence in the harsh north central plains. It was the father who went to town for supplies and had all important contact with the outside world; the mother stayed home, worked hard, was close to the children, but seemed to have little say in running things. Yet in the cities this patriarchy began to crumble. Oscar Handlin (1951) in a tableau of the uprooted's immigrant experience depicts the loss of status that came to husbands used to male domination in the old country. In the city these men had to rely on the help of working wives and children to meet their basic needs. They thereby suffered a certain loss of pride. They were also confused about how to behave under the changed circumstances. A contemporary picture of surviving peasant-family patterns emerges in a study of Boston's West End Italians who were displaced by new apartment buildings in the 1960s. Gans (1962: 47-53) shows how segregated were the activities of husbands and wives. Rather than relying on each other for close and intimate relationship, each was more likely to find support and companionship among workers, cousins, or friends of the same sex. Men avoided interaction with women, fearing domination by the women's greater verbal facility, and retreated into companionship with other men. Only among the younger generation did this pattern seem to be on the wane. There, particularly as couples moved out to the suburbs, each was more likely to turn to the other rather than to outsiders for support.

These descriptions of immigrants show certain tensions between traditional family life of peasant origins and the style of interaction now common to modern urban America. The peasant is used to a family life intertwined with economic activities such as prevailed in a small landholding. The father was in charge of the principal productive enterprise, whereas the mother was in charge of the garden, the chickens, and/or the pig. Together with their children the couple sustained the family by their own efforts without much need for money or travel to and from work or market. In that system the father had final authority, perhaps because production had to take priority over consumption so that the family would not endanger its supply of seed or consume its capital. Although they contributed to production, women were nonetheless more identified with the emotional and nurturant dimension of life, as perhaps best symbolized in the image of the Virgin Mary, who was venerated in Catholic countries from the late feudal period onward.

By comparison with this preindustrial peasant family, the family of the modern period became more separated from economic production, more specialized in emotional functions, and more egalitarian in its relations between the sexes. As productive work moved outside the family and men became the "breadwinners," women's position within the household was consolidated. They became specialists in the emotional domain and gained more authority inside the household by virtue of the division of labor between husbands' duties and their own. John Stuart Mill (1869, 1970: 178-179), who is generally regarded as one of the great supporters of feminism, advocated this form of family life as indeed a step forward into modern society:

> When the support of the family depends not on property, but on earnings,
> the common arrangement, by which the man earns the income and the wife

superintends the domestic expenditure, seems to me in general the most suitable division of labour between the two persons. If, in addition to the physical suffering of bearing children, and the whole responsibility of their care and education in early years, the wife undertakes the careful and economical application of the husband's earnings to the general comfort of the family; she takes not only her fair share, but usually the larger share, of the bodily and mental exertion required by their joint existence. If she undertakes any additional portion, it seldom relieves her from this, but only prevents her from performing it properly. The care which she is herself disabled from taking of the children and the household, nobody else takes; those of the children who do not die grow up as they best can, and the management of the household is likely to be so bad as even in point of economy to be a great drawback from the value of the wife's earnings. In an otherwise just state of things, it is not, therefore, I think, a desirable custom that the wife should contribute by her labour to the income of the family.

As Young and Willmott (1973: 275) have commented, in the sort of marriage that Mill was praising "there was symmetry between the sexes in respect, love, and legal rights but not in the tasks performed within the family, let alone in the work done beyond it." If we imagine in our mind's eye what is the division of labor and the relationship between husbands and wives in the 34 percent of contemporary American families who rely on a single breadwinner, we realize that the form of life we picture has not departed very far from Mill's ideal. The breadwinner is the husband; the home caretaker is the wife. Each has authority in his or her own sphere. Men are conceded to be experts in external affairs; women are the major consumers. A survey of household decision making between 1955 and 1971 in Detroit showed little deviation from this pattern over a recent fifteen-year period:

> Three functions—straightening the living room, doing the dishes, and getting breakfast—remain predominantly the wife's. Four functions are done either by both spouses or by the wife primarily: grocery shopping, deciding on the food budget, taking care of the money and bills, and deciding whether the wife should work. Five items fall heavily to the husband, or are shared by both spouses but rarely are assigned to the wife primarily. These include decisions about the house, the car, life insurance, and the husband's job, and the task of doing household repairs. This classification is as clear in the 1971 statistics as it is in the 1955 data. [Duncan et al., 1973: 18]

Despite the persistence of the early modern family over the past century, there do now seem to be real changes taking place. Particularly in professional segments of the population where each member of a couple has a career, and in working-class groups where wives are lately working not just of necessity but for a higher standard of living, the traditional marriage norms are subject to strain, and we may expect that they will undergo gradual transformation toward greater similarity between the roles of husband and wife.

THE SYMMETRICAL FAMILY FORM

One sign of ferment in the family division of labor comes from American opinion surveys conducted between 1964 and 1974. Over that decade women's attitudes toward the traditional division of labor between husbands and wives showed a consistent trend. In every major segment of the population, the proportion of women supporting the traditional pattern declined. At the same time the proportion supporting women's rights in the labor market and their options for a life without marriage or motherhood increased (Mason et al., 1976: 585).

Newspapers report instances of commuting professional couples, one of whom may work in Cleveland, the other in New York City, yet who manage to share a marriage and perhaps even children. Less attention has been given the life patterns of husband and wife in the blue-collar classes. Historical studies, however, suggest that the sharing of work and family responsibilities between husbands and wives employed in the mills may have had some of the characteristics of the modern symmetrical family. Children were expected to help with household tasks and care for younger siblings. Schedules were stretched and complicated. People found various adaptive routines for making do (Hareven, 1975).

Symmetrical families are a phenomenon of modern society not just in the United States but in Europe as well. Househusbands are not common in Sweden, but they do exist there and their roles are accepted. Dual-career families in Great Britain are the subject of a major study by Rhona and Robert Rapoport (1976). Other countries of Eastern and Western Europe where high numbers of women are in the labor force have for the time being put women under a heavy overload if they have both families and careers. The way out of this stressful situation has not yet resulted in full institutionalization of the symmetrical family. But a rising divorce rate and growing insistence by women on revising the roles within marriage point in that direction (Fogarty et al., 1971: 96; Sokolowska, 1977; Silver, 1977).

Why is the symmetrical family the likely wave of the future? The answer comes from an analysis of modern society and the kind of capacity for role flexibility that a highly differentiated structure requires. Moreover, when society is changing rapidly and circumstances are uncertain, a high degree of flexibility is more adaptive than rigid adherence to one pattern of activity or another. This is true not only of individuals but of the family itself as well. The family performs its function best when it handles nonuniform tasks that are not easily farmed out to bureaucratic institutions, which can perform them more expertly or more efficiently. But as Litwak (1970: 354-359) has pointed out, what are defined as nonuniform functions change as fast as technology and the social environment change. For the family to perform at its best, it must therefore be able to take on functions that are at the moment defined as nonuniform and to drop them when they become routine.

For example, early in the century laundry was a routine menial task, and there were outside laundry establishments prepared to provide the service; even working-class women sent out their wash. When, however, the home washing machine appeared and new fabrics and automatic washers were introduced, laundry returned to the home. The household could then meet the special requirements of each individual's laundry needs and care for each fabric type better than could the commercial establishment. Litwak (1970: 358-359) concludes analysis of the laundry example with a general rule that gives a clue to the type of family that may be best adapted to our rapidly changing society:

> [The] one key structural need of the family—given a rapidly changing technology—is the capacity to deal with changing functions, the capacity to rapidly change what are legitimate and what are nonlegitimate activities, or most generally the capacity to be flexible.

One of the main sociological consequences of flexibility in the family is role substitutability between husband and wife rather than fixed sex-typed roles. The wife cannot just be an expressive leader in the family and let the husband be the instrumental leader in the world of work outside. She may be the instrumental leader in bringing up the children or managing household affairs. She needs the husband's expressive help to handle the tensions that may result, just as he needs her expressive help with anxieties about work. Furthermore, by Litwak's reasoning, the family has major commitments in all areas of life, not just to the care of young children. It is the most effective agent for handling other types of nonuniform problems, such as peculiar circumstances of health or emotional depression, sudden loss of income by some member, some failure in school or work, or some threat to the local neighborhood. To meet such unexpected needs, the "family clockwork" must be able to respond appropriately.

As each family experiments to produce a workable formula of interaction, certain common themes emerge. One is that couples are still more likely to put primary emphasis on the husband's job as a basis for choosing a residential location or timing major family events. The wife's role more often contains the compromises that keep the family flexible. Yet even this pattern may characterize only one point in time, when the children and couple are relatively young. Later on the wife's career may in fact take precedence. Families move in and out of different forms, and it is difficult to keep remembering that their very flexibility makes it difficult to capture a snapshot of them that is true for more than a moment. It is therefore important to examine some of the forms that families may take over a period of time.

In a twelve-country survey of the uses of time, Szalai (1973: 21–22) found that there was an unmistakable trend toward a more modern family structure. The modern family differs from the traditional or early modern type in the following ways: (1) it tends to allocate tasks in a neutral rather than sex-linked way, (2) it is democratic rather than autocratic in reaching decisions, (3) it balances power and distributes it rather than relying on hierarchy, and (4) it depends on a cooperative coordination of roles rather than a specialized and solitary role performance by each sex.

Szalai's survey extended into Belgium, Bulgaria, Czechoslovakia, France, East and West Germany, Hungary, Peru, Poland, the United States, the U.S.S.R., and Yugoslavia, and it collected data from 30,000 respondents. Nowhere had the modern family structure actually been achieved. Husbands helped with household care and important peripheral activities such as maintenance and repair to a degree that almost equaled wives' hours spent in cooking and primary housework. But the two sexes still rarely crossed over to help in each other's domain. Perhaps most telling was the consistent finding that employed men after their contributions to the household still had 50 percent more leisure than the employed women (Szalai, 1973: 28–30).

Where fairness and equity had proceeded farthest, however, was in those societies that were at a high level of socioeconomic development and in those families that had a more comfortable standard of living. Among marriage partners that were better educated and in those couples where the wife was more involved outside the home as a breadwinner or otherwise, the symmetrical ideal was also closer to being realized (Szalai, 1973: 31).

Dual-career families.
Numerous studies of professional couples where the wife also has a career have shown consistently that even in this type of marriage the husband's career is accorded somewhat greater priority than that of the wife. Yet Holmstrom (1972: 40), who interviewed twenty two-career couples, notes:

The wives accommodated to their husbands' careers more than vice-versa, when deciding where to live. But the more surprising finding is how much the husbands' decisions were affected by the career interests of their wives. In quite a departure from middle-class norms, many husbands went out of their way to live in places where their wives could also obtain desirable employment.

In addition, the internal division of labor evolves so that some husbands and children are drawn into household tasks. As a wife goes to work, the husband takes on more chores around the house, and the wife's power in the household domain diminishes somewhat (Bahr, 1974: 185). One of the couples described by the Rapoports was very effective in getting each of their two boys to pitch in as was needed. According to the wife,

> the main rule we've tried to work to ever since we were married is that if there is a job to be done, we do it together so that there isn't one person working and feeling 'there's me slaving over a hot stove and there's him sitting with his feet up.' Unless the person who is specifically doing the job says 'Right, you go and sit down,' we do it together and nobody sits down and does nothing until everybody sits down and does nothing. The children join in this plan and they are expected to work when we are working and we don't expect them to work and us sit down but we all do it together. [Rapoport and Rapoport, 1976: 65]

In some families a wife's work may become more important later in the life of the couple than it was at the beginning. Established male professors, for example, have been known to relocate in another sometimes less famous university center because it offered more opportunity for the wife's career. Data on women's labor-force participation by age certainly suggest that the life pattern whereby older married women are employed is rapidly becoming the norm.

However, it would be a mistake to suppose that the ideal patterns of role symmetry and sharing that are occasionally realized in a few dual-career families are yet in fact a reality for the great majority of two-worker families. With respect to sharing of household work, data reported in 1969 and 1970 by Kathryn Walker are sobering: women at that time still performed considerably more home work than men—4.8 hours a day for the married women employed 30 hours a week or more as compared with 1.6 hours for the employed men who were married to working wives. Child-care routines still assume that the mother is the parent primarily responsible for coming to school conferences, delivering the child to weekday extracurricular activities, and being at home when the child is sick. Joseph Pleck (1977) perceives the differential permeability of men's and women's careers to the demands of family as patterned in such a way as to reinforce the priority of husband's commitment to work and wife's commitment to family.

In their recent reexamination of dual-career families whom they studied in the late 1960s, the Rapoports (1976: 301) list overload dilemmas as the number one stressor. How the overload dilemma is solved depends on the priorities of the couple involved. Other research on such families shows three major patterns: in some families the household work is shared by husband and wife; in others it is divided along conventional lines with the wife responsible for both housework and child care; in still others the husband becomes involved equally in care of children but not household chores. What is different in the 1970s as compared with the 1960s, according to the Rapoports, is that now the issues of how to solve the overload dilemma are actively discussed. Ideas about job sharing, joint job holding, part-time work for both partners, alternating job involvement, and split residence during the work week have been developed through the press or personal knowledge. In addition the myth of the necessity of full-time motherhood is on the wane; the male role has broadened somewhat, and there is a wider variety of acceptable family forms available. Although these people still have the problem of finding time for all they want to do, keeping up their social networks, or deciding to move or not for the sake of one person's career, they are reported to be happy—happier than they would be if one member of the couple were not employed.

Whether sexual activity is also happy is not altogether clear. As compared with the rather sexually oriented studies of communes and other variant family forms, the research on dual-career families tends to be work-oriented (Giele, 1976). The Rapoports (1976: 342) do, however, report Grønseth's finding from a Norwegian study of dual-career families that one-quarter of them reported improved sexual relationships as a result of their work arrangements. In Lillian Rubin's (1976: 131–150) intensive study of working-class wives compared with middle-class wives, I find a complex pattern that shows persistent differences in male and female sexual expression lingering alongside an emerging norm that there should be equality and similarity of response. On the one hand, in both classes there seems to be a difference in the nature of male and female sexuality. The women want to talk, take time, explore the psychological relationship. The men do not talk so much, are more direct and physical in their orientation. But on the other hand, there seems to be an emerging norm that the nature of sexual gratification should be more similar between men and women. The women feel they should be getting physical sexual gratification equal to their husbands'—through achieving orgasm, enjoyment of greater frequency and experimentation in intercourse, and so on. They also want their husbands to talk to them more, to be more subtle and diffuse and sensitive to their emotions. In both classes there seems to be an emerging norm of equality in sexual matters, though only imperfectly realized.

Working-class families.

New efforts to understand working-class families in the United States closely parallel the findings of Young and Willmott in London. Working-class people in some ways give more devotion to family than middle-class people, presumably because their work lives are less stimulating and all-consuming. The 1974 Virginia Slims Poll, partly summarized in Table 5, found for example that, when women were asked what they wanted most for a son, a happy marriage or an interesting career, far more of the less-educated women gave priority to family than to work.

Of course, it is also true that the older respondents gave more priority to family than to work, and, to the extent that age and lower education are associated, differential responses by education may not be related just to social class but to age as well. Yet such results seem to make sense out of what some have found to be the puzzling rejection by working-class women of women's liberation. College women and their husbands have the education that would open interesting careers to them. Educated women thus feel frustrated when doing housework, because they compare it with the work that they might do for pay. But working-class women, whose alternatives are repetitive factory work or menial service occupations, find their liberation through independence in home life, cooking, and household work. To them being a good wife and mother is one of the few routes to significant satisfaction, and the middle-class women's liberation rhetoric seems to them to be devaluing a world they consider to be of primary importance (Seifer, 1975; Levison, 1974; Meade, 1975; Coles, 1973: 106).

Nevertheless, there may soon perhaps be a convergence between the working class and the middle class in their attitudes toward family life and the roles of husbands and wives. In reviewing what is

T A B L E 5. Results of Poll on Women's First Goal for Their Sons—A Happy Marriage or an Interesting Career

ANSWER	WOMEN WITH 8TH-GRADE EDUCATION, %	WOMEN WITH HIGH-SCHOOL EDUCATION, %	WOMEN WITH COLLEGE EDUCATION, %
A happy marriage first	64	56	53
An interesting career first	18	26	34

SOURCE: Roper Organization (1974: 82). Reprinted with the permission of The Roper Organization, Inc.

known about blue-collar women, Victoria Samuels (1975) finds signs that there has been some change since Rainwater and Komarovsky surveyed working men's wives in 1959. At that time working-class women lived a routine life segregated from much companionship with men. One day was pretty much the same as another. Husbands resisted wives' working, and wives seemed to lack self-confidence (Rainwater et al., 1959; Komarovsky, 1964). In the 1970s more working-class women view themselves as being competent in the role of housewife than the number reporting such competency in 1959. They show more interest in work and freedom to work. And they seem to feel that they can be more assertive in the home (Samuels, 1975). Even in the drabness and frustration that Rubin finds in the lives of working-class women, there is an underlying theme that more egalitarian relationships within the family are desired. The implicit ideal is more talking, more understanding, and more sharing of emotional life between wives and husbands. Ann Oakley (1975) contends that housework is also boring to working-class women. And among the working class Lein et al. (1974) finds that a significant number of husbands share in housework and child care when their wives are working (see also Working Family Project, 1978).

In her studies of working-class women, Nancy Seifer (1975) got to know a few women in various parts of the United States—for example, the wife of a coal miner in Alabama and a secretary in a steel mill in Gary, Indiana. Each of these women became an activist for women's rights through some catalyzing experience that touched her own job or her family's interests. They all had been turned off by middle-class feminist rhetoric that devalued the wife and mother role, but when they perceived their common interests with other women over issues such as equal pay, opportunities for promotion, or the family health-insurance plans of their unions, they became involved.

Just why such changes have occurred is still hidden. Many have speculated that a wife's working actually changes the power relationship in any couple. The husband has less opportunity to dominate when the wife also brings in a paycheck (Bahr, 1974: 184-185). In the past a wife's employment might have threatened a husband's self-esteem. But rising participation of women in the work force is now apparently changing that norm. Short-term unemployment or a cutback in working hours or overtime is such a common threat to the working class that a wife's work is unquestionably an asset for tiding the family over lean times. Seifer (1975: 14) has recently estimated that the *majority* of women in working-class families are now employed for at least some part of the year. Dougherty et al. (1977) found in a study of fourteen Boston area dual-worker blue-collar families that *every family had experienced at least one layoff* of either husband or wife in the recession period since 1972-1973. Husbands tremendously valued a wife's contribution when her wages helped keep the family income up to the standard they desired.

OTHER EMERGING FAMILY FORMS

High rates of marital breakdown have put large numbers of women "at risk" of forming single-parent households. Divorce has also given rise to remarriage and reconstituted nuclear families. In addition, communal experiments and individuals in transition between single or married states have created intimate networks and other variant forms. Of these we shall give most attention to the single-parent households, reconstituted marriages, and experiments with communal and modified extended families because they have the most far-reaching implications for women's status. Each of these variant forms can provide information on the structural conditions that are conducive to equality in household and work roles, legal provisions, child-care arrangements, and leisure.

Single-parent households.

From the point of view of women, the significant feature of single-parent families, particularly where a woman is head of the household, is that resources may be less than in the nuclear or extended form, and as a result the woman head may be unusually burdened with responsibility. Much effort has been devoted to lowering the number of such women on the welfare rolls by means tests or by getting them into the labor force. But not even the majority of single heads of family are on welfare. Those not on welfare also have needs that should be met for the sake of the family and the children.

The proportion of white families headed by women has not changed in forty years, although it has doubled for blacks. What has changed markedly is the proportion of these families in younger age groups *with children*. It is the presence of children that makes the difference between poverty and an adequate standard of living for the families with a single head. In 1972 the Michigan Panel Study of Income Dynamics studied 5,000 families over a period of several years and found that 65 percent of all families with mother heads had *no* income from welfare and no more than a fifth of all mother heads received as much as half of their income from welfare. Only 47 percent received any alimony or child support from fathers, and the median amount of such support was only $1,350 (Heclo et al., 1973: 12-13). But a relatively high percentage of even college-educated female heads of family are poor, 18 percent as compared with 3 percent of college-educated male heads. Lack of male support coupled with women's frequent lack of marketable skills and much lower earning power, even if they are fully employed, makes it more likely that a female-headed family will be poorer than either the male-supported nuclear family or the reconstituted family.

How do these women and their families survive then? More than half (56 percent) derive at least $500 or more from their own earnings and receive no welfare income. Furthermore, many of these female-headed families (10.2 percent of all families with children) reconstitute themselves into nuclear families with a husband and wife within five years. The single-parent state thus seems definitely transitional.

But the possibility that single headship is a transitional state should not make us forget that, in the difficult years, parents without partners need emotional support, help with household chores, flexible working hours so that they can meet their dual-family and work responsibilities, and publicly available provision for child care so that they can meet emergencies, get away on occasion, and see that their children get proper attention while the parent attends to other responsibilities. Cogswell and Sussman (1972) note the prevailing assumption that a mother will be available to come to school during the day for a parent-child conference, take time off to get children to the doctor or dentist, chauffeur children to recreational areas, or be available to fix lunch and supper. For some working women, heading a household and meeting these expectations can prove a loss to working hours and needed income. Rather than impose on such persons the system designed for the nonemployed wife in the husband-wife family, Cogswell and Sussman suggest that mobile health-care units come to school yards, recreational facilities be in walking distance for young children, round-the-clock child care be available for emergencies, and eating facilities be present in the neighborhood where children can take morning and evening meals either accompanied or unaccompanied by parents. While there might not be sufficient demand for such services in suburban middle-class areas to be feasible, one can easily imagine what a boon such facilities would offer to poor working-class or middle-class single-parent families in regional subgroupings of large urban areas. We shall see in the next chapter how current suggestions for policy reform address these issues.

Reconstituted families.

While the income outlook for reconstituted families is definitely better than for single-parent families, other problems remain in legal impediments and psychological drain. Established legal routines have generally given custody to the mother, thereby causing fathers a sense of loss of their children. If custody is not awarded to the mother, there is a common tendency to assume that something must be wrong with her. Visitation rights for either parent may provoke inconvenience and further conflict.

Division of property between the former spouses is likely to be a further bone of contention, particularly where a couple entered the marriage arrangement unprepared for any possible termination and so merged their assets that an equitable reckoning at the end is made difficult.

Finally, continuing provision for support of children or a dependent wife of a former marriage may constitute an almost intolerable burden for the husband who has also to contribute support to a second marriage. Undoubtedly in a few cases fathers do not support their legitimate offspring by a former marriage because of such a dual burden. However, this reason should not be exaggerated. One study done in 1970 in five California counties found that nonsupporting fathers were similar in their occupational distribution to the entire male population, neither predominant in low-income occupations nor more heavily represented among the unemployed: 10 percent were professional or managerial and 8 percent were craftsmen or foremen. Usually these fathers were living in the same county as their children. And they were not supporting any other children; 92 percent of the nonsupporting fathers had a total of three or fewer children, and only 13 percent were married to other women. Furthermore, the amount of child support awarded was not unreasonable, typically on the order of $50 a month (Winston and Forsher, 1971: 15- 16). Heclo et al. (1973: 33- 36), however, explain nonsupport largely as the inability of fathers to pay. They note that four-fifths of the fathers involved receive less than $10,000 a year. Many administrative and legal factors also contribute to nonsupport—the attitudes of the judges who make the awards, the lack of incentive for officials to enforce the order, and the lack of legal interest in the problem.

Aside from these economic complexities, which may underlie reconstituted marriages, there are also knotty interpersonal issues that may arise. The kinship terms are lacking for referring to one's spouse's children by another marriage or to the second wife whom one's father married. Household avoidance patterns and the incest taboos have to be redefined (Bohannan, 1970). As with the communes and extended family experiments that we consider next, the structural problems have just begun to be identified. Satisfactory solutions still have to be found.

Communes and extended-family experiments.

In the last decade a number of variant family forms have arisen. Their sheer variety and the amount of popular attention they have aroused suggest that their significance is larger than the mere curiosity factor. Some students of the phenomenon in fact contend that these experiments are a sign of strains in the traditional nuclear family and a clue to the mutations that it must undergo if it is to be adapted to contemporary society (Cogswell, 1975: 391).

A great deal of interest has centered upon the unconventional sexual arrangements that are found in the new family forms. Some people have tried "swinging," intimate networks, and multilateral marriage as alternatives to the sexual exclusivity of the nuclear family. However, it turns out that sexual activities have lower priority than obligations of work, child care, and home duties even in the new intimate networks (Ramey, 1975). It is with respect to these daily household obligations that the new family experiments offer the most innovative alternatives for the changing domestic roles of women and men.

Betty Cogswell (1975: 401) makes the insightful observation that traditional family forms emphasize constraints, while the participants in the experimental forms speak primarily of freedom and opportunity. Yet any viable social system sets constraints as well as offers opportunities. Both age-old limits and new possibilities have been discovered by experimentation. The main innovations revolve around (1) flexible work opportunities for female and male alike, (2) ways of sharing cooking, cleaning, shopping, and other household duties, and (3) new approaches to maternity, pregnancy, and child care.

Shared living arrangements among a group of adults or couples can result, for example, in rotation of responsibility for meal preparation and home maintenance, thus particularly freeing women for job responsibilities. Such experiments have been tried most notably in the kibbutzim, the Chinese collective enterprises, and the contemporary urban communes in the United States.

There is a tendency, however, toward a more traditional assignment of women to the home and kitchen tasks when children arrive. This happened when the Israeli kibbutzim were transformed from revolutionary frontier communities to more settled establishments that began to have families with young children. Women were more and more assigned to the kitchens and nurseries as part of their communal work (Talmon, 1972). Contemporary rural communes in the United States have generally had a more traditional division of labor from the beginning (Schlesinger, 1972; Berger et al., 1972). When the contemporary urban communal households begin to have children, there is some tendency for men to desert, leaving women to handle the responsibility (Bernard, 1974: 309–310). Or people do not choose to have children and are ambivalent about their care. Kanter found that there were remarkably few (only ten) "full-time children" in fifty-eight Boston area communes that she studied (Kanter, 1972: 27). It may also be that, viewed in terms of the life cycle, the experimental marriage or commune is primarily a transitional state and that people will leave when they decide to set up their own households or marry and have children (Giele, 1976). Nevertheless, recent feminist interest in public child-care facilities has drawn considerable impetus from foreign communal experiments in child care, particularly in China, Israel, and the U.S.S.R. (Sidel, 1972; Bettelheim, 1969; Bronfenbrenner, 1970).

Curiously, the idea of communal eating facilities has never caught on to the same degree among the noncommunal family population. One of the leading theorists of feminism, Charlotte Perkins Gilman (1898; 1966), in the last century visualized a day when there would be neighborhood kitchens that would save each family's making its meal separately. Perhaps the hamburger chains, the frozen dinner, prepared mixes, and other convenience foods, together with advanced household appliances such as the gas or electric stove and the refrigerator, have obviated this alternative. By contrast, no such comparable shortcut for child care has yet appeared or, for that matter, is likely to.

Although communes have received considerable attention, there is one family form to which perhaps more examination is due than it has yet received, what Litwak (1970) has called "modified extended families." If we picture that many of the needs families are called to fill are personal, emotional, and physical, and that the individuals who fulfill them are at best in a trusting and intimate relationship to those receiving help, it is usually a relative or group of relatives who turn out to have the deepest and longest-lasting loyalties that will sustain these demands. One possibility for modifying the nuclear family, therefore, is to extend it in ways that activate and maintain these ties with a larger group of relatives. This would not be the traditional extended family of patriarchal legend, but a more flexible and egalitarian group, able to help its kin with crises of child care, illness, or financial distress. It would probably be maintained by geographical proximity, impromptu visiting, and perhaps even common economic or ethnic ties that prevail in certain farming, mining, manufacturing, or professional milieux. The nineteenth-century pattern of taking in roomers and boarders may have helped to sustain such an extended network in a tight economy. Communes in the Canadian West (which are similar to those in the United States) apparently even now take in former members on a temporary basis, much as a kinship group would operate in the past (Gagné, 1975). There may be other networks sustained through church, lodge, or colleague relationships that operate in similar fashion and of which social scientists as yet have little formal knowledge.

Affluence may allow people to buy services and support separate living arrangements in a way that diminishes the human ties based on noneconomic exchange. Or geographical mobility may be so great that even relatives who wish to maintain helping ties are prevented from doing so by their distance from each other. If this is so, we will have to decide whether such a trend is to be allowed or encouraged or whether it in the end promotes an antifamilial policy.

SUMMARY

Changes in the life cycle of women have made the shape of their lives more similar to that of men. Longer life and shorter childbearing are combined with women's greater participation in the paid labor force. At the same time men's labor force participation has declined slightly, and there is greater *ideological* (if not behavioral) acceptance of the principle that men should participate more equally in child care and household work.

Trends in family form suggest that the modern symmetrical family is more favorably structured to permit crossover between male and female roles than was the preindustrial or early industrial family. At the same time, however, other various forms are emerging or are appearing with greater frequency: the single-parent household, reconstituted households, and variant communal forms. Whether or not any one of these forms is successful in supporting sex equality depends on circumstances. The single parent is frequently hampered by inadequate economic resources and overburdening of time. Some communal forms apparently do not successfully sustain sex equality when children are born; other such communities have very few children. Even the dual-career families, who seem to promise greatest symmetry between the roles of husband and wife, typically put the wife's career second and fail to involve the husband in household work in many cases. In all these new forms there is a repeated underlying theme—the question of who will take care of the children and whether the care will be satisfactory where it is done in a nontraditional way.

The contemporary experience of individuals and families now suggests that a new norm of flexibility is emerging in the roles that men and women take on at different stages of their lives. These new expectations appear to be somewhat less rigidly age- and sex-stereotyped than in the past. They make it more possible for a man or woman to delay and then later decide to be a parent, to change career in midstream, to drop out or reenter the labor force, and, in general, to negotiate a life pattern that meshes with the changing needs of other individuals in the family as well as with the changing needs of the self.

But these new life patterns and the family forms that make them possible are not yet fully institutionalized. Innovators still face difficulties, as do deviants from the preferred life cycle. The implicit and explicit rules that governed and reinforced the Victorian family are still to a large degree in operation. These rules govern the timing and scheduling of education, work, and leisure. They impose costs on the people and families who deviate. The costs may manifest themselves as poverty, isolation, overburdening, or rejection. But our growing awareness of viable family alternatives makes us look for ways to change laws and social policies so that they better accommodate the wide variety of individual and family behavior that now exists.

REFERENCES FOR CHAPTER FOUR

Bahr, Stephen J. 1974. "Effects on Power and Division of Labor in Family." In *Working Mothers*. Edited by L. W. Hoffman and F. I. Nye. San Francisco: Jossey-Bass.

Bane, Mary Jo. 1976. *Here to Stay: American Families in the Twentieth Century*. New York: Basic Books.

Beard, Mary R. 1946. *Woman as Force in History: A Study in Traditions and Realities*. New York: Macmillan.

Beecher, Catherine. 1841-1857; 1977. *A Treatise on Domestic Economy*. With an introduction by K. K. Sklar. New York: Schocken Books.

Bell, Carolyn Shaw. 1975. "The Next Revolution." *Social Policy* 6 (September-October): 5-11.

Berger, Bennett M.; Hackett, Bruce M.; and Millar, R. Mervyn. 1972. "Child-rearing Practices in the Communal Family." In *Family, Marriage, and the Struggle of the Sexes*. Edited by H. P. Dreitzel. New York: Macmillan.

Berkner, Lutz. 1972. "The Stem Family and the Developmental Cycle of the Peasant Household." *American Historical Review* 77 (April): 398-418.

Bernard, Jessie. 1974. *The Future of Motherhood*. New York: Dial Press.

Bettelheim, Bruno. 1969. *The Children of the Dream*. New York: Macmillan.

Blake, Judith. 1974. "The Changing Status of Women in Developed Countries." *Scientific American*, September, pp. 137-147.

Blenkner, Margaret. 1963. "Social Work and Family Relationships in Later

Life." In *Social Structure and the Family: Generational Relationships.* Edited by E. Shanas and G. Streib. Englewood Cliffs, N.J.: Prentice-Hall.

Bohannan, Paul, ed. 1970. *Divorce and After.* Garden City, N.Y.: Doubleday-Anchor.

Brim, Orville G., Jr. 1976. "Theories of the Male Mid-life Crisis." *Counseling Psychologist* 6, no. 1: 2–9.

Bronfenbrenner, Urie. 1970. *Two Worlds of Childhood: U.S. and U.S.S.R.* New York: Russell Sage Foundation.

———. 1975. "The Next Generation of Americans." Paper presented at the Annual Meeting of the American Association of Advertising Agencies, March 20, Dorado, Puerto Rico.

Bureau of the Census, U.S. Department of Commerce. 1975. *Historical Statistics of the United States, Colonial Times to 1970, Bicentennial ed., Part 1.* Washington, D.C.: U.S.G.P.O.

Campbell, Angus; Converse, Philip; and Rodgers, William. 1976. *The Quality of American Life.* New York: Russell Sage Foundation.

Carter, Hugh, and Glick, Paul C. 1970. *Marriage and Divorce: A Social and Economic Study.* Cambridge, Ma.: Harvard University Press.

Chevan, Albert, and Korson, J. Henry. 1975. "Living Arrangements of Widows in the U.S. and Israel, 1960 and 1961." *Demography* 12 (August): 505–518.

Cochran, Heidi, and Strasser, Susan. 1974. "The Efficient Home: The Technology and Ideology of Housework in the Early Twentieth Century." Paper presented at the Second Annual Conference on Marxist Approaches to History, New Haven, Ct., 23–24 February.

Cogswell, Betty E. 1975. "Variant Family Forms and Life Styles: Rejection of the Traditional Nuclear Family." *Family Coordinator* 24 (October): 391–406.

Cogswell, Betty E., and Sussman, Marvin B. 1972. "Changing Family and Marriage Forms: Complications for Human Service Systems." *Family Coordinator* 21 (October): 505–516.

Coles, Robert C. 1973. "Statement." In *American Families: Trends and Pressures, 1973: Hearings before the Subcommittee on Children and Youth, U.S. Senate.* Washington, D.C.: U.S.G.P.O.

Cowan, Ruth Schwartz. 1973. "A Case Study of Technology and Social Change: The Washing Machine and the Working Wife." Paper presented at the Berkshire Conference of Women Historians, Douglass College, New Brunswick, N.J.

Cutright, Phillips. 1972. "Illegitimacy in the United States: 1920–1968." In *Research Reports, Demographic and Social Aspects of Population Growth,* vol. 1. Commission on Population Growth and the American Future. Edited by C. F. Westoff and R. Parke, Jr. Washington, D.C.: U.S.G.P.O.

———. 1974. "Components of Change in the Number of Female Family Heads Aged 15–44: United States, 1940–1970." *Journal of Marriage and the Family* 36 (November): 714–721.

Davis, Kingsley. 1972. "The American Family in Relation to Demographic Change." In *Research Reports, Demographic and Social Aspects of Population Growth*, vol. 1. Commission on Population Growth and the American Future. Edited by C. F. Westoff and R. Parke, Jr. Washington, D.C.: U.S.G.P.O.

Demos, John. 1974. "The American Family in Past Time." *American Scholar* 43 (Summer): 422–446.

Dougherty, Kevin; Howrigan, Gail; Lein, Laura; and Weiss, Heather (Working Family Project). 1977. *Work and the American Family*. Chicago: National Parent Teachers Association.

Duncan, Greg, and Morgan, James N., eds. 1976. *Five Thousand American Families—Patterns of Economic Progress. Vol. IV: Family Composition Change and Other Analysis of the First Seven Years of the Panel Study of Income Dynamics*. Ann Arbor, Mi.: Institute for Social Research, University of Michigan.

Duncan, Otis D.; Schuman, Howard; and Duncan, Beverly. 1973. *Social Change in a Metropolitan Community*. New York: Russell Sage Foundation.

Elder, Glen H., Jr. 1974. *Children of the Great Depression: Social Change in Life Experience*. Chicago: University of Chicago Press.

——. 1975. "Family History and the Life Course." Paper presented at the Family Life Course in Historical Perspective conference, Williams College, Williamstown, Ma., July.

Elder, Glen H., Jr., and Rockwell, Richard C. 1976. "Marital Timing in Women's Life Patterns." *Journal of Family History* 1 (Autumn): 34–53.

Engels, Frederick. 1884; 1972. *The Origin of the Family, Private Property, and the State*. Edited by E. B. Leacock. New York: International Publishers.

Fogarty, Michael P.; Rapoport, Rhona; and Rapoport, Robert N. 1971. *Sex, Career, and Family*. London: Allen and Unwin.

Frisch, Rose E., and Revelle, Roger. 1970. "Height and Weight at Menarche and a Hypothesis of Critical Body Weights and Adolescent Events." *Science*, 24 July, pp. 397–399.

Frisch, Rose E., and McArthur, Janet W. 1974. "Menstrual Cycles: Fatness as a Determinant of Minimum Weight for Height Necessary for Their Maintenance or Onset." *Science*, 13 September, pp. 949–951.

Furstenberg, Frank. 1976. *Unplanned Parenthood: The Social Consequences of Teenage Childbearing*. New York: The Free Press.

Gagné, Jacques. 1975. Interview with Janet Zollinger Giele at the Vanier Institute of the Family, Ottawa, Canada, February.

Gans, Herbert. 1962. *The Urban Villagers*. New York: The Free Press.

Gauger, William. 1973. "Household Work: Can We Add It to the GNP?" *Journal of Home Economics*, October, pp. 12–23.

Giele, Janet Zollinger. 1961. "Social Change in the Feminine Role: A Comparison of Woman's Suffrage and Woman's Temperance, 1870–1920." Ph.D. dissertation, Radcliffe College.

——. 1976. "Changing Sex Roles and the Future of Marriage." In *Contempo-*

rary Marriage: Bond or Bondage. Edited by H. Grunebaum and J. Christ. Boston: Little, Brown.

Gilman, Charlotte Perkins. 1898; 1966. *Women and Economics.* Edited by C. N. Degler. New York: Harper and Row.

Glick, Paul C. 1977. "Updating the Life Cycle of the Family." *Journal of Marriage and the Family* 39 (February): 5-13.

Goody, Jack. 1972. "The Evolution of the Family." In *Household and Family in Past Time.* Edited by P. Laslett, with the assistance of R. Wall. Cambridge, Eng.: Cambridge University Press.

Gove, Walter R. 1973. "Sex, Marital Status, and Mortality." *American Journal of Sociology* 79 (July): 45-67.

Grabill, Wilson H.; Kiser, Clyde V.; and Whelpton, Pascal K. 1958; 1973. "A Long View." In *The American Family in Social-historical Perspective.* Edited by M. Gordon. New York: St. Martin's Press.

Haller, William, and Haller, Maleville. 1941-1942. "The Puritan Art of Love." *Huntington Library Quarterly* 5: 235-272.

Handlin, Oscar. 1951. *The Uprooted.* Boston: Little, Brown.

Hareven, Tamara K. 1975. "Family Time and Industrial Time: Family and Work in a Planned Corporation Town, 1900-1924." *Journal of Urban History* 1 (May): 365-389.

Havens, Elizabeth M. 1972. "The Relation between Female Labor-Force Participation and Fertility Rates." Paper presented at the American Sociological Association Annual Meeting, New Orleans, August.

Hayghe, Howard. 1976. "Families and the Rise of Working Wives—An Overview." *Monthly Labor Review* 99 (May): 12-19.

Heclo, Hugh; Rainwater, Lee; Rein, Martin; and Weiss, Robert. 1973. "Single-parent Families: Issues and Policies." Prepared for the Office of Child Development, Department of Health, Education, and Welfare.

Hedges, Janice N., and Barnett, Jeanne K. 1972. "Working Women and the Division of Household Tasks." *Monthly Labor Review* 95 (April): 9-14.

Henretta, James A. 1973. "The Morphology of New England Society in the Colonial Period." In *The Family in History: Interdisciplinary Essays.* Edited by T. K. Rabb and R. I. Rotberg. New York: Harper Torchbook.

Hoffman, Lois Wladis. 1974. "Effects of Maternal Employment on the Child: A Review of Research." *Developmental Psychology* 10, no. 2: 204-228.

Hoffman, Lois W., and Nye, F. Ivan. 1974. *Working Mothers.* San Francisco: Jossey-Bass.

Holmstrom, Lynda Lytle. 1972. *The Two-career Family.* Cambridge, Ma.: Schenkman.

Hornblower, Mary T. 1973. "Divorce Rate Still Spirals." *Boston Evening Globe,* p. 37.

Kanter, Rosabeth Moss. 1972. "Communes, the Family, and Sex Roles." Paper presented at the annual meeting of the American Sociological Association, New Orleans, August.

———. 1977. *Work and Family in the United States: A Critical Review and*

Agenda for Research and Policy. New York: Russell Sage Foundation.

Kobrin, Frances E. 1976. "The Primary Individual and the Family: Changes in Living Arrangements in the United States since 1940." *Journal of Marriage and the Family* 38 (May): 233–239.

Komarovsky, Mirra. 1964. *Blue-collar Marriage.* New York: Random House.

Kreps, Juanita M., and Clark, Robert. 1975. *Sex, Age, and Work: The Changing Composition of the Labor Force.* Baltimore, Md.: Johns Hopkins University Press.

Laslett, Barbara. 1973. "The Family as a Public and Private Institution: A Historical Perspective." *Journal of Marriage and the Family* 35 (August): 480–492.

Laslett, Peter, ed., with the assistance of R. Wall. 1972. *Household and Family in Past Time.* Cambridge, Eng.: Cambridge University Press.

Leacock, Eleanor B. 1972. "Introduction." In *The Origin of the Family, Private Property, and the State* by Frederick Engels. Edited by E. B. Leacock. New York: International Publishers.

Lein, Laura; Durham, M.; Pratt, M.; Schudson, M.; Thomas, R.; and Weiss, H. 1974. *Final Report: Work and Family Life.* Cambridge, Ma.: Center for Study of Public Policy, National Institute of Education Project no. 3–33074.

Lekachman, Robert. 1975. "On Economic Equality." *Signs* 1 (Autumn): 93–102.

Lerman, Robert I. 1973. "The Family, Poverty, and Welfare Programs: An Introductory Essay on Problems of Analysis and Policy." In *The Family, Poverty, and Welfare Programs: Factors Influencing Family Instability.* Paper no. 12 (Part I). Joint Economic Committee, U.S. Congress. Washington, D.C.: U.S.G.P.O.

Lerner, Gerda. 1969. "The Lady and the Mill Girl: Changes in the Status of Women in the Age of Jackson." *American Studies Journal* 10 (Spring): 5–15. Reprinted in Bobbs-Merrill American History Series H–43.

Levine, James A. 1976. *Who Will Raise the Children? New Options for Fathers (and Mothers).* Philadelphia: Lippincott.

Levison, Andrew. 1974. "The Working-class Majority." *New Yorker*, 2 September, pp. 36–61.

Litwak, Eugene. 1970. "Technological Innovation and Ideal Forms of Family Structure in an Industrial Democratic Society." In *Families in East and West.* Edited by R. Hill and R. Konig. Paris: Mouton.

Loeser, Herta. 1974. *Women, Work, and Volunteering.* Boston: Beacon Press.

Lynn, David B. 1974. *The Father: His Role in Child Development.* Monterey, Ca.: Brooks/Cole.

Mason, Karen Oppenheim; Czajka, John; and Arber, Sara. 1976. "Change in U.S. Women's Sex-role Attitudes, 1964–1974." *American Sociological Review* 41 (August): 573–596.

Meade, Ellen. 1975. "Role Satisfaction of Housewives." Paper presented at Annual Meeting of Eastern Sociological Association, New York City, August.

Melder, Keith. 1967. "Ladies Bountiful: Organized Women's Benevolence in Early Nineteenth-Century America." *New York History* 48 (July): 231–256.

Mill, John Stuart. 1869; 1970. "The Subjection of Women." In *Essays on Sex Equality* by John Stuart Mill and Harriet Taylor Mill. Edited by A. S. Rossi. Chicago: University of Chicago Press.

Modell, John, and Hareven, Tamara K. 1973. "Urbanization and the Malleable Household: An Examination of Boarding and Lodging in American Families." *Journal of Marriage and the Family* 35 (August): 467–479.

Morgan, Edmund S. 1944; 1966. *The Puritan Family: Essays on Religion and Domestic Relations in Seventeenth-Century New England*. New York: Harper and Row.

Oakley, Ann. 1975. *The Sociology of Housework*. New York: Pantheon.

O'Neill, Nena, and O'Neill, George. 1972. *Open Marriage: A New Life Style for Couples*. New York: Evans.

O'Neill, William. 1969. *Everyone Was Brave*. Chicago: Quadrangle.

Oppenheimer, Valerie Kincade. 1977. "Women's Economic Role in the Family." *American Sociological Review* 42 (June): 387–406.

Packard, Vance. 1972. *A Nation of Strangers*. New York: McKay.

Pleck, Elizabeth. 1976. "Two Worlds in One: Work and Family." *Journal of Social History* 10: 178–195.

Pleck, Joseph H. 1977. "The Work-Family Role System." *Social Problems* 24: 417–427.

Presser, Harriet B. 1975. "Social Consequences of Teenage Childbearing." Paper presented at the Conference on the Consequences of Adolescent Pregnancy and Childbearing, Bethesda, Md., 29–30 October.

Preston, Samuel, and Richards, Alan Thomas. 1975. "The Influence of Women's Work Opportunities on Marriage Rates." *Demography* 12 (May): 209–222.

Rainwater, Lee; Coleman, Richard P.; and Handel, Gerald. 1959. *Workingman's Wife*. New York: Oceana.

Ramey, James W. 1975. "Intimate Groups and Networks: Frequent Consequences of Sexually Open Marriage." *Family Coordinator* 24 (October): 515–530.

Rapoport, Rhona, and Rapoport, Robert N. 1976. *Dual-Career Families Reexamined*. New York: Harper and Row.

Riley, Matilda W., and Foner, Anne. 1968. *Aging and Society. Vol. 1: An Inventory of Research Findings*. New York: Russell Sage Foundation.

Rölvaag, O. E. 1927. *Giants in the Earth*. New York: Harper and Row.

Roper Organization. 1974. *The Virginia Slims American Women's Opinion Poll. Vol. 3: A Survey of the Attitudes of Women on Marriage, Divorce, the Family, and America's Changing Sexual Morality*. New York: Roper Organization.

Ross, Heather, and Sawhill, Isabel V. 1975. *Time of Transition: The Growth of Families Headed by Women*. Washington, D.C.: Urban Institute.

Rossi, Alice S. 1977. "A Biosocial Perspective on Parenting." *Daedalus* 106 (Spring): 1–31.

Rubin, Lillian. 1976. *Worlds of Pain: Life in the Working-class Family.* New York: Basic Books.

Sacks, Karen. 1974. "Engels Revisited: Women, the Organization of Production, and Private Property." In *Women, Culture, and Society.* Edited by M. Z. Rosaldo and L. Lamphere. Stanford, Ca.: Stanford University Press.

Safire, William. 1973. "On Cohabitation." *New York Times,* 29 September, p. 31.

Samuels, Victoria. 1975. "Nowhere to Be Found: A Literature Review and Annotated Bibliography on White Working-class Women." New York: Institute on Pluralism in Group Identity.

Sawhill, Isabel V. 1977. "Economic Perspectives on the Family." *Daedalus* 106 (Spring): 115–125.

Scanzoni, John H. 1975. *Sex Roles, Life Styles, and Childbearing.* New York: The Free Press.

Schlesinger, Benjamin. 1972. "Family Life in the Kibbutz of Israel: Utopia Gained or Paradise Lost?" In *Family, Marriage, and the Struggle of the Sexes.* Edited by H. P. Dreitzel. New York: Macmillan.

Schoen, Robert. 1975. "California Divorce Rates by Age at First Marriage and Duration of First Marriage." *Journal of Marriage and the Family* 37 (August): 548–555.

Schoen, Robert; Greenblatt, Harry N.; and Mielke, Robert B. 1975. "California's Experience with Non-Adversary Divorce." *Demography* 12 (May): 223–243.

Schottland, Charles I. 1968. "Government Economic Programs and Family Life." *Journal of Marriage and the Family* 29 (February): 71–123.

Seifer, Nancy. 1975. "The Working Family in Crisis: Who Is Listening?" Project on Group Life and Ethnic Americans, American Jewish Commission. New York: Institute on Pluralism in Group Identity.

Shorter, Edward. 1973. "Illegitimacy, Sexual Revolution, and Social Change in Modern Europe." In *The Family in History: Interdisciplinary Essays.* Edited by T. K. Rabb and R. I. Rotberg. New York: Harper and Row.

Sidel, Ruth. 1972. *Women and Child Care in China.* New York: Hill and Wang.

Silver, Catherine Bodard. 1977. "France: Contrasts in Familial and Societal Roles." In *Women: Roles and Status in Eight Countries.* Edited by J. Z. Giele and A. C. Smock. New York: Wiley.

Sklar, June, and Berkov, Beth. 1974a. "Teenage Family Formation in Postwar America." *Family Planning Perspectives* 6, no. 2: 80–90.

Sklar, June, and Berkov, Beth. 1974b. "Abortion, Illegitimacy, and the American Birthrate." *Science,* 13 September, pp. 909–995.

Sklar, Kathryn Kish. 1973. *Catherine Beecher: A Study in American Domesticity.* New Haven, Ct.: Yale University Press.

———. 1977. "Introduction." In *A Treatise on Domestic Economy* by Catherine Beecher. New York: Schocken Books.

Smelser, Neil J. 1959. *Social Change in the Industrial Revolution.* Chicago: University of Chicago Press.

Smith, Daniel Scott. 1974. "Family Limitation, Sexual Control, and Domestic

Feminism in Victorian America." In *Clio's Consciousness Raised*. Edited by M. Hartman and L. Banner. New York: Harper and Row.

Sokolowska, Magdalena. 1977. "Poland: Women's Experience under Socialism." In *Women: Roles and Status in Eight Countries*. Edited by J. Z. Giele and A. C. Smock. New York: Wiley.

Statistical Abstract of the United States, 1973. Washington, D.C.: U.S. Department of Commerce, Social and Economic Statistics Administration.

Sweet, James A. 1971. "The Living Arrangements of Separated, Widowed, and Divorced Mothers." Madison, Wi.: University of Wisconsin, Center for Demography and Ecology, Working Paper # 71-4.

Szalai, Alexander. 1973. "The Quality of Family Life—Traditional and Modern: A Review of Sociological Findings on Contemporary Family Organization and Role Differentiation in the Family." Paper presented at the United Nations Interregional Seminar on the Family in a Changing Society: Problems and Responsibilities of its Members, London, 18-31 July, ESA/SDHA/ AC. 3/6.

Taeuber, Irene B., and Taeuber, Conrad. 1971. *People of the United States*. Washington, D.C.: U.S. Department of Commerce, Bureau of the Census.

Taeuber, Karl A., and Sweet, James A. 1976. "Family and Work: The Social Life Cycle of Women." In *Women and the American Economy*. Edited by J. M. Kreps. Englewood Cliffs, N.J.: Prentice-Hall.

Talmon, Yonina. 1972. *Family and Community in the Kibbutz*. Cambridge, Ma.: Harvard University Press.

Tilly, Louise A.; Scott, Joan W.; and Cohen, Miriam. 1976. "Women's Work and European Fertility Patterns." *Journal of Interdisciplinary History* 6 (Winter): 447-476.

Uhlenberg, Peter R. 1969. "A Study of Cohort Life Cycles: Cohorts of Native-born Massachusetts Women, 1830-1920." *Population Studies* 23 (November): 407-420.

——. 1974. "Cohort Variations in Family Life-Cycle Experiences of U.S. Females." *Journal of Marriage and the Family* 36 (May): 284-292.

U.S. Senate, Subcommittee on Children and Youth. 1973. *American Families: Trends and Pressures, 1973: Hearings*. Washington, D.C.: U.S.G.P.O.

Van Dusen, Roxann, and Sheldon, Eleanor Bernert. 1976. "The Changing Status of American Women: A Life Cycle Perspective." *American Psychologist*, February, pp. 106-116.

Vanek, Joann. 1974. "Time Spent in Housework." *Scientific American*, November, pp. 116-120.

Walker, Kathryn E. 1969. "Time Spent in Household Work by Homeworkers." *Family Economics Review*, September, pp. 5-6.

——. 1970. "Time Spent by Husbands in Household Work." *Family Economics Review*, June, pp. 8-11.

Weinstein, Fred, and Platt, Gerald M. 1969. *The Wish to Be Free*. Berkeley, Ca.: University of California Press.

Wells, Robert V. 1971. "Demographic Change and the Life Cycle of American Families." *Journal of Interdisciplinary History* 2 (Autumn): 273–282.

Welter, Barbara. 1976. "The Cult of True Womanhood, 1820–1860." In *Dimity Convictions.* Edited by B. Welter. Athens, Oh.: Ohio University Press.

Winston, Marian P., and Forsher, Trude. 1971. "Nonsupport of Legitimate Children by Affluent Fathers as a Cause of Poverty and Welfare Dependence." Santa Monica, Ca.: Rand Corporation.

Working Family Project. 1978. "Parenting." In *Working Couples.* Edited by R. N. Rapoport and R. Rapoport. New York: Harper and Row.

Wortis, Rochelle P. 1971. "The Acceptance of the Concept of the Maternal Role by Behavioral Scientists: Its Effects on Women." *American Journal of Orthopsychiatry* 41 (October): 733–746.

Young, Michael, and Willmott, Peter. 1973. *The Symmetrical Family.* New York: Pantheon.

5

FAMILY POLICY

Society has not considered it proper to provide for the discontinuity in women's lives and their risks in marriage by assuming social responsibility for their support. If marriage is no longer an economically profitable status, some fundamental rearrangements in marriage itself and in its connection with work and support have to be demanded

—Alva Myrdal, *Nation and Family*, 1941; 1968.

All the angles from childbearing to role integration are engaging the attention of thoughtful men and women throughout the industrial world. . . . [M]others continue to gerrymander their own little self help . . . to spell one another off from time to time. They devise a mosaic of arrangements to spare themselves from collapse, exchange baby-sitting services with one another . . . set up their own cooperative child-care facilities. . . . Their children though, will be spared at least some of the trauma. Many different kinds of help are on the way

—Jessie Bernard, *The Future of Motherhood*, 1974a.

No modern society can avoid policies that influence the family. But the effects of such policy are usually concealed and unconscious rather than open and deliberate. Feminism and alternate family life styles are two forces, however, that have recently uncovered the effects of past hidden policies on men and women.

In earlier chapters we have seen how changes in women's political and labor-force participation eventually put a strain on norms that kept women out of high office and well-paid jobs. Ultimately, court decisions, antidiscriminatory legislation, and efforts for affirmative action followed.

We shall now trace a similar process in family matters. As we saw in chapter 4, changing demographic patterns of *individual* behavior (marriage, divorce, fertility, and length of life) have brought change to the *family system* (smaller households, fewer children, and role sharing). In this chapter we shall see how these changes in turn

188

subject *law and social policies* (child care, welfare, Social Security, family law) to considerable strain and attempts at revision. Finally, these developments raise a larger *value* question: the relative priority that household and family considerations should hold in a society ruled by the market economy.

Family policy is still a relatively new and unfamiliar term. The concept first developed in European countries. During the 1930s, Sweden and France, for example, tried to halt declines in their birthrates (Myrdal, 1941). By instituting family allowances, housing subsidies, and health benefits, those countries hoped to strengthen and support family life and give parents help in the care of children. More recently in Great Britain Margaret Wynn (1970) presented the concept of family policy as a device by which the whole society can help bear the disproportionate investment that parents alone now make in rearing a future generation of citizens.

Similar concern for the effects of social policy on children has appeared in the United States. In 1973 the U.S. Senate Subcommittee on Children and Youth chaired by Senator Walter Mondale (Democrat, Minnesota) held hearings on the state of the American family. Witnesses described unintended harmful effects on family life of such policies as frequent transfers in the army or overly bureaucratized and centralized systems of foster care, health care, and other social services. More recently President Carter, both in his campaign and in the early months of his administration, has shown strong interest in the state of the American family.

In the face of these developments we may well ask what *is* family policy? Whom does it concern, and how is it related to changing sex roles?

Family policy is that set of support programs created by the larger society that supplements functions once performed by the family. Basic family functions are organized in a contextual pattern with nurturance and care of individuals at the center. Ranging outward from the individual members are next the family group that shares resources with the individual, and then the neighborhood or larger ecological niche from which the family derives its resources. Encompassing the whole is a symbolic system of communication or culture that is based on various religious, racial, or other traditions. Corresponding with each one of these basic family functions is a type of social policy that provides public supports for that function. For example, certain programs support the *nurturance* function: child care, health care, services to the elderly or handicapped. Other programs support the *economic* functions of the family by providing welfare benefits to people in need or stimulating employment for certain categories of family members such as women. The *ecological* function of the family is served by programs and policies that promote helping arrangements, social networks, and exchange of services among families. Finally, certain aspects of family law and social policy clarify the boundaries and strengthen the identity of the family as a *legal and cultural* entity.

The evolution of these social policies for the family is intertwined with the history of changing sex roles. We saw in the last chapter how as women's lives lengthened and the period of their lives devoted to childbearing diminished, more of them entered the labor force. The new flexibility in women's lives, however, subjected family policies to considerable strain. Hidden assumptions embedded in child-care programs or economic supports—that most women are full-time wives and mothers—were no longer entirely valid. At the same time the proliferation of a wider variety of family types (dual-worker, single-parent, reconstituted) invalidated the traditional conjugal pattern (husband-breadwinner, wife-homemaker) as the single appropriate family ideal.

This chapter, then, is a review of the changes in social policies for the family that have been either proposed or adopted as a response to changes in women's roles. It begins with a brief history of the societal changes that caused social programs for the family to proliferate. It then takes up the four major types of family policy in which the significance of changing sex roles is evident: personal services, economic support policies for the family, housing and community development, and changing family law. The final section raises some speculative questions concerning national priorities, particularly the relative value that individuals and the society accord to economic and work-related pursuits as distinguished from noneconomic and family-related activity.

FAMILY CHANGE AND SOCIAL POLICIES

During the last hundred years the effects of social programs on the family have been almost entirely indirect. Until the 1930s, when various European countries began to adopt programs of family allowances that would deliberately stimulate population growth, the concept of family policy did not exist. However, in the United States between 1935, when the Social Security Act was passed, and 1969 to 1972, when the Family Assistance Plan was brought before Congress in various forms and defeated, there emerged a growing sense that government should explicitly try to protect and foster family life.

Social insurance programs constitute a very significant part of the government's present social policy for families. These programs began with changes in the underlying structure of the family and its relation to the larger economy. In the eighteenth and nineteenth centuries the family became less able to perform independently a wide variety of functions such as economic production, provision for old age, and social placement of the young. Family efforts to provide for old, sick, and handicapped members were gradually supplemented (though not supplanted) by public programs and facilities. Charitable institutions multiplied. The general-purpose almshouse appeared. It was joined by shelters, asylums, and hospitals, each serving specialized populations of the needy. At the same time a patchwork of retirement plans, workmen's compensation, and other forms of social insurance slowly developed to provide more reliable protection against the prospect of old age and poverty. By the Depression of the 1930s such techniques of mutual assistance had become so familiar that the nation could review, rationalize, and consolidate earlier programs.

The Social Security Act of 1935 began the consolidation by providing an umbrella of insurance coverage which protected the old, the permanently and totally disabled, the unemployed, and their survivors.* In the 1950s self-employed persons and domestics were covered. The proportion of employees covered by the system stood at 60 percent in 1939 but had risen to 95 percent by 1970 (Social Security Administration, U.S. Department of Health, Education, and Welfare, 1973*b*: 1, 2). Medicare and Medicaid brought health care to the aged and indigent in 1965. The War Against Poverty from 1964 to 1968 expanded welfare to provide income supplements to families and aged below the poverty line. In 1973–1974 Supplemental Security Income (S.S.I.) payments were transferred to the Social Security program. In 1974 Supplemental Income (as distinct from earnings-based old-age and pension plans and Medicare) clients were about one-eighth of the total recipients of Social Security checks (Drucker, 1976: 40). In 1929 the United States spent 3.9 percent of its Gross National Product (G.N.P.) on social welfare. By 1975 the proportion had risen to 20.1 percent of GNP. As a proportion of government

---

* Other countries generally recognize nine broad types of social security. Of these the 1935 Social Security Act in the United States established (1) unemployment insurance, (2) workmen's compensation, (3) old age, and (4) survivor's insurance. Family allowances (5) of a limited form were available in Aid to Dependent Children. Disability insurance (6) was added in 1956. In 1965 Medicare and Medicaid (7) established a form of national health insurance limited to the old and medically indigent. Maternity benefits (8) and temporary sickness and disability insurance (9) are not, however, available under U.S. Social Security (Social Security Administration, U.S. Department of Health, Education, and Welfare, 1973*b*).

spending, social-welfare expenditures rose from 36.3 percent in 1929 to 58.4 percent in 1975.

While Social Security was consolidating retirement insurance and welfare programs in the public sector, pension funds and health-insurance plans emerged in the private sector. General Motors began a modern pension program in 1950, and the idea spread. There are now some 50,000 private pension plans. By 1975, pension funds held stock that amounted to one-third of the equity capital of American business (Drucker, 1976: 3, 6, 7).

CHANGE IN THE TRADITIONAL FAMILY

No history has yet been written that shows how the rise of government-provided social insurance and welfare programs were related to changes in the family. We do know that throughout the Western world the first programs for workmen's compensation, rail-road workers' retirement, and insurance for survivors began to appear in the 1870s (Schottland, 1967; Lubove, 1968). Smelser (1959: 342–383), in a study of the Industrial Revolution in the English textile region, shows that workers began savings banks, friendly societies, and cooperative societies as early as the 1830s and 1840s. These facts alert us to the changing relation between work and family life that must have stimulated the invention of social insur-ance. Workmen's compensation and security in old age must have become pressing concerns either because the risks of income loss became greater or because traditional patterns of sharing risk were no longer to be counted on. It was indeed the case, Smelser shows, that structural differentiation between family and workplace both raised the risk of unemployment and weakened the family's resources for meeting catastrophe when it occurred.

THE INCREASING AUTONOMY AND INSECURITY OF WOMEN

When the agrarian family gave way to a family dependent on outside wages, women probably experienced a rise in autonomy and independence relative to what had been possible in the peasant family. But probably they also experienced a drop in their sense of security. The ideal family advocated by John Stuart Mill (1869; 1970) was based on a model of the male as breadwinner who worked outside the home. The woman was to be in charge of domestic expenditure and child care, and she had considerable opportunity for independent action in management of the household. However, the woman of Mill's ideal family was extraordinarily vulnerable if her husband was unemployed. If he was injured or died, or if he was improvident and drank his earnings away, she and her children might be destitute.

Between the Civil War and the First World War, women expressed this contradictory trend in their status. In the suffrage movement they asked for greater autonomy in the public sphere. They conveyed that they were somehow superior and particularly well qualified to oversee health care, child rearing, education, community housekeeping, and personal and political morality. Through the hospital board and the school committee, they enlarged their roles as homemakers to bring good influence into local government.

On the other hand, these same women tried to avoid vulnerability to dependency and the loss of a breadwinner husband. The Women's Christian Temperance Union tried to remove corner saloons to protect women and families from men's intemperance. They were also concerned for the women and young girls who were sexually exploited. Through their work in charitable organizations and missionary and temperance societies, women sought means to erect other social supports where the family was absent or inadequate (Giele, 1961).

But their solutions did not try to change the Victorian family so much as to restore it to ideal functioning. Social reform, religious and charitable activity, and private social-insurance programs were the only "family policy" of the immediate post- Civil War era. Major assumptions went unchallenged—men were breadwinners and women were homemakers and child rearers. Insurance was against loss of a job or loss of a breadwinner. The husband earned the benefits; they were paid to survivors and dependents.

SEX-ROLE SYMMETRY AND CHANGING FAMILY POLICY

Changes in family life over the last fifty years now alert us to the rather narrow range of assumptions that governed early policy and programs. Rising numbers of married women in the labor force are now a challenge to the traditional male "breadwinner" concept. Large numbers of households headed by women (65 percent of whom are *not* on welfare) call for new programs such as day care, flexible hours in industry, or entitlements to social insurance based on household work. The trend is toward symmetry with *wife* and husband *working* and *husband* and wife *doing household chores.*

Should present tax policies and social programs then stand? In which regulations does the older Victorian model still persist, and how can they be changed to support alternative models? These questions guide the following examination of current social policies.

CHANGING SEX ROLES AND CURRENT FAMILY POLICY

The traditional family model (husband-breadwinner, wife-houseworker) is imbedded in at least four major areas of established law and social policy: (1) services to care for children, handicapped, sick, or other dependent persons in the family; (2) economic programs that affect welfare and work; (3) community services and community design; and (4) laws and policies defining the family as a legal entity. Each of these facets of social policy is now due for critical review in light of changing sex roles and family forms.

CHILD CARE

At the most concrete level of daily activity, families provide care and personal services to individuals. With the development of the welfare functions of the state, public programs are increasingly available to augment or replace the family's nurturant functions in the care of children and older people, the sick, the handicapped, and other dependents. Recently some of this trend has been reversed in a process known as *de-institutionalization.* The mentally disabled and the handicapped are being returned to their families and the local community to receive as much care through them as can be given. With an increasing proportion of women in the labor force, a pressing issue arises: who will take care of the dependents who were once cared for by families, then were shifted to public care, and now are shifted back again? We saw in the last chapter how middle-aged women, primarily daughters, were called on to look after the needs of older people. We know that young children have traditionally been in the charge of the mother. The most pressing question with respect to all these nurturant functions is who will take care of the children.*

Of all wives who were working from 1948 to 1974, the highest participation rate was for women with school-age children, and this rate rose during that period from 26 percent to 51 percent. Thus as

* An important related issue is policy toward reproductive freedom and abortion. Congress in 1977 again considered a ban on the use of Medicaid funds for abortion. Policy related to reproduction is outlined in chapter 1.

John O'Riley (1976: 1) comments, "we have already passed the point where more than half of the wives with school-age children are either holding jobs outside the home or looking for such jobs." The rate for wives with no children under eighteen was 43 percent, but for women with children under six it was not that much lower—34 percent.

There are two major responses to the question of who will take care of children. One group recognizes the change in women's roles and calls for more child-care facilities, services to children, or other offsetting adjustments (Bronfenbrenner, 1975; National Research Council, 1976: 76-78). Another group surveys present child-care arrangements, finds that most are worked out informally with relatives, and concludes that the debate over child care is a secondary issue (Woolsey, 1977: 143).

Evidence to support both viewpoints is presented below. Finally, it is possible to list certain reforms on which there appears to be widespread agreement among the major contending interest groups—the ones concerned with the changing roles of women, or the ones concerned with the welfare of children, and, last, the ones who have to pay the bill.

Scope of the problem.

Measured by a number of indices, the United States is apparently falling behind in the quality of care given its young children. Our ranking among nations in combating infant mortality has declined steadily in recent decades until it now stands fourteenth among the nations. Bronfenbrenner (1975: 17) contends that "a similar situation obtains with respect to a maternal and child health, day care, children's allowances, and other basic services to children and families."

To explain what seems to be a worsening situation for children (higher delinquency, rising rates of suicide among the young, and so on) a recent report by the National Research Council (1976: 14-39) links these phenomena to changes in the American family—the rising rate of maternal employment, the smaller number of adults in the home, the increase in single-parent families, divorce and remarriage, and larger numbers of children born to unmarried mothers. After perusing these statistics it is not difficult to conclude with Bronfenbrenner (1975: 32) that a key factor in the changing welfare of children is the changing position of women. Bronfenbrenner, a leading authority on child development, says:

> These concerns bring me to what I regard as the most important single factor affecting the welfare of the nation's children. I refer to the place and status of women in American society. Whatever the future trend may be, the fact remains that in our society today the care of children depends

overwhelmingly on women, and specifically on mothers. Moreover, with the
withdrawal of the social supports for the family to which I alluded above,
the position of women and mothers has become more and more isolated.
With the breakdown of the community, the neighborhood, and the extended family, an increasing responsibility for the care and upbringing of
children has fallen on the young mother. Under these circumstances it is not
surprising that many young women in America are in revolt. I understand
and share their sense of rage, but I fear the consequences of some of the
solutions they advocate, which will have the effect of isolating children still
further from the kind of care and attention they need. There is, of course, a
constructive implication to this line of thought, in that a major route to the
rehabilitation of children and youth in American society lies in the enhance-
ment of the status and power of women in all walks of life—in the home as
well as on the job.

From an association between women's changing status and the
changing state of children, however, it cannot be simply concluded
that women should return to the home. Exhaustive reviews of the
effects of maternal employment on children show that positive or
negative results depend largely on whether the mother is satisfied and
happy to be working, whether the family is supportive of her
employment, and whether satisfactory household and child-care
arrangements have been worked out (Hoffman and Nye, 1974;
Howell, 1973a, 1973b).

The question is whether it is easily possible to work out these
satisfactory child-care arrangements, or whether they are difficult to
come by. Woolsey (1977: 135, 142–143) contends that it is primarily middle-class people who perceive the working out of informal
arrangements with relatives as difficult. They are more likely to be far
removed from family, whereas the working or lower class are able to
find alternative arrangements with nearby relatives without difficulty.

Still other evidence gives a contrary impression—that there is
greater demand for care of young children than can be satisfied by
the places available in preschools. The National Research Council
report (1976: 68, 72) concludes that the supply gap is clearly visible,
especially for children over three, where there is a growing tendency
for parents to seek some care arrangement for their children. Between 1964 and 1974 the proportion of all children three to five
years old who were enrolled in nursery school and kindergarten rose
from one-quarter (25.5 percent) to nearly half (45.2 percent). This
pattern is similar to that of other Western countries. The Finer report
(1974: 457–459) on one-parent families in Great Britain mentions
long waiting lists for places in nursery schools. A Swedish report
indicates that the common method of solving the child-supervision
problem there is for parents to stagger their working hours. But the
method is hard on both children and parents. The reporter com-

ments, "Presumably many people stagger their working hours in this fashion precisely because the public sector falls short of meeting the demand for child-care facilities" (Sandberg, 1975: 68).

Existing solutions.

In fact the actual growth of preschool places for children grew remarkably from 4,000 licensed facilities providing care for 140,000 children in 1960 to 16,600 centers providing care for more than 600,000 children in 1970 (Keyserling, 1972: 72). But of all the care arrangements used for children under six between 1965 and 1971, only one-quarter was provided outside homes in a day-care center or another such arrangement. This compares with a third of all families who have day care in their homes provided by a father or some other relative. One-quarter arrange care in their homes to be given by a combination of relatives or nonrelatives. The remaining fraction (17 percent) are cared for in another person's home (Jusenius and Shortlidge, 1975: 82). These figures are consistent with a finding from the *Five Thousand American Families* study showing that nearly half of all the families with children under the age of twelve do not pay anything for child care; they are able to rely on family members instead (Dickinson, 1975: 224).

Between 1965 and 1971 the average proportion of children under six cared for in the home rose from 48 to 56 percent. The proportion cared for in other persons' homes dropped from 28 to 18 percent, and the number cared for by some other arrangement such as day care rose only two percentage points from 24 percent to 26 percent (Jusenius and Shortlidge, 1975: 82).

How to interpret these findings is not clear. It can be argued either that people prefer home care or, on the other hand, that out-of-home alternatives are too expensive or too scarce. A survey by the Stanford Research Institute in 1975 showed that people preferred child care in their own homes (see Woolsey, 1977). Lillian Rubin's (1976: 84–85) interviews with working-class couples show their reluctance to place their children in an institutional setting. The staggered schedules of working-class couples described by Lein et al. (1974) seem to be a strategy for having children cared for by family members in the home.

However, these facts do not banish an impression that present American child-care arrangements are not entirely satisfactory— whether from the viewpoint of the working parents, the child, or the state. Between 1965 and 1971, for example, the proportion of white children aged six to thirteen who took care of themselves doubled from 11 percent to 22 percent; the proportion of children under the age of six looking after themselves rose from 1 to 3 percent (Jusenius and Shortlidge, 1975: 82). The Keyserling report (1972) on day-care centers around the country reported some examples of three-year-old children left alone to fend for themselves while the mother was away at work. Members of the National Council of Jewish Women who gathered these field observations reported other examples of propri-etary day-care centers where twenty or thirty children were strapped in chairs or confined to double-decker makeshift cribs under the care of one or two inadequately trained older children or a lone woman (Keyserling, 1972: 13-26).

Proposals for change.
In response to the working-mother trend (as well as to the concern for general child welfare and poverty), Congress has in the last decade considered several major proposals for subsidizing child-development programs and day care. As early as 1966 Representative Patsy Mink (Democrat, Hawaii) had proposed preschool centers. But it was in 1971 that the joint Mondale-Brademas Senate/House bill, attached to the Economic Opportunity Amendments of 1971, passed the Senate and House and went to the president. The bill would have provided for comprehensive child-development services to children to meet their physical, mental, social, cognitive, and nutritional needs. It also provided for prenatal care and special activities for the handicapped. The legislation would have allowed any family of four under a certain income level to qualify for free services and would have charged those with higher incomes on a sliding scale. Centers would have been established in every community of over 10,000 population. In December of 1971, President Nixon vetoed the bill, saying that it threatened to substitute communal-based child care for the family-centered approach. An attempt to override failed (Schultze et al., 1972: 286-290).

Since the 1971 veto, a number of bills similar to the defeated bill have been introduced. In the 93rd Congress, Representative Brade-mas (Democrat, Indiana) and Senator Mondale (Democrat, Minne-sota) sponsored the Comprehensive Child Development Act. Repre-sentatives Abzug and Chisholm (Democrats, New York) cosponsored an almost identical bill (Streuer, 1973: 56-57). The Mondale-Brade-mas bill, the Child and Family Services Act (S. 626, H.R. 2966), lay dormant through the 94th Congress and was the target of a right-wing pamphleteering campaign in the Midwest, which raised the specter that day care and comprehensive services would "sovietize" education (Bowman, 1975).

Explanations for the defeat of comprehensive plans for day-care and child development services largely focus on the competing ideo-logical and political interests that are involved. The middle-class intellectuals wish to improve child development. The workfare conservatives want to put welfare mothers to work. The adherents of the women's movement are interested in day care as a supportive service (Steiner, 1976; Woolsey, 1977).

If legislation were somewhat differently drawn, it might have a better chance of being adopted. There are several theories on what the proposed provisions should contain. One common thread seems to be that more care is needed; the question is how much more. Should new programs be primarily addressed to the unlucky child who has nowhere to go, as Gilbert Steiner (1976: 254-255) suggests? Or should services be provided instead across the board to avoid stigma for any one group of children and to act as a preventive screening device to identify health and developmental problems early enough to do something about them? The latter view has long been advocated by the pioneer of family policy, Alva Myrdal (1941; 1968: 133-153), who supports the concept of services "in kind" to all children as preferable to payments "in cash" to a few. Recently the National Research Council (1976: 63) also voiced its position in favor of comprehensive health services to all children. In addition, scholars who have studied fatherless families in the United States suggest that greater availability of housekeeping services, community kitchens, and home help would be a great aid to the burdened mother (Herzog and Sudia, 1973: 216-227.)*

All the proposals for change emphasize that a parent should have the option of remaining in the home to look after the children. The first device by which this option appeared was through the "mother's pension" movement at the turn of the century. In the late 1960s and early 1970s David Gil (1973: 59-135) refurbished the idea under the term "mother's wages." Today the National Research Council (1976: 77) states as its first recommendation for child care, *"Parents should have the option, first and foremost, of raising their children at home, without sacrificing a reasonable standard of living."* For certain families this will require a form of income support. Caution must be taken, however, in how such a program is designed. In Great Britain the Finer report (1974: 267) notes that a supplementary benefit available to one-parent families has had the effect of keeping mothers from taking up part-time work even when they find it desirable because the low disregard in calculation of taxes on added earnings acts as a disincentive to work.

* George and Wilding (1972: 149), however, in a study of motherless families in England conclude that the "personal social services were at best peripheral to the problems of most fatherless families." Some way or other, through friends and relatives, the father managed to look after the children. The social services were slow to identify people who needed help, and the help they provided was not always meaningful.

For the time being the least controversial remedy appears to be tax relief for families who need child care. The tax law, revised in 1976, now permits a tax credit of 20 percent of work-related child-care expenses up to a maximum of $2,000 for one child and $4,000 for two or more children. Such tax deductions may primarily help families with high incomes, however, especially if low-income families rely heavily on informal unpaid arrangements with relatives.

The persistent question is how to design programs with sufficient provisions for both need and work incentives while at the same time keeping open a wide set of options for a mother either to be employed or to stay at home to care for her children. Changing sex roles are thus as directly relevant to any workable system of economic supports for the family as to the provision of personal services.

ECONOMIC SUPPORTS TO THE FAMILY

In most developed countries of the world, social policies affecting individual and family well-being are closely intertwined not only with employment but also with some system of entitlements, the benefits of which are partly based on earnings and partly based on need (Wilensky, 1975). Yet sociologists and historians have largely failed to address the connections among changing sex roles, family structures, and the economic policies that determine eligibility for such benefits. What is now needed is an extension of the theory of crossover in contemporary sex roles to show how future welfare and employment policies might more appropriately be drawn. The question is how these policies could be made to reinforce flexibility and interchangeability of tasks between male and female rather than project the breadwinner-husband and homemaker-wife as unique role ideals.

Much of the debate over women's roles and welfare reform during the last decade has dealt with crossover in sex roles, but only implicitly. Concern to strengthen the *father's place in the family* is at the bottom of efforts to redraw welfare policies so that they do not give the father incentive to desert. Concern to promote *mother's employment* lies just below the surface of the day-care debate and of various efforts to cut welfare costs by putting women to work. Although stated harshly, these expectations are actually in line with the direction of change in modern sex roles toward greater overlap. Traditional sex roles defined woman's place as in the home and man's position as the sole or primary breadwinner. Under the 1930s legislation for Aid to (for) Dependent Children (ADC, now AFDC), income support was provided to families on the theory that it substituted for the breadwinner who was the dead or the disabled father. The fact that in the last two decades growing numbers on the welfare rolls were not caused by death or disability but by divorce and separation has forced revision of the older theory.

Not only did the welfare reform attempts of the 1960s try to restore fathers to the home in order to restore their economic support to the family; but also, the arguments as to the deleterious effects of father absence for children and the positive benefits of father presence were to some extent psychological. The Moynihan report drew a connection between a child's performance in school and whether or not a father was present in the home. The children with fathers present did better (Rainwater and Yancey, 1967: 82- 84). Such an argument began to lay a foundation for crossover of the father into the realm of child care.

Also in the 1960s welfare rules began to change in a way that no longer treated women as categorically dependent. To put the matter in the words of Myrdal (1941; 1968: 332), there began to be questioning of "a social philosophy under which a woman should be able to claim lifelong support just because she has once been married." From society's point of view such a question was beginning to extend to mothers as well; the employment of mothers (albeit welfare mothers) began to seem reasonable. By 1962 and 1967, amendments of the Social Security Act required that a woman register for work or training in the Work Incentive Program. Contrary to expectations, more women voluntarily applied for admission to the program than there were places available; compulsion was unnecessary (Marmor and Rein, 1973: 11).

Welfare and income maintenance.

The program for Aid to Dependent Children at its founding in 1935 assumed an ideal family structure in which the father would earn adequate income. In the absence of that structure, ADC provided an alternative source of security. Thirty years later, however, the number of families receiving aid had grown so large that there was fear the program itself had created a class of people dependent on it.

First signs of crisis appeared in rising numbers of AFDC cases during the 1960s. Between 1950 and 1970 the number of families receiving assistance more than quadrupled, rising from two and a quarter million persons in 1950 to more than nine and a half million in 1970. By contrast the number of persons receiving public assistance because of age, blindness, or disability grew by only 150,000 persons, less than 4 percent (see Table 6).

The causes of the rapid rise in AFDC families are still not altogether clear. Rising divorce and separation rates make more people qualify. In addition, program rules may provide a perverse incentive to family splitting and a disincentive to work. Thus the variables in our present welfare structure that require critical attention are changes in eligibility, effects of the benefit structure on the family unit, and effects on work incentives.

Eligibility. Several aspects of eligibility explain changes in the welfare load: (1) whether a greater proportion of the eligible people choose to participate; (2) whether underlying changes in family structure make more people qualify for aid; and (3) how the rules for eligibility are stated. Particularly relevant to sex roles are the second and third of these elements. Changes in the actual number of people who qualify suggest significant changes in sex roles and family structure so as to produce many more female-headed households. Changes in eligibility requirements suggest a shift in the national consciousness so as to legitimate a wider variety of family types (and, implicitly, sex-role patterns) that qualify for aid.

Ross and Sawhill (1975: 104–118) quantified the relative contribution of all three factors in the rise of AFDC case loads. Surprisingly almost half the rise (46 percent) was due to increased participation by eligible people in the program (Boland, 1973). Another 27 percent of the growth was due to increase in the number of households headed by women. Only 7 percent was due to broader eligibility requirements.

Of particular interest to Ross and Sawhill were the effects that welfare regulations had on the stock and flow of female-headed

T A B L E 6. Number of Persons Receiving Public Assistance and AFDC for Selected Years 1950-1970

DESCRIPTION	NUMBER, IN THOUSANDS				
	1950	*1955*	*1960*	*1965*	*1970*
Persons receiving public assistance because of age, blindness, or disability	2,953	2,883	2,781	2,729	3,098
Families receiving AFDC	651	602	803	1,054	2,553
Total recipients receiving assistance under AFDC	2,233	2,192	3,073	4,396	9,660

SOURCE: Schultze et al. (1972: 188). Reprinted with permission from *Setting National Priorities: The 1973 Budget,* edited by Charles L. Schultze, Edward R. Fried, Alice M. Rivlin, and Nancy H. Teeters. Copyright © 1972 by The Brookings Institution.

households. While availability of AFDC did not appear to *cause* illegitimacy and family dissolution, it did appear to delay marriage or remarriage. AFDC could thus *maintain* more families with a female head than would otherwise be the case. This aspect of the eligibility issue ultimately links up with the question of whether the program has undesirable side effects on family structure and is considered in that connection.

Changes in the eligibility requirements are relevant to sex roles in connection with AFDC-UF, the program established in 1961 to broaden coverage to unemployed fathers. What is particularly interesting in connection with this program is the low rate of enrollment by those families who are eligible. Only twenty-five states have adopted the program (as compared with all fifty states who have adopted the regular AFDC). But even in those states with AFDC-UF, only 15 percent of the eligible families are enrolled.

Lidman (1975) speculates that nonparticipation in AFDC-UF is due to an unknown combination of gate keeping by welfare officials and voluntary nonparticipation by the eligible families. Although his explanation of voluntary nonparticipation is highly speculative, it sounds plausible and is directly related to sex-role patterns in poor families. He reasons that certification for eligibility entails such a confession of failure on the part of the male breadwinner that families avoid this degree of disruption in their internal division of responsibility if at all possible. Only where males can somehow perceive their unemployment as systemic and not personal, as among West Virginia coal miners, does the rate of participation rise. By contrast participation in the regular AFDC program is very high. Between 1967 and 1973 the rate rose from 63 to 91 percent of those people eligible who were enrolled, largely, it is believed, because of the activity of welfare-rights organizations among welfare mothers. Similar rights of unemployed fathers to claim welfare support is not yet, however, fully institutionalized.

Effects on family structure. The issue of eligibility is in some sense simply an example of a larger issue whereby welfare-benefit schedules vary for different types of family units. The family-unit rules that are intended to ensure equity among families unfortunately sometimes have the effect of creating undesirable incentives. For example, AFDC rules discourage marriage and encourage separation by making intact families ineligible for benefits. This is the nature of the family-unit problem in transfer programs: it involves questions of whether the individual, the family (legally or naturally related), or the household is the recipient of benefits. If an individual is the unit, and individual benefits are pooled by the family, the resulting total income for the family unit may be higher than needed, creating problems of equity among families. If the family is taken as the unit, formation of larger households with unrelated individuals may be discouraged. A number of goals—family cohesiveness, economy, equity, and freedom of association—all good, are in potential conflict (Lerman, 1973: 22-24). How to design a program with an optimum amount of attention to each goal is the problem. Current programs are said to treat many families and individuals unfairly, but no very clear alternatives have emerged since the 1972 defeat in the Senate of the Family Assistance Plan (F.A.P.), a program for a minimum income guaranteed to all families regardless of type.

Sex roles are directly relevant to family unit rules because they determine the underlying family dynamics by which responsibility for gaining income, pooling resources, and child care are carried out. Just as benefit schedules should take into account economies of scale and the actual patterns of family expenditure, as Rainwater (1974) has argued, or take into account sharing patterns within extended kin networks, as Blaydon and Stack (1977) have argued, so I would contend that such programs should also take changing sex roles into account. Remarkably little direct attention has been given to this issue. The following outline of relevant issues is therefore of necessity still in a formative stage.

In the past our welfare structure assumed that women were wives and mothers and, if not accompanied by a male breadwinner, should be treated as a dependent class. However, steadily increasing rates of marital dissolution force a reexamination of this perspective because they indicate that a different model may be more appropriate. Rather than uncontrollable factors such as death or disability, a woman's situation may be the product of some choice on her part, some preference to be independent of her husband. As a consequence the present welfare system must be revised so that the rules will better accommodate a variety of family models and their accompanying sex-role types—traditional, symmetrical, and transitional.

In 1935 most mothers of children who received ADC were widows. The program allowed mothers to stay at home to care for their children. By 1971, however, less than a quarter of all children receiving aid had fathers who were dead, incapacitated, or unemployed while three-quarters had fathers who had left their families through divorce, separation, or desertion (Rein and Wishnov, 1971; Lerman, 1973: 34). Many intact male-headed families of the same size and income received no benefits. The forces that had "broken" families between 1935 and 1970 had changed. The state's role as substitute for the husband-provider became more questionable as rates of family dissolution rose due to forces that might be interpreted as "choice" rather than uncontrollable forces such as death, disability, or unemployment. Between 1950 and 1974 the number of

Figure 3.   Growth of Female-Headed Families with Children (FHFCH) and Husband-Wife Families with Children (HWFCH) 1950-1974 (1950 = 100)

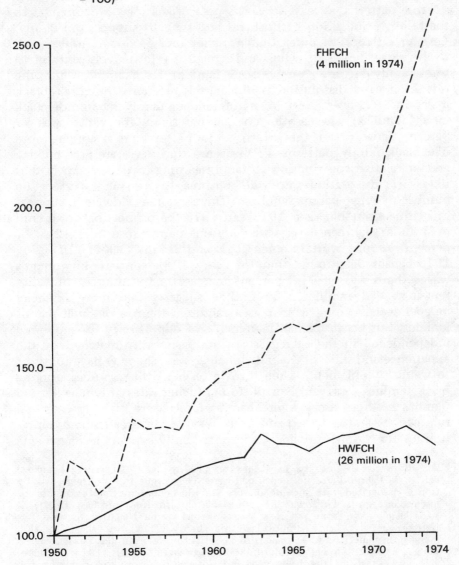

SOURCE: Carnegie Commission (1973:2). Reprinted with permission from *Opportunities for Women in Higher Education,* a report by the Carnegie Commission on Higher Education, © 1973 by McGraw-Hill Book Co.

female-headed families with children grew by 250 percent (see Figure 3).

At the same time the rates of dissolution appear related to sex-role patterns, at least to that aspect of sex roles which relates to the relative obligation of husband and wife to support the family. Lerman (1973: 22) notes that a higher rate of dissolution is positively correlated with a husband's relatively lower contribution to total family income. Among black families, for example, where the rate of marital dissolution is higher, the median earnings of black males in 1971 were 68 percent of median family income of black intact families, whereas the comparable figure for whites was 77 percent. If we reason that white family patterns are becoming more like black family patterns, in the sense that wives are now making greater relative contribution to family earnings, we may expect that the white dissolution rate will continue to rise, and with it the number of single-parent families.* There is some evidence to support this projection. Between 1970 and 1975 the proportion of all children under eighteen living with only one parent rose from 12 to 17 percent. Among white women Ross and Sawhill (1975: 117) using 1970 census data found that for every 10 percent rise in women's wages there was an 11.3 percent increase in the number of white female-headed families. The finding suggests that more financial independence among women is a factor in the rise of single-parent families. But because small increments of opportunity for economic independence in the aggregate are not necessarily matched by the experience and skills of the individual woman, she may have to resort to welfare supplements when thrown on her own resources. Among black families Ross and Sawhill found higher rates of female-headed families in those areas where benefit levels were higher. A general rule can be stated to explain these results: "greater income opportunities for women outside traditional family support arrangements

---

* An alternative hypothesis by Rainwater (1973) and Cutright and Scanzoni (1973: 56) should also be mentioned here. They argue that marriage dissolution is associated with income factors and that economic improvements for low-income units will lower the rate of dissolution. Ross and Sawhill (1975: 125) using data from the New Jersey–Pennsylvania Negative Income Tax Experiment give some support to this theory. They note that a $1,000 increase in benefits and extension of benefits to intact families was associated with a 2 percent lower dissolution rate. However, Lerman (1973: 22) convincingly questions the Rainwater and Cutright-Scanzoni thesis. I have followed his lead when he says, "Rainwater is probably closer to the right track when he emphasizes the relatively low income contribution of the father. [D]iminishing importance of the father's financial contribution to total income may be the more significant economic explanation of broken families than is low combined income of some husbands and wives relative to average family income."

are associated with higher proportions of women heading families"
(Ross and Sawhill, 1975: 115).

The association between women's opportunities for independent
income, marital dissolution, and rising AFDC levels may, of course,
be only transitional. Until such time as women are better educated
and trained before they marry, have more continuous participation
in the labor force, and are able to find placement in as wide a range
of jobs as men, with a pay scale higher than the present 60 percent of
men's pay, women may indeed have to rely on welfare benefits to
tide them over. And it will be some time before all these conditions
are obtained. The question then is how to change welfare policy in
the interim so that it will point toward egalitarian sex roles while at
the same time being able to accommodate women in transition
between traditional and future patterns.

Perhaps the best solution is one of neutrality toward sex-role
patterns much as Ross and Sawhill (1975: 178) recommend a welfare
policy that is neutral with respect to family form:

> The proper objective in structuring public policy with respect to family
> organization is neutrality. Policy should not attempt to promote one family
> living pattern over another, and policy directed at other purposes should be
> structured with an eye to minimizing incentives for people to live or appear
> to live in any particular family arrangement.

A standard of neutrality toward sex roles helps us to evaluate
various welfare and income-maintenance proposals. By this standard
a guaranteed annual income calculated on the basis of needs and
available to all families regardless of their form appears far superior
to such a program as AFDC. While AFDC implicitly reinforces the
model of the dependent wife and breadwinner husband, a program
such as the Family Assistance Plan would help intact families as well
as single-parent families, thus leaving open the possibility of including more unemployed fathers and more dual-worker families in
the program.

Effects on work incentives. Tax deductions for child-care costs
or provision of subsidized day care can enable a woman to enter the
labor force and thereby increase family income. Statistics since the
Second World War in fact suggest that a wife's earnings are often the
key to a family's relative ranking in total income. Between 1949 and
1966, for example, the percentage of husband-wife families in the
paid labor force increased by 15 to 18 percent in the three highest
income quintiles. But the rate of wife's labor-force participation in
the lowest and second-lowest quintiles increased by only 2 and 9
percent, respectively (Merriam, 1968: 749, Table 10). In 1966 of all
female-headed families where the woman did not work, was unem-

ployed, or worked only part of the year, 44 percent were poor.* But in such families where the woman was able to work all year, only 18 percent were poor (Merriam, 1968: 758, Table 17).

Increasingly, women have been defined as potentially "able-bodied" participants in the work force. Yet established employment and welfare policy put more barriers on the side of taking a job than on the side of receiving welfare. Betty Burnside (1968: 16-18), in a review of studies of women heading families with children who were receiving welfare, found that many such women were employable but that formidable obstacles stood in their way if they sought employment. Principal difficulties were poor health and domestic responsibilities, especially child care.

Rein and Heclo (1973), in an analysis of income support for female heads of families in Sweden, Great Britain, and the United States, found a noticeably higher proportion of such women in Sweden who had jobs. They concluded that public attitudes and institutional supports favored a higher work response in Sweden than in either England or America. In the latter two countries, prevailing ideology allowed a mother to engage in full-time housework in order to be with her children. In the United States there has been a running debate over whether public money should go to supporting a mother to stay at home with her children or should be used in combination with strategies to help the mother go to work.

Recently several negative income-tax experiments have provided a new source of data on the relation between welfare-benefit levels and women's work response. These experiments, conducted by the Poverty Research Center at the University of Wisconsin and the Stanford Research Institute, have collected data from families in four locations: Seattle, Denver, New Jersey-Pennsylvania, and Gary, Indiana. To date their most important single finding with respect to sex roles is that women's work response is lower (by about 20 percent) in those families who received cash payments as compared with the women in families of the control group who did not. The effect was particularly strong among white families, of whom 50 percent fewer of the wives were likely to work if the family received benefits (Office of Economic Opportunity, 1973: 34).

Manpower training programs have attempted to raise the level of work response among welfare recipients. Both the Work Incentive Program (W.I.N.) and the Manpower Development and Training Act established means by which women could train for employment. The

* Poverty was defined according to the Social Security Administration index that takes family size into account. The property level for a nonfarm family of four averaged $3,130 for 1962 incomes (Merriam, 1968: 755).

WIN program early admitted a considerably lower proportion of women than were in the eligible pool. (Over 90 percent of AFDC recipients are women, but only 62 percent of WIN enrollees were women.) Such discrimination was ruled against by the state Supreme Court of Washington in 1971 (*Thorn* vs. *Richardson*). Programs for on-the-job training under the Manpower and Development Training Act have proved more effective, however. The latter have a considerably better record on placement and pay of female graduates (Heclo et al., 1973: 36–43).

Work and earnings.

Observers of low-income families repeatedly emphasize the importance of jobs as the alternative to welfare. Where unemployment is high, job opportunities may be widened by government action. Training opportunities can improve the job seeker's chances in the labor market. Entitlements based on employment can bring income security, health care, and other benefits without carrying stigma. Recently there has been particular interest in whether women's work carries equitable entitlements in Social Security and private pension plans. A new issue is coverage of the homemaker, whether she should be covered in her own right, irrespective of her relation to her husband.

Manpower policy and women. The overall supply of jobs strongly affects women's earning power. During periods of national crisis such as wars and depressions, women are drawn into the labor market. Lipman-Blumen (1973) terms the phenomenon sex-role "de-differentiation." Needed resources are thereby released that enable either men or women to do those jobs which help society to adapt to the crisis. Chafe (1972: 161–173) in his history of women's roles from 1920 to 1970 shows how a great variety of day-care accommodations were erected during the Second World War to permit women to work in the defense plants. When the war was over, however, there was a precipitous drop in the number of nurseries and similar facilities. By 1970 the total capacity of the nation for day care was one-sixth what it had been at the height of the war. Roles that had been dedifferentiated and resources that had been freed for adaptation to crisis were suddenly reshaped along lines similar to the precrisis era (U.S. Civil Rights Commission, 1973).

In the postwar trend toward sex-role symmetry, roles have expanded to include a wider range of specialized tasks much as in the war era. Strains have inevitably followed, but without a sense of national crisis that would throw more resources into an effort to make women's jobs compatible with their family roles. Particular attention should be paid to two matters: flexible and part-time scheduling and supportive services such as maternity leaves or further opportunity for education.

Proposals for flexible hours aim to provide inducements both on the supply side (by attracting women into jobs with more convenient schedules) and on the demand side (by encouraging employers to make the efforts necessary to institute changes, and perhaps in the process create more jobs). Recent hearings before the Senate Subcommittee on Employment, Poverty, and Migratory Labor, chaired by Senator Gaylord Nelson, heard testimony on both these aspects of the issue. Such organizations as New Way to Work, supported by Bay Area governments in California, described their experience in setting up a talent bank, a job-sharing project, and workshops for job-seekers, 85 percent of whom were women (U.S. Senate, Committee on Labor and Public Welfare, 1976: 440–448). It was apparent that a few employers had made considerable effort to institute innovative schedules. Organizations such as Nestlé, Harman Industries (who make the Harman mirror in Bolivar, Tennessee), Northwestern Mutual Life Insurance, and the U.S. Civil Service Commission reported favorable results from innovations in scheduling. Across all U.S. industry it was reported that in 1974 one million workers had a four-day, forty-hour week. Within the Federal Government in 1976, 28,000 employees from thirty different organizations were engaged in some type of flexible hours program.

Several proposals for flexible hours were put forward in the Ninety-fourth Congress. The Part-Time Career Opportunities Act (H.R. 7174) would give federal agencies a mandate to make more part-time jobs available at all government service levels up to grade 15. The Flexible Working Hours Bill (H.R. 5451, Abzug) would permit all federal civil service employees to participate in an experimental two-year program with a variety of schedules, arrival and departure times, and flexible numbers of hours of employment. The Baltimore Office of the Social Security Administration has already tried such a plan, and in two locations productivity rose by 11 and 40 percent, respectively. Proponents of "flexitime" plans contend that adult men and women can better pursue both employment and household responsibilities. At the same time government can benefit by having experienced personnel available who might otherwise have to withdraw because of family obligations. As the White House Conference on Children in 1970 also suggested, such schedules also better permit a parent to handle children's illness or care when the child is home from school (Bernard, 1974a: 337).

A somewhat different though related issue is the right to maternity leave. A recent report by the Pennsylvania Commission on

Women finds that the United States lags far behind other countries in provisions for maternity leave, pay, and benefits. As early as 1911 the International Labor Organization set minimum standards for maternity protection that included: six weeks employment leave after" (*Women Today*, 1977*b*: 47- 48). Indeed, in the eyes of many breaks during work hours to allow nursing mothers to feed their infants; and medical care, cash benefits, and security of employment during the period of pregnancy. But the Pennsylvania Commission finds that "in this country we expect pregnant women either to withdraw from the labor force entirely, no matter what their financial needs, or else to be 'super women' and work up until the day they give birth and then be back on the job almost immediately after" (*Women Today*, 1977: 47- 48). Indeed, in the eyes of many the 1976 Supreme Court Decision in *Gilbert* vs. *General Electric* barring use of company medical disability insurance for workers' maternity costs was a movement away from the concept of guaranteed maternity protection.

Theoretically, according to dual labor-market analysis, one should not be surprised at difficulties in establishing flexible hours, part-time arrangements, or maternity leaves. The secondary sector made up of persons in part-time or seasonal jobs has always missed its share of promotions, salary increases, or coverage of benefits. It is the core full-time workers who typically benefit, while the part-time workers remain subject to the lower pay and insecurity of the periphery. To ease these tendencies, Urie Bronfenbrenner (1973: 169, 175) several years ago suggested a "Fair Part-time Practices Act" that would prohibit such institutionalized discrimination and would institute tax-benefit arrangements to employers who modify work schedules so that parents can be with their children when they return from school. Another purpose for which employers might institute more flexibility is to permit employees time to obtain further education through a leave of absence or some other arrangement (Bernard, 1974*a*: 337).

The question is how the cost of such programs will be borne. The Pennsylvania Commission on Women warns that, if an employer is forced to bear the full cost of maternity protection, the results may in the long run work against women's employment by making it too costly. The most workable arrangement seems to be one that relates such a program as maternity protection to the Social Security system, thereby dividing the costs among government, employers, and the insured persons themselves.

Work-related entitlements. If having a job is a principal key to health care, Social Security, pension funds, and training opportunities, then it is important to get a job that carries those benefits.

Because of their family responsibilities, women have generally had less access to jobs with fullest benefits. Many jobs in which women are found either do not entitle the holder to benefits such as unemployment insurance (domestic or part-time work) or do not entitle the holder to a very wide range of benefits. Laura Lein and her associates (1976) in their study of Boston area working-class families found that a wife might have worked in a series of part-time jobs because of family duties and therefore had accrued no benefits. A husband, on the other hand, might thoroughly dislike his job but stay in it because he could not afford to leave behind the benefits he had accumulated. If a family stays together, these differences are a basis for the division of labor between the couple. If, however, the husband is unemployed or disabled, or the marriage dissolves, and the wife is thrown on her own resources, sex-related differences in entitlements become a crucial factor in individual and family welfare.

One solution to women's relative disadvantage in benefits is increased employment of part-time workers and inclusion of them in insurance plans. This is difficult to do because employers use the dual-labor market (full-time workers at the core and part-time, part-year workers at the periphery) to meet peak demand at certain periods and yet keep costs at a minimum through ordinary times. It is likely that some system of tax incentives would be necessary to make employers adopt a more liberal program for part-time workers.

Another solution is through a more universal, more flexible, and portable insurance system. In several of her books, Jessie Bernard has mentioned the concept of "generalized drawing rights" first proposed by Gösta Rehn (1973) in a publication of the Common Market countries. European countries have given considerable attention to international social-security agreements that would permit a worker who has migrated from Italy to France, say, to draw benefits to which he may be entitled in either country (Social Security Administration, U.S. Department of Health, Education, and Welfare, 1973a). Rehn's suggestion is a variation on that theme, applied not to workers moving between countries but to workers moving within their own life cycle from one period of leisure, education, family building, or employment to the next. According to such a plan, the individual would deposit all those "fees, taxes [unemployment, Social Security], study-loan payments and other compulsory savings" in a single unified account. Future increases in hourly earning could also be directed into the account. In periods of nonemployment, childbearing, child care, education, leisure, and retirement, the person could draw on the account, much as a person has the right to borrow on private life insurance (quoted in Bernard, 1975: 274).

Another variation on generalized drawing rights is to allow workers to move more easily from one job to another without losing pension rights or health-care coverage that are vested in the former employer's institution. Known by the term *pension preservation*, this feature is also related to *vesting* (limitations on who is qualified) and *portability* (the right to transfer pension credits from one plan to another). Among all current private pension systems, the Teachers' Insurance and Annuity Association (T.I.A.A.) and the National Health and Welfare Retirement Association (N.H.W.R.A.) are the principal ones that allow a person to move from one educational or health and welfare agency to another and still retain and accrue benefits. If the person goes to work for a profit-making concern, benefits accumulated in the past are still retained (Srb, 1973). Outside of these examples other approximations are to be found in Keogh plans and Individual Retirement Accounts (I.R.A.s). A proposal is currently pending that would permit a housewife to accumulate benefits in an independent account.

Problems of vesting and portability are not women's alone; thousands of men share them. But to the extent that women are more likely to be in and out of the labor force and work in part-time positions that carry no pension rights, then pension issues are of heightened importance for them. Solutions entail redefinition of part-time status, discontinuity, and the housewife's role so that the true value of each is recognized and reflected in provisions that are more generous to women. Such issues as portability and coverage for the housewife lead directly to considerations of the treatment of women under Social Security and the issue of the so-called displaced homemaker.

Social Security. In our present national system of social insurance Social Security is the key element. Participation in covered employment permits the worker later to draw retirement, health, and disability benefits. Exclusion is a handicap. Housewives are included indirectly through a husband who is a covered employee, but a wife cannot claim her benefit if she is divorced from her husband before she has been married ten years.

Recently two aspects of Social Security coverage for the dependent spouse have been under intense scrutiny. The first concerns whether a husband has the same right as a wife to claim benefits as a surviving spouse. Several important Supreme Court rulings in the spring of 1977 have settled this issue. In *Califano* vs. *Goldfarb* and several follow-up judgments the court ruled that a surviving husband has the same right as a surviving wife to claim benefits without passing a dependency test.

The second issue is whether a homemaker should be able to qualify for Social Security benefits in her own right and maintain an independent account to accumulate credits toward such benefits on the basis of work performed inside the home. Both issues are of particular significance in connection with changing roles of women. The court's rule that a surviving husband might claim benefits under his employed wife's coverage is a clear example of the crossover principle. In this case crossover operates to allow the husband to claim a role that had once been confined to wives. On the other hand, the issue of independent Social Security coverage for home-makers is an example of crossover of another kind. Here the principle would operate to extend the pattern of covered employment into the wife's housekeeping realm where her work had formerly been defined as beyond the reach of economic calculation. Of course, in the latter case some important questions yet remain: how does one put a value on the housewife's earnings; when is she not working; when does she retire; who will make the contributions that fund the benefits?

Coverage of women under Social Security has gradually increased. Merriam (1968: 739) found that by 1966 a slightly larger percentage of older women received income from social security (85 percent) than did men (83 percent), as is shown in Table 7. Merriam concluded that though women's income as a percentage of men's had

TABLE 7. Percentage of All Persons Age 65 and Over Receiving Any Income for Selected Years 1947-1966

	NUMBER OF PERSONS, %				
GROUP	1947	1953	1957	1964	1966
Men, all sources	84	92	95	98	99
OASHDI*	14	38	59	78	83
Women, all sources	47	59	72	82	83†
OASHDI*	9	30	49	74	85†

*Old Age, Survivors, Health, and Disability Insurance.

†Slight discrepancy because data come from different sources; an aged husband and wife receiving joint benefit checks would be counted as two OASDHI beneficiaries, but census income data could show wife with zero income if she did not state that part of the check was hers.

SOURCE: Derived from Current Population Survey, Series P-60, and unpublished data from the Social Security Administration. This table taken from Table 2 in "Welfare and Its Measurement," by Ida C. Merriam, in *Indicators of Social Change: Concepts and Measurements*, edited by Eleanor Bernert Sheldon and Wilbert E. Moore, © 1968 Russell Sage Foundation, New York.

declined since 1947 because more women now have income, women as a group are still better off than they used to be. More of them are covered by Social Security; therefore, they have some money of their own and can be independent at least to a degree.

Some feminist organizations have, however, questioned whether women as a class have been discriminated against in the nature and amount of Social Security benefits that they receive. A special Task Force appointed by the Senate Special Committee on Aging chaired by Senator Frank Church (Democrat, Idaho) has recently studied current Social Security rules as they apply to women. The Task Force concludes that women workers as a group, though they do receive lower average benefits than men, are not being shortchanged. Because their benefits are higher in relation to the amount they paid into the system, women actually now receive a somewhat higher ratio of benefits to earnings than men. This is true because of their longer life expectancy and the weighted benefit formula. These advantages more than balance the greater number of secondary beneficiaries (wives or widows) generated by male workers (U.S. Senate, Special Committee on Aging, 1975: 16–18).

Among female beneficiaries, special issues arise for the single retired woman and the retired widow. The Senate Task Force proposes to raise the relative value of the single, retired woman's benefits by increasing the primary benefit based on earnings and lowering the proportion paid as a wife's benefit to couples. This solution would also keep the single person from having to pay a significantly higher proportional contribution than results for the couple. To help widows, the Task Force recommends that contributions before retirement be related to average wages, and benefits after retirement to prices. This would help widows whose retirement benefits may be tied to low earnings of a husband long deceased (U.S. Senate, Special Committee on Aging, 1975: 40–44).

How to credit household work on its own merits is still a resistant puzzle. There seems to be no objective standard available. One homemaker may do a good job; her role may be demanding. The work of another may be inadequate. There are no visible dollar earnings that set a value on the work. Yet definite savings accrue to a family from cooking, washing, and lodging in the household rather than eating every meal in a restaurant, sending all laundry out, or living in a hotel. Such savings are made possible through household work. But this work does not at present entitle a person to Social Security (health insurance or retirement benefits). Only through the covered employment of another worker can the homemaker be covered.

Kathryn Walker (1973: 473), in a statement of the American

Home Economics Association before the Griffiths Committee, summarized the problem as follows:

> Failure to include the value of household production in economic indicators has contributed to discriminatory national and state policies in such areas as taxation, employment, Social Security, insurance regulations, family welfare, and child-care services. Partly because policymakers do not realize that household work has monetary value, and that this value varies over the life cycle, employment policies for women have not been equitable with those of men.

Walker suggests as a first step toward valuation of household work the use of a method that has been adopted in the Netherlands. It uses substitute wage rates for employment at a job that the women is qualified to do and calculates the opportunity cost that results from her working in the home instead. The Netherlands in addition uses an arbitration board to evaluate the theoretical and practical knowledge required of the housewife to do the services she performs. Robert Lekachman (1975: 96) suggests another approach. Just as the national income-accounting system imputes rents to owner-occupied houses, a weekly salary could be imputed to the manager of the home. Even though a woman were not actually paid this salary, she would thereby become eligible for Social Security coverage in her own right, workmen's compensation, and full tax credit for the business expenses of administering the household. The technique would also be a correction to what Lekachman terms the "outrageously inequitable" difference in treatment given profit-making firms and households by the Internal Revenue Service. Just as businesses are allowed to deduct for tax purposes the costs of rent, light and power, and materials, he would advocate a system whereby the household could deduct the costs of homemaking and child care. A somewhat similar proposal comes from an economist, Jessie Hartline, who suggests that housewives should exchange services and pay each other salaries so that they can claim employment benefits such as Social Security and tax deductions for materials and depreciation costs (*New York Times*, 1976: 81).

One of the most inequitable aspects of Social Security coverage for women may be the low benefits due them even though they have been employed. Even if women average their earnings over twenty years to calculate their benefits, as present legislation allows, many will have years in which they had zero earnings because of discontinuity in their labor-force participation (O'Grady, 1977: 47-48). Coverage of the housewife would help fill those gaps.

Suggestions for crediting the work of the housewife are directly relevant to a new issue, the "displaced homemaker." The divorced or widowed woman without work experience but not on welfare has no particular supports to count on during her job training and placement. The U.S. Senate Special Committee on Aging (1975: 43) recently touched on the problems of this group but found that it could not agree on any proposal. Because homemaking is not defined as employment that accrues earnings, the committee found it difficult to assign responsibility for the problem. Should it be the Social Security Administration, Manpower, or other programs that should look after the interests of this group? No decision was reached. Early in 1977, however, Senator Birch Bayh (Democrat, Indiana) introduced the Displaced Homemaker's Act (S. 418) to accompany similar legislation sponsored by Representative Yvonne Braithwaite Burke (Democrat, California) in the House. The bill would establish centers in each state to aid women aged thirty-five to sixty-four who through most of their adult lives have been homemakers and who—through death, divorce, or the loss of traditional family income—find themselves cast into the labor market without training or marketable skills. In addition the bill calls for a study to be made of the appropriate procedures by which displaced homemakers could be included under unemployment compensation programs (*Women Today*, 1977a: 13-14).

In sum, treatment of women under Social Security is a guide to major sex-role trends in all the welfare legislation and work-related programs that have been reviewed here. The trend is away from policy based on a sex-typed two-role model of family life. It is being replaced by policies that imply a more flexible and interchangeable role structure where men can be both breadwinners and dependents and where women can be both homemakers and wage-earners. Efforts to keep fathers in the home, to put mothers to work, to adopt flexible hours for both parents, or to cover homemaking under Social Security all point to the growing interpenetration of the world of work and the world of the family. Accompanying this change is gradual legitimation of crossover between men's and women's roles.

COMMUNITY SUPPORTS TO THE FAMILY

Services for the family (such as child care) and economic support policies (such as welfare and work) are in turn embedded in a larger ecological and institutional framework. At the community level the family has access to resources and facilities by virtue of the fact that it is housed in a certain location and is part of larger social groups linked by residence. These ecological functions of the family are affected by social policies that determine the shape of the physical community, such as policies for housing or transportation. In addition a family's links to volunteer associations and neighborhood or kin networks affect the social environment in which it lives.

Changing roles of women are relevant to community context surrounding the family in two ways. First, women have traditionally been the key pillars on which many community services and volunteer activities have rested. Second, as women spend more time in the paid labor force the community work they have done will have to be performed in other ways.

Theoretically, on the basis of the crossover model, we would expect to find that women will increasingly seek to rationalize and routinize their informal service functions in the community. At the same time we would also expect to find on behalf of the larger bureaucratic society a new interest in the informal aspects of community life. It is too soon to report any more than impressionistic support for these hypotheses. Evidence for women's ambivalence toward the traditional volunteer role is plentiful in the women's movement (Carden, 1974: 117-118). On the other hand, apparently more men than in the past are interested in taking up volunteer roles (Loeser, 1974: 150). But further discussion of tendencies toward sex-role crossover in community activity will have to await more concrete data.

In the interim, we review here some of the positive roles that women have taken in furthering the larger ecological functions of the family. It is important to consider some of the changes in these roles that are likely to come about as a result of women's increased independence from the housewife role. In general, it appears that women have been able to organize cooperatively at the local level by building their own networks of exchange with women in other families. Now, as more of them are engaged in paid employment, there is pressure to institutionalize the services that they once performed on an informal basis.

Helena Lopata (1971) has shown how the occupational role of housewife is directly associated with the process of building community. In a large survey of Chicago-area housewives conducted during the early 1960s, Lopata discovered three major types of housewives, each different with respect to degree of community involvement. The first followed a narrowly defined "restricted" and passive role modeled after that of the traditional peasant wife. The second was in an emerging "uncrystallized" state where she was newly mobile but had not yet explored the full possibilities for expanding her role. The third "multidimensional" housewife took an active role in the community; her home no longer contained "wallbound" people, but she carried its concerns into the larger ideological and social world:

The modern housewife is very likely to define homemaking as extending into the community, mothering as utilizing all social facilities to expand the world of the young, and wifehood as many-leveled involvement in the various social roles of the husband.... [She is] most likely to think of self-expressive and creative roles for herself and to feel obligations to the society and the community in which she functions.... She gives the impression that the role of housewife provides her a base for building a many-faceted life, an opportunity few other vocational roles allow, because they are tied down to single organizational structures and goals.... The newly developing competent housewife is utilizing multiple sources for the acquisition of knowledge and skill in the performance of that role, building unique patterns of action from items selected out of the large fund of interpersonal and secondary material she now has available to her. [Lopata, 1971: 373–374]

Lopata's "multidimensional" modern housewife creates many of the community support systems that surround her family. For more than a century women have expanded their home concerns into the community through the women's missionary societies, temperance and suffrage organizations, and women's clubs. But the *institutionalization* of women's community efforts is a constantly advancing frontier. Women's community processes (volunteer work and neighboring) have helped to establish such community services as day care. Recent research also reveals that women have engaged in exchange of services and other informal mechanisms to give economic support to each other's families.

Network building and community services.

Lopata gives useful clues to the way that women build community networks and thereby provide social support to each other. They know how to neighbor with each other; they know interaction rituals. By contrast, the isolated are themselves deprived of easy contact with others, are unable to establish ties with others because they do not know how. Lopata (1973) illustrates these differences by a study of widows. Having lost a partner, some widows are able to make rational choices and chart a new life. Others continue living in a stable inner-city ethnic or suburban neighborhood where their life does not change much. But the isolated widow drops contacts when the couple ceases to exist and retreats into a narrow and restricted world. As in the contemporary women's movement with its sharing of information and resources, either in a neighborhood group, in caucuses, or among "new girl networks," widows appear to do better when in contact with others.

One of the most common practical applications of such cooperation has been among young mothers who work out arrangements for child care. A full history of the nursery-school movement and the ethnography of local women's individual efforts has yet to be written. But a theme running throughout is women's organizational prowess repeated in community after community to get a nursery school established, and their willingness to donate time and effort to make it go. The nursery schools and kindergarten movement began in the 1880s and reached a kind of plateau in the 1920s. Today the frontiers have moved to informally organized "play groups" handled on a rotating basis by mothers of preschool children and to organized day care. All major recent studies of day care show that a very large proportion of it is paid for "in kind." Parents pay very little for the care their children get, often from a relative or neighbor and usually for less than $10 a week. (Only 5 percent of all users pay more than that for day care.) Of the care children get in organized centers, about 25 percent is supported by the work of volunteers, donation of parent time, or the time of student trainees (Rowe and Husby, 1973).

Women's cooperative experience with child care teaches several lessons. First, cooperation succeeded when there was agreement that the service was both desirable and necessary; an ever rising proportion of mothers in the work force made child care more acceptable. Second, when women believed that such service was needed, they organized cooperatively to get it done, in the church basement, or at somebody's house. Third, once the informal organization had developed, the pattern could be repeated in other communities on an institutionalized basis. Now the number of places in nursery schools and kindergartens is more than four times what it was in 1961. Last, the question could then be raised whether child-care services should be made comprehensive and universal with support from the public purse.

Caring for very young children has up to now been considered a very private and personal affair. Local organization on a small scale therefore seemed appropriate to accomplish it. Women, by their ties to traditional family roles, had the opportunity to represent the interests of both worlds—individual-personal and community-associational. In the future some of the same techniques may be used by men and women to deal with other social challenges—being a single parent, being widowed, having a handicapped child, caring for an aged parent. Finding others with similar situations, making contact, and giving each other support is central to the process. Already, Parents Without Partners and the Widow-to-Widow programs in Boston and New York City have taken such steps (Lopata, 1973: 274-275).

Support networks and sharing.
Just as women's networks have started community-based services for individual care, so also can they form the basis for economic

exchange of goods and services among families. The best description that we have of this process is to be found in Carol Stack's (1974: 33, 41) account of the swapping relationships among poor black people: "They trade food stamps, rent money, a television, hats, dice, a car, a nickel here, a cigarette there, food, milk, grits, and children." In the words of Ruby Banks, one of Stack's informants:

> When I first met you, I didn't know you, did I? But I liked what you had on about the second time you seen me, and you gave it to me. All right, that started us swapping back and forth. You ain't really giving nothing away because everything that goes round comes round in my book. It's just like at stores where people give you credit. They have to trust you to pay them back, and if you pay them you can get more things.

These swapping relationships have implications for economic support policies because they make clear what a vital part of the poor family's survival is provided by a large network of kindred or friends. Persons who are penniless can ask for help from others with whom they have an exchange relationship. The goods received are a needed supplement to welfare benefits. Blaydon and Stack (1977) therefore persuasively argue that welfare rules should be drawn so as not to impair informal exchange by expecting it to be formalized through legal marriage, formal recognition of paternity, or fixed demands for support payments from an absent father.

What have these exchange relationships to do with women's roles? While the sociological literature makes clear that such exchanges between kin occur in all segments of the society, their implications for women's roles have not been clearly spelled out. It is clear, however, that women are usually at the focal points of these networks.

The full potential of such nonmarket exchange has yet to be explored. Because modernization of society has always seemed to point toward increasing formality and universalism in exchange, sociologists and economists are not in the habit of imagining that the trend might go in the opposite direction, toward increase in non-monetized transactions. Yet at least one economist with a futurist bent, Scott Burns (1975: 22), finds that it is precisely the household economy that is the most rapidly growing sector of the true gross national product. A calculation of estimated national household income as $212 billion in 1968 showed that women were responsible for almost 75 percent, or $155 billion. Moreover, the largest single contribution to this figure was made by so-called unemployed house-wives, who were responsible for $124 billion. These figures pose an interesting question: will this proportion of the presently nonmone-tized part of the household economy hold steady, rise, or fall as more women enter the labor force? If the household economy continues to grow, as Burns speculates, an interesting related question will be whether informal economic exchange at the community level will also gain greater public recognition and response.

Women's networks and family policy.

In her pioneer work on family policy, Alva Myrdal (1941; 1968: 133-153) devoted a whole chapter to whether help should be given families "in cash or in kind." Myrdal's position was that it is easier in the short term to give cash allowances. But in the long run cooperative services organized on a community level are more efficient, more equitable, and better fitted to a preventive rather than merely curative strategy. Cash allowances, because they favor the needy population, fail to win the support of the middle class. Only community services such as schools or health clinics that serve everyone can mobilize cooperative effort, achieve economies of scale, and avoid attaching stigma to any one group.

Community provision of services is relevant to women's role in the family in two ways. Not only have women, by their voluntary efforts and lobbying, helped to create the services. But also, it is principally women who stand to benefit when certain family functions that had to be done by each woman privately are undertaken by collective effort. A review of various communal and family experiments reveals that some of their principal innovations had to do with sharing precisely those functions that were formerly the duty of women within each private household. Examples come from the cooperative living arrangements and child-care practices of China, Russia, the Israeli kibbutz, and various historical and contemporary communes in the United States. Out of these accounts emerge several important elements of family life that typically are rearranged to serve a number of individuals rather than the single nuclear family. The dimensions are (1) housing arrangements and architectural design, (2) meals and food service, (3) sexual privileges and family planning, (4) child care, (5) health care, and (6) emergency help during illness or other crises.

Yet the very nature of the collective experiments makes them difficult to apply in America. Collective organization of child care in Russia or China arouses fear in many Americans that the system requires group conformity. The Israeli kibbutz is composed of like-minded individuals committed to a set of religious, political, or moral values that would be difficult to duplicate on a large scale anywhere. In her study of communes in America, Kanter (1972: 229) concluded that

> there are no answers in the experience of utopian communities of the past or present to the problem of building large and complex structures out of

very small ones. . . . In fact, history suggests that the process by which large social systems are constructed out of small, intimate ones is the very process by which Gesellschaften (societies or complex organizations or cities) are created out of Gemeinschaften (close, family-like communities). How communal and utopian ideals can be translated to large-sized units is therefore a difficult question, one that will be found often by social planners of the future.

Kanter suggests that the process may in part be accomplished by a federation of small communes to "create cooperative facilities and organizations that are suitable to urban life, such as schools, day-care centers, food cooperatives, or shared enterprises that employ commune members." In this connection, network building and community volunteer effort by women continue to be important processes to create services in kind (such as day care) that will support sex-role liberation in the future.

CHANGING LEGAL DEFINITIONS OF THE FAMILY

As the activities of the family have changed—in care of its dependents, in gaining a living, and in use of community services—the law of the family has begun to reflect the change. The change is momentous for women, because it is built on an underlying process of individuation in marriage with greater autonomy and risk for each partner that such a shift implies. Evidence for this transformation in legal perspective may be found in the rules governing marriage, divorce, and the rights of children.

Deregulation of marriage.

Present trends are interpreted by Glendon (1976: 701) to be evidence of the growing delegalization of marriage. The current tendency within the law is to define the marriage relationship as one between autonomous partners rather than as either a hierarchical or a communal relationship. In Glendon's opinion this tendency toward dejuridification of marriage may be as important as the shift during the Reformation of jurisdiction over matrimonial causes from the ecclesiastical authorities to the state.

In a growing number of instances the law appears to look on marriage as a matter of individual choice, not to be barred by excessive preliminary formalities nor to be dissolved with undue difficulty. In the last few decades, impediments to marriage such as racial restrictions, simultaneous marriage, and rules prohibiting marriage between cousins or certain other degrees of kin have gradually been chipped away. In the process it has become clear that the state's posture toward the family has changed to allow greater rein to individual choice and feeling. As a consequence it has become increasingly difficult to distinguish among the married state, the umarried state, and informal de facto marriages (Glendon, 1976: 684).

For women this change has had a two-sided effect. On the one hand, the state is now less likely to treat the wife as a dependent, subject to the husband's authority. On the other hand, the state is also less likely to guarantee that the marriage will form the basis of a husband's obligation to support the wife if the marriage fails. Rules for management and taxation of the marital property are moving toward recognition of the spouses' interests as separate and autonomous. Women interested in keeping their own names have revived the ancient common-law practices that allow the matter to be regulated by individual choice rather than the more recent custom of taking the husband's name. The right to determine domicile is no longer so clearly the province of the husband. The principle has been upheld and extended that a wife can independently establish her own credit (Babcock et al., 1975: 575–645).

It logically follows from the reconceptualization of marriage that the husband is less likely to be expected to provide alimony and child support at the time of divorce. The pressure to provide support will be divided between his old family and his new family if he remarries. The consequence of women's new thoretical autonomy in marriage is autonomy also after divorce.

In the past, marriage was to be for life, and divorce was an adversary procedure based on finding fault with one of the partners. Custody of children, alimony, and support were commonly awarded in ways that acted as a penalty for the person whose behavior presumably led to the breakdown of the marriage. In 1970, California revised its divorce law to replace the idea of fault with the principle of irretrievable breakdown of the marriage as a sufficient ground for divorce. Since then a number of other states have adopted some form of no-fault divorce; some others have a combination of no-fault grounds and fault grounds. Reform had established the no-fault concept as early as 1915 in Sweden and 1922 in Denmark. England passed its Divorce Reform Bill in 1969 (Rheinstein, 1970: 167; Kay, 1970: 275).

Associated with divorce reform has been a steady rise in the divorce rate and declining compliance with child-support orders. In addition, the award of spousal support appears on the way to becoming the exception dictated by a particular need rather than the expected rule (Jones et al., 1976: 29, 31; Glendon, 1976: 706). In California in 1970, the first year under the new no-fault law, the number of dissolutions rose by 46 percent. In Michigan in 1972 the rate rose by 10 to 15 percent (Wheeler, 1974: 27, 34). Goddard, a California lawyer, surveyed judges' attitudes toward support payments under the new law and concluded, "There is some evidence which suggests that the Act has accelerated the growing tendency among judges to award a wife less support, both in duration and amount." One judge explained, "Changing social attitudes about divorce and about employment of women have, in reality, been reflected increasingly in the courtroom, where it is often expected that a wife not encumbered with small children should contribute her own support. . . . The increasing emphasis on equality for women is incompatible with the idea of life-long spousal support from an ex-husband" (Wheeler, 1974: 60).

Even before divorce reform, data on actual settlements for child support showed women bearing a heavy burden of responsibility. As is shown in Table 8, the probability of a divorced woman's collecting any child-support money was less than half within two years of the court order and declined to only 20 percent at the end of ten years (Weitzman, 1974: 1195). A recent review of national data by the Urban Institute finds that approximately 20 percent of all divorced and separated mothers receive child support regularly; 7 percent receive it sometimes; and only 8 percent of all divorced women receive alimony (Jones et al., 1976: 29).

TABLE 8. The Probability of A Divorced Woman's Collecting Any Child Support Money

Years Since Court Order	Number of Open Cases	Full Compliance %	Partial Compliance %	No Compliance %	Nonpaying Fathers Against Whom Legal Action Was Taken %
One	163	38	20	42	19
Two	163	28	20	52	32
Three	161	26	14	60	21
Four	161	22	11	67	18
Five	160	19	14	67	9
Six	158	17	12	71	6
Seven	157	17	12	71	4
Eight	155	17	8	75	2
Nine	155	17	8	75	0
Ten	149	13	8	79	1

SOURCE: Weitzman (1974: 1195). Based on Eckhardt (1968: 473). Reprinted with the permission of *Social Problems*, the Society for the Study of Social Problems, and Kenneth W. Eckhardt.

Nature of the state's involvement.

Accompanying the deregulation of marriage by the state is, however, a new and, Glendon finds, somewhat ominous involvement of the family with the state. If a husband is now less likely to be expected to support his wife and children by a former marriage, those families not otherwise able to sustain themselves after separation and divorce will have to rely on public support. Since the state has goot out of the marriage business and made divorce easier, the number of single-parent families has grown, and with it the welfare load. Moreover, the proportion of AFDC families receiving monthly contributions from absent fathers has dropped from 31 percent in 1961 to 13 percent in 1973 (Jones et al., 1976: 29). Apparently among fathers there has been a declining sense of obligation to pay. Some states have also been lax in their enforcement of support orders.

The 1975 Social Security Amendments Law made it possible for states to enforce support orders by placing at their disposal the forces of the Social Security system, the Internal Revenue Service, and various other federal agencies to ensure collection. Thus while the state has taken less interest in the rules governing marriage and dissolution, it is taking an ever more active role in pragmatic economic matters related to family obligations. In addition, as regards children, emerging state policy has broadened to approximate the status of the child born outside the marriage to that of one born within, thereby making dependency rather than legitimacy and family relationship the basis for entitlement to benefits (Glendon, 1976: 714- 715).

The future of marriage for women.

These trends pose at least two extreme possibilities for women. On the one hand, they can become dependent on the state. But the role of being a poor welfare mother wangling her way through the system does not seem particularly easy or pleasant. Or women can prepare themselves for both the autonomy and the risks of the new form of marriage. Two types of suggestion have recently been put forward to prepare for these eventualities—the so-called marriage contract and divorce insurance.

In the face of the implied dependence of women in the older marriage form some reformers have suggested a new form of more explicit partnership arrangements that they have termed "marriage contracts." Each member of the pair would ahead of time rationally examine his or her reciprocal obligations to the other with respect to such important decisions as location of residence, decision to have children, duration of the agreement, and ownership and control of wages and property (Weitzman, 1974). Such explicit discussion of terms would presumably alert each party to many of the hidden and unexamined expectations of traditional marriage. The financial aspects of marriage and divorce would be treated like a business partnership from the beginning: each partner who brings certain assets, debts, and earning capacity would list these facts explicitly and discuss directly how financial decisions will be made and who will exercise control. Although such "contracts" have no legal standing so far as enforcement by the state is concerned, discussion of them has nevertheless served an important function in the popular understanding of marriage, particularly in the women's movement. The idea of a negotiation process ahead of time makes clear that each member of the pair, the wife especially, must develop skills and earning capacity. Each can also at that time negotiate the details of responsibility for child care and household chores (Babcock et al., 1975: 647-658).

Some type of family insurance is another possible hedge against the future. Several years ago Alice Rossi pictured the possibility of a national insurance contract or policy for childbirth and child rearing (Bermant, 1972: 44). She was interested in providing a way for women to maintain some connection with the occupational world during the experience of maternity. Like Jessie Bernard's "generalized drawing rights" or Alice Cook's "Maternal Bill of Rights," such a plan would facilitate women's movement from one type of activity to another over the life cycle. In the context of changing marriage and divorce patterns child-rearing insurance might have attraction for fathers as well.

A system of divorce insurance proposed by a lawyer, Dianna DuBroff in New York State, would pay a lump sum during the transitional period after divorce when the family's economic resources are most strained. Pursuit of alimony and support payments would no longer be necessary. New York State Senator Halperin, who has supported the idea, suggests that divorce insurance could be publicly funded, possibly through Social Security or income taxes, in the long run saving money on Aid to Dependent Children payments under the welfare system (Wheeler, 1974: 70). Others have proposed that the portion of family income allotted to the wife as salary could be used to buy an annuity or pension that might be drawn upon if the marriage were dissolved (Babcock et al., 1975: 722-729).

With this brief review of changes in the marriage law and their impact on women, our consideration of changing family policies draws to a close. The large trends in each major area of family policy—child care, economic support policies, community organization, and family law—obscure many complex details. Nevertheless, several strong threads run through the whole: women's roles are becoming more differentiated, offering a wider variety of choice, more autonomy, and independence both within and outside the family. A corresponding change is occurring in men's roles: though the trend is less pronounced because their range of choices has always been broader, their roles are being enlarged to include behaviors and statuses similar to those of women in the past; they are more likely to be encouraged to take a role in child care; they are less clearly obligated to support the family than was once the case. Overall, the involvement of the state in support of essential family functions is becoming more pronounced. Whether we define these trends as good or bad depends on the larger context within which they are viewed. That judgment requires consideration of the major value alternatives.

VALUE ISSUES IN FAMILY POLICY

A radical value position in the field of family policy is quite in contrast with its counterpart in the field of work. In the case of the economy an enlarged role for women is congruent with humanization of the workplace, the recovery of intimacy and fuller expression of feelings among workers, and the endowment of work with larger meanings.

In matters of family life, however, strange as it may seem, the radical value alternative points toward rationalization, monetization, and individuation—all those aspects of the differentiation process that in history were linked with development of the economy during the nineteenth century. In the case of the family this shift is congruent with an enlargement of women's role beyond the family and the rationalization of tasks still left within it. Is this not exactly the way national policy toward the family is developing? But is it the way that the families and the nation should be going? Much to my surprise, when I worked out these questions on a theoretical basis, I found that the logic of the crossover model led directly to monetization of the nurturant functions that the family performs, calculation of the nonmarket work that the household produces, and calculation of the economic value inherent in community support systems. All these unpaid activities that families do are now being discovered to have a value, and a price is being put on them.

In her recent review of research on the relation of work to family, Rosabeth Kanter (1977: 71-74) made a plea for looking at work and intimacy not as distinct structures or activities located separately in the firm or the household but as processes or modes of organizing experience that can be found everywhere. This perspective leads her to examine the growing rationalization that has occurred in the household since the turn of the century, from the inception of home economics to modern-day interest in wages for housework and time-limited, highly specific "marriage contracts." These developments show that "even though most housework has remained private and privately 'managed,' it is interesting to note that 'industrial' standards were applied and continue to be applied to activities in the family sector."

Such rationalization of the family sector contrasts with an opposite trend toward humanization in the workplace. A new work ethic is in the making "due to the expansion of the service sector, with its people-serving, relational ethos. Such an ethic may function to reintroduce or reinforce familial kinds of relationships and familial norms in the occupational world" (Kanter, 1977: 76).

Kanter's perspective is distinctively contemporary: it manifests the new ideology of crossover between family and work; it criticizes the older mode of thought typified by Parsons and Bales's (1955: 35–131) theory that expressive concerns are confined primarily to the family and instrumental pursuits to work. By contrast, the contemporary perspective perceives the possibility of interpenetration between work and family. It is precisely compatible with differentiation of sex roles when segregated activities become more interchangeable.

If rationalization of the family is an appropriate alternative value, what then does it entail? In actuality, the processes outlined in the foregoing review of developing family policy are some examples of what is possible: Nurturant functions such as child care can to some extent be universalized and routinized in ways that are beneficial not only to a family with working parents but to their children as well. Nonpaid productive activities of wives and mothers in the home and the community are proposed as bases for entitlements to benefits such as Social Security. The individuation of the marriage relationship leads to proposals for negotiation of the marriage agreement and better provision for future contingencies such as dissolution.

At first glance the rationalization process may seem to *cause* the "breakdown of the family," a phenomenon that many believe is an actual fact. Bronfenbrenner (1975) and the National Research Council (1976) detail the declining number of adults in the family, the increase in single-parent families, the rise in juvenile delinquency, child abuse, and suicides among children. In fact, however, it may be that rationalization, at least in the state's response to the family, is the only workable *solution* to these problems. It may be that the state should invest *more rather than less* in the family. If it can only learn how to do so properly, investment in support of families with children would probably save more in the long run than the cost of ameliorating social problems later on.

At the moment we are instead spending proportionately much more on our older people than on our children, partly because their benefits under Social Security are defined as earnings-related rather than as welfare. But we may well ask whether this is either equitable among age groups or a wise order of priorities for investment in the future. Mary Jo Bane (1976: 119–120) provides a striking comparison between the amounts now spent on benefits for the aged as compared with benefits for dependent children:

> In 1973, $51 billion was paid out in Social Security payments, most of it to old people. Only $7 billion was paid out to Aid to Families with Dependent Children (AFDC). The total amount of AFDC funds paid out in 1973 averages only $700 per child in female-headed families.
>
> Between 1965 and 1973 . . . the relative income position of the aged has improved, while the relative income position of children in one-parent families has deteriorated. In 1967 the income of white female-headed families averaged 57 percent of the income of white male-headed families; the income of black female-headed families averaged 52 percent of the income of black male-headed families. By 1973 . . . the average income of white female-headed families was 49 percent, that of black female-headed families only 44 percent, of the income of male-headed families. In contrast, the relative income position of the aged improved over the period 1967 to 1973. Families with heads over 65 had incomes of 51 percent of the median family income in 1967 but 55 percent of the median family income in 1973. The improvement in the position of the aged and deterioration in that of female-headed families is consistent with trends in transfer payments.

How can the situation be changed? How can society give up its tendency to romanticize families of the past and instead learn to pursue a rational attitude toward its investment in the family of the present and future? The investment should pay off in lowered crime rates, less rather than more dependency, and improvement in the total quality of life. But some changes in political and psychological attitudes are necessary to get this transformation under way. What is needed is an enlargement of identification so that the whole nation sees all the children as its children.* This process has occurred in several other instances, particularly in the evolution of aid to the aged under the Social Security program, and in the modernization of developing countries.

---

* I am indebted for this insight to Alva Myrdal, with whom I discussed the concept of family policy in February 1976.

The institution of Social Security is one of the most striking examples of enlargement in identification. Responsibility of individual children to their parents was transferred to a national system whereby all children paid into an insurance scheme that supported a whole nation of parents. A number of states had laws requiring that adult children support their indigent parents. The requirement of filial support affected administration of benefits under two programs for the aged. A dependent parent could qualify for benefits under an adult child's Old Age, Survivors, and Disability Insurance (O.A.S.D.I.) if it could be proved that the parent was receiving at least one-half of his support from the worker prior to the worker's death.* In 1960 there were 35,000 such dependent parents receiving benefits. Second, an older person not covered by OASDI could qualify for Old Age Assistance (O.A.A.). In 1960, 2.4 million persons received some sort of minimum assistance from OAA. However, at that time fourteen states required a contribution from adult children in order for a parent to receive benefits from the program. Twenty-one other states required a contribution by law or policy but did not withhold assistance if children did not meet their responsibilities. Only sixteen states did not have a support requirement (Schorr, 1960: 20–24).

The requirement of support from adult children raised questions similar to those at present surrounding collection of payments from absent AFDC fathers: Did the children live out of state? Were their incomes sufficient to support a dependent parent? Did the needs of their own families and children compete with the needs of their parents? Were collection efforts worthwhile to stem the rise of soaring public-assistance costs? In his review of evidence on these matters, Alvin Schorr (1960) concluded that most children whose dependent parents were eligible for assistance were not themselves able to provide needed support. Moreover, the requirement that children support their parents or take them into their homes probably introduced undesirable strains in the relationship. The parents' dependency could result in a loss of dignity and capacity for independent action. Furthermore, many old people preferred to live alone and direct their own affairs.

That this set of issues is no longer salient in the 1970s is testimony to a dramatic shift in the national attitude toward support of the elderly. Not only is the demographically eligible pool for these

---

* The one-half–support rule resulted from a 1950 amendment to the law. In the 1939 law that introduced availability of benefits to dependent parents of a worker, the parents had to be *wholly* dependent on and supported by the worker. In 1946 the law was liberalized to say "*chiefly* dependent upon and supported by" (Schorr, 1960: 20–21).

two types of assistance probably proportionately smaller now because more old people qualify for OASDI in their own right as workers. But also there is a greater feeling, I judge, that the old are *entitled* to a pension that supports them in some kind of independent dignity rather than in a dependent relation to their children. This shift in attitude could be termed a universalization of the concept of filial responsibility. The obligation to support the old is transferred from the shoulders of their particular children to the entire younger generation.

Such enlargement of identification and consciousness may be a distinctively modern accomplishment. In *Becoming Modern* Inkeles and Smith (1974: 315) note that men in the six developing societies that they studied, who had been exposed to the factory system or other modernizing influences, had broader loyalties than the traditional men. The modern men were in addition more knowledgeable about the community and nation, whereas the traditional men were preoccupied with their own personal and family affairs to the exclusion of larger community concerns. This example suggests that experience with rationalized, differentiated social structures need not lead to anomie or isolated self-interest, but may in fact have exactly the opposite effect. A kind of affective flexibility may emerge that allows people to transfer affection and loyalty from their particular origin group to others with whom they live and work. Such flexibility, analogous to the freedom of contract that Max Weber (1947: 275) associated with a rational economy, is a prerequisite to the identification with others that permits very diverse groups to join in common cause.

While a broadened concern for others may be necessary to accomplish a national policy for investment in family life, it appears that a different manifestation of rationality is required at the household level. In the past housewives did good works. In Jessie Bernard's language, they inhabited the "integry," where, unlike the economy, work was done for love rather than money.* Now what is happening is the monetization of the integry (Bernard, 1974b: 81-93). In a society where people tie identity and value to their work, not their family, the housewife was in a particularly weak position (Berley, 1973: 47; O'Toole, 1973: 104). But now efforts are being made to calculate the value of housework in the national accounting system (Kreps, 1971: 68; Walker, 1973). Soon there may also be an interest in putting a price on women's network-building activity and volunteer work in the community (Loeser, 1974: 117-131).

---

* Bernard uses this term originally coined by Kenneth Boulding to refer to all those productive activities that go unpaid because they fall outside the boundaries of the market economy.

To the extent that a price is put on her component activities, the housewife's role is differentiated to reveal a set of discrete tasks that are capable of being performed by others. Then the stage is set for greater interchangeability of tasks between those located inside the home and those outside, between those done ordinarily by women and those done by men, between the jobs that are paid and unpaid. The flexibility in task assignment that results from this differentiation process can have many consequences—for reallocation of tasks between the public and private sector, between the sexes, and among different age groups. One possible outcome is greater sharing of work, family, and community-building tasks between men and women over the life span.

Possibly the sharing will be accomplished by a *timing* pattern that governs when men and women undertake these different tasks. Married women may engage in more family activity and network building in their early years. Single women and men may concentrate more narrowly on work while they are young, then turn to some of the generative tasks of caring for friends, helping protégés, and taking on community responsibility when they reach their middle years.

By this perspective the regeneration of family and community values will come about through choice of the individual rather than by force of parochial or family tradition or an ascribed age or sex role. The work-involved individual, programed not just for individualistic and self-interested success, will say after a period of productive achievement, "there's more to life than that." The family-involved individual (usually a woman entering her middle years), programed for more than selfless devotion to the needs of others, will say, "I want to do my own thing for a while." Greater flexibility in age and sex roles over the life span will facilitate these shifts. At the same time these individual choices should be able to accomplish the family and community work that needs to be done.

SUMMARY

Family policy is now an issue because traditional family patterns have changed. As family life has become more differentiated from work life and women have moved into the paid labor force, there are no longer clear solutions to certain age-old questions. Who will do the work of the family? Who will support the wife and children if a marriage dissolves? Who will provide a woman old-age security or other benefits if her entire productive life has taken place within the confines of the home?

In the context of family life, sex-role differentiation leads to greater individuation and autonomy for women. It also encourages rationalization of family tasks. As household work is divided into discrete tasks to be shared, women are freed for other activities outside the home, and it becomes more possible for others to help with work that once fell entirely on them.

Rationalization is now evident at four different levels of family life and social policy: (1) nurturance and personal services; (2) economic support mechanisms; (3) family involvement in the community; and (4) changing legal obligations of family members. Current developments in each of these fields reveal two complementary themes—one, the continuing individuation and growing autonomy of women; the other, their need to develop compensating schemes for mutual help, support, and sharing through such mechanisms as social insurance and informal networks.

Current proposals for child care reveal steady pressure to find ways that the family (particularly the mother) can share her nurturant responsibilities with others. Some proposals rely on government or community provision of the service; others depend on informal helping arrangements between relatives and neighbors.

Welfare programs and other forms of economic support for women and families are also in flux. The welfare regulations are being revised to accommodate a wider variety of families than was possible using a single model of the breadwinner-husband and homemaker-wife. As these changes occur, there is effort to support both the father's role as parent and the mother's role as worker. In addition, there is a search for ways to give women work-related entitlements that are based on their actual productive contributions in the home.

The family's location in the community is a springboard for developing intermediate support mechanisms that require neither complete family self-sufficiency nor full dependency on the state. Through experiments with various neighborhood helping arrangements and volunteer groups, women have learned how to provide social services to each other. Often these informal organizations and networks have then become the basis of formal organizations in the wider community. In that respect they provide a model for possible future community-based supports to the family.

Finally, changing legal definitions of the family allow women more autonomy, but they also impose new risks. No longer is the husband seen as the only major source of support for wife and children. As a result the state may have to take a larger role in such matters as child support. Or individuals may devise their own intermediate solutions such as "marriage contracts" or marriage insurance to prepare themselves for future uncertainty.

All of these developments in specific areas of family policy raise larger philosophical and moral questions. Are these changes for the good? Will they serve the best interests of individuals and families?

To the extent that autonomy and individuation are accompanied by a wider identification of each person with other people, the trend toward rationalization of family concerns can be welcomed. The nation is gradually learning to think of all its elders and all its children as members of the public household.

In addition, new attempts to put value on unpaid family work will make it more feasible for both women and men to move back and forth between the public and private spheres. In the process greater flexibility will be realized not only in the roles of each sex but also in the activities permitted them at different stages in the life cycle.

What in the end is desired is a better balance between humane and material concerns in the lives of all individuals and families. While humanization and job enlargement are needed in the work place, the direction of progress in families is somewhat different. There, the trend to be encouraged is toward greater individuation and autonomy for every member. With humanization of work and rationalization of family life, the whole society will once again be in a position to rejoin work with leisure and love.

REFERENCES FOR CHAPTER FIVE

Babcock, Barbara A.; Freedman, Ann E.; Norton, Eleanor H.; and Ross, Susan C. 1975. *Sex Discrimination and the Law: Cases and Remedies.* Boston: Little, Brown.

Bane, Mary Jo. 1976. *Here to Stay: American Families in the Twentieth Century.* New York: Basic Books.

Barth, Michael C.; Carcagno, George J.; and Palmer, John L. 1974. *Toward an Effective Income Support System: Problems, Prospects, and Choices.* Madison, Wi.: Institute for Research on Poverty, University of Wisconsin.

Berley, Edith Radlich. 1973. "In Defense of Housewives." Letter to *Radcliffe Quarterly* 37 (June): 47.

Bermant, Gordon. 1972. "Alice Rossi, Sisterhood Is Beautiful." *Psychology Today,* August, pp. 40–46ff.

Bernard, Jessie. 1974a. *The Future of Motherhood.* New York: Dial Press.

——. 1974b. "Women and New Social Systems." In *The American Woman: Who Will She Be?* Edited by M. L. McBee and K. Blake. Beverly Hills, Ca.: Glencoe.

——. 1975. *Women, Wives, Mothers.* Chicago: Aldine.

Bettelheim, Bruno. 1969. *The Children of the Dream.* New York: Macmillan.

Blaydon, Colin C., and Stack, Carol B. 1977. "Income Support Policies and the Family." *Daedalus* 106 (Spring): 147–161.

Boland, Barbara. 1973. "Participation in the Aid to Families with Dependent Children Program (AFDC)." In *Studies in Public Welfare*. Paper no. 12 (Part I). Joint Economic Committee, U.S. Congress. Washington, D.C.: U.S.G.P.O.

Bowman, Elizabeth. 1975. "Child Care Programs: Federal Role Debated." *Congressional Quarterly Weekly Report* 33 (December): 2635–2640.

Bronfenbrenner, Urie. 1970. *Two Worlds of Childhood: U.S. and U.S.S.R.* New York: Russell Sage Foundation.

———. 1973. "Statement." In *American Families: Trends and Pressures, 1973: Hearings before the Subcommittee on Children and Youth, U.S. Senate.* Washington, D.C.: U.S.G.P.O.

———. 1975. "The Next Generation of Americans." Paper presented to the Annual Meeting of the American Association of Advertising Agencies, March 20, Dorado, Puerto Rico.

Burns, Scott. 1975. *The Household Economy: Its Shape, Origins, and Future.* Boston: Beacon Press.

Burnside, Betty. 1968. "Employability of AFDC Mothers in Six States." *Welfare in Review* 9 (July-August): 16–19.

Caldwell, Bettye M. 1973. "Infant Day Care—The Outcast Gains Respectability." In *Child Care—Who Cares?* Edited by P. Roby. New York: Basic Books.

Carden, Maren Lockwood. 1974. *The New Feminist Movement.* New York: Russell Sage Foundation.

Chafe, William. 1972. *The American Woman: Her Changing Social, Economic, and Political Roles, 1920–1970.* New York: Oxford University Press.

Chilman, Catherine. 1973. "Public Social Policy and Families in the 1970s." *Social Casework* 54 (December): 575–585.

Cutright, Phillips, and Scanzoni, John. 1973. "Income Supplements and the American Family." In *Studies in Public Welfare.* Paper no. 12 (Part I). Joint Economic Committee, U.S. Congress. Washington, D.C.: U.S.G.P.O.

Dickinson, Katherine. 1975. "Child Care." In *Five Thousand American Families—Patterns of Economic Progress.* Vol. 3: *Analyses of the First Six Years of the Panel Study of Income Dynamics.* Edited by G. J. Duncan and J. N. Morgan. Ann Arbor, Mi.: Survey Research Center, University of Michigan.

Drucker, Peter F. 1976. "Pension Fund Socialism." *Public Interest* 42 (Winter): 3–46.

Eckhardt, Kenneth W. 1968. "Deviance, Visibility, and Legal Action: The Duty to Support." *Social Problems* 15: 470–477.

Finer, Morris. 1974. *Report of the Committee on One-parent Families*, vol. 1. London: Her Majesty's Stationary Office.

George, Victor, and Wilding, Paul. 1972. *Motherless Families.* London: Routledge and Kegan Paul.

Giele, Janet Zollinger. 1961. "Social Change in the Feminine Role: A Comparison of Woman's Suffrage and Woman's Temperance, 1870-1920." Ph.D. dissertation, Radcliffe College.

——. 1971. "Changes in the Modern Family: Their Impact on Sex Roles." *American Journal of Orthopsychiatry* 41 (October): 757-766.

Gil, David. 1973. *Unraveling Social Policy*. Cambridge, Ma.: Schenkman.

Glendon, Mary Ann. 1976. "Marriage and the State: The Withering Away of Marriage." *Virginia Law Review* 62 (May): 663-720.

Heclo, Hugh; Rainwater, Lee; Rein, Martin; and Weiss, Robert. 1973. "Single-parent Families: Issues and Policies." Working paper prepared for the Office of Child Development, Department of Health, Education, and Welfare.

Herzog, Elizabeth, and Sudia, Cecilia E. 1973. "Children in Fatherless Families." In *Child Development and Social Policy*. Edited by B. M. Caldwell and H. N. Ricciuti. Chicago: University of Chicago Press.

Hoffman, Lois W., and Nye, F. Ivan. 1974. *Working Mothers*. San Francisco: Jossey-Bass.

Howell, Mary C. 1973*a*. "Employed Mothers and Their Families (I)." *Pediatrics* 52, no. 2 (August): 252-263.

——. 1973*b*. "Effects of Maternal Employment on the Child (II)." *Pediatrics* 52, no. 3 (September): 327-343.

Inkeles, Alex, and Smith, David. 1974. *Becoming Modern: Individual Change in Six Developing Countries*. Cambridge, Ma.: Harvard University Press.

Jones, Claire Adaire; Gordon, Nancy M.; and Sawhill, Isabel V. 1976. *Child Support Payments in the United States*. Washington, D.C.: Urban Institute.

Jusenius, Carol L., and Shortlidge, Richard L., Jr. 1975. *Dual Careers: A Longitudinal Study of Labor Market Experience of Women*, vol. 3. Columbus, Oh.: Center for Human Resource Research, Ohio State University.

Kay, Herma Hill. 1970. "A Family Court: The California Proposal." In *Divorce and After*. Edited by P. Bohannan. Garden City, N.Y.: Doubleday-Anchor.

Kanter, Rosabeth Moss. 1972. *Commitment and Community*. Cambridge, Ma.: Harvard University Press.

——. 1977. *Work and Family in the United States: A Critical Review and Agenda for Research and Policy*. New York: Russell Sage Foundation.

Keyserling, Mary Dublin. 1972. *Windows on Day Care*. New York: National Council of Jewish Women.

Kreps, Juanita M. 1971. *Sex in the Marketplace: American Women at Work*. Baltimore, Md.: Johns Hopkins University Press.

Lein, Laura. 1976. "The Working Family Project." Research Colloquium at Radcliffe Institute. Wellesley, Ma.: Center for Research on Women.

Lein, Laura; Durham, M.; Pratt, M.; Schudson, M.; Thomas, R.; and Weiss, H. 1974. *Final Report: Work and Family Life*. Cambridge, Ma.: National Institute of Education Project no. 3-33074, Center for Study of Public Policy.

Lekachman, Robert. 1975. "On Economic Equality." *Signs* 1, no. 1 (Autumn): 93-102.

Lerman, Robert I. 1973. "The Family, Poverty, and Welfare Programs." In

Studies in Public Welfare. Paper no. 12 (Part I). Joint Economic Committee, U.S. Congress. Washington, D.C.: U.S.G.P.O.

Levinson, Perry. 1969. "A Study of Children in AFDC Families." *Welfare in Review* 7, no. 2 (March-April): 1–9.

Lidman, Russell M. 1975. "Why Is the Rate of Participation in the Unemployed Fathers Segment of Aid to Families with Dependent Children (AFDC-UF) So Low?" Madison, Wi.: Institute for Research on Poverty, University of Wisconsin.

Lipman-Blumen, Jean. 1973. "Role De-differentiation as a System Response to Crisis: Occupational and Political Roles of Women." *Sociological Inquiry* 43, no. 2: 105–129.

Loeser, Herta. 1974. *Women, Work, and Volunteering.* Boston: Beacon Press.

Lopata, Helena Znaniecki. 1971. *Occupation Housewife.* New York: Oxford University Press.

———. 1973. *Widowhood in an American City.* Cambridge, Ma.: Schenkman.

Lubove, Roy. 1968. *The Struggle for Social Security 1900–1935.* Cambridge, Ma.: Harvard University Press.

Marmor, Theodore R., and Rein, Martin. 1973. "Reforming 'The Welfare Mess': The Fate of the Family Assistance Plan, 1969–1972." In *Policy and Politics in America: Six Case Studies.* Edited by A. P. Sindler. Boston: Little, Brown.

Merriam, Ida C. 1968. "Welfare and Its Measurements." In *Indicators of Social Change.* Edited by E. Sheldon and W. E. Moore. New York: Russell Sage Foundation.

Mill, John Stuart. 1869; 1970. "The Subjection of Women." In *Essays on Sex Equality* by John Stuart Mill and Harriet Taylor Mill. Edited by A. S. Rossi. Chicago: University of Chicago Press.

Moynihan, Daniel Patrick. 1965; 1967a. "The Negro Family: The Case for National Action." In *The Moynihan Report and the Politics of Controversy.* Edited by L. Rainwater and W. Yancey. Cambridge, Ma.: MIT Press.

———. 1965; 1967b. "A Family Policy for the Nation." In *The Moynihan Report and the Politics of Controversy.* Edited by L. Rainwater and W. Yancey. Cambridge, Ma.: MIT Press.

———. 1968. "Introduction." In *Nation and Family: The Swedish Experiment in Democratic Family and Population Policy* by Alva Myrdal. Cambridge, Ma.: MIT Press.

Myrdal, Alva. 1941; 1968. *Nation and Family: The Swedish Experiment in Democratic Family and Population Policy.* Cambridge, Ma.: MIT Press.

National Research Council. 1976. *Toward a National Policy for Children and Families.* Washington, D.C.: National Academy of Science.

National Women's Political Caucus. 1975. *Newsletter,* 3 December.

New York Times. 1976. "Employment Plan for Housewives Is Urged by a Rutgers Economist." 12 December, p. 81.

O'Grady, Regina A. 1977. "Social Security Coverage for Caring Work." Waltham, Ma.: Heller School, Brandeis University, mimeographed.

Office of Economic Opportunity, U.S. Department of Health, Education, and Welfare. 1973. *Summary Report: New Jersey Graduated Work Incentive Experiment.* Washington, D.C.: U.S.G.P.O.

Oppenheimer, Valerie. 1970. *The Female Labor Force in the United States.* Berkeley, Ca.: University of California at Berkeley, Population Monograph Series, no. 5.

O'Riley, John. 1976. "The Outlook: Review of Current Trends in Business and Finance." *Wall Street Journal,* 2 February, p. 1.

O'Toole, James. 1973. "Statement." In *American Families: Trends and Pressures, 1973: Hearings before the Subcommittee on Children and Youth, U.S. Senate.* Washington, D.C.: U.S.G.P.O.

Parsons, Talcott, and Bales, R. F. 1955. *Family, Socialization and Interaction Process.* New York: The Free Press.

Rainwater, Lee. 1973. "Poverty, Living Standards, and Family Well-being." In *Studies in Public Welfare.* Paper no. 12 (Part II). Joint Economic Committee, U.S. Congress. Washington, D.C.: U.S.G.P.O.

———. 1974. *What Money Buys.* New York: Basic Books.

Rainwater, Lee, and Yancey, William, eds. 1967. *The Moynihan Report and the Politics of Controversy.* Cambridge, Ma.: MIT Press.

Rapoport, Robert, and Rapoport, Rhona. 1965. "Work and Family in Contemporary Society." *American Sociological Review* 30 (June): 381–394.

Rehn, Gösta. 1973. "For Greater Flexibility in Working Life." *OECD Observer,* February, pp. 3ff.

Rein, Martin, and Heclo, Hugh. 1973. "What Welfare Crisis?: A Comparison among the United States, Britain, and Sweden." *Public Interest,* no. 33 (Fall), pp. 61–73.

Rein, Mildred, and Wishnov, Barbara. 1971. "Patterns of Work and Welfare in AFDC." *Welfare in Review* 9 (November-December): 7–12.

Rheinstein, Max. 1970. "Divorce Law in Sweden." In *Divorce and After.* Edited by P. Bohannan. Garden City, N.Y.: Doubleday-Anchor.

———. 1972. *Marriage, Stability, Divorce, and Other Law.* Chicago: University of Chicago Press.

Ross, Heather L., and Sawhill, Isabel V. 1975. *Time of Transition: The Growth of Families Headed by Women.* Washington, D.C.: Urban Institute.

Rossi, Alice S. 1964. "Equality between the Sexes: An Immodest Proposal." In *The Woman in America.* Edited by R. J. Lifton. Boston: Beacon Press.

Rowe, Mary P., and Husby, Ralph D. 1973. "Economics of Child Care: Costs, Needs, and Issues." In *Child Care—Who Cares?* Edited by P. Roby. New York: Basic Books.

Rubin, Lillian Breslow. 1976. *Worlds of Pain: Life in the Working Class Family.* New York: Basic Books.

Sandberg, Elisabet. 1975. *Equality Is the Goal: A Swedish Report.* Stockholm: Swedish Institute.

Schorr, Alvin. 1960. *Filial Responsibility in the Modern American Family.* Washington, D.C.: Social Security Administration, U.S. Department of

Health, Education, and Welfare.

Schottland, Charles I. 1967. "Government Economic Programs and Family Life." *Journal of Marriage and the Family* 29 (February): 71-123.

Schultze, Charles L.; Fried, Edward R.; Rivlin, Alice M.; and Teeters, Nancy H. 1972. *Setting National Priorities: The 1973 Budget.* Washington, D.C.: Brookings Institution.

Sidel, Ruth. 1972. *Women and Child Care in China.* New York: Hill and Wang.

Smelser, Neil J. 1959. *Social Change in the Industrial Revolution.* Chicago: University of Chicago Press.

Social Security Administration, U.S. Department of Health, Education, and Welfare. 1973a. *International Social Security Agreements.* Research Report no. 43. Washington, D.C.: U.S.G.P.O.

———. 1973b. *Social Security Programs in the United States.* Washington, D.C.: U.S.G.P.O.

———. 1975. *Social Welfare Expenditures, Fiscal Years 1970-1975.* Washington, D.C.: U.S.G.P.O., DHEW Publication no. (SSA) 76-1170.

Srb, Josetta H. 1973. "Portable Pensions." *Key Issues Series*, no. 4. Ithaca, N.Y.: New York State School of Industrial and Labor Relations, Cornell University.

Stack, Carol B. 1974. *All Our Kin: Strategies for Survival in a Black Community.* New York: Harper and Row.

Steiner, Gilbert. 1976. *The Children's Cause.* Washington, D.C.: Brookings Institution.

Streuer, Erika. 1973. "Current Legislative Proposals and Public Policy Questions for Child Care." In *Child Care—Who Cares?* Edited by P. Roby. New York: Basic Books.

Talmon, Yonina. 1972. *Family and Community in the Kibbutz.* Cambridge, Ma.: Harvard University Press.

U.S. Civil Rights Commission. 1973. "Fact Sheet no. 8: Working Mothers with Children under 18." In *Eight Fact Sheets; Statistics on Effects of Racism and Sexism in the United States.* Washington, D.C.: U.S.G.P.O.

U.S. Senate, Committee on Labor and Public Welfare. 1976. *Changing Patterns of Work in America, 1976: Hearings before the Subcommittee on Employment, Poverty, and Migratory Labor.* Washington, D.C.: U.S.G.P.O.

U.S. Senate, Special Committee on Aging. 1975. *Women and Social Security: Adapting to a New Era.* Washington, D.C.: U.S.G.P.O.

U.S. Senate, Subcommittee on Children and Youth. 1973. *American Families: Trends and Pressures, 1973.* Washington, D.C.: U.S.G.P.O.

Walker, Kathryn E. 1973. "Statement of the American Home Economics Association on 'National Income Accounting of Household Work'." In *Economic Problems of Women: Hearings of the Joint Economic Committee of Congress*, part 3. Washington, D.C.: U.S.G.P.O.

Weber, Max. 1947. *The Theory of Social and Economic Organization.* Translated by A. M. Henderson and T. Parsons. Edited by T. Parsons. New York: The Free Press.

Weinstein, Fred, and Platt, Gerald M. 1969. *The Wish to Be Free.* Berkeley, Ca.: University of California Press.

Weitzman, Lenore J. 1974. "Legal Regulation of Marriage: Tradition and Change." *California Law Review* 62 (July-September): 1169–1288.

Wheeler, Michael. 1974. *No-fault Divorce.* Boston: Beacon Press.

Wilensky, Harold. 1975. *The Welfare State and Equality.* Berkeley, Ca.: University of California Press.

Women Today. 1977a. "Bayh Introduces Displaced Homemakers' Legislation." Vol. 7, no. 3 (7 February): 13–14.

——. 1977b. "Pennsylvania Commission Study Shows U.S. Lagging in Maternity Protection." Vol. 7, no. 8 (18 April): 47–48.

Woolsey, Suzanne H. 1977. "Pied Piper Politics and the Child-Care Debate." *Daedalus* 106 (Spring): 127–145.

Wynn, Margaret. 1970. *Family Policy: A Study of the Economic Cost of Rearing Children and Their Social and Political Consequences.* Hammondsworth, Eng.: Penguin.

6

EDUCATION FOR THE FUTURE

Is liberation to be achieved by mastering the skills of the dominant culture, or is it to be found through achieving the capacity to confront, analyse, and articulate another kind of experience which commands no place in the institutions which are the guardians of the dominant culture? . . . On the one hand, to be in command of that culture women must master skills in mathematics and the hard sciences. . . . On the other hand, if these skills are to be applied in a manner which draws on the inner springs of creativity, they must be acquired in a way which is no threat to the female identity. This can be achieved by an educational experience which is critical of many of the assumptions of a male-controlled culture and which takes the female as the norm rather than the deviant exception to the life of the mind

—Jill Conway, "Coeducation and Women's Studies . . . ," 1974.

Education is the crucial process in preparing for the future. The fate of individuals hangs on each person's preparation for occupation or larger lifetime career. The fate of society hangs on the creation and transmission of a culture that will provide solutions to such general problems as the diminishing supply of resources or the twin economic hazards of inflation and recession.

The present educational disadvantage of women highlights problems in both these realms. Because women are currently so underrepresented in politics and the high reaches of all business and nonprofit institutions, one possible explanation is that they have chosen not to strive for such positions. Another explanation is that they have been denied equal access and opportunity for education. Still a third possibility is that the culture that educational institutions project is out of date, training women for a world where occupational and family life are still segregated by sex roles, rather than permeable to crossover.

As is hinted in the epigraph to this chapter, women's lack of progress through the educational system may not alone be the fault of women's effort or of unequal opportunity to learn. It may be the

242

imbalance of the culture itself, its heavier emphasis on "male" rather than "female" elements, that puts women at a disadvantage. By this analysis the problem of educational equality between the sexes will not be solved simply by raising women's aspirations or by countering "discrimination" with compensatory educational programs for women. Rather, if a skewed set of values lies at the root of the problem, the educational establishment will have to reassess its heavy emphasis on scientific and occupational advancement and perhaps give greater place to familial, community, and humanistic concerns.

On the average in every major sector of society, women's educational attainments are considerably lower than men's. Being a female is second only to being from a lower socioeconomic status (S.E.S.) as a handicap for getting education beyond high school. On the basis of the experience of 9,000 randomly selected Wisconsin high-school students whom he surveyed first in 1957 and then in 1964, William Sewell (1971: 795) concluded that the educational chances of males were uniformly greater than the opportunities of females at every socioeconomic level:

> For example, in the bottom SES category males have a 26% advantage over females in obtaining any further schooling, a 58% advantage in attending college, an 86% advantage in completing college, and a 250% advantage in attending graduate or professional school. Likewise, in the top SES category males have an 8% advantage over females in obtaining any further schooling, a 20% advantage in attending college, a 28% advantage in completing college, and a 129% better chance of attending graduate or professional school.

Among women who have attained higher degrees, there is still inequality in the academic positions where they are employed. They tend to be found in the lower ranks and in the faculties of less prestigious institutions than men of comparable educational background. Moreover, between 1930 and 1970, the position of academic women appeared to worsen rather than improve. During those four decades a progressively smaller proportion of women received doctorates and were employed in the highest academic ranks.

These facts depart from the common-sense American expectation that women have equal educational opportunity with men. How can the women's record be explained? One theory emphasizes the importance of women's choice. In her book *Academic Women* Jessie Bernard (1964) described the differences in men's and women's academic careers at that time. Although she suspected that the women who received the doctor's degrees were superior insofar as "test-intelligence" was concerned because they were more highly selected, she found them less productive, as measured by published work, than men. The phenomenon was explained by the type of college or university where the women were found—not in the first-rate research-oriented institutions but in the less prestigious schools oriented primarily to teaching. Bernard (1964: viii) raised the possibility that their location was the result of women's choice:

> The question must then be raised as to why women tend to gravitate to positions which are less productive. It seems to me that many women have a vocation for college teaching; they prefer teaching to research. The concept of the fringe benefit status has interested me; it is a status whose occupants are on the fringes of their professions but of enormous benefit to the institutions that use them. These women combine marriage, children, and career according to one pattern.*

A decade after Bernard's book, Thomas Sowell (1976: 63) noted that "never married" academic women do relatively well in salary and publications. He then concludes:

> This lends support to the belief that many able women end up in non-research institutions because they prefer teaching. . . . The preference of women for teaching over research is not only significant in itself, [but] it also highlights the crucial element of individual *choice* which is routinely ignored in syllogistic arguments which go directly from statistical "under-representation" to "exclusion" or "discrimination."

On the other hand, forces external to the woman can be used to explain the same phenomena. Using data from the Wisconsin high-school seniors, William Sewell notes that girls in high school have higher aspirations than boys, but parent and peer pressure and the realities of marriage concerns in the immediate post-high-school years apparently interfere with girls' educational attainment. Sewell (1971: 804) endorses policy recommendations that not only would assure equal access by women to fellowships and other forms of financial support but would also allow women greater flexibility to combine education with family responsibilities over their life span:

> Existing rules covering residency, full-time enrollment, and credit transfers should be revised to accommodate the needs of women, and child-care centers should be established at all institutions. Also there should be courses in the schools to broaden the conceptions of male and female roles, to reduce prejudice toward women's full participation in all institutional areas, and particularly, to further encourage women to form (and men to accept) a life-long commitment to educational and occupational achievement.

* Bernard also notes another emerging pattern: women combining marriage, children, and career not in the fringe institutions but in the mainstream. These women, unlike the earlier generation described in *Academic Women*, appear to represent the emerging pattern of family-work crossover that becomes much more prominent after 1964 when Bernard's book appeared (Bernard, 1964: 231-240).

In the final analysis it is probably a combination of individual "choice" and institutional "discrimination" that determines the course of a woman's educational career. Both are summed up in the prevailing societal expectations about the connection between work and family life. Until recently educational assumptions were based on a sex-segregated model of work and family responsibility in which women's primary commitment was to the family and men's to work. Now those assumptions are undergoing a severe strain as more women enter the labor force and emphasize *both* family and career achievement. The educational system is subject to pressure for change that will accommodate the new pattern.

The educational response required is one typically found where social differentiation makes demands for a higher level of performance. Talcott Parsons (1966: 22) has described the process as *adaptive upgrading*.* Differentiation of tasks within sex roles has resulted in the phenomena demonstrated in earlier chapters—women's greater participation in politics, their massive entry into the labor force, and their rationalization of household duties and child care to permit greater activity outside the home. Such differentiation makes greater demands not only on the individuals involved but also on collectivities such as the workplace and the household to facilitate movement across the boundaries of private and public life. The problem for society is one of *generalizing* and transmitting these individual and collective capacities so that the means for adaptation do not have to be learned *de novo* by every single man and woman attempting the new behavior, or by every single firm or household where they work or live. The educational system is society's specialized institution for discovering and codifying such new knowledge and passing it on.

---

* According to Parsons (1966: 22),

> Adaptive upgrading requires that specialized functional capacities be freed from ascription within more diffuse structural units. There is, then, a reliance upon more *generalized* resources that are independent of their ascriptive sources. For these reasons, differentiation and upgrading processes may require the *inclusion* in a status of full membership in the relevant general community system of previously excluded groups which have developed legitimate capacities to "contribute" to the functioning of the system. . . . Differentiation, particularly, produces cases in which the necessities for integrating newly differentiated subsystems strongly indicate including otherwise excluded elements.

Although the example Parsons gives is inclusion of inferior social classes in the definition of citizenry, his theoretical formulation is applicable, I believe, to the situation currently obtained in the sex-role revolution. The ability to combine "masculine" or "feminine" knowledge or traits such as child care or paid employment are in my view examples of newly "specialized functional capacities."

The present chapter describes educational adaptation to the new pattern of sex-role differentiation. It begins with a historical review of the circumstances that contributed to a decline in women's portion of higher degrees and top faculty and administrative posts after 1920. It then considers four different aspects of the contemporary educational scene that appear to impede women's educational progress. At the *personality* level early socialization appears to put a brake on women's educational motivation and occupational aspiration; remedies include greater involvement by both parents in the child-rearing process, exposure to a greater variety of sex-role possibilities, and greater opportunity for education over the entire life span. Within the *classroom* setting formal education may carry subtle messages that reinforce women's tendency to cluster in "women's" fields and curtail their achievement; suggested remedies involve special encouragement to women in "men's" fields and provision of female role models in the classroom and in the administration. The more general context of women's education is regulated by *administrative* policies that set schedules, rules for granting credit, and other conditions that affect the ease with which women students (and men as well) can integrate educational demands and family obligations. Administrative policies of another kind affect the hiring and promotion of women faculty. For improving the attainments of both students and faculty, suggested reforms in administrative standards would institute both greater flexibility and enlargement of the criteria by which performance is judged. Finally, encompassing all these other levels are the ultimate *value* commitments of the educational enterprise. Critical scrutiny for balance between emphasis on "male" and "female" behavior styles and types of knowledge should be given such commitments. In this realm reform proposals suggest that, where the emphasis on one type is lopsided, it should be enlarged to include the other.

HISTORY OF WOMEN'S EDUCATIONAL DISADVANTAGE

It is immediately apparent to anyone who reviews the statistics that girls have done relatively well at primary and secondary school levels. In 1890 over 60 percent of high-school graduates were female. As more boys finished high school and thereby attained educational equality with girls, their percentage approached that of girl graduates and in 1968 stabilized at nearly 50 percent, where it remains today (Women's Bureau, 1969: 13). However, women show a lower proportional representation in education after high school.

The proportions of women enrolled in post-secondary education rose briefly during the 1920s and 1930s, then dipped during the postwar period and did not regain previous levels until after 1970. Women comprised 34 percent of the undergraduate student body in colleges and universities in 1920. After the war, with the sharp rise in returning veterans, women's proportion fell to nearly 20 percent, not to return to its prewar level until 1970. Among those getting doctorates in 1970, only 13 percent were women as compared with 15 percent in 1920 (Women's Bureau, 1969: 16; Carnegie Commission, 1973: 2, 35, 37). While the *number* of women obtaining degrees at all levels increased steadily during this century, the percentage of degrees awarded to women dropped particularly sharply after the Second World War (Burstyn, 1973: 175). The GI Bill undoubtedly contributed to this shift, as probably did heavy government funding of science and engineering. Only in the late 1960s and early 1970s, coincident with the new woman's movement, did increased entry of women begin to redress the imbalance. The numbers of women entering law and medical schools showed a sharp rise after 1970. Medical schools reported that at least one in six of all 1973-74 freshmen were women (Association of Governing Boards, 1974: 3). Although in 1971 women lawyers constituted only 3 percent of the profession, they made up 10 percent of the entering class (as compared with 5 percent in 1967) and probably today are at least 20 to 30 percent of the student body in most law schools (American Bar Association, 1972). In 1974-75 the proportion of doctorates awarded to women rose to a new high of 21 percent.

The proportion of women schoolteachers and administrators also changed after the early part of the century. In 1928, for example, 55 percent of all elementary school principals were women. By 1973 that figure stood at only 20 percent (Estler, 1975: 364). The percentage of women on school boards also declined. In Boston, for example, women held four of the twenty-four school board positions from 1890 to 1894. After 1905 when the board was reduced to five members, only one token woman (except for 1952-53) served until 1976-77, when at least two members of the board were again women (Kaufman, 1978).

Among women faculty in colleges and universities the drop in percentages was less striking but nonetheless real. Women had constituted 26 percent of faculties in 1920, 27 percent in 1930 and 1940, but stood at only 22 percent in 1976. Perhaps more surprising and ominous still are the short-term declines that have taken place just within the last decade. The proportion of tenured women faculty fell from 17 percent in 1971-72 to 13 percent in 1974-75 (Kilson,

1976). However, an optimistic interpretation could be that an older cohort of professionals has just passed through the system and a new wave of recruits is about to achieve greater representation than before. Between 1959 and 1975 the number of women at the instructor level rose from 29.3 to 47.8 percent.

Proportions of women top administrators in higher education also declined rather sharply in recent years. Between 1969- 70 and 1971- 72 the number of women presidents fell from 11 percent to 3 percent, and the number of women academic deans from 18 to 2.8 percent. Many small Catholic women's colleges closed. In 1973 the total number of women's colleges in the country was one-half the number in 1960, down from 298 to 146. Moreover, movement toward coeducation was associated with a decline rather than an increase in women faculty (Kilson, 1976).

Explanation for these trends is tied to four other phenomena that changed during the same period. First, an "academic revolution" altered the nature of higher education to give it a highly specialized focus on scientific advancement. Second, the enormous growth of educational institutions resulted in a sifting out of leading universities known for their research, which were distinguished from a wide range of other schools primarily devoted to teaching. Third, a rising marriage rate among the college-educated women diminished the number of unmarried women who had traditionally been more likely to complete the doctorate or reach high faculty rank. Finally, the broadening of educational access to include more people of lower socioeconomic background probably increased the number of women seeking higher education either for practical vocational reasons or to enrich women's conventional role within the home. The net effect of all these changes was evident in women's failure to sustain a record of improved performance both as students and as faculty.

EFFECTS OF THE ACADEMIC REVOLUTION ON WOMEN

In their recent studies of changes in the American university, the historian Veysey (1965) and the sociologists Jencks and Riesman (1968) and Parsons and Platt (1973) are all generally agreed that a transformation has occurred since the turn of the century. Colleges and universities have tried to emancipate themselves from the parochialism of region, ethnicity, or religion. Devotion to service, vocation, or the arts has been forced to take second place behind the central and most prized activity of "doing research." Measurement of a university's quality or the prestige of its faculty increasingly relies on the number of faculty publications rather than on quality of teaching or loyal service to the institution.

In Parsons and Platt's phrase (1973: 38), the university has become ever more single-mindedly devoted to the value of "cognitive rationality." That is, science and knowledge gained by the scientific method has gained ascendancy over expressive concerns or more intuitive modes of knowing. In addition, the transmission of knowledge through teaching has been downgraded relative to the pursuit of new knowledge that will help illuminate still unsolved problems. These trends coupled with the realities of women's other roles have apparently worked to women's disadvantage. Women, who have generally been taught to serve the needs of others before their own, thereby receive less recognition for their teaching and service to an institution, while productivity in research, which they have fewer opportunities to perform, receives greater reward.

A recent survey of more than 3,500 men and women doctorates found that 7 percent more women than men expressed their interest as "very heavily in teaching" (Centra, 1974: 62-63). Yet a 1972-73 national survey of more than 50,000 faculty members showed that the most significant predictor of faculty rank was number of articles published, and in this respect women did far less well than men. Among men, 35 percent had published at least five articles as compared with only 12 percent of women (Bayer and Astin, 1975: 801).

At the same time, a drive for "professionalization" and higher standards in almost every field has worked for uniform standards in assessing credentials. The position of the strong schools has been consolidated and the marginal ones have been weeded out. In connection with the women's medical colleges, for example, the 1910 Flexner Report on medical education had the effect of closing many peripheral schools where women had earlier been able to gain at least a foothold.

CORE AND PERIPHERY: THE DUAL EDUCATION MARKET

As a result of changes in the university's mission, sharper internal differentiation occurred in the various organs providing different types of education to different segments of the population. The college with an entirely undergraduate body became more sharply distinguished from the university with its professional and graduate schools and elite university college. The old normal schools were swept into large state systems, where they generally became four-year colleges. At the same time a new crop of two-year community colleges sprang up. The standards at each type of college varied; the ideal of research productivity was more easily realized at the center of the system among the great research universities and elite colleges than at the peripheral two-year colleges, where the faculty had fewer doctorates and did more teaching than research and the students terminated their education after two years.

Data on sex differentials in rank and salary by type of institution support this hypothesis. Kilson (1976) reports, for example, that "the more prestigious and influential an institution is . . . the greater is the inequality between men and women in American higher education." The gap is wider at universities between the proportion of men and women in the two highest-ranking positions than at colleges and two-year institutions (see Table 9).

Salary differences between men and women faculty show the same pattern. Inequality is greater in the more prestigious institutions: women's median salary was only 77.8 percent of the men's in the universities in 1974-75, as compared with 90 percent of the men's at the two-year institutions (Kilson, 1976).

The data suggest that women have done less well in relation to men in the institutions that value research productivity most highly. One possibility is that women's academic behavior runs along lines like teaching that are relatively more rewarded in the peripheral sectors of the system and therefore women do better there in comparison with men.

TABLE 9. Percentage of Men and Women Faculty Who Are Professors and Associate Professors, by Type of Institution, 1974-75

Type of Institution	Professors and Associate Professors among Male Faculty, %	Professors and Associate Professors among Women Faculty, %	Proportion of Women Faculty, %
Universities	60	30	50
Other four-year institutions	54	30	56
Two-year institutions	17	11	65

Source: Vetter and Babco (1975: 145).

EFFECT OF MARRIAGE AND FAMILY DEMANDS

The effect of all these changes in the academic world was to make the college or university an especially greedy institution. In the competition to produce research results, publish, attend distant meetings, and still meet the formal demands of the teaching schedule for which one was being paid, males had a considerable advantage. A wife who could type, assist with research, and perform consumer maintenance tasks at home was an asset that no women enjoyed (Hochschild, 1975). Only in communities of Catholic sisters was there perhaps a parallel, or in Hull House at the turn of the century, where such famous scholars as Alice Hamilton, the pioneer in industrial medicine, and Edith Abbott, the woman economist, found companionship and mutual aid.

After 1920 the declining rate of spinsterhood among the highly educated may have put personal demands on women's time that worsened their outlook for success in professional competition. Between 1920 and 1960 a higher proportion of educated women were marrying. The 1960 census showed that among women with five years or more of college, the proportion of single women had dropped from 46 percent of those sixty-five and older to 25 percent for those thirty-five to forty-four years old (Carter and Glick, 1970: 311). After the Second World War there was also a surge in the birthrate.

The problem of role conflict dominated literature on women and education in the 1950s. Role conflict meant that young women wanted *both* educational and occupational advancement *and* a happy family life. They were no longer willing to choose between marriage or the cloister. There perhaps lies the significance of the recent revolution in "parietals" and "coresidence." At the everyday levels of the educational experience, students are now learning to put work (learning, study) obligations together with the private details of life. Unlike the first experiment in coeducation at Oberlin, in which men students did the farm work and women did the laundry and cooking, the patterns of integrating academic and nonacademic life are now becoming similar for each sex.

EFFECT OF EQUAL ACCESS AND DEMOCRATIZATION

One further aspect of change in women's roles combined with the academic revolution to push down the proportion of women's doctorates and professorships. This was the paradoxical effect that greater access to higher education apparently had on women's educational attainments. Although the earlier reforms that permitted women access to colleges and professional schools had a generally positive effect, later democratization of opportunity was ironically associated with women's declining proportion of highest professional degrees and with their diminishing proportions among the top ranks of faculties.

Women had been admitted to ever higher levels of education, primary then secondary schools, colleges, and finally doctoral programs and professional schools. The curriculum accessible to girls was consistently broadened through coeducation and emergence of parallel women's institutions of higher learning. Before 1700 in Virginia, only a third of females were literate as compared with almost twice as many males. Girls could for the first time get a secondary education equivalent to that of boys when in 1821 Emma Willard opened her special seminary for girls in Troy, New York. Then the colleges and universities began to open to women, some from the time of their founding. Oberlin admitted women in 1837, Iowa in 1856, Wisconsin in 1860, and Michigan in 1870. Women's colleges such as Mount Holyoke opened in 1847, Vassar in 1865, Wellesley and Smith in 1875, and Bryn Mawr in 1885. The professional schools were some of the last bastions of male exclusivity. Harvard, Yale, and the University of Chicago admitted women to doctoral programs in the 1890s, but in 1920 some of the most prestigious professional schools, such as the Columbia and Harvard law schools, were still closed to women.

The effect of these changes was to increase sharply the proportion of women gaining higher education in relation to their own previous record. Dolan (1972: 23) reports that in 1969 the proportion of women earning doctorates *in relation to the total population of women* was greater than at any previous time in the century and had improved by 75 times, whereas the number of men earning doctorates improved only 14 times in relation to the total population of men.

At the same time that women's educational opportunities were improving in relation to men's, higher education itself was becoming more democratic. Following the Civil War an ever larger proportion of each birth cohort attended college. From 8 percent of all women aged eighteen to twenty-one in college in 1920, the figure rose to 46 percent in 1970. Ironically, however, this upward trend may have contributed to a shift by highly educated women away from single-minded devotion to career. It is Patricia Albjerg Graham's (1976) theory that broader admissions had the effect of associating higher education for women with the prevailing expectations of the feminine role rather than with the less conventional pattern of career achievement. As more women entered college, higher education became less of a stepping stone to a distinguished professional occupation for those women who had it.

In addition the GI Bill provided educational subsidies for 17 million persons after the Second World War, only 1.8 percent of whom were women. It is now believed that men's educational attainment rose more rapidly than women's during the postwar period in large part because of the enormous impetus to men's higher education that was provided by the GI Bill (Citizen's Advisory Council, 1973: 15-16, 44-48; 1974: 55; Common Cause, 1973: 30-31). Comparable resources were not available to girls until the National Defense Education Act of 1958.

In sum, these four historical trends—establishment of scientific productivity as an ideal, consolidation by the great research universities of their leading position, the impact of declining spinsterhood, and mass admissions to higher education—had the effect of slowing rather than advancing women's educational progress. Analysis of present circumstances cannot rest, however, with this historical analysis. It is now necessary to examine possibilities for changing the behaviors both of women and of educational institutions to enhance women's educational attainments in the future.

INDIVIDUAL FACTORS IN EDUCATIONAL ATTAINMENT

Beyond any historical change in women's educational attainment lies the persistent fact of contemporary sex differences in school performance, aspirations, and attainment. Girls consistently do well in primary school. Their marks are generally higher than boys'. Their median educational level in the total population is slightly higher than that of men, averaging about three-tenths of a percent more than men across all age groups in 1960 (Riley and Foner, 1968: 112).

Participation in educational activities in 1961-62 showed only slight differences in the percentage of men and women studying. Among both men and women between thirty-five and fifty-four years of age, 21 percent were studying, if one counted studying any subject by any method (Riley and Foner, 1968: 116).

Fewer girl high-school graduates, however, aspire to go to college or professional school, and fewer of them actually do so. In 1961 a national survey of more than 33,000 college seniors showed that 39 percent of the men and 24 percent of the women expected to attend graduate school the following year. Among the top-ranking fifth, 68 percent of the men but only 36 percent of the women planned to continue (Davis, 1964). Ten years later a similar study of more than 20,000 college seniors in 1970–71 asked what the person expected to be doing in the fall of 1971. Three-fourths of the women as compared with only 52 percent of the men planned to be working. Nearly twice as many of the men (33 percent) expected to be doing graduate or professional study as compared with the women (18 percent) (Baird, 1973: 97).

The lower representation of women at every succeeding level of educational attainment after high school is apparent in Figure 4, a bar graph prepared by the Carnegie Commission (1973: 2). In 1974–75 roughly half the high-school graduates were women, and 43 and 45 percent of bachelor's and master's degrees went to women. But, though there had been great improvement since 1970, still only 21 percent of the doctoral degrees went to women (National Center for Education Statistics, 1977: 3).

One possible explanation for women's attrition is that individual sex differences—biological, psychological, or role related—account

Figure 4.   Women as a Percentage of Persons at Selected Levels of Advancement within the Educational System, 1970.

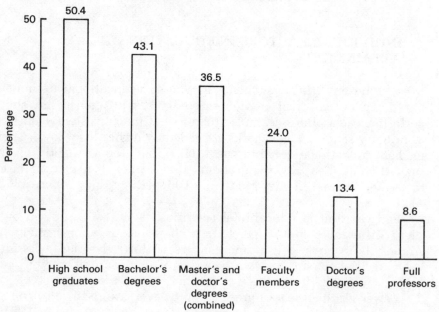

Some data gathered from *Current Population Reports,* Series P-20, "Household and Family Characteristics," Washington, D.C.: U.S. Bureau of the Census.

for these patterns. During the fifties, consistent with the function-alist sociology of the period, social scientists found women's lower achievement consistent with the adult expressive role of women (Parsons and Bales, 1955). The mood of the period was what Betty Friedan (1963) labeled the "functionalist freeze," a disposition in the social sciences to explain (and justify) the patterns in women's lives by their congruence with the existing social order. See, for example, Tiedemann (1959: 64-68) and Monsour (1963: 9-20).

Functionalist explanations evoked from critics a response that women perform below their ability because of anxiety caused by role conflict. If plans for a future career, continuing education, part-time study, and child care are assured, the bright girls whose marks or aspirations suddenly drop with prospect of family responsibilities will in many instances resume their former high level of performance and perhaps even do better (Senders, 1963: 25-26).

Two major questions thus emerged in the effort to explain women's educational aspirations and performance. The first focused on *pervasive differences between the sexes* and referred to biological differences, psychological functioning, and early socialization. The second focused on *differences in educational attainment among women* and referred to achievement conflicts, role ideology, and available financial or other resources. More recently a third line of inquiry has begun to emerge: a focus on *differences in the socialization experience and the life cycle of both men and women*. Each of these different theoretical orientations selects a different part of the reality for emphasis and suggests different remedies.

SEX DIFFERENCES

Whether consistent sex differences in intellectual performance exist is still a topic open to further research. Prior to the massive review of the psychological literature on sex differences published by Maccoby and Jacklin in 1974, a number of investigators had suggested that boys showed more field independence and were better able to sort out irrelevant cues and pursue an analytic mode of reasoning than girls (Bardwick, 1971; Lynn, 1972; Freedman and Omark, 1973). Maccoby and Jacklin (1974: 350), however, found that boys do not excel at tasks that call for "decontextualization" or disembedding, except when the task is visual-spatial. Instead they contend that "boys and girls are equally likely to respond to task-irrelevant aspects of a situation, so that neither sex excels in ana-lyzing or selecting only those elements needed for the task." However, a critical review of the Maccoby and Jacklin analysis seriously questions this interpretation of the available evidence (Block, 1976: 286, 307).

Intellectual dimensions that definitely do show sex differences are (1) verbal ability, (2) visual-spatial ability, and (3) mathematical reasoning. Girls have greater verbal ability than boys, particularly after about age eleven. The female superiority increases throughout high school and possibly beyond. Boys, however, excel in visual-spatial and mathematical ability. Though the sexes are similar in mathematical and visual-spatial tasks in childhood, about the age of twelve or thirteen boys begin to show superior ability. How much of boys' increase in mathematical skills is due to their greater exposure to math courses is not well understood. But Maccoby and Jacklin (1974: 351–352) suggest that the difference is probably not all due to training. They also note, however, that boys' general advantage in these tasks should not be understood to mean that all girls lack the ability. Instead the distributions overlap. While 50 percent of the boys have high visual-spatial ability, only 25 percent of the girls do. As Maccoby and Jacklin comment, this is more than enough to fill the engineering schools with girls if other factors are favorable.

One might think that boys' mathematical and visual-spatial advantage would be balanced by girls' greater verbal ability. Similar ability in analytic tasks would further equalize their educational aptitudes. Boocock (1972: 80) reminds us, however, that while a majority of the high-school students who take the National Merit Scholarship tests are girls, 69 percent of the awards actually go to boys. David B. Lynn (1972: 241–243) says that girls' grades are higher, but that boys score higher in standardized achievement tests and "also surpass in almost any aspect of actual intellectual achievement—books and articles written, artistic productivity, and scientific achievement." How is such a discrepancy to be explained? Past explanations can generally be grouped into three types, which focus on different factors: (1) mathematical ability and training, (2) early socialization for independence, and (3) differences in the resulting sense of competence.

Mathematical skills.

Boys' mathematical edge at puberty could be reinforced during high school by cultural pressures giving them more encouragement to take math courses and thereby giving them a much bigger advantage in tests and entry into science courses later on. Sells (1976: 1, 3) found at the Berkeley campus of the University of California that men's and women's applications for admission differed significantly in the number of years of high-school mathematics that they recorded. Of women entering in the fall of 1973, 68 percent of the women did not qualify for the freshman calculus sequence as compared with 35 percent of the men. Sells argued that mathematical training thereby served as an important filter for women's entry into other fields such as engineering, the physical sciences, architecture, and engineering.

Intrigued by Sells's findings, Ernest (1976: 9–10) carried out a similar study at the University of California at Santa Barbara and found that there too many more men entered as freshman with four years of high-school mathematics (36 percent as compared with 16 percent of women). When one looks at the fields where the proportion of Ph.D.s earned by women is below 10 percent, they are found to be fields that, except for religion, require a strong mathematics background: geography, astronomy, economics, mathematics, computer science, applied mathematics, geology, atmospheric science, business administration, physics, engineering, and operations research (McCarthy and Wolfle, 1975). However, a number of programs for increasing the number of women in mathematics have found that, given special encouragement, more women will enter mathematics courses and perform very well (Ernest, 1976).

Early independence training.

Early socialization differences in the relations between mother and child might provide basic psychodynamic forces behind later sex differentials in performance. Because both male and female early identify with the mother, but the male has later to break away while the girl does not, certain differences in intellectual style result. Lynn (1972: 248) suggests that boys' cognitive style involves primarily (1) defining the goal, (2) restructuring the situation, and (3) abstracting principles. Girls, on the other hand, develop a cognitive style that involves primarily (1) a personal relationship and (2) lesson learning. Unlike the boys, the girls are not forced to transcend the immediate conditions in order to learn. Nancy Chodorow (1974: 44) comes to somewhat similar conclusions. Because of the universal difference in the nature of a relationship between mother and child of same sex and mother and child of different sex, the "feminine personality comes to define itself in relation to people more than the masculine personality does." Women thus have a less individualized style of performance than men. They have a more flexible sense of ego, seeking communion rather than agency, and they handle dependency differently. While for men the problem of overcoming dependency is tied up with the problem of achieving masculinity, the same formula for achieving femininity does not hold for women. Adult women have particularly high self-esteem when surrounded by social networks that assure mutual support. The implication for cognitive style is that men may develop a more "stimulus-centered, parts-specific orientation to reality," whereas women may develop a more " 'relational' cognitive style, responding to the global characteristics of a stimulus in reference to its total context" (Chodorow, 1974: 57). Although Maccoby and Jacklin state that there is no inherent sex difference in analytic ability, Chodorow suggests that males and females will habitually choose different *styles* of analysis.

Sense of competence.

Finally, small innate differences in ability, coupled with the unconscious process of early socialization, may result in a different sense of reward and competence on the part of boys and girls in dealing with the educational system. The process can in part be explained by Maccoby and Jacklin's unexpected finding that boys have a more intense socialization experience than girls. They receive more attention, both positive and negative, than do girls. Perhaps the difference is due to a greater value put on boys than on girls. Or it may be due to the greater strength and aggressiveness of boys, or their tendency to depart from rules, which possibly makes their behavior qualitatively more interesting. They also receive more pressure against sex-inappropriate behavior than girls (Maccoby and Jacklin, 1974: 348–349). Such attention, more demanding, more controlling, yet communicative, appears associated with development of a greater sense of competence (Smith, 1968: 309–310). The boys would thus have an advantage.

Furthermore, a sense of competence in certain areas of expertise may be strengthened or weakened by sex-role expectations in the school and surrounding culture, particularly after puberty and in young adulthood when adult identity is being established. The largely female environment of the primary school may particularly reward girls up to the age of twelve or thirteen (Lynn, 1972). Then adult sex-role expectations may begin to encroach, making school a kind of "pseudo training" which is not meant to interfere with the training to be "feminine" and a wife and mother (Chodorow, 1974: 55). By the time a young woman reaches the age of eighteen to twenty-two, she may feel serious internal conflict over demands from the two systems, and, if she is unable to resolve the dilemma simply and quickly, her sense of competence may be lowered. Maccoby and Jacklin (1974: 350–359) found that each sex had a somewhat specialized area where each felt competent: girls felt greater social competence; boys rated themselves higher in power, domination, and strength. There was also a tendency for young women of college age to lack confidence in their ability to do well on a new task; they also had less sense of control over their own fates than men. But *this sex difference in self-confidence in the eighteen- to twenty-two-year-old group was not noted in either older or younger groups.* This latter finding points to the importance of role demands, which may differ either among women or among people at different stages in the life cycle.

DIFFERENCES AMONG WOMEN

To explain differences among women who distinguish themselves intellectually from those who do not, investigators have commonly pointed to one or more of the three following factors: achievement motivation, role ideology, or realistic financial or time constraints. Of particular relevance has been the statistical fact that girls of high socioeconomic background seem much less handicapped relative to boys of their class than girls of working-class origins. In 1967 in the lowest socioeconomic quartile, *15 percent more of the boy high-school graduates* of top-ranking ability went to college than the girls (75 and 60 percent, respectively). In the highest socioeconomic quartile, *1 percent fewer of the boys* went to college than the girls (92 and 93 percent, respectively) (Carnegie Commission, 1973: 40). The training of daughters and/or the investment of resources may be different according to the social class of the family from which a girl comes.

Achievement motivation.

Of great interest in the field of psychology for the last twenty years has been the concept of an achievement motive that predisposes some individuals to extraordinary effort and accomplishment (McClelland et al., 1953). Findings that emerged powerful and consistent for men, however, were not equally clear in the case of women (Alper, 1973). Then for a brief period Matina Horner's discovery of a motive to avoid success (which she observed in 62 percent of her female group as compared with only 10 percent of the males) offered the possibility that a key factor had been isolated. Horner (1969: 38) furthermore reported a highly significant finding that women high in fear of success performed better in working alone as compared with those low in fear of success, who performed better in competition. Subsequent efforts to replicate Horner's findings have been disappointing, however, leading investigators to conclude for the moment that fear of success is a popular but unproven concept that at the outset may have been in part the artifact of methodological flaws in the original study (Tresemer, 1973; Levine and Crumrine, 1975).

Close examination of Horner's work suggests that she may not be dealing with an underlying predisposition (motive) to avoid success so much as with anxiety, fear of failure, or other negative feelings that arise from envisioning performance in a deviant role. For example, black women turn out to show lower fear of success imagery than black men or white women (Horner, 1972; Tresemer, 1973). The finding suggests that differences in role expectations may be a powerful variable for explaining educational aspirations and performance.

Role ideology.

Throughout the 1950s and 1960s a paradox developed. Although it was fashionable for women to have low occupational commitment, their participation in the labor force continued to rise. As psychologists and sociologists sought clues to the phenomenon, they happened on bits and pieces of evidence that women's ideology toward the feminine role differed, depending on their social background or the nature of their employment. Douvan (1959) discovered that adolescent girls gave different reasons for attending college: some wanted to achieve in the professions; others were interested in a traditional female job and marriage; still others looked almost exclusively to marriage. Hoffman (1963) found that women who worked had a different ideology about male dominance and sharing of household tasks than those who did not. Dornbusch (1966: 209-210), in an afterword to Maccoby's volume *The Development of Sex Differences*, suggested that sex-role ideology itself might account for many historical and cultural variations in male and female behavior:

> [W]e must demonstrate that the shared norms influence the socialization practices, thereby linking role behavior with normative expectations ... all that early socialization can do is lay a foundation that is compatible with the most probable later experiences.

In 1972, Lipman-Blumen reported a clear relationship between female role ideology and the educational aspirations of young women. In a 1968 survey she gathered data on educational and employment plans of 1,012 wives in the Boston area who had some college education. Significantly, more of those with a "contemporary" role ideology (who held a belief that wife and husband should share work and family responsibilities) had medium and high educational aspirations (69 percent) than those with a "traditional" role ideology (47 percent) that a husband should support the family and the wife should do domestic tasks. In addition, more women with contemporary role ideology were likely to have completed college before marrying and to choose as their ideal role a combination of family responsibility and paid work (Lipman-Blumen, 1972).

Additional research is necessary to determine how such role ideology is distributed in the population by socioeconomic status, employment, and age group. It is interesting that Horner (1972: 67) reports that more of her upper-middle-class subjects with successful professional fathers showed fear of success than her working or lower-middle-class respondents. Perhaps role ideology differs in the two classes.

Constraints in time and money.

Of all the background factors influencing an individual woman's educational and career decisions, some of the simplest, most accessible, and yet powerful may be the availability of money and time to pursue her interests. More young women than young men when asked why they are not studying immediately after high school answer that they "cannot afford it" (Baird, 1973: 126). Roby (1973: 45) notes that parents provide a much larger share of college costs for girls than for boys; men students are more apt to rely on savings or their own earnings to help pay for their education. Such a pattern would seem to put the girl of lower socioeconomic background at a particular disadvantage, unless some countervailing cultural expectations about earning her own way were operating.

Time and mobility are also practical constraints, especially for older women with family obligations. Centra (1974: 47) found in his study of men and women doctorates that half the reasons for unemployment given by the women had to do with marriage and family obligations: pregnancy (20 percent), no jobs available in locale of the husband's job (16 percent), lack of domestic help or day care (9 percent), or husband's opposition (4 percent).

AGE-RELATED CHANGES IN WOMEN'S ACHIEVEMENTS

Even if socialization, ideology, and current role affect educational performance, there is still the inexorable march of time, which changes all things. The body ages, the labor market expands or contracts, and fashion shifts. In recent years an emerging psychology of the life cycle has begun to ask how socialization, work, and education affect the adult. Central to this inquiry is an examination of the effects of *time* and *age* on individual aspiration and performance (Brim and Abeles, 1975).

Through the middle years, important changes may take place in the physiological and psychological makeup of the individual and in the surrounding social and cultural milieu. There is a possibility that some of these age-related changes may soften sex differences, allowing the male to explore the emotional and affective side of his

personality, and the female to meet her competitive and achieve-
ment-oriented needs.

In one of the few studies suggesting age-related changes in wom-
en's motivation, Baruch (1967) showed that achievement motivation
in a group of Radcliffe graduates was lower in the group ten years
out of college than in those women who were either younger or
older. Although the findings were from a cross-sectional comparison
of different age groups (rather than a longitudinal analysis), Baruch
hypothesized that women's achievement motivation began to rise
after the age of about thirty-five, when major family responsibilities
were lessening. She tested the generality of her results on a larger
body of data. A national survey conducted in 1957 by Gurin et al.
(1960) showed that achievement motivation was slightly higher
among the college-educated women past thirty-five. Among the non-
college educated, however, the older age groups showed lower
achievement motivation.

From her observation of normal middle-class college-educated
women seeking counseling, Martha S. White (1973) has suggested
that women encounter a midlife crisis about the age of thirty-seven
or thirty-eight, when they begin to review their present roles and
plan for the future. Some seek further education and a job; others
look for enrichment of their lives by further learning; all raise issues
of identity as they move away from heavy family responsibility
toward the possibility of using their time differently. White finds the
period to be one of enormous opportunity for growth and reorganization of the personality.

We have already seen in chapter 4 how the number of women's
years free of child rearing has doubled in the last century owing to
the shortening of the childbearing period and the lengthening of life.
Yet the way a woman chooses to use these years may vary widely
depending on her own life cycle and shifts in the economic cycle or
labor supply. Before the recent recession Cartter (1971) warned that
due to a decline in the birthrate the number of faculty positions
would shrink in the colleges and universities just as the number of
the doctorates graduating from the universities was at an all-time
high. On the other hand, previous wartime experience had shown
that sharp increases in demand for labor could greatly increase
opportunities for women in politics and employment (Dodge, 1966;
Lipman-Blumen, 1972). Graham (1970) similarly argued that wom-
en's opportunities in higher education expanded during every period
when colleges and universities were short of money and students.
Change in the sex composition of the cohort flow thus results in
social change in the opportunities open to women, sometimes expanding them and other times contracting (Waring, 1975: 240).

Those who are members of a small cohort may invest in conformity, whereas those of an age where there are too many for the existing roles may drop out and differentiate their responses in either innovative or deviant ways.

Depending on general social conditions, persons may discover or invent a response that becomes part of the cultural repertoire of a whole generation. In a follow-up survey of children studied during the Great Depression, Elder (1974) found that young women growing up in the Depression in poor families developed a somewhat different adaptation to the feminine role from those who grew up in more affluent circumstances. The former group married younger and viewed their marriage as an avenue to freedom from the confines of the parental home, whereas the latter group delayed marriage somewhat longer, got more education, and experimented more with family-job combinations. Evidence from alumnae of an Eastern women's college similarly suggests that women who graduated in peak years of the economic cycle, when presumably work opportunities were more available, were more likely to hold jobs in the early 1960s than those who graduated during the Depression, when jobs were scarce and marriage and volunteer work were acceptable alternatives (Giele, 1973). Both examples suggest that the adaptation of a generation during a formative period may be a distinctive mode that shapes choices through the remainder of the life course.

REMEDIES ORIENTED TO THE INDIVIDUAL

In the matter of sex differences in educational attainment, one possible response is to accept and enhance sex differences. Current suggestions turn much more to compensatory solutions, however. Maccoby and Jacklin (1974: 366-367) point to the desirability of strengthening a child in weak skills rather than building only on the strong. They thus advocate special encouragement for girls to develop visual-spatial skills and for boys to develop verbal skills. Boys' aggressive behavior could be toned down, while somewhat more aggressive activity among girls might be encouraged.

If the mother as primary caretaker creates a quite different cognitive style in girls from boys, it is possible to argue that this form of socialization is as it should be to train a future generation of mothers. However, another possibility is to argue from the work of Lynn (1972) and Chodorow (1974) that more caretaking by fathers would give girls the advantages of conditions that permit analytic thinking and boys the conditions that promote relational and contextual thinking, resulting in a better balance for each sex between the two modes of thought. Furthermore, the preparation of boys to undertake more child care and household tasks in later life might better be accomplished if the boy could identify with a same-sex parent who at the same time is doing household work.

If role ideology is a central factor in women's educational accomplishment, then exposure to the women's movement and a variety of female models should usefully broaden the possibilities that a young woman considers.

Finally, if changes over the life course promote greater flexibility in the future, good counseling for adults, continuing education programs, leaves of absence from work, and part-time study arrangements should be made easily available to all.

Although any one of these changes is aimed at individual factors, it is immediately evident that larger institutional changes are ultimately involved. The next section considers educational practices in schools and colleges.

FACTORS IN THE LEARNING SITUATION

Observers of the educational system in America have lately begun to propose that it has properties which make it dovetail with the dual-labor market. Indeed James O'Toole (1975a; 1975b) refers to the college-bound and vocational education track as a dual system that funnels some people of favored class, race, or sex into the college preparation that will get them good jobs, while it at the same time channels people of less favored characteristics to specific short-term training that will prepare them only for the second-rate positions. O'Toole's remedy is to reorganize education so that it better prepares everyone with the basic skills of reading and writing, some broad theoretical understanding, and a zest for learning. Training in the specific skills would be left to the job and be certified by the educators as the person progresses. Such a solution, if successful, would move the society toward greater equality by changing those aspects of the present education system that now promote inequality.

Whether there is a comparable dual-education system that directs the two sexes into fields of different prestige and remuneration has not been clear, although many observers have found *differences* in the treatment of male and female in almost every aspect of education—from textbooks to athletics. An important reality is the concentration of professional women in a few overcrowded fields, such as teaching, library science, and social work. Well before the present shortage of academic and teaching positions, Rossi (1970; 1973) and

Kahne (1973) were warning of the impending crisis that women teachers would face when the supply of positions in these fields would outrun demand. Rossi counseled active resistance to discrimination and affirmative action; Kahne counseled diversification.

If a dual-educational system that feeds a dual-labor market which is sex typed does exist, then one would expect to find mechanisms that channel one sex into the year-round full-time occupations that are predominantly male and the other sex into part-time part-year jobs that are female. Bits and pieces of evidence have begun to accumulate that such a process does exist, that "maleness" is associated with core high-status positions and "exciting" academic fields and that "femaleness" is associated with peripheral applied fields that have lower status and little research activity but demand considerable commitment to teaching. Sorting by sex then occurs both at the level of curriculum and student attrition and at the level of hiring and promotion of faculty.

CURRICULUM, LEARNING PROCESS, AND STUDENT ATTRITION

Before a boy or girl reaches postsecondary education, the primary and secondary schools already appear to have exerted some subtle sorting. Textbooks and basal readers picture male characters more than three times as often as female characters; this tendency increases the higher the grade level and the more adult the characters. The occupations of the female and male characters are sex stereotyped. The women are more likely portrayed in a family role or in a narrow range of occupations, such as teacher or nurse (Weitzman and Rizzo, 1974; Levy and Stacey, 1973). Adult males are more often depicted in problem-solving behavior, while adult females show significantly higher proportions of conformity and verbal behavior (Saario et al., 1973: 396).

The courses that males and females take are also likely to be different in the primary grades and high school. More boys will turn out to have an interest in math courses than girls. (This is less true in England, Belgium, and Sweden than in a number of other Western countries [Keeves, 1973].) Boys will have played on school athletic teams that a male coaches, girls cheer for, and in which the community invests far more resources than in any comparable girls' sport. Vocational training will disproportionately have exposed boys to agriculture and shop, while girls will have had training in home economics, which does not prepare them for a paid job (Trecker, 1973: 111; Saario et al., 1973: 405, 409). Informal mechanisms that guide students into sex-typed courses of study may be so accepted in the community that no one thinks to question them. Consciousness is then raised only when boys are encouraged to take the "creative living" and girls the "industrial arts" courses, as is now happening in some progressive, junior high schools. But sex-linked expectations in straight academic courses may be hidden and difficult to unearth. In many colleges and graduate programs, for example, an equal proportion of men and women applicants are admitted, but attrition rates differ. To understand the reasons, an analysis of sex labeling of fields and the social-psychological support mechanisms in each is helpful.

Sex differentiation of the curriculum.

A cursory examination of undergraduate or graduate enrollment or of doctorates enrolled by field will reveal clear differences in the sex ratio by discipline. The sciences and all professions like law and medicine are heavily male. The humanities, English, Spanish, French, and professions like elementary education, nursing, and social work are heavily female. Furthermore, a very large proportion of the female undergraduates receive their first degree in one field—education. Between 1948 and 1970 the proportion of women who received their first degree in education increased from 24 to 36 percent (Carnegie Commission, 1973: 64). Within any major branch of social science, physical science, or humanities, there is still further tendency for females to be disproportionately represented in some specialties and not in others. Patterson (1973) found by analysis of doctorates received between 1960 and 1969 that in the social sciences women were twice the expected number in anthropology but half the expected number in economics. In the physical sciences they were much more likely to be in astronomy or chemistry than in metallurgy, oceanography, or meteorology. Within the field of anthropology, they were more often in cultural and linguistic subspecialties than in physical anthropology or archaeology, from which they were in fact likely to be discouraged. Women physicians were significantly more often pediatricians or psychiatrists and less often surgeons. While half of all male lawyers were in general practice, only one-third of women lawyers were, and there were over three times as large a proportion of women in trusts and estates as men.

Seeing in the sex typing of fields a much more general pattern of status allocation, Feldman (1974) recently carried out an imaginative analysis of income and prestige correlates for every major academic discipline. Using a measure based on the semantic differential, Feldman first had 352 students characterize each of forty-five academic fields. Using a scale of 1 to 7, he then ranked the fields from masculine to feminine. Next he compared the list with the actual proportions of women in the student body and on the faculty in each field and found a close correspondence (see Table 10).

Feldman then examined the relationship between sex typing of a field and signs of its power and status in the academic community. He noted the extent to which people in the field felt that they got the best students, the extent to which they believed that "exciting things were happening," the proportion who felt that teaching was important, the proportion of faculty who did paid outside consulting, and the proportion of faculty who made over $20,000 a year from their academic salary.

From all these measures of status, Feldman discovered the remarkable fact that more people in the most "masculine" fields were enjoying high prestige and financial reward. They perceived themselves as getting the best students, doing "exciting things" (research), and not highly committed to teaching. More of their members did outside consulting, and more earned over $20,000 a year (Feldman, 1974: 47- 66). Moreover, within each field these measures were more characteristic of the males than of the females.

Such sex differentiation of the curriculum appears to be stronger in the more prestigious and research-oriented colleges and universities (Carnegie Commission, 1973: Table C-2, 200- 201). These findings lend general support to the concept of a dual-educational system composed of (1) a scientific research-oriented core that receives high rewards and where the majority of students and faculty are men and (2) an educational service-oriented fringe that receives lesser rewards and where a much larger proportion of students and faculty are women. If sex discrimination exists, it remains to show that people are queued into one of these sectors rather than the other not just on the basis of their abilities or preferences, but on the basis of being male or female.

Sorting students.

Because women students generally have higher grades than men in high school and college and are a smaller portion of the total pool entering graduate school, it seems fairly safe to assume that differences in ability are not sufficient explanation for recurring sex differences in attrition rates. Yet in a study of the most select graduate students, Woodrow Wilson fellows between 1958 and 1963, Sells found that 64 percent of the women as compared with 44 percent of the men had dropped out before the end of their graduate training (Carnegie Commission, 1973: 91). Significantly their rates differed by field of study. Although the overall drop-out rates were highest in the humanities (about two-thirds did not finish) and lowest in the sciences (about one-third did not finish), the *sex*

T A B L E 10. Sex Typing of Academic Disciplines

Field	Score on Semantic Differential, 1 = Most Masculine, 7 = Most Feminine	Female Graduate Students 1968-69, %	Female Bachelor's Degree Recipients, 1968-69, %	Female Faculty, %
Masculine				
Electrical engineering	1.58	0.6	0.4	0.6
Mechanical engineering	1.59	0.6	0.4	0.5
Civil engineering	1.62	0.9	0.5	0.1
Chemical engineering	1.72	1.0	0.9	0.9
Agriculture/forestry	1.93	5.6	3.1	0.9
Law	1.94	5.8	—	4.3
Physics	2.00	4.8	5.9	3.6
Dentistry	2.03	1.1	—	—
Business	2.10	4.0	8.2	16.3
Architecture	2.18	11.7	4.3	4.3
Geology	2.34	7.9	10.4	4.2
Chemistry	2.36	14.1	18.3	9.3
Medicine	2.50	8.8	—	7.7
Mathematics	2.61	23.2	37.6	13.6
Biochemistry	2.69	22.6	24.8	6.6
Economics	2.72	10.6	10.6	5.9
Political science	2.90	18.7	20.8	10.7
Educational administration	2.99	22.7	—	9.4
Neutral				
Bacteriology	3.05	30.8	47.2	16.6
Physiology	3.17	21.1	24.2	10.0
Zoology	3.18	23.9	21.9	7.3
Philosophy	3.23	17.8	22.3	11.5
History	3.34	28.2	35.3	11.3

TABLE 10. (Continued)

	Score on Semantic Differential, 1 = Most Masculine, 7 = Most Feminine	Female Graduate Students 1968-69, %	Female Bachelor's Degree Recipients, 1968-69, %	Female Faculty, %
Botany	3.39	26.2	34.7	9.0
Geography	3.44	15.6	21.6	10.7
Psychology	3.57	33.8	43.1	18.5
Journalism	3.61	30.8	40.7	10.1
Anthropology	3.63	41.4	57.6	13.4
Physical and health education	3.66	34.3	40.8	40.9
German	3.71	51.6	59.4	27.7
Sociology	3.80	35.6	61.1	20.2
Feminine				
Educational psychology	4.10	47.0	35.0	21.4
Speech	4.19	49.5	58.5	23.4
Spanish	4.29	57.3	75.5	39.2
Art	4.31	51.0	67.9	20.7
Dramatic arts	4.36	42.8	58.5	23.4
Music	4.39	44.1	57.3	23.5
Secondary education	4.59	45.5	60.8	39.7
Social work	4.71	61.5	80.5	43.1
English	4.83	54.5	67.7	33.5
French	4.98	68.7	82.7	45.0
Library science	5.50	81.8	93.6	60.2
Elementary education	6.01	78.9	90.7	39.7
Nursing	6.47	98.5	98.6	96.1
Home economics	6.51	90.6	97.3	89.2

SOURCE: Feldman (1974: 40-45, Tables 10 and 11).

differences in attrition were least in the humanities and greatest in the natural sciences (Sells, 1973*b*). Stark (n.d.), also analyzing data on graduate student attrition rates at Berkeley from 1951 to 1963, concluded that most students who left were "starved out." He conjectured that drop-out rates were lowest in the natural sciences because fellowships were more readily available there and the years required to complete a doctorate were fewer.

Anecdotal evidence suggests that social-psychological factors are also at work to discourage entry of women into predominantly male fields and to confine them to the more female professions. *Opportunities for Women in Higher Education* (Carnegie Commission, 1973: 240–241) includes in its appendix an informal report from Stanford University in which young women in science courses relay discouraging remarks on the part of the professors. One professor said to a woman premed student that he did not expect to see her around the following year, another that he could not stand women who thought they could be scientists; still others questioned women's seriousness and nudged them toward high-school teaching, which would be "more flexible for a woman."

Wallach (1975: 100–101) notes the disparagement of women that regularly occurred in law schools before the recent surge of feminism:

> When I entered law school in 1969, many women students were as alienated as I by a pervasive classroom attitude that considered the entire student body, legal profession, indeed the world, to be male. Male professors often ignored the presence of women by addressing the class as "Gentlemen." Or they used illustrations insulting to women: "A system of procedure is just like a woman; if you've seen one, you've seen them all." Or as a professor in a course on corporations said, calling on a male student, "Suppose you *guys* want to start a 6-*man* firm. How would you form a partnership?"
>
> ... Moreover, [there were the] standard derogatory female stereotypes ... auxiliary players to male central characters in illustrative hypotheticals ... the helpless widow, the dependent wife, the deceptive bitch, the pure virgin, the irrational or hysterical female, the silly consumer who is easily conned by male exploiters, the rape victim who secretly wanted to be raped, or any stupid loathsome creature.

The net effect of ignoring the female as a professional or disparaging her as a client appears to be one in which the network of mutual support, the alliance of powerful professor and student protégé, does not work well for women because there is no sense of identification with them or hope in investing in their future for its later rewards. Weiss (1972: 31) and Sells (1973*a*) found that professors were more likely to regard men students as "colleagues" than they did women students. A study of microbiologists conducted in 1971 revealed that more than three times as many women doctorates as men reported that they had received discouraging advice during their graduate careers (Kashket et al., 1974: 492).

The pattern is perhaps first evident in fellowship support. For whatever reason, men are more likely to have fellowships in graduate school than women; half the women students receive support from a spouse, as compared with one-fourth of the men (Carnegie Commission, 1973: 95). The reasons for the difference are various: women may be more "dependent" than men (Roby, 1973: 48); perhaps getting fellowship support is nearly impossible for those women who choose part-time study (University of Michigan, 1974: 16, 32- 34; Carnegie Commission, 1973: 83); perhaps cultural expectation causes the committee making the awards to perceive the men (and divorced women?) as "needing" the fellowship more than the married women (Harris, 1970; 1973: 400- 401).

But the more powerful and obvious underlying cause may be in the simple ratio of women undergraduate students to women professors. In her survey of 188 graduate departments of sociology in the U.S. in 1968- 69, Alice Rossi (1970: 10- 11) reported the example of one West Coast public university in which women made up 43 percent (n = 64) of the graduate Ph.D. students, 14 percent (n = 3) of the junior faculty, and 0 percent of the senior faculty. If some of the sixty-four women students preferred to air personal-professional problems with one of the three junior faculty members of the same sex, they would have to compete for the time of those women faculty in a ratio of 21 to 1, whereas the males would be competing for the time of a comparable male junior faculty member on the basis of 2.5 to 1. Rossi (1970: 11) concluded:

> Thus the women graduate students in this department have no local feminine model for advancement to the top of academic sociology; they must compete for time with the few women on the faculty; and they are probably subjected to subtle disapproval or overt ridicule from some proportion of the male faculty. *Quite apart from the more usual explanations of faculty vs. career conflicts, this example suggests that the structure of a typical graduate department may itself exert a negative influence on both women students and women faculty, leading to higher levels of career anxiety and attrition among women students, and among the women faculty members a heavier burden of student counseling, a lower rate of publication, and more anxiety about job security and advancement.*

FACULTY HIRING AND PROMOTION

A number of studies on the status of women have now been done, either in different universities such as the University of Michigan, University of Illinois, Harvard, and Brandeis, or in different disciplines such as microbiology, political science, and sociology. These studies are now beginning to be codified, and their findings are consistent and powerful: the higher one goes in the hierarchy of academic teaching and administration, the lower the number of women found there. Overall, about half of all male faculty are in the top two ranks of professor and associate professor, while less than a quarter of all female faculty are in these senior positions (Robinson, 1973: 207).

To understand the processes that produce this pattern, one strategy is to examine variations by type of institution as Robinson (1973) has done. The disparity between the proportion of women faculty and women graduate students is greatest at the top universities (Rossi, 1970: 6- 7). We have earlier hypothesized that the ideal of research productivity puts women at a particular disadvantage in these universities. Indeed the Carnegie Commission found that *sex differentiation by fields* was more pronounced in the top research universities than in the less selective colleges and community colleges (see Table 11).

Using the concept of a dual education system in which research institutions function at the core and teaching institutions at the periphery, one can imagine a sorting of faculty that channels those people with certain characteristics such as research orientation, full

T A B L E 11. **Amount of Sex Differentiation in Disciplines, by Level and Type of University, 1969**

	DEVIATION OF PERCENT FEMALES FROM 50 PERCENT			
LEVEL	Under-graduate	Graduate Student	Assistant Professor	Professor
Research universities I	29.9	25.5	37.9	44.9
Other universities	24.3	27.6	36.4	39.2
Comprehensive universities	20.1	26.6*	28.7	39.6
Liberal arts colleges I	20.5	37.0*	26.6*	38.5*
Liberal arts colleges II and two-year colleges	17.6		25.2*	33.8*

SOURCE: Carnegie Commission (1973: 200-201, Table C-2).
NOTE: The Carnegie table gives percent female in each category by disciplines. I have found the deviation of percent female from 50 percent, summed across fields, and computed an average deviation, whether it be positive or negative.
*Some fields had fewer than fifty respondents.

devotion to career, and an early and fast publishing record into the core institutions. To the extent that males possess marked characteristics that serve as cues to these qualities, one might expect to find a disproportionate number of them encouraged toward the "top-quality" institutions. On the other hand, because women express slightly more interest in teaching, may take more time before publishing, and frequently work part-time because of family commitments, they may be marked for deflection toward the peripheral institutions. (For insight into how this process works, Richard Lester's [1974] book on the dangers of affirmative action provides an incomparable glimpse of how a powerful academic and former dean sorts people according to just such sex-linked marker characteristics as mentioned here.)* One would expect that surveys done after this dual-streaming process has occurred would show women less well represented at all levels of the faculty in the core research institutions than in the peripheral teaching institutions.

By the dual-system theory one would furthermore expect future productivity of men and women to accentuate and perpetuate the initial differences, like a self-fulfilling prophecy. Men in core institutions with secretarial help, research assistance, expensive laboratory and computer facilities, and institutional clout for getting additional research grants would have an advantage in piling up a record of research productivity and publication. Their teaching and advising would be specialized, so as to help rather than deflect from their "work." On the other hand, the women in the peripheral institutions, teaching a variety of courses (none of which may be their "specialty"), seeing many students, and working far from the heavily capitalized scientific apparatus that promotes productivity, would be at considerable disadvantage in accumulating a record of accomplishments on their vitae that "counts" for promotion in other than second-level all-purpose educational institutions. (An analogous process may operate when women are put in "off-ladder" marginal positions such as lecturer and research associate within core institutions. They may never have full access to the role structure and technology that would make them fully productive in a scientific sense.)

Another strategy for explaining the difference in women's promotion rate is to examine the process of attrition by discipline. Here some curious results emerge. On the one hand, as Sells and Stark have demonstrated for Berkeley graduate students, overall attrition rates are lower in the sciences, medium in the social sciences, and

---

* The book has received sharp and deserved criticism (Sandler, 1975; Tobias, 1974).

highest in the humanities, but the pattern of *sex differences in attrition rates* run in exactly the opposite direction, greatest in the sciences and least in the humanities. Another curious piece of information should be added to this puzzle: women's sense of being discriminated against seems to be highest in the social sciences, and lower in the sciences and humanities. For example, only 15 percent of women doctorates in physics felt they had suffered discrimination, as compared with 41 percent in psychology, 66 percent in anthropology, and 85 percent in American studies. Using a rough scale from 1 (low relative status of women) to 3 (high), and summarizing several parity measures such as salary differences and reports of discrimination, Morlock characterized several disciplines as follows, in the status they accorded women: physics, 2.6; anthropology, 2.5; political science, 1.8; sociology, 1.2; and modern languages, 2.0 (Morlock, 1973: 293, 302).

If one graphs the relationship between discipline and these three dependent variables—overall attrition of graduate students, sex differences in attrition of graduate students, and a feeling on the part of mature women scholars of having been discriminated against—the patterns emerge that are sketched in Figure 5.

No one has yet proposed a theory to explain these puzzling relationships. Using the dual-system theory as it applies to the educational system, the results may be explained by two types of

Figure 5. Attrition Rates and Discrimination, by Discipline

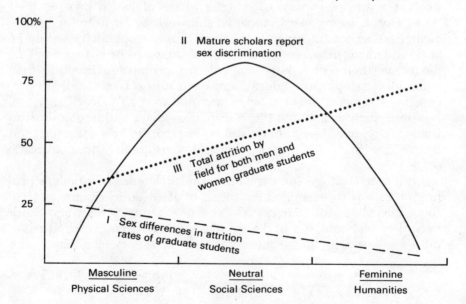

differentiation. The first type early sorts people between core and peripheral sectors and explains higher attrition of females in the sciences (Line I on the graph). Hours per week spent working and research productivity are the critical factors in this differentiation. To the extent that sex is related to these indices, sex differences are related to attrition early in the career, but when that hurdle is passed sex differences are less important. Such an explanation would make sense of the findings that women's *perception* of sex discrimination is lower in the natural sciences and that the status of women in physics is rated high.

A second type of differentiation may occur later in a person's career. This would explain the high amount of perceived sex discrimination among social scientists (as indicated by the peak on Line II of the graph). The fields where the peak occurs have an ambivalent identity and an ambiguous position with respect to the scientific core and the teaching periphery. One part of a field may be research and science oriented; another enormous segment may prepare students for fields such as law, nursing, teaching, and social work. This is particularly the case in a discipline such as sociology and a number of other social sciences such as history, anthropology, and political science. For graduate students and faculty in these fields, the process of deciding career direction may continue much longer than in the sciences. Social-science doctorates who are neither helped to do productive work by a laboratory setting or a clear research paradigm, nor "starved out," may have to continue vying for professional prestige, university placement, and sponsorship for a longer time than those in the natural sciences. Though the social sciences show intermediate attrition rates and intermediate sex differences in their drop-out rates, they show the strongest sex differences in *faculty promotion.* Perhaps speed and early individual promise (markers that people may link to sex) are more decisive for attaining a core position in these social-science fields with less clear scientific paradigms than in either the sciences (where the laboratory structure and paradigm consensus of the field make individual differences less important, once past the doctorate) or the humanities (where research and publication are on the whole less important for promotion than in either the sciences or social sciences).

Like the sciences, the humanities fare relatively well with respect to sex discrimination at the faculty level. Note, however, that the humanities have the highest overall attrition rates for both men and women (as is shown by Line III). These rates may give a clue to the structure of knowledge in the field. If there is less consensus on the fundamental research paradigm in the humanities, it may take longer to finish the doctorate or make research contributions. Women are then perhaps at less of a disadvantage because fast, voluminous, and early contribution is less likely to be a distinguishing mark of promise.

REMEDIES

Although the sex typing of educational fields is well recognized, it is not clear what strategies will effectively remedy the situation. It is easy enough to argue that men and women are naturally different, or that little can be changed without changing the entire economy or family system. The intermediate approach is direct: encourage more women to take mathematics or enter the sciences. Institute affirmative action to change the faculty ratios in the direction of parity within every field.

All such tactics have something to contribute, but none directly addresses the underlying dualism of the educational system. Only reform efforts directed at reconciling core and periphery appear to promise such radical change. Only structural change of educational regulations and policies promises to reorganize the context in which teaching and learning occur.

INSTITUTIONAL REFORMS

Following the example of the civil-rights movement, one important means for improving women's education has been through legislation. Law enforcement has given some recourse against sex discrimination in hiring, promotion, pay, and accommodations. At the same time spontaneous experiments have sprung up. Admissions policies have been altered by coeducation; curriculum has expanded through introduction of women's studies; the relation between work and education has changed through expansion of continuing education programs. Each of these experiments has at first aroused enormous enthusiasm as though it might turn out to be the primary means to sex equality in education. In each instance, however, such grand hopes have been disappointed. Coeducation, for example, in a formerly all-male bastion such as Yale only revealed a deeper and more pervasive male orientation in the entire university, damaging to the self-confidence of some women who went there, and requiring more extensive changes than a mere shift in the admissions ratio could accomplish.

Summing up the impact of such experiments, Jill K. Conway, now president of Smith College, stated a basic formula for understanding the significance of these reforms based on an ascending hierarchy of generality. Each reform, when instituted, points to a deeper organizational principle that must ultimately be confronted and modified if true equality is to be realized. At the moment, coeducation is one of the most visible changes, but it represents only the first rung of educational organization:

Coeducation obviously involves a social policy with regard to access to educational institutions. If genuinely equal treatment of the sexes were an educational goal, then it should also involve changes in the content of the curriculum, what is taught, and the varieties of human experience examined. It might also affect the very creation of knowledge because a new group with new social perspectives would be recruited into the research activities of the universities which are today the major creators of knowledge. Finally if coeducation were really to result in equal treatment for males and females, there would be the same pattern of career development for men and women into the professional elites of the society. *Up to the present, however, attention has been focused on the access of women to institutions of higher education, with little or no thought given to the relationship of women students to the curriculum, women scholars to research activity, or women graduates to the occupational structure of society.* [Conway, 1974: 239; emphasis added]

Besides coeducation, other innovations such as women's studies and affirmative action have been tried. But success is still limited. Each experiment has worked primarily to bring women into the male world of scholarship and education. As women have tried to succeed by emulating male patterns, they have discovered that "women-centered" methods and values must also be identified. Only with such a vision can they propose major alternatives to the present system and in turn establish the equality of their own achievements.

COEDUCATION AND THE WOMEN'S COLLEGES

During the 1960s selective all-male colleges such as Yale, Princeton, and Dartmouth began to admit women undergraduates. In 1968-69 Yale admitted 500 women to the college, establishing a ratio of 1 female to 8 males. Some of the early results were negative. A number of young women experienced a loss of self-confidence, confusion about their feminine identity, and debilitation from fighting a constant battle of proving their intellectual capacity in an environment that seemed to recognize only the achievements, values, and style of males (Schwartz and Lever, 1973; Getman, 1974; Deinhardt, 1974). Yet one of the young women who went through this process concluded that "only later, through losing a sense of myself as a woman, did I come to consider womanhood all the more thoughtfully. By trampling on my self-image, Yale freed me to assert my femaleness, to discover myself as a whole human being" (Jelly, 1974: 62).

What is the deeper theoretical significance of changing the sex ratio in the student body? Both consciously and unconsciously, the experiments were designed to promote crossover between the educational worlds of the two sexes. On the one hand, women were to learn and imitate the more aggressive male style of discussion and be put on the road to career success that Yale's tradition of producing a thousand male leaders a year was supposed to assure. On the other hand, the "stag" world of the all-male college was to be humanized by the introduction of female expressiveness. Grant and Riesman (1975: 172, 185) tell us that in fact this latter aim was to some extent accomplished by coeducation:

> Polarization in terms of sex which left creative expression as a female domain has greatly moderated; with men encouraged to develop what would once have been thought "feminine" aspects of themselves, colleges specializing in aesthetic expressivity for women have had to reconsider their mandate. Bennington and Sarah Lawrence, along with most formerly women's colleges, have gone co-ed. . . . What the aesthetic-expressive colleges have to teach has been in considerable measure incorporated everywhere.

Like diploma-holders of old, students of both sexes have become the diplomats of our age, communicating across America's many subcultures. In Jencks and Riesman's (1968: 26) terms, they have gained the "diplomatic passports they need to cross the borders of their racial, religious, economic, sexual, or generational parish."

An important difficulty remains, however. Since males hold a disproportionate part of power and prestige, females may be pressured to emulate male style at the expense of their own creativity. At the same time there may be insufficient pull on the male world toward the aesthetic-expressive pole. The balance may tip even farther in the masculine direction because the coeducational institutions have largely absorbed even those last outposts of female culture that were embodied in women's colleges.

In the face of such a possibility, it is significant that institutions like Smith, Mount Holyoke, and Wellesley have decided to remain women's colleges. Tidball's (1973) research on the educational background of women listed in *Who's Who of American Women* gave support to the decision. She found that a significantly higher proportion of women notables were graduates of the women's colleges than one would expect from their numbers in the college-educated population. She related the finding to two structural properties of the women's schools—their much higher proportion of women faculty to serve as role models, and their absence of men in the student body. Another positive effect of the women's college is its apparent encouragement of women to major in "male" fields such as the sciences. In 1969, 13 percent of the women's college graduates majored in natural sciences and mathematics, as compared with only 7 percent of all women receiving bachelor's degrees that year (Carnegie Commission, 1973: 72). Tidball and Kistiakowsky's (1976) subsequent research using the Doctorate Records File since 1920 confirmed the earlier finding that women's colleges produced a disproportionate number of high achievers. Of the top twenty-five institutions producing the highest proportions of doctorates in relation to the size of their female student body, all the Seven Sisters (Bryn Mawr, Radcliffe, Barnard, Mount Holyoke, Wellesley, Vassar, and Smith) were represented, as well as Goucher. Yet coeducational colleges are five times more numerous in the entire nation than women's colleges.

Female colleges, rather than emphasize sex differences, tend to foreclose their negative impact on women's intellectual attainment by denying sex differences. The strategy seems to work because they *prevent* sex differentiation. By barring men they forestall the sex labeling of subject matter and of intellectual styles and thereby ease some of the conflict between women's feminine self-image and participation in a field elsewhere labeled masculine.

From this analysis, however, it is apparent that *no major institutions presently stand for woman's part of the culture or "woman's point of view."* Some would say no such point of view exists; others would say that institutional segregation is not the way to foster it. Yet leading exponents of feminism are beginning to recognize the vacuum and to articulate the need for positive alternatives to the present male-dominated culture of higher education. Adrienne Rich (1975) calls for a "woman-centered university." Arlie R. Hochschild (1975) asks recognition of life patterns not fashioned around "the clockwork of the male career." Florence Howe (1975: 167) argues that the feminist vision must be allowed to surface in traditional female professional fields such as teaching, social work, and nursing. These insights point to the need for reorganizing education to treat women's experience seriously. A beginning has been made in a new field called "women's studies."

WOMEN'S STUDIES AND TRADITIONAL DISCIPLINES

Beginning in 1969 a number of women's courses sprang up across the country. By 1972-73 their number had reached more than 800

(Howe and Ahlum, 1973). During the civil-rights movement, future women's studies teachers like Florence Howe had learned to draw on students' own experience. Using this same outlook in the new women's courses, teachers of history, literature, sociology, and psychology discovered springs of women's experience and consciousness hitherto untapped in the traditional curriculum. There was resistance to be sure; Howe (1975: 150) says that, even as late as 1971, she did not mention "women" as the topic of her literature course, "Identity and Expression," at Goucher College.

Why has interest in women's studies been so great? Will it be a lasting phenomenon? It was in the women's studies courses that women's everyday experience could be raised to a level of consciousness where it might become subject to the "cognitive rationality" of the university. Women's studies courses thus did what the women's colleges alone could not do: they labeled certain activities, feeling states, and experience as important that had been ignored and undervalued because they were primarily in the woman's domain. Women poets and authors suddenly took on new significance; the history of the family became as exciting as diplomatic and intellectual history; the sociology of discrimination extended beyond race and ethnicity to sex.

Two limitations on these developments should be noted, however. Women's studies, by and large, did not extend into the sciences; the established paradigm of "objective" science made these fields seem less fertile ground for discovering a distinctively female point of view. At the other end of the continuum in the extremely "feminine" specialties, feminists ignored the radical possibilities for tapping women's experience in the fields where women were heavily represented—teaching, social work, nursing, child care, and housework.

What do these omissions signify about the larger significance and future of women's studies? First, it is interesting that the academic study of sex differences began earliest and proceeded farthest in fields like sociology, history, psychology, and anthropology, which fall in the sex-neutral range of disciplines where the sense of overt sex discrimination is highest. The ambiguous intellectual position of these fields with respect to masculine or feminine label, teaching or research orientation, makes them especially able to justify intellectually a position that takes women's experience into account.

The second observation is that it may be only a matter of time until the perspective of "women's studies" reaches both the sciences and the "female professions." Like sex-role crossover in other realms, the sciences are ripe for inclusion of more humane issues in their research, and the "feminine" specialties can well encourage women to become the masters of rational technique. Ruth Hubbard (1976) has already reported the introduction of a biology course at Harvard subtitled "Biology and Social Issues," which addresses the relationship between science and society. She gives a sample issue:

> If women had constituted half the scientific work force since the time Western science broke away from its medieval precursors, its structure and content would be different—it would have addressed different questions and probably found different answers. One of the easiest places to see this is in medical science, for here the fact that the definitions of health and disease have been established by men has had the odd result that all woman's normal but specifically feminine functions—menstruation, pregnancy, childbirth, lactation, menopause—have been defined as diseases requiring medical attention and/or intervention . . . but the specialty of andrology—diseases of men—was considered briefly and deemed unnecessary. As defined by male doctors, woman is sick; man isn't. [Hubbard, 1976: 9-10]

In another "male" field, the law, courses on women and the law had by 1972 spread to half of all law schools (Wallach, 1975: 107).

At the other end of the spectrum in the traditional women's fields there are also recent signs of interest in extending the concept of women's studies. Florence Howe (1975: 165) has stated the case as follows:

> Instead of bemoaning the fact that women numerically dominate the teaching, nursing, and social work professions, why not consider that fact important strategically? Why encourage the most talented women to enter a physics laboratory rather than a school superintendent's office or a department of educational administration? Why is it more important to spread a thin tokendom of women through the nontraditional kingdoms than to attempt a transformation of the traditional ghettos themselves—especially if one of those, the public school system, is responsible for the perpetuation of sex stereotyping and the low aspirations of women?

The health professions have begun some critical self-appraisal through women's eyes. *Our Bodies, Ourselves*, published by the Boston Women's Health Book Collective (1971; 1973), advocates a less hierarchical and more woman-centered approach to women's health issues; it also encourages women to take a dispassionate look at their own bodies. A recent issue of *Social Policy* (September-October, 1975) gives a scholarly consideration to the health-care field from the standpoint of feminist social scientists. Various workshops among schoolteachers have begun to raise consciousness and encourage innovations to avoid sex stereotyping in the classroom (McCune, 1973).

Faculty who teach women's studies courses, however, are still heavily concentrated in the nontenured ranks (Sicherman, 1974: 171-172). Until their efforts enter into the mainstream of course offerings and their jobs become secure, the women's studies phenom-

enon must yet be regarded as an experiment not fully institutionalized.

CONTINUING EDUCATION

During the early 1960s a remarkable amount of innovation took
place in women's education. Programs for an older population,
principally made up of women, appeared in a variety of college and
university centers. The University of Minnesota established a center
for continuing education of women in 1960. Radcliffe College
opened the Radcliffe Institute for independent study in 1961. Sarah
Lawrence College offered two courses in 1960-61 and four courses
in 1961-62 to former Sarah Lawrence students who had dropped
out and wished to continue for the degree (Raushenbush, 1961:
268). A decade later Jean Campbell (1973: 109), director of the
women's center at the University of Michigan, reviewed the changes
accomplished and reported that in 1971, 376 programs existed at the
college and university level for returning women.

The growth of continuing education has important structural
implications, for as Campbell implied, its very nature requires commitment to helping students get an education despite the institutional mores that have confined such effort to the age from seventeen to twenty-one. The new programs have all made adjustments in
schedules, financial aid, counseling, and residence requirements
(Women's Bureau, 1971; 1972; 1974). They have instituted new
courses and used new techniques that have recently become available
for assigning credentials to nontraditionally acquired knowledge. The
process helps the educational institution to "universalize" particular
interests and past experience of women and gives them a stepping-
stone to other roles. Vast needs still exist among that population of
women who might finish their high-school education and enter the
skilled trades if adequate counseling and vocational education were
made available to them (Roby, 1976).

But a more radical possibility is also present. The educational
process can move in the opposite direction. In addition to taking
women into the institution and credentialing their experience, educators can extend the learning process into "real life" and thereby
particularize knowledge in ways that make it useful to specific jobs.
James O'Toole (1975b: 31-33) tells us that the opportunity to keep
learning is a key to job satisfaction:

> Career education can deal with the unemployed self by encouraging learning
> through experience. This means that the schools would prepare youth for
> their life careers by building a basis for future growth. With such a back-
> ground, as one grows older one knows how to look for stimulation and how

to find rewards both in one's leisure and in one's work. . . . Acquiring skill without understanding its theoretical background [is] not learning. . . . At the same time, theoretical knowledge is useless and quickly lost by all but the brightest if it is not acquired in the context of practical experience.

By this formula, women's participation in adult education is an important paradigm for how workers in other kinds of occupations might continue their learning. An experiment such as the College of Human Services in New York City is a landmark example. Devoted to new career opportunities for disadvantaged women, it creates as close a possible relationship between fieldwork and classroom in a two-year work-study program. It has discovered "a vast reservoir of unused talent in the . . . neighborhoods" and sought to channel it toward needed services (Campbell, 1973: 101). In addition, the College Entrance Examination Board has since 1968 administered the College-Level Examination Program (CLEP) to give credit for learning that persons may gain outside the classroom, through reading or on-the-job experience.

Women participating in continuing education in mid-life have been found to use the experience in several ways. Some move into different occupations. Others find the educational experience satisfying in and of itself and enlarge or modify the roles they presently occupy at work or in the community (M. S. White, 1970; 1973; Markus, 1973). As John Dewey would have hoped, they have learned to carry over the dead spots in life. Learning becomes self-improvement where there is no fixed or final plateau. It also embodies what Willard Wirtz and the National Manpower Institute (1975: 52) refer to as "career education." By this concept first priority is placed "on infusing—in the truest sense—'liberal arts' and 'vocational' education."

Conway pictured the ultimate realization of sex equality in education as equal access of women graduates to the occupational structure of society. Of all the educational reforms under way, continuing education comes closest to accomplishing this end. It challenges existing modes of teaching based on age difference. It questions fast and early accomplishment as a sign of excellence. It replaces the central traditional assumptions that education comes *before* life and work. If the philosophy of continuing education can eventually win acceptance at the core of universities and colleges, many current structural barriers to women's achievement will vanish at the same time.

NEW LAWS FOR EDUCATIONAL EQUITY

Changes in the law express many of the educational innovations that have taken place during the last decade. The civil-rights move-

TABLE 12. Federal Laws and Regulations on Sex Discrimination and Equity in Educational Institutions Since 1960

Effective Date	Law or Regulation	Institutions Covered	Enforcement
June 1964 (for nonprofessional workers) July 1, 1972 (for professionals)	EQUAL PAY ACT of 1963. (Amended by Education Amendments in 1972). Prohibits discrimination in salaries, benefits on basis of sex. Now covers all employees.	All institutions. None exempt.	Enforced by Wage and Hour Division, Dept. of Labor. Does not require affirmative action other than salary increases and back pay.
July 1965 (for nonprofessional workers) March 24, 1972 (for professionals)	TITLE VII of the CIVIL RIGHTS ACT of 1964. (Amended by the Equal Employment Opportunity Act in 1972). Prohibits discrimination in employment (hiring, upgrading, salaries, benefits, training, etc.) on basis of race, color, religion national origin, or sex. Now covers all employees.	All institutions with 15 or more employees. Religious institutions exempt with respect to hiring persons of particular religion or religious order (including those limited to one sex). Not exempt, however, from prohibition of discrimination based on sex, race, etc.	Equal Employment Opportunity Commission (EEOC). Affirmative action not required unless charges have been filed or included in conciliation agreement or court order.
October 13, 1968	EXECUTIVE ORDER 11246 (as amended by 11375). Prohibits discrimination in employment (hiring, upgrading, salaries, benefits, training, etc.) on basis of race, color, religion, national origin, or sex. Covers all employees.	All institutions with federal contracts of over $10,000. None exempt.	Policy formulated by Office of Federal Contract Compliance (OFCC), Dept. of Labor. HEW has responsibility for contract compliance in all educational institutions. Office for Civil Rights (HEW) conducts reviews, investigations.
November 18, 1971 (Regulations went into effect August 6, 1975)	TITLE VII (Section 799A) & TITLE VIII (Section 845) of the PUBLIC HEALTH SERVICE ACT. (Amended by the Comprehensive Health Manpower Act & the Nurse Training Amendments Act of 1971). Prohibits discrimination in admission of students on basis of sex and against some employees.	All institutions receiving grant, loan, interest, or a contract under Title VII or VIII of the Public Health Services Act. None exempt.	HEW'S Office for Civil Rights (OCR) conducts reviews, investigations. Affirmative action may be required after discrimination is found. OCR may institute proceedings to withdraw or bar future award of federal monies.

TABLE 12. (Continued)

Effective Date	Law or Regulation	Institutions Covered	Enforcement
July 1, 1972 (regulations went into effect July 2˙, 1975)	TITLE IX of the EDUCATIONAL AMENDMENTS of 1972. Prohibits discrimination against students or others on basis of sex in recruiting, admissions, financial aid, student rules, housing rules, health care, insurance benefits, student employment, textbooks, curricula, and athletics.	Covers all educational institutions receiving federal aid. Prohibits discrimination in admissions in vocational, graduate and professional, and public undergraduate institutions. Exempts some religious and military institutions and voluntary single sex youth organizations.	Institutions must undertake self-evaluation, assure government of compliance, keep records and notify others of nondiscrimination policy. OCR to have primary enforcement powers; may institute proceedings to withdraw or bar future award of federal monies.
1974 (guidelines issued August 11, 1975)	WOMEN'S EDUCATIONAL EQUITY ACT. Institutes positive action for women's educational equity. Provides grants to review curricula, texts, tests, preservice and inservice training for educational personnel, and design educational programs for adult women.	Covers all levels including preschool, elementary, secondary, and adult education; also vocational and career education, physical education, and educational administration.	Commissioner of Education authorized to make grants and contracts with public and private nonprofit agencies and individuals to design activities that will promote educational equity. An Advisory Council on Women's Educational Programs in the Office of Education will oversee the program.
October 12, 1976	EDUCATION AMENDMENTS of 1976. Extends and revises Vocational Education Act of 1963, Higher Education Act of 1965, and Title IX of Education Amendments Act of 1972.	Affects national, state and local administration of Vocational Education Law. Gives support for educational research on women's education and jobs.	Consolidates vocational education through block grants to the states. Commissioner of education required to collect data on sex stereotyping in vocational education programs. Some grants for overcoming bias in curriculum, guidance, and testing materials. States are to monitor effort to eliminate sex bias in counseling and curriculum.

Source: Sandler (1973: 456-462); Dunkle and Sandler (1975); Section 408 of Public Law 93-380; *Federal Register* (1975b: 33802-33809); National Advisory Council on Women's Educational Programs (1977a; 1977b). General format of table adapted with changes from one prepared by Project on the Status and Education of Women (1977).

ment provided the women's movement with important tools and precedents for fighting sex discrimination. Women first used the civil-rights law to press for affirmative action and equal treatment as educational employees. Then, after 1970, other laws were devised to achieve equity in educational programs.

Affirmative action.

The Equal Pay Act of 1963 as early as 1964 protected nonprofessional workers against sex discrimination in salaries and benefits. The Civil Rights Act of 1964 also protected nonprofessional workers against discrimination in employment (hiring, training, and so on) on the basis of sex. But until these acts were amended in 1972 to cover professional workers, women faculty members and researchers had no recourse against unfair treatment except through a nonobvious route based on Executive Orders 11246 and 11375, which became effective in 1968. These orders barred sex discrimination in employment in any institution receiving over $10,000 in federal contracts. (See Table 12.)

It was Bernice Sandler and a small group of women working principally through WEAL who hit upon the strategy of contract compliance. In a few years, they helped to generate hundreds of complaints against sex discrimination in universities (Freeman, 1975; Sandler, 1973). By early 1975 no federal funds had ever been actually withheld from a university on the basis of sex discrimination, however. Nor had any complaint ever been refuted (Sandler, 1975).

The concept of affirmative action has been central to efforts at changing the sex composition of faculties and administration. According to the HEW Guidelines for enforcing Executive Order 11246 and Revised Order No. 4 in the field of higher education, affirmative action requires the employer to "make additional efforts to recruit, employ, and promote qualified members of groups formerly excluded. . . ." (Carnegie Council, 1975: 116). Affirmative action means a good faith effort on the part of an employer to hire minority employees in proportions consistent with their numbers in the pool of qualified applicants. Such a proportion is defined as a positive *goal* against which past and present efforts can be measured.

Resistance to the concept of affirmative action has been based on two arguments. The first is that a goal is really a quota that keeps out the majority group. The de Funis case crystallized the issues. It was based on the complaint of a law student who claimed that he had been denied admission to the University of Washington law school because his place had gone to someone from a preferred minority group who was less qualified and had lower test scores. Then Alan

Bakke made a similar claim with respect to his being denied admission to the University of California Medical School at Davis. The California Supreme Court ruled that burden of proof was on the University of California to show that Bakke would not have been admitted even in the absence of a special minority admissions program.

The other argument against affirmative action is primarily represented by Richard Lester's *Antibias Regulations of Universities* (1974). Lester maintains that the pool of qualified minority candidates for elite academic positions is so small that concerted affirmative action (here meaning preferential treatment) would result in a decline in quality of students in top academic institutions.

Lester's arguments have been effectively answered by two women who have been active on behalf of women in higher education. Sandler (1975) points up factual errors in Lester's account of how affirmative action works. She also addresses his hidden assumption that equal access to job opportunities by minorities will result in a lowering of standards. Tobias (1974) uncovers an implicit age bias in Lester's work, that young faculty of promise will be identified between the ages of twenty-five and thirty and few women will be found then because of their family obligations. As Tobias shows, women of promise could presumably be identified at some later point in their life cycle if hiring practices were properly designed to find rather than exclude them. As the American Association of University Professors (A.A.U.P.) has said in its statement of affirmative action, "standards of competence and qualification [should] be set independently of the actual choices made . . . for otherwise, a fatal circularity ensues. . . ." Effort should be made not to "inadvertently foreclose consideration of the best qualified persons by untested presuppositions." (Carnegie Council, 1975: 247, 249).

Practical measures for locating qualified minority candidates include rosters, open job advertisements, and checks by the college or university to see that a proper effort has been made. In addition organizations like the Higher Education Resource Services (H.E.R.S.), with offices both in New England and the Middle Atlantic region, have served as clearinghouses for bringing together job openings and qualified women applicants.

Still missing from all these efforts, however, is any sustained critical examination of the faculty role as it is now structured, or of the "standards of excellence" that presumably fill it with the best-qualified candidates. Yet it can be argued that both the role and the standards of excellence are somewhat arbitrary and relative, that they do not always operate to produce either the most significant research or the best teaching. The educational ironies produced by the present system are described by Arlie R. Hochschild (1975: 63):

If a Cuban or a Wintu Indian happened to walk down the fourth floor of Barrows Hall at Berkeley, she might get the impression of a bare mustard yellow tunnel, long and dimly lit from above, casting ghostly shadows on the under-eyes of its "trespassers." Closed doors to left and right offer a few typed notices of class meeting schedules, envelopes containing graded examinations, and one wry sign, posted several months earlier by a man who had just won tenure: THIS MACHINE IS NOT IN ORDER. It might be experienced as a place where no one lives. It's the one place professors are supposed to be available to students, but since students unwittingly block the extension of one's vita, it's the one place from which professors are curiously absent. Only instructors not yet in the tenure race and older professors on the other side of it might answer to a knock. The rest are seemingly lost between their several offices (the institute, the department, the home). Often they pick up their mail at dawn or dusk when the department office is closed. . . . On a day when the printed notice says a middle-rank professor will be in, a small society of students will assemble on the floor against one wall. They have penciled their names on a posted sheet that marks time in 15-minute pieces; and they may be rehearsing their lines.

The deserted faculty offices and the waiting students raise questions about the present organization of teaching and research. Are there perhaps other and better ways by which the university could organize the work of its faculty, teach its students, and meet the needs of the larger society?

The answer from the established institutions still comes back that research is the criterion to be given first priority. Derek Bok, in the 1975-76 President's annual report to the Harvard Board of Overseers, states the position:

Some critics have suggested that the most useful step to strengthen the College would be to encourage the appointment of professors whose strength lies in teaching rather than research. But I am persuaded that this is a superficial view of the matter. There is no way of knowing whether the enthusiastic dedicated young teacher will continue to be successful after the age of forty-five. Thus, scholarship must remain the decisive factor, not only because it is intrinsically important but [also] because it offers the most reliable assurance that even dull teachers will continue to have something of value to communicate. [Bok, 1977: 102]

The feminist critic of the modern university might ask whether the research of the enthusiastic, dedicated young scholar may not as often turn out to be arid as the exciting young teacher turns out to be dull.

Educational programs.

After 1971 women had laws available to support educational equity in matters broader than employment alone. The Public Health Service Act, Title IX of the 1972 Education Amendments, and the

Women's Educational Equity Act of 1974 gave recourse against discrimination in admissions, financial aid, textbooks, and curriculum. The Women's Educational Equity Act also supports efforts to devise counseling, continuing education, and other innovative programs that would broaden women's career options. The Educational Amendments of 1976 particularly support new data collection and efforts to eliminate sex stereotyping from vocational education (see Table 12).

Guidelines for enforcing Title IX were slow to materialize. After three years of debate they were finally published in the summer of 1975 (*Federal Register*, 1975a: 24127-24145). The sports provisions of Title IX have generated particular resistance and publicity. Universities with major football teams have tried to argue that antidiscriminatory regulations do not apply to revenue-producing sports (even though they may run a deficit made up by the educational institution). Women's groups have noted that women's sports budgets nationwide are only 2 percent as much as men's budgets (Dunkle, 1975). Brigham Young University, a Mormon institution, has argued that prohibitions against sex-differentiated dress codes and inquiry regarding marital or sexual life interferes with the religious and moral principles by which the university is governed (Walsh, 1976).

In the first year following the publication of the Title IX guidelines the most important consequence was perhaps the institutions' own self-evaluation. Dunkle (1975) predicted that institutions would discover sex discrimination in a number of heretofore unrecognized areas such as admissions, scholarships (including athletic scholarships), physical education classes, and "equal benefits" provisions for employees.

Guidelines for enforcing the Women's Educational Act of 1974 were also published in the summer of 1975 (*Federal Register*, 1975b: 33801-33809). The legislation provided for action in three areas: (1) removal of sex stereotypes from curricula and textbooks, (2) critical evaluation of educational policies and practices that result in women's underrepresentation in certain jobs such as educational administration, and (3) development of positive programs for women's "career education" through in-school programs, counseling and guidance, and later continuing education in the community or on the job.

The Education Amendments of 1976 extended and revised earlier legislation contained in the Vocational Education Act of 1963, the Higher Education Act of 1965, and Title IX of the Education Amendments of 1972. Particularly significant were new provisions to change vocational education by attempting to remove sex bias. The legislation authorizes support for efforts to counter sex stereotyping in curriculum and guidance. Some federal grants to the states will be used to support programs that encourage *both* males and females to combine the roles of homemaker and wage earner (National Advisory Council on Women's Educational Programs, 1977*a*; 1977*b*).

As implementation of the new legislation proceeds, it will be important that its leaders are guided by some vision of the crossover ideal. Experiments of the last decade suggest that educational equity for women is a two-part process resulting in enlargement of both "male" and "female" realms of learning. One aspect is movement of women into the educational system, toward the "male" disciplines, into the core programs where they have the same privileges and encouragement as men. The other aspect that is less obvious and more recent is the movement of men into the particular worlds of work and family life, toward the service vocations where women have been concentrated. There men may share some of the inevitable problems of underemployment and repetitious work that women long have known. As more are educated but the number of "interesting" jobs remains relatively small and finite, both sexes will have to cope together with ways of continuous learning that occupy the unemployed self. To envision what, under such conditions, it would be worthwhile to learn, it is finally necessary to consider more general life goals and values against which the purpose of our present educational system can be measured.

INSTRUMENTAL AND EXPRESSIVE VALUES IN EDUCATION

Education has two major purposes. It shapes and continues the culture itself by creating and passing on knowledge. At the same time it forms the personality of the students who pass under its influence. Educational institutions give them information, a sense of competence, and standards of judgment that they will use at work or in the rest of their lives.

The sex-role revolution raises possible alternative standards by which to measure both these educational functions. With respect to the science and culture of the nation, the emergence of "feminine" concerns suggests the possibility that our knowledge has been all too instrumental in the service of narrow utilitarian goals. An important alternative to consider is whether social and humanitarian considerations should be given more emphasis.

With respect to personality formation, the sex-role revolution raises the theoretical possibility that the socialization process has been too "masculine" in its insistence on objectivity, de-emphasis of feelings, and inattention to the moral and political community.

Unbalanced emphasis on achievement and competition for its own sake can overshadow the ultimate purpose of the knowledge itself, as in the case of premed students who have in some universities reportedly sabotaged each other's experiments in the chemistry lab in order to undermine their competitors.

One possible response is, of course, to insist on more "ethical" behavior. Robert K. Merton (1957: 140) pointed out some years ago, however, that sharp practices by a deviant are ultimately a clue to imbalance between more general ends and means. The remedy is to recover a clearer vision of educational purpose so that winning a competition ceases to be an end in itself.

The final purposes of education are to keep human beings and society functioning as well as they possibly can within the limitations of present resources. Science and the arts must not mislead people by putting current academic fashions ahead of ultimate truths. Nor should educational institutions mislead students by rewarding them for behavior that is unrelated to the real tests of life.

Feminist analysis of educational institutions suggests there may be danger ahead if purpose and standards are skewed too far in the instrumental direction, to the detriment of humanistic and expressive values. Certain scientific and educational achievements may be rewarded that are in the long run maladaptive. The alternative is to recover those aspects of human feeling and experience that have been cut away, both in the creation of science and culture and in the educational process itself.

JOINING SCIENCE AND FEELING

In the seventeenth and eighteenth centuries, the first scientists took nature into the laboratory to understand it by separating it from complex and confusing background events. Today, however, biologist Ruth Hubbard (1976: 11) notes that students very frequently plant their first seed in the "science corner" of the nursery school or touch their first frog or piglet on the dissecting table. Hubbard's example points up the value of specific, objective procedures for the early scientists who had a rich experience of nature; it also suggests the danger to modern-day students and researchers who may pursue the "scientific method" without the necessary diffuse backdrop of experience that their predecessors enjoyed. For the contemporary scientist, discovery may now best occur by moving observation out of the laboratory, back to the confusing and complex worlds from which laboratory experiments select only a thin slice of reality.

Some years ago Robert K. Merton showed why Nazi science was doomed to less than lasting validity. It failed to adhere to central normative safeguards in the scientific community, such as universalism, sharing of results, disinterestedness, and organized skepticism (Merton, 1957: 553). Using a Mertonian type of analysis, we might consider how our present science may be invalid because it fails to take into account certain broader ecological or humanistic principles that inhere in the larger community of which science is a part. Wilma Scott Heide (1974), an outspoken feminist critic of higher education, has gone so far as to suggest that the "objectivity" of certain disciplines is not only a delusion but also works against the long-range usefulness of science and social science to people. Instead, she argues, the scholarly disciplines must take into account the "subjective" definitions of what people themselves consider desirable and work to implement these values. Otherwise society will reward doctors for reinforcing a definition of "health" that keeps people alive by superhuman technology while allowing others to become sick and die through lack of attention and simple preventive care. Or the educational system will continue to reward professors whose "work" is interrupted when they see their students.

The history of past science shows that systems of thought have flourished within accepted paradigms until it became apparent that important assumptions were left out (Kuhn, 1962; 1970). What caused shifts in paradigm to occur? Why were Copernicus or Pasteur not heard at first, even resisted, then understood and applauded later on? Scientific paradigms change in part because social and scientific attitudes change (McDonagh, 1976). The sex-role revolution promises to introduce such an attitude shift that will have long-term effects on the course of scientific and cultural development. With increased appreciation of the expressive and "feminine" aspects of culture, there is likely to be an ever growing effort in science to recover the diffuse aspects of nature.

In the arts and humanities and human-service professions, on the other hand, "masculine" self-assertion and instrumental approaches may be the new lessons that adherents of these disciplines will learn. Florence Howe's (1975: 165) admonition that women discover their self-worth in the traditional "female" professions—teaching, homemaking, child care, nursing, and social work—is part of this development.

JOINING EDUCATION AND LIFE

As a person is educated, it is not just the weak areas that need filling out. The sense of self, of individual identity, should also be nourished and encouraged. The sex-role revolution has had three types of impact on the formation of persons. It has exposed women to the male world and helped them try to enter it more than ever before; it has exposed males to women's culture and invited them to accept it as part of their own; and, in a few instances that are becoming increasingly frequent, it has identified "feminine" qualities and affirmed their value in women (and men).

The greatest tension and uncertainty have surrounded the relative emphasis that should be given each of these themes. Continued emphasis on male culture for women could result in detriment to both women and men. They could end up feeling fragmented, competitive, numb, or out of touch with their own larger senses and feelings. Yet for women not to learn some of the professionalism and objectivity, affective neutrality, and stratagems of the male world appears to doom them forever to second place in the hierarchy of success. So coeducation and affirmative action have been supported for these reasons.

The other two themes are more radical, however. To discover the expressive in women and men and to assert its value runs counter to the major assumptions of American culture, which have centered around mastery, self-control, and achievement. Yet changed social conditions may now make a shift from the material production of goods to a concern for the quality of life a necessary adaptation for long-term survival of society. Several recent trends in higher education such as "coresidence" and the new vocationalism seem related.

Coresidence of males and females in the same dormitory implicitly recognizes that people have to go on eating and sleeping and attending to the daily necessities of life even as they work and think. Talcott Parsons (1974: 273) has said this development, together with the loosening of "parietal" regulations, is "perhaps the most conspicuous area in which something like a revolution" has occurred in the last decade on the American academic scene. The new type of college living pushes pressure for integration of work and living demands to a younger age.

New efforts to combine jobs with study also implicitly teach that learning and thoughtful living are processes that continue throughout life and are not just to be segregated in four years of college or preprofessional training. Symbolically, women had been associated with families, men with work; men had been associated with learning and rationality, women with all the rest of life. Now continuing education is helping to break down the boundaries of sex-stereotyped territories. Greater flexibility in educational schedule makes it possible for each sex to combine both work and family life. At the same time the new educational process may also make possible "career education" that joins liberal studies with practical learning in a vocation.

None of these trends are yet, however, entirely secure. While greater opportunity for males to express their feelings and females to be self-assertive and instrumental is generally thought to be a good thing, no one can say quite why. This chapter has suggested that any culture which becomes too one-sided with regard to either instrumental or expressive values runs the risk of being maladapted for the future unknown. The current revolution in sex roles promises to recover the diffuse and expressive dimension of life and to restore it to a place of respect alongside instrumental modes of action. The result promises to be a more humane and effective balance in the culture among science, humanities, and the arts, and in the person among thought, feeling, and action.

SUMMARY

The sex-role revolution has brought to education searching questions about how women can be better prepared to take advantage of occupational and political opportunities. At the same time, the feminist perspective raises the possibility that improved education alone will not be sufficient to catapult women into positions of power and equal responsibility with men. Instead, a more radical critique of our science and culture may be in order, a critique that points up the sterility of narrow preoccupation with numbers of articles published or tenure battles to the detriment of teaching, learning, and pursuit of difficult but significant questions that may not lead to quick results.

The history of educational institutions since the turn of the century indicates that the value of cognitive rationality as applied to the development of science and culture has been of growing importance, particularly at the great universities of national renown. While research power and fame of the universities have grown, however, the position of women has declined. The percentage of women both in senior ranks of the faculty and in students receiving doctoral degrees was lower in 1960 than in 1930. Plausible reasons for the drop include the greater percentage of educated women marrying, the advantage given men by the GI Bill, and the broadening of higher education to include less elite and less professionally committed women. Added to all these is the possibility that the standards of academic accomplishment themselves changed, requiring more mobility, more research production, and greater emancipation from involvement with students, families, and local communities. These changing standards put women at a particular disadvantage because of their heavier responsibility for families, their lower mobility, devotion to students, and lack of access to research networks and communities that were heavily male-dominated.

If the rules of the present educational enterprise are accepted as they are, there are two major routes by which to remedy women's situation: (1) by provision of better training opportunities and (2) by efforts to remove discrimination and to institute affirmative action. If the rules of the educational enterprise are themselves subjected to critical review, there are two other more radical possibilities to be reconsidered: (3) the restructuring of the educational process through admissions, curriculum, and continuing education and (4) the reorganization of knowledge to put greater emphasis on expressiveness in the scientific and technological realms and greater emphasis on instrumentalism in the humanistic and artistic realms. This analysis implies that all four types of action are not only possible but desirable, for the good of both women and the whole society.

Giving women access to more equitable training opportunities is the most popular solution to the problem of education equity between the sexes; it is also the least threatening to the established social structure. Proposals at this level frequently include improvement of girls' training in mathematics, better access to scholarships and fellowships, team sports, and professional education, better counseling, and more female role models. Of all the remedies at the psychological and pedagogical level that appear most promising, the new psychology of the life cycle offers most hope to women. It suggests alternative ways to organize education over the entire life span to permit movement among family, work, and study.

At the next more general level of social structure, the classroom or actual learning situation, standards for measuring performance or the style of some disciplines may put women at a disadvantage. These subtle factors may explain higher attrition rates for women students and the cluster of women in the nontenured and peripheral positions at the bottom of the academic pyramid. Up to now, criticism of the dual educational structure that channels women so heavily into one set of activities and men into another has focused on obvious sex-related exclusions from admissions or eligibility. But a more penetrating analysis of discipline style and content shows that the educational structure may give the male an advantage in "male" disciplines and access to on-the-job training for research while it relegates females to the periphery.

The third level of analysis, focusing as it does on general patterns of institutional structure, suggests several avenues of reform. Restructuring the educational process through admissions, curriculum, staff, and relations to the adult occupational world has elicited a great many attempts at change during the past decade. Single-sex colleges went coed; major professional schools began to admit more women; the curriculum saw women's studies emerge and grow. Continuing education programs for older women students became a model for the ways in which four-year undergraduate institutions could change to compensate for declining enrollment in the 1970s. Finally, Title IX of the Higher Education Amendments of 1972, the Women's Educational Equity Act of 1974, and the Educational Amendments of 1976 gave legal precedent for reviewing the implicit structure of education—schedules, courses, counseling, credit for past work, and sex stereotyping of curriculum—to see how it could be changed to bring greater advantage to women.

Ultimately, even these reforms are doomed to the periphery of the educational establishment unless some more radical reappraisal of the purpose and quality of education is undertaken. When that is done, it turns out that traits usually stereotyped as feminine—expressiveness, humanistic concern for the whole person and the community—are in undersupply in much of the scientific and technological research community. On the other hand, cosmopolitan and liberal values, objectivity and universalism usually stereotyped as "masculine" values are in undersupply in the professions involving primary care of persons—teaching, nursing, child care, family life, social work, and local community activity. We need not only to find out how to promote crossover between masculine and feminine in our science and human-service professions; but we need also to learn how to teach males expressive qualities while we teach females self-confidence and assertive behavior.

It is not the purpose of this chapter to choose any one analysis as more fitting nor to say any one solution is more important than all the others. By contextual analysis that delineates ever wider pools of influence surrounding the individual, however, we see that mere retraining of women is not enough; mere removal of discrimination is not enough; fiddling with the admissions ratio or numbers of women's studies courses is not enough. Nothing less than a commitment to the equal value of male and female, of research and teaching, of the instrumental and the expressive, of the specialized and the general will do. When this truth is grasped, the practical steps of working out the means for achieving educational equity will follow in due course.

REFERENCES FOR CHAPTER SIX

Alper, Thelma. 1973. "The Relationship between Role Orientation and Achievement Motivation in College Women." *Journal of Personality* 41 (March): 9-31.

American Bar Association. 1972. *Review of Legal Education: Law Schools and Bar Admissions Requirements in the United States 1967-1971.* Chicago: A.B.A.

Association of Governing Boards of Universities and Colleges. 1974. *AGB Notes* 5 (October): 3.

Astin, Helen S. 1972. "Sex Differences in Mathematical and Scientific Precocity." Paper presented to the American Association for the Advancement of Science, 26-31 December, Washington, D.C.

Baird, Leonard L. 1973. *The Graduates: A Report on the Characteristics and Plans of College Seniors.* Princeton, N.J.: Educational Testing Service.

Bardwick, Judith. 1971. *Psychology of Women: A Study of Bio-cultural Conflicts.* New York: Harper and Row.

Baruch, Rhoda. 1967. "The Achievement Motive in Women: Implications for Career Development." *Journal of Personality and Social Psychology* 5, no. 3: 260-267.

Bayer, Alan E., and Astin, Helen S. 1975. "Sex Differentials in the Academic Reward System." *Science,* 23 May, pp. 796-802.

Bernard, Jessie. 1964. *Academic Women.* University Park, Pa.: Pennsylvania State University Press.

Block, Jeanne H. 1976. "Issues, Problems, and Pitfalls in Assessing Sex Differences: A Critical Review of *The Psychology of Sex Differences.*" *Merrill-Palmer Quarterly* 226, no. 4: 283-308.

Bok, Derek. 1977. "The President's Report." *Harvard Magazine,* March-April, pp. 98-113.

Boocock, Sarane S. 1972. *An Introduction to the Sociology of Learning.* Boston: Houghton Mifflin.

Boston Women's Health Book Collective. 1971; 1973. *Our Bodies, Ourselves: A Book by and for Women.* New York: Simon and Schuster.

Brim, Orville G., Jr., and Abeles, Ronald. 1975. "Work and Personality in the Middle Years." *Items* 29 (September): 29-33.

Burstyn, Joan N. 1973. "Women and Education: A Survey of Recent Historical Research." *Educational Leadership* 31 (November): 173-177.

Campbell, Jean W. 1973. "Women Drop Back In: Educational Innovation in the Sixties." In *Academic Women on the Move.* Edited by A. S. Rossi and A. Calderwood. New York: Russell Sage Foundation.

Carnegie Commission on Higher Education. 1973. *Opportunities for Women in Higher Education.* Hightstown, N.J.: McGraw-Hill.

Carnegie Council on Policy Studies in Higher Education. 1975. *Making Affirmative Action Work in Higher Education.* San Francisco: Jossey-Bass.

Carter, Hugh, and Glick, Paul C. 1970. *Marriage and Divorce: A Social and Economic Study.* Cambridge, Ma.: Harvard University Press.

Cartter, Allan M. 1971. "Scientific Manpower for 1970-1985." *Science,* April, pp. 132-140.

Centra, John A. 1974. *Women, Men, and the Doctorate.* Princeton, N.J.: Educational Testing Service.

Chodorow, Nancy. 1974. "Family Structure and Feminine Personality." In *Woman, Culture, and Society.* Edited by M. Z. Rosaldo and L. Lamphere. Stanford, Ca.: Stanford University Press.

Citizens Advisory Council on the Status of Women. U.S. Department of Labor, Employment Standards Administration. 1973. *Women in 1972.* Washington, D.C.: U.S.G.P.O.

——. 1974. *Women in 1973.* Washington, D.C.: U.S.G.P.O.

Common Cause. 1973. *Action Program for Ratification of the Equal Rights Amendment.* Washington, D.C.: Common Cause.

Conway, Jill K. 1974. "Coeducation and Women's Studies: Two Approaches to the Question of Women's Place in the Contemporary University." *Daedalus* 103 (Fall): 239–249.

David, Opal G., ed. 1959. *The Education of Women: Signs for the Future.* Washington, D.C.: American Council on Education.

Davis, James A. 1964. *Great Aspirations: The Graduate School Plans of America's College Seniors.* Chicago: Aldine.

Deinhardt, Barbara. 1974. " 'Mother of Men'?" In *Women in Higher Education.* Edited by W. T. Furniss and P. A. Graham. Washington, D.C.: American Council on Education.

Dennis, Lawrence E., ed. 1963. *Education and a Woman's Life.* Washington, D.C.: American Council on Education.

Dexter, Elizabeth Anthony. 1924. *Colonial Women of Affairs: A Study of Women in Business and the Professions in America before 1776.* Boston: Houghton Mifflin.

Dodge, Norton T. 1966. *Women in the Soviet Economy.* Baltimore, Md.: Johns Hopkins University Press.

Dolan, Eleanor F. 1972. "A Century for Equality." *Improving College and University Teaching* 20, no. 1: 23–27.

Dornbusch, Sanford M. 1966. "Afterword." In *The Development of Sex Differences.* Edited by E. E. Maccoby. Stanford, Ca.: Stanford University Press.

Douvan, Elizabeth. 1959. "Adolescent Girls: Their Attitudes toward Education." In *The Education of Women: Signs for the Future.* Edited by O. G. David. Washington, D.C.: American Council on Education.

Dunkle, Margaret C. 1975. "Title IX: New Rules for an Old Game." *Teachers College Record* 76 (February): 385–399.

Dunkle, Margaret C., and Sandler, Bernice. 1975. "Sex Discrimination against Students: Implications of Title IX of the Education Amendments of 1972." Washington, D.C.: Association of American Colleges, Project on the Status and Education of Women.

Elder, Glen H., Jr. 1974. *Children of the Great Depression: Social Change in Life Experience.* Chicago: University of Chicago Press.

Ernest, John. 1976. "Mathematics and Sex." Santa Barbara, Ca.: University of California at Santa Barbara, Mathematics Department.

Estler, Suzanne E. 1975. "Women as Leaders in Public Education." *Signs* 1, no. 2 (Winter): 363–386.

Federal Register. 1975*a*. "Nondiscrimination on Basis of Sex: Education Programs and Activities Receiving or Benefiting from Federal Financial Assistance." 4 June, pp. 24127–24145.

——. 1975*b*. "Women's Educational Equity Program." 11 August, pp. 33801–33809.

Feldman, Saul D. 1974. *Escape from the Doll's House: Women in Graduate and Professional School Education.* New York: McGraw-Hill.

Freedman, Daniel G., and Omark, Donald R. 1973. "Ethology, Genetics, and Education." In *Cultural Relevance and Educational Issues.* Edited by F. A. J. Ianni and E. Storey. Boston: Little, Brown.

Freeman, Jo. 1975. *The Politics of Women's Liberation.* New York: McKay.

Friedan, Betty. 1963. *The Feminine Mystique.* New York: Norton.

Furniss, W. Todd, and Graham, Patricia Albjerg, eds. 1974. *Women in Higher Education.* Washington, D.C.: American Council on Education.

Getman, Lisa. 1974. "From Conestoga to Career." In *Women in Higher Education.* Edited by W. T. Furniss and P. A. Graham. Washington, D.C.: American Council on Education.

Giele, Janet Zollinger. 1973. "Age Cohorts and Changes in Women's Roles." Paper presented at the annual meeting of the American Sociological Association, August, New York City.

Graham, Patricia Albjerg. 1970. "Women in Academe." *Science,* 25 September, pp. 1284–1290.

——. 1975. "So Much to Do: Guides for Historical Research on Women in Higher Education." *Teachers College Record* 76 (February): 421–429.

——. 1976. "Women in Higher Education: Historical Perspective." Paper presented at the annual meeting of the American Association for the Advancement of Science, Boston.

Grant, Gerald, and Riesman, David. 1975. "An Ecology of Academic Reform." *Daedalus* 104 (Winter): 166–191.

Gurin, Gerald; Veroff, Joseph; and Feld, Sheila. 1960. *Americans View Their Mental Health: A Nationwide Interview Survey.* New York: Basic Books, Monograph Series, no. 4 of the Joint Commission on Mental Illness and Health.

Harris, Ann Sutherland. 1970; 1973. "Statement." In *Discrimination against Women: Congressional Hearings on Equal Rights in Education and Employment.* Edited by C. R. Stimpson. New York: Bowker.

Heide, Wilma Scott. 1974. "Wellesley—Education for What?" Speech, 20 November, Wellesley College.

Heilbrun, Carolyn G. 1976. "Point of View." *Chronicle of Higher Education,* 15 November, p. 32.

Hochschild, Arlie Russell. 1975. "Inside the Clockwork of Male Careers." In *Women and the Power to Change.* Edited by F. Howe. New York: McGraw-Hill.

Hoffman, Lois W. 1963. "Parental Power Relations and the Division of Household Tasks." In *The Employed Mother in America.* Edited by F. I. Nye and

L. W. Hoffman. Chicago: Rand McNally.

Horner, Matina. 1969. "Fail: Bright Women." *Psychology Today* 3 (November): 36, 38, 62.

———. 1972. "The Motive to Avoid Success and Changing Aspirations of Women." In *Readings on the Psychology of Woman*. Edited by J. Bardwick. New York: Harper and Row.

Howe, Florence. 1975. "Women and the Power to Change." In *Women and the Power to Change*. Edited by F. Howe. New York: McGraw-Hill.

Howe, Florence, and Ahlum, Carol. 1973. "Women's Studies and Social Change." In *Academic Women on the Move*. Edited by A. S. Rossi and A. Calderwood. New York: Russell Sage Foundation.

Hubbard, Ruth. 1976. "Sexism in Science." *Radcliffe Quarterly* 62 (March): 8-11.

James, Edward T., and James, Janet Wilson, with P. S. Boyer. 1971. *Notable American Women, 1607-1950*, 3 vols. Cambridge, Ma.: Harvard University Press.

Jelly, Katherine L. 1974. "Coeducation: One Student's View." In *Women in Higher Education*. Edited by W. T. Furniss and P. A. Graham. Washington, D.C.: American Council on Education.

Jencks, Christopher, and Riesman, David. 1968. *The Academic Revolution*. Garden City, N.Y.: Doubleday.

Johnson, Miriam M.; Stockard, Jean; Acker, Joan; and Naffziger, Claudeen. 1975. "Expressiveness Re-evaluated." *School Review* 83 (August): 617-644.

Kahne, Hilda. 1973. "Women in Science: Employment Prospects and Academic Policies." *Annals of the New York Academy of Science* 208 (March): 143-153.

Kashket, Eva Ruth; Robbins, Mary Louise; Leive, Loretta; and Huang, Alice S. 1974. "Status of Women Microbiologists." *Science*, 8 February, pp. 488-494.

Kaufman, Polly. 1978. "Boston Women and City School Politics, 1872-1905: Nurturers and Protectors in Public Education." Ed.D. dissertation, Boston University.

Keeves, J. P. 1973. "Differences between Sexes in Mathematics and Science Courses." *International Review of Education* 19, no. 1: 47-62.

Kilson, Marion. 1976. "The Status of Women in Higher Education." *Signs* 1, no. 4 (Summer): 935-942.

Kuhn, Thomas S. 1962; 1970. *The Structure of Scientific Revolutions*. Chicago: University of Chicago Press.

Lerner, Gerda. 1969. "The Lady and the Mill Girl: Changes in the Status of Women in the Age of Jackson." *American Studies Journal* 10 (Spring): 5-15. Reprinted in Bobbs-Merrill American History Series H-43.

Lester, Richard A. 1974. *Antibias Regulations of Universities: Faculty Problems and Their Solutions*. New York: McGraw-Hill.

Levine, Adeline, and Crumrine, Janice. 1975. "Women and the Fear of Success:

A Problem in Replication." *American Journal of Sociology* 80 (January): 964–974.

Levy, Betty, and Stacey, Judith. 1973. "Sexism in the Elementary School: A Backward and Forward Look." *Phi Delta Kappan* 55 (October): 105–109.

Lipman-Blumen, Jean. 1972. "How Ideology Shapes Women's Lives." *Scientific American*, January, pp. 34–42.

Lynn, David B. 1972. "Determinants of Intellectual Growth in Women." *School Review* 80: 241–259.

McCarthy, Joseph L., and Wolfle, Dael. 1975. "Doctorates Granted to Women and Minority Group Members." *Science*, 12 September, pp. 856–859.

Maccoby, Eleanor E., ed. 1966. *The Development of Sex Differences*. Stanford, Ca.: Stanford University Press.

Maccoby, Eleanor E., and Jacklin, Carol N. 1974. *The Psychology of Sex Differences*. Stanford, Ca.: Stanford University Press.

McClelland, D. C.; Atkinson, J. W.; Clark, R. A.; and Lowell, E. I. 1953. *The Achievement Motive*. New York: Appleton-Century-Crofts.

McCune, Shirley. 1973. Personal communication to Janet Zollinger Giele and materials available from the Resource Center on Sex Roles in Education, National Foundation for the Improvement of Education, Washington, D.C.

McDonagh, Eileen. 1976. "Attitude Changes and Paradigm Shifts: Social Psychological Foundations of the Kuhnian Thesis." *Social Studies of Science* 6: 51–76.

Markus, Hazel. 1973. "Continuing Education for Women: Factors Influencing a Return to School and the School Experience." University of Michigan, unpublished paper.

Merton, Robert K. 1957. *Social Theory and Social Structure*. New York: The Free Press.

Monsour, Karem J. 1963. "Education and a Woman's Life." In *Education and a Woman's Life*. Edited by L. E. Dennis. Washington, D.C.: American Council on Education.

Morlock, Laura. 1973. "Discipline Variation in the Status of Academic Women." In *Academic Women on the Move*. Edited by A. S. Rossi and A. Calderwood. New York: Russell Sage Foundation.

National Advisory Council on Women's Educational Programs. 1977a. "The Education Amendments of 1976: Impact on Women and Girls Concerning Title IX and Other Amendments." Washington, D.C.: N.A.C.W.E.P.

———. 1977b. "The Education Amendments of 1976: Impact on Women and Girls Concerning Vocational Education." Washington, D.C.: N.A.C.W.E.P.

National Center for Education Statistics, U.S. Department of Health, Education, and Welfare. 1977. *Earned Degrees Conferred 1974–75, Summary Data*. Washington, D.C.: U.S.G.P.O.

O'Toole, James. 1975a. "The Reserve Army of the Underemployed, I, The World of Work." *Change* 7 (May): 26–63.

———. 1975b. "The Reserve Army of the Underemployed, II, The Role of Education." *Change* 7 (June): 26–63.

Parsons, Talcott. 1966. *Societies: Evolutionary and Comparative Perspectives.* Englewood Cliffs, N.J.: Prentice-Hall.

——. 1974. "Stability and Change in the American University." *Daedalus* 103: 269-277.

Parsons, Talcott, and Bales, Robert F. 1955. *Family, Socialization, and Interaction Process.* New York: The Free Press.

Parsons, Talcott, and Platt, Gerald M. 1973. *The American University.* Cambridge, Ma.: Harvard University Press.

Patterson, Michelle. 1973. "Sex and Specialization in Academe and the Professions." In *Academic Women on the Move.* Edited by A. S. Rossi and A. Calderwood. New York: Russell Sage Foundation.

Project on the Status and Education of Women. 1977. "Federal Laws and Regulations Concerning Sex Discrimination in Educational Institutions." Washington, D.C.: Association of American Colleges.

Raushenbush, Esther. 1961. "Unfinished Business: Continuing Education for Women." *Educational Record* 42 (October): 261-269.

Rich, Adrienne. 1975. "Toward a Woman-Centered University." In *Women and the Power to Change.* Edited by F. Howe. New York: McGraw-Hill.

Riley, Matilda W., and Foner, Anne. 1968. *Aging and Society. Vol. 1: An Inventory of Research Findings.* New York: Russell Sage Foundation.

Robinson, Lora H. 1973. "Institutional Variation in the Status of Academic Women." In *Academic Women on the Move.* Edited by A. S. Rossi and A. Calderwood. New York: Russell Sage Foundation.

Roby, Pamela. 1972. "Women and American Higher Education." *Annals of the American Academy of Political and Social Science* 404 (November): 118-139.

——. 1973. "Institutional Barriers to Women Students in Higher Education." In *Academic Women on the Move.* Edited by A. S. Rossi and A. Calderwood. New York: Russell Sage Foundation.

——. 1976. "Toward Equality: More Job Education for Women." *School Review* 84 (February): 181-211.

Rossi, Alice S. 1970. "Status of Women in Graduate Departments of Sociology, 1968-1969." *American Sociologist* 5, no. 1 (February): 1-12.

——. 1970; 1973. "Women in the Seventies: Problems and Possibilities." In *Discrimination against Women: Congressional Hearings on Equal Rights in Education and Employment.* Edited by C. R. Stimpson. New York: Bowker.

Rossi, Alice S., and Calderwood, Ann, eds. 1973. *Academic Women on the Move.* New York: Russell Sage Foundation.

Saario, Terry N.; Tittle, Carol K.; and Jacklin, Carol N. 1973. "Sex Role Stereotyping in Public Schools." *Harvard Educational Review* 43 (August): 386-416.

Sandler, Bernice. 1973. "A Little Help from Our Government: WEAL and Contract Compliance." In *Academic Women on the Move.* Edited by A. S. Rossi and A. Calderwood. New York: Russell Sage Foundation.

———. 1975. "Backlash in Academe: A Critique of the Lester Report." *Teachers College Record* 76 (February): 401–419.

Sanford, Nevitt. 1966. *Self and Society*. New York: Atherton.

Schwartz, Pepper, and Lever, Janet. 1973. "Women in the Male World of Higher Education." In *Academic Women on the Move*. Edited by A. S. Rossi and A. Calderwood. New York: Russell Sage Foundation.

Sells, Lucy W. 1973*a*. "Sex and Discipline Differences in Doctoral Attrition." University of California, Department of Sociology, unpublished paper.

———. 1973*b*. "Sex Differences in Graduate School Survival." Paper presented at the annual meeting of the American Sociological Association, New York City, 28 August.

———. 1976. "Mathematics, Minorities, and Women." *ASA Footnotes* 4 (January): 1, 3.

Senders, Virginia L. 1963. "Discussion Group 2." In *Education and a Woman's Life*. Edited by L. E. Dennis. Washington, D.C.: American Council on Education.

Sewell, William. 1971. "Inequality of Opportunities for Higher Education." *American Sociological Review* 36 (October): 793–809.

Sicherman, Barbara. 1974. "The Invisible Woman: The Case for Women's Studies." In *Women in Higher Education*. Edited by W. T. Furniss and P. A. Graham. Washington, D.C.: American Council on Education.

Smith, M. Brewster. 1968. "Competence and Socialization." In *Socialization and Society*. Edited by J. A. Clausen. Boston: Little, Brown.

Social Policy. 1975. "Women and Health, Special Issue." 6 (September–October).

Sowell, Thomas. 1976. " 'Affirmative Action' Reconsidered." *Public Interest* 42 (Winter): 47–65.

Stark, Rodney. N.d. "Graduate Study at Berkeley: An Assessment of Attrition and Duration." Berkeley, Ca.: Survey Research Center, University of California.

Tidball, M. Elizabeth. 1973. "Perspective on Academic Women and Affirmative Action." *Educational Record* 54 (Spring): 130–135.

Tidball, M. Elizabeth, and Kistiakowsky, Vera. 1976. "Baccalaureate Origins of American Scientists and Scholars." *Science*, 20 August, pp. 646–652.

Tiedeman, David V. 1959. "Career Development of Women: Some Propositions." In *Education of Women: Signs for the Future*. Edited by O. G. David. Washington, D.C.: American Council on Education.

Tobias, Sheila. 1974. "Richard Lester's Book on *Affirmative Action*." Middletown, Ct.: Wesleyan University, mimeographed.

Trecker, Janice Law. 1973. "Sex Stereotyping in the Secondary School Curriculum." *Phi Delta Kappan* 55 (October): 110–112.

Tresemer, David. 1973. "Fear of Success: Popular But Unproven." In *The Female Experience*. Edited by C. Tavris. Del Mar, Ca.: Communications/Research/Machines.

University of Michigan. 1974. "The Higher, the Fewer: Report Prepared by the

Committee to Study the Status of Women in Graduate Education and Later Careers." Ann Arbor, Mi.: University of Michigan, Horace Rackham School of Graduate Studies.

Vetter, Betty M., and Babco, Eleanor L. 1975. *Professional Women and Minorities: A Manpower Data Resource Service.* Washington, D.C.: Scientific Manpower Commission.

Veysey, Laurence R. 1965. *The Emergence of the American University.* Chicago: University of Chicago Press.

Wallach, Aleta. 1975. "A View from the Law School." In *Women and the Power to Change.* Edited by F. Howe. New York: McGraw-Hill.

Walsh, John. 1976. "Brigham Young University: Challenging the Federal Patron." *Science,* 16 January, pp. 160–163.

Waring, Joan. 1975. "Social Replenishment and Social Change." *American Behavioral Scientist* 19 (November-December): 237–256.

Weiss, Carin S. 1972. "The Development of Professional Role Commitment among Graduate Students." Master's thesis, University of Washington.

Weitzman, Lenore J., and Rizzo, Diane. 1974. "Biased Textbooks: A Research Perspective." Washington, D.C.: Resource Center on Sex Roles in Education, National Foundation for the Improvement of Education.

White, Martha Sturm. 1970. "Psychological and Social Barriers to Women in Science." *Science,* 23 October, pp. 413–416.

——. 1973. "Intervention in Women's Transitional Stages." Paper presented at the Conference on Human Development: Issues in Intervention, 30 May to 2 June, Pennsylvania State University, College of Human Development.

Wirtz, Willard, and the National Manpower Institute. 1975. *The Boundless Resource: A Prospectus for Education/Work Policy.* Washington, D.C.: New Republic Books.

Women's Bureau, U.S. Department of Labor, Wage and Labor Standards Administration. 1969. *Trends in Educational Attainment of Women.* Washington, D.C.: U.S.G.P.O.

——. 1971. *Continuing Education Programs and Services for Women.* Washington, D.C.: U.S.G.P.O., pamphlet no. 10, revised.

——. 1972. "Plans for Widening Women's Educational Opportunities." Paper prepared for the Wingspread Conference on Women's Higher Education: Some Unanswered Questions, 13 March, Racine, Wi.

——. 1974. "Continuing Education for Women: Current Developments." Washington, D.C.: U.S.G.P.O.

Woody, Thomas. 1929. *A History of Women's Education in the United States,* 2 vols. New York: Science Press.

7

SYMBOLIC PORTRAYAL OF
MALE AND FEMALE

Then God said, "Let us make man in our image and likeness; and let him have dominion over the fish of the sea, and over the fowl of the air, and over the cattle, and over every creeping thing that creepeth upon the earth." So God created man in His own image; in the image of God created he him; male and female created he them

—Genesis, 1: 26–27.

This is the task we are undertaking today, the creation of a true symbol of ourselves out of our special, lived experience, which will explain our identities, both to others and to ourselves

—Elizabeth Janeway,
Between Myth and Morning: Women Awakening, 1974.

Sex roles are now changing in every major institution of American society. But ancient and traditional patterns of action continue alongside new and emerging modes of behavior. Inevitably the question arises, are the changes permanent? Will present contradictions and strains eventually disappear? Will a new coherent and authentic culture emerge that provides models for action in the future?

As Catharine R. Stimpson (1977: 229) in a recent essay on "Sex, Gender, and American Culture" has said,

> The arts and media are instruments of consciousness, and they cannot reflect, though they may anticipate, a new reality about sex and gender unless that new reality is there. When schools, the work force, the family, the military, government, and economics change, the arts will change. Until then, some of the time, in their anticipatory mode, they will allow their audience a chance to apprehend new forms of sex and gender, to experience them vicariously, to rehearse for the new reality.

Culture can enable people to cope with changing circumstances and even in some cases anticipate them. If it is coherent, culture provides human beings with that distinct capacity to order behavior even in the face of changing conditions that has long been recognized as man's principal advantage over the animals. When, however, culture is inconsistent or poorly fitted to the actual realities that people face, it hinders a sense of meaning and integration. Stimpson, following the English critic Raymond Williams, says culture has three meanings: (1) "culture refers to an ideal world" where absolute or universal values express moral, intellectual, and aesthetic standards of the good for a particular society, (2) "culture refers to a documentary world" that records experience through intellectual and artistic works, and (3) "culture refers to a social world"; it describes social situations and sets forth rules for ordinary behavior. In sum, "culture is the totality of significant patterns of action of a specific group" (Stimpson, 1977: 201).

To these three dimensions of culture may be added a fourth, psychological aspect, which social scientists describe as the "modal personality" or typical life pattern of individuals in a particular society.* Individuals as a result of internalizing values and norms of a culture, are likely to develop a characteristic mode of life, an organization of traits and motives that is in turn passed on to the next generation (Inkeles and Smith, 1974; Erikson, 1950, 1976; Campbell, 1968: 633).

As the invention of authentic images for the modern period goes forward, society will make a selection from past available models as well. The challenge will be to develop a coherent definition of male and female that is at once adequate for tying together past human experience and the new insights that emerge for contemporary society. To accomplish effective symbolic portrayal, these images will have to satisfy four requirements that Joseph Campbell (1968: 609–623), a historian of comparative religion, says are necessary to any complete belief system. These functions are related to the four major components of culture just identified—ideal, documentary, social, and individual. A complete imagery of men and women will have to serve four functions: First, the metaphysical-mystical will define the *ideal* woman or man and the links between female and male modalities of behavior and societal values. Second, the cosmological aspect will link those ideal images to the documentary world and environmental context in which individuals live, thereby tying masculine and feminine behavior to attitudes toward nature. Third, the sociological aspect will link ideal images to the functions and social roles available in the society. Finally, the psychological aspect

---

* These four dimensions of culture correspond with the basic components of "social action" identified by social scientists in the early 1950s. See Parsons and Shils (1951) and the work of Parsons that came afterward.

will represent the ideal personality traits of persons of each sex and will chart the model life course that individuals will ideally follow.

The reader will here recognize in these four aspects of ideal image a correspondence (in reverse order) with the major levels of social structure that have been analyzed throughout this book. Whether in the polity, the economy, the family, or the educational system, evidence of change in sex roles has emerged at the individual level in changing attitudes, in organizations and collectivities where less conventional role assignments have been made, in institutional regulation and policy, and finally in the most abstract principles or values that guide the subsystems of society. This chapter, by taking up the problem of symbolic representation and culture per se, must analyze the relevant components "horizontally" as well as "vertically." That is, it must deal with certain common themes that run across the economy, government, family, and other institutions. These cultural themes as they relate to sex roles are here approached through analysis of the ideal images of men and women. The analysis also deals with the vertical specification of these images through progressively more concrete layers of social structure, taking into account historical location, organizational milieu, and constraints imposed by individual personality.

The point of this analysis is to gather together various strands of social criticism and reform to examine them for the existence of common underlying themes. Such a sifting should identify elements of a usable past, elements that provide continuity and authenticity in the present. It should also indicate the aspects of contemporary ferment that appear most likely to give useful direction for the future.

This chapter proceeds through five steps. The first is to examine the wide array of cultural alternatives for defining sex roles that now confront American women and men. These alternatives are then tested by four standards for judging their coherence and viability under contemporary social conditions. The most general standard poses the question, "Which alternative best contributes to the long-term well-being of society, to human goodness, to fullest realization of the highest human potential?" Relevant evidence has to do with continuities in the human ideal across time periods and across cultures. A somewhat more specific standard asks, "Which alternatives are most consistent with institutional changes in American culture at this point in history?" Relevant evidence here has to do with differences in sex-role images across historical time periods and among major types of society. The third standard, still more concrete, compares actual assignment of sex roles across institutions within a society. Do such organizations as the church or the media project images of men and women that are consistent with actual lived experience in other parts of the society such as the economy and the family? The fourth standard is based on the individual; it asks whether popular psychology accurately portrays the traits and capacities that are known to exist in the two sexes.

Such questions assume that culture is both "active" and "passive." On the one hand, it constitutes the set of symbols, values, images, knowledge, and artifacts that shape individual and societal perceptions of reality. On the other hand, it is modified, however slowly, by the changing experience of individuals and institutions. Throughout the following review this double view should be borne in mind. In some instances culture leads; in others it lags. The problem for society is to select those aspects of both culture and behavior that best promise realization of its ultimate goals.

MALE AND FEMALE IMAGES IN CONTEMPORARY AMERICA

Recent opinion polls reveal some of the prevailing images of women and men in American society. They share several common themes: (1) the images of male and female are strongly differentiated in consistent ways, (2) there is a clear tendency to associate superiority with the male, yet (3) there is at the same time a powerful countercurrent of opinion—belief in the essential similarity of the sexes in some important respects; and (4) there is strong support of equal opportunity for women especially in matters of employment, such as hiring and equal pay.

Differentiation between the sexes is a strong and recurrent theme in studies of personality and role ideals. Clarkson et al. (1970) reported asking forty-eight male and thirty-nine female college-age students to rate a list of personality characteristics for social desirability. The male traits formed a "competency" cluster which described "a rational, competent, active and mature individual . . . capable of functioning effectively in our society." By contrast, the female items fell into a "warmth and expressiveness" cluster that described a gentle, sensitive, expressive individual.

A 1972 study by *Redbook* magazine suggests similar beliefs about personality differences between the sexes. The magazine received 120,000 replies to its questionnaire on women's attitudes about children, marriage, discrimination, sex, pregnancy, and childbirth. Analysis of a subsample of 2,500 returns showed that the great majority of women believed aggressiveness and independence were more common in men and nurturing capacity and empathy and intuition more common in women (see Table 13).

Several national opinion surveys based on probability samples also reveal that a majority of respondents believe career achievement is the primary responsibility of men and child care of women. More than two-thirds of the respondents say that it is more important for a man to have a career than for a woman and that the wife should take care of the home and family (Mason, 1973; Mason et al., 1976). Nearly half reveal that they believe a working mother cannot establish as warm and secure a relation with her children as a mother who does not work (see Table 14).

Cross-cultural studies further suggest that boys and girls are different in their actual behavior. The Whitings found in their studies of childhood in six cultures that boys were more aggressive and dominant than girls. The girls were more likely than the boys to offer help and support to other children. In addition, psychologists have discovered that if a picture is flashed rapidly on a screen, women have greater difficulty recognizing aggressive scenes and men have greater difficulty recognizing the dependency themes (Kagan, 1973).

Besides differentiating between traits and expectations of males and females, people tend to associate *superior value with the male* cluster. Broverman and associates (1970) have made this point dramatically by asking their respondents to check traits of a normal

TABLE 13.   Sex-Typed Traits Reported by A 1972 *Redbook* Questionnaire

TRAITS	TOTAL ANSWERING "MORE COMMON," %	TOTAL ANSWERING "FOR BIOLOGICAL REASONS," %	TOTAL ANSWERING "FOR CULTURAL REASONS," %
*Traits Believed More Common in Men**			
Aggressiveness	59.6	13.8	45.8
Indpendence	68.2	7.1	61.1
Traits Believed More Common in Women			
Nurturing capacity	69.6	42.5	27.1
Empathy and intuition	68.3	46.2	22.1

SOURCE: *Redbook*, "How Do You Feel about Being a Woman? The Results of a *Redbook* Questionnaire" (1972: 9, 10).

*The question was worded as follows: "Some people believe that personality differences between the sexes are biological in origin, others think that they are learned; others say that there are no differences at all. Which of the statements listed best expresses your viewpoint about the traits in entries 4 through 11?" (Other traits listed were: a capacity for deep feeling, objectivity, and rationality, ability to reason abstractly, preference for monogamy. For results, see below.)

TABLE 14. Sex-Role Attitude Items in Four U.S. Sample Surveys

			PERCENTAGE AGREEING		
ATTITUDE ITEM	1964 NORC* SENIORS STUDY MEN, %	WOMEN, %	15-YEAR[†] FOLLOW-UP 1970 (WOMEN ONLY), %	1970 NATIONAL[‡] FERTILITY STUDY (WOMEN ONLY), %	NORTH CAROLINA[s] 1973 STUDY (WOMEN ONLY), %
Achievement-Related					
It is much better for everyone involved if the man is the achiever outside the home, and the woman takes care of home and family.	‖	‖	......	78	65
It is more important for a wife to help her husband ('s career) than to have (one) a career herself.	76	76	81	......	68
Child Care					
A working mother can establish just as warm and secure a relationship with her children as a mother who does not work.	35	54	......	47	55

TABLE 14. (Continued)

	1964 NORC* SENIORS STUDY		PERCENTAGE AGREEING		
ATTITUDE ITEM	MEN, %	WOMEN, %	15-YEAR[†] FOLLOW-UP 1970 (WOMEN ONLY), %	1970 NATIONAL[‡] FERTILITY STUDY (WOMEN ONLY), %	NORTH CAROLINA[§] 1973 STUDY (WOMEN ONLY), %
A preschool child is likely to suffer (emotional damage) if his mother works.	66	60	......	71	49

SOURCE: Mason (1973: Table 1, pp. 138-139).

*Based on a national probability sample of graduating arts and science college seniors of June 1961, who were followed up by mail questionnaire in 1964. The sample contains very few nonwhites. Most persons in the sample were age twenty-four in 1964.

[†]The initial sample for this study was a probability sample of high school sophomores and seniors residing in small- and medium-size metropolitan areas as of 1955. These individuals were followed up by mail questionnaire in 1970. This sample also includes very few nonwhites.

[‡]Based on a national probability sample of ever-married women in 1970. Information was collected through household interviews. This sample contains a representative proportion of blacks and other nonwhites, and it is far more heterogeneous with respect to educational attainment than are the other three samples.

[§]Based on a quota sample of women residing in three North Carolina metropolitan areas who have been married only once and were still married (husband present) as of 1973. Information was collected through household interviews; approximately one-quarter of the sample is black. Over 90 percent of the women in this sample fall into the twenty-five to thirty-four age range; their educational attainment is somewhat higher than that of the comparable age group in the 1970 Census.

[‖] Item asked in 1964, but marginals currently unavailable.

male, a normal female, and a healthy adult. The traits of a "healthy adult" were nearly the same as those of a "normal male," but noticeably different from the stereotypic cluster of female traits.

Perhaps not surprisingly, the *Redbook* survey reveals considerable feelings by women that their work is undervalued and that they are not taken seriously. The results are shown in Table 15. A sizable majority of women in 1972 felt that they were not taken seriously by men, were paid less than men for their ability, and were denigrated by the media.

Nevertheless there are signs of change: surveys show trends that can be interpreted optimistically. Mason's summary of data in Table 14 shows that both in the 1964 NORC study of college seniors and the 1970 fifteen-year follow-up study of high-school students, over four-fifths of women said they would encourage as much independence in their daughters as their sons. Moreover, surveys taken in 1970 and 1973, showed that over three-fourths of the respondents believed in equal pay and employment opportunities for women and more than half believed that a husband should help with the housework (Mason et al., 1976).

The *Redbook* survey shows a number of traits in which women believe there are substantial similarities between the sexes. Over half the respondents believe that no sex differences exist at all in such personality traits as capacity for deep feeling (55.5 percent), objectivity and rationality (61.6 percent), and ability to reason abstractly (58.5 percent). When asked which sex has more advantages or privileges, the majority (56.9 percent) reply that there are advantages and disadvantages for each sex (*Redbook*, 1972: 8-10).

In her review of effects of the contemporary women's movement, Edmiston (1975) asserts that it is "beginning to be accepted

TABLE 15. Discrimination Against Women Reported by A 1972 *Redbook* Questionnaire

ITEM	AGREE, %	DISAGREE, %
Many women who do the same work as their male colleagues earn substantially less money.	90.7	9.2
Most men do not take women seriously	72.3	27.6
The communications media (for example, television and the press) degrade women by portraying them as sex objects or mindless dolls.	73.6	26.4

SOURCE: *Redbook* (1972: 11).

not only for women to function as independent, strong-minded individuals, but also for them to *look* as if they're independent and strong-minded." Programing and commercials on television are beginning to improve. In 1974 the percentage of time that women were depicted in "subservient" roles (housewife, secretary, cook, domestic) dropped to 50 percent as compared with 70 percent in 1971. Some observers go so far as to suggest that the new social movements of the early seventies, with their emphasis on sensitivity and caring, are perhaps signs of the feminization rather than the masculinization of the larger society (Lewis, 1973).

Using data gathered from a national sample of 3,000 women and 1,000 men by the Roper Organization (1974: 19), Joseph Pleck (1977b: 21) notes that there is great similarity in the qualities admired in women and in men as shown in Table 16.

First, for all thirteen traits, and for both male and female respondents, the proportions of respondents indicating admiration for each was on the same side of 50 percent for both sexes. That is, there were no traits admired by a majority for one sex and not admired by a majority for the other. Next, the

T A B L E 16.   Qualities Admired by Women and Men

	QUALITIES MOST ADMIRED IN A MAN (IN PERCENT)		QUALITIES MOST ADMIRED IN A WOMAN (IN PERCENT)	
	Women's Opinions	Men's Opinions	Women's Opinions	Men's Opinions
Intelligence	66	66	57	55
Being sensitive to the feelings of others	51	36	52	38
A sense of humor	46	38	42	38
Gentleness	44	16	37	43
Self-control	37	47	41	37
Being able to express feelings and emotions	22	16	25	24
Leadership ability	21	36	11	10
Willingness to compromise	21	18	21	25
Independence	19	20	24	17
Frankness—speaking out on opinions	18	36	21	20
Competence	11	17	12	14
Sex appeal	6	2	5	26
Being competitive	3	7	4	4

SOURCE: Roper Organization (1974: 19). Reprinted with permission of The Roper Organization, Inc.

rank orders of the traits admired in each sex are quite similar. Women's lists of the five most admired traits for men and women included the same items, and the same lists for men include four traits in common (with gentleness being the important exception). . . .

Further, the most admired traits for both sexes include both masculine and feminine elements. The most admired trait for both is intelligence, presumably masculine. "Feminine" sensitivity to the feelings of others, and gentleness (in women's ratings), are also highly valued.

Pleck (1977a: 186) suggests that nothing less than a major paradigm shift has occurred not only in the popular mind but in the scholarship of sex roles as well. From an earlier view that emphasized the importance of such differences as strength and aggression in which males rank higher, both the society at large and the psychologists who study sex roles have now retreated. Today they are more likely to stress importance of interpersonal skills, traits that both sexes need to acquire.

At the same time that such a shift has occurred in psychology, it is evident in sociology, anthropology, and history as well. While they earlier gave primary emphasis to biological determinants of sex-differentiated behavior, social scientists are now more apt to look for historical and cultural influences on sex roles. The change is to a large extent associated with the introduction of systems theory and cybernetic principles into the social sciences. The earlier paradigm conceived of all behavior, sex roles included, as heavily influenced by their biological underpinnings as follows:

$$Body \longrightarrow Mind \longrightarrow Action$$

Modern social science, however, conceives of action by the individual as heavily influenced by interactions with others in a social context. Furthermore, such action feeds information back to the individual and the group. This has the effect of either modifying or reinforcing present behavior (Giele, 1972a: li). Rather than being unidirectional, this model thus incorporates a number of feedback loops as follows:

$$Body \longrightarrow Mind \longrightarrow Social\ Context \longrightarrow Action$$

This systemic framework for understanding behavior makes understandable how behavior of males and females could be in some contexts sex-differentiated and in others similar. The outcome would depend in large part on the *social context*, which could emphasize either the differences or the similarities. Pleck demonstrates convincingly that a large proportion of traits now expected of males and females in American society are in fact perceived as common to both sexes. In addition, material from the *Redbook* survey, as summarized in Table 13, indicates a large proportion of women believed that men's independent and aggressive behavior was culturally determined. Apparently important elements of the American cultural experience reinforce similarities between the sexes. Still others reinforce differentiation and inequality. The present question then is, What is wanted? What is desirable? Assuming that sex-differentiated behavior need represent only a small residual if the culture so directs, what in fact seems to be the most coherent, consistent, and workable position for Americans to adopt with respect to the nature of innate sex difference and similarity?

One way to answer these questions is by reference first to metaphysical standards, values, and ideals. Following that, we shall consider in turn the relevant historical, sociological, and psychological constraints and opportunities that exist in contemporary America.

IDEAL IMAGES: MALE, FEMALE, AND HUMAN

"The first function of a living mythology, the properly religious function," says Joseph Campbell (1968: 609), "is to waken and maintain in the individual an experience of awe, humility, and respect, in recognition of that ultimate mystery transcending names and form, 'from which . . . words turn back'."

The closest culture can approach to this "ultimate mystery" is through its ideals and values, and, more specifically, through its links between male and female traits and the ultimate goals of the society and its people. These ideal images are of a whole and perfect society and the persons within it that individuals desire to become. To the extent that these ideals are shared, they are cultural ideals and may be found in origin myths, literary classics, and visual representations in classical or popular art. "Images are," in Nancy Goldenberg's (1976: 449) view, "our psychic pictures of action."

Shared images of the ideal society and the ideal person always carry direct or indirect messages about sexuality and gender. The images may be undifferentiated by sex, or they may be clearly male or female, or they may include both male and female elements. This sexuality—undifferentiated, differentiated, or combined—is linked to the order of the larger universe. Two aspects of sexual image are thus of special interest: First, how are traits or qualities of the ideal male or female defined? Second, how are the cultural priorities of the entire society, its values and ideal goals, associated with qualities of the ideal man and woman, with "male" and "female" principles?

Observers who have tried to unravel these connections have generally noted a strong and near universal association between women and nature. Whether this connection should be undone or strengthened, whether society should give greater place to nature rather than to its control, has been at the center of modern debate about how contemporary women and men can achieve wholeness. Accompanying the debate has been a search for more usable images from the past and authentic positive images in the present, both in religion and in literature. Ultimately all these efforts converge on a strong central theme of androgyny, but variously elaborated, each version implying a somewhat different strategy for its achievement.

WOMEN AND NATURE

Since Simone De Beauvoir produced her stunning historical and philosophical analysis of sex roles in *The Second Sex*, first published in America in 1952, a number of other authors have tried to explain prevailing stereotypes of women. Each has noted the strong association of male with culture that transcends nature and with adulthood rather than childhood. In contrast, women are linked to the givens of nature; they are associated with both the happy aspects of childhood and the immaturity left behind when one becomes adult. Two tactics are frequently suggested to change these associations: Women are encouraged to participate in the male world of transcendence and mastery, and they are asked to reject the limited and inferior roles to which they have traditionally been confined.

De Beauvoir (1949; 1968: 63) makes the following association between woman and nature, woman and immanence:

Birth and suckling are not *activities*, they are natural functions; no project is involved; and that is why woman found in them no reason for a lofty affirmation of her existence—she submitted passively to her biological fate. The domestic labors that fell to her lot because they were reconcilable with the cares of maternity imprisoned her in repetition and immanence; they were repeated from day to day in an identical form, which was perpetuated almost without change from century to century; they produced nothing new.

Man's case was radically different; he furnished support for the group, not in the manner of worker bees by a simple vital process, through biological behavior, but by means of acts that transcended his animal nature.

Two solutions are then offered by De Beauvoir (1949; 1968: 679-680, 717, 731)—transcendence through woman's employment and refusal to be confined to a self-centered, narcissistic role:

> It is through gainful employment that woman has traversed most of the distance that separated her from the male; and nothing else can guarantee her liberty in practice. Once she ceases to be a parasite, the system based on her dependence crumbles; between her and the universe there is no longer any need for a masculine mediator. . . . When she is productive, active, she regains her transcendence. . . .
>
> . . . instead of wishing to put man in a prison, woman endeavors to escape from one; she no longer seeks to drag him into the realm of immanence but to emerge, herself, into the light of transcendence. . . . To emancipate woman is to refuse to confine her to the relation she bears to men, not to deny them to her. . . . Let her have her independent existence. . . . Her relations to her own body, to that of the male, to the child will never be identical with those (of the) male. . . .

In her essay, "Is Female to Male as Nature Is to Culture?," Sherry Ortner (1974: 72) also finds association between woman's universal inferior status and her association with nature: "[W]oman is being identified with—or, if you will, seems to be a symbol of—something every culture devalues, something that every culture defines as being of a lower order or existence than itself." This thing is "nature," and to it women are seen as being *closer* than men, as "mediators," whose biology, social roles, and psychological penchant toward emotion and concrete thinking distinguish them from the objective and rational style of men's thinking and of culture itself. Ortner's solution, like that of De Beauvoir, calls for transcendence: "Ultimately both men and women can and must be equally involved in projects of creativity and transcendence" (Ortner, 1974: 87).

Recently a new interpretation of male-female distinctions has begun to compete with the De Beauvoir-Ortner synthesis. Several authors have independently begun to question the universality of women's second-class status as resulting from a closer association between women and nature. Psychologist Zella Luria (1974: 5, 7) questions that childbearing and child rearing are any less "transcendent" than production:

> I think the formulation by De Beauvoir of what is transcendent and what is immanent has elitist and idiosyncratic aspects that luckily have not been pressed by the modern women's movement. De Beauvoir makes clear that biological reproduction is not, by her definition, transcendent. Yet for most of us—men and women—the only continuity with the future will be through

our children. Some few among us—artists, scientists, writers—may leave significant products for the future. Most of us leave only our children, the products of our genes and our care. . . . It seems implied that only a narrow set of productions—literary, scientific, artistic—qualify for transcendence. If that is in fact so, then again women and men are caught in the same net of immanence.

Implicitly also Luria is questioning that women are associated with nature any more than men, for the procreative function is just as important as a means of transcendence to most men as it is to most women.

The unity rather than the opposition between nature and transcendence is more fully developed by theologians Christ (1976) and Plaskow (1976) in their commentary on Margaret Atwood's novel *Surfacing* (1972). Atwood traces connections between a woman's consciousness, the sense of her power that comes from an identification with nature, and the possibilities for self-realization that can result from giving birth, facing death, celebrating or denying the connections between oneself and the animals, the woods, and the water. In a special section of *Signs*, Christ and Plaskow note the symbolic connections between the protagonist's emerging sense of identity and her identification with nature. It is as though she discovers and affirms her own power through recognizing the links between herself as woman and the natural world.

The contemporary passion for controlling nature, however, may automatically put women in an inferior position if they are identified with it. In contrast with De Beauvoir's suggestions that women attain equality through transcendence over nature, another possible strategy is to reorder society's priorities to give greater importance to natural processes, to the ripening and waiting that are required by the natural order. Rosemary Ruether in *New Woman/New Earth* (1975: 186, 204) suggests such a radical change in the social order; because the man/nature dualism is associated with rapacious use of resources, a more responsible stewardship of the earth is fundamentally tied to egalitarian and reciprocal relations between the sexes:

Since women in Western culture have been traditionally identified with nature, and nature, in turn, has been seen as an object of domination by man (males), it would seem almost a truism that the mentality that regarded the natural environment as the object of domination drew upon imagery and attitudes based on male domination of women. . . .

Women must see that there can be no liberation for them and no solution to the ecological crisis within a society whose fundamental model of relationship continues to be one of domination. They must unite the demands of the women's movement with those of the ecological movement to envision a radical reshaping of the basic socioeconomic relations and the underlying values of society.

The practical question then is how to establish new, more complete images of women. The process requires reference to past usage as well as to contemporary lived experience.

THE CONTEMPORARY QUEST FOR AUTHENTIC IMAGES

Americans who write about male and female images are all centrally concerned with one issue. It is the search for a credible image, the "search for a usable past" (Russell, 1974: 73), or "the creation of a true symbol of ourselves" (Janeway, 1974: 180). Some, like Warren Farrell, the champion of "male liberation," and Jessie Bernard, a leading feminist sociologist, assert that not just image but society is at fault: male values are defined as the superior values, whereas female values are ignored or given lower priority (Farrell, 1974: 16-17; Bernard, 1973). Mary Daly, the radical Catholic theologian, believes that "the most basic change has to take place in women—in our being and self-image" (Daly, 1973: 19).

An examination of false and true images of women seems to be in order. "Image," says Elizabeth Janeway (1974: 167), "connotes all the cultural associations—religious, artistic, intellectual, and normative—that define what a person is expected to be and against which a person may indeed rebel." In a changing society, the outlines of the true image are constantly subject to redefinition. "Symbols," says Joseph Campbell (1968: 625), "hold the mind to truth, but are not themselves the truth, hence it is delusory to borrow them. Each civilization, every age, must bring forth its own." Janeway suggests that true images will come about only when women and men of the age listen to their own inner experience. Mary Daly (1973: 157) says they must form an *exodus community* and write a new covenant, which is "the deep *agreement* that is present within the self and among selves. . . ." who find harmony in an environment that is beyond the limits of established institutions.

Contemporary efforts to reject images that no longer fit and to construct a new expression of the self are particularly evident in religion and literature. One common thread runs through them: a rejection of patriarchal representations that are stifling and ill-fitting, and a discovery of equalitarian and androgynous images that offer inspiration and promise.

Religious images.
New theological work and research in the history of religion has turned up an extensive array of negative and positive images of women, not only in the Bible but also in institutionalized religion.

Ancient Christian texts associated with the Gnostic tradition gave prominent place to women, not only in their secret versions of the gospels but in the roles accorded women in the early congregations. This tradition was, however, declared heretical, and a more patriarchal view therefore gained ascendance in the early church (Pagels, 1976). The misogynist images in Judeo-Christian religion turn out to be dualistic, splitting the spirit apart from the body, the worshiper from the godlike, the laity from the clergy. Usually women are identified with one side of the split, and men with the other. Rosemary R. Ruether (1974: 150–183) has traced the elevation of the celibate ideal and the parallel emergence of the image of Mary to late antiquity and the early Church. Although the emergence of the Virgin Psyche (feminine spirit) allowed women a "spiritual personhood" not possible in an earlier period, when only men could commune with the divine, it was bought at a terrible cost: all real physical women, sex, and fecundity were despised with the result that religious images of women were wholly etherealized "into incorporeal phantasms."

Theologians, critical of this tradition, Catholic, Protestant, and Jewish alike, call for bridging religious dualisms identified with sex differentiation. Their reexamination of the creation myth reveals that the human being, *anthropos* (that is, *both* man and woman), is created in God's image. The ancient associations of man with the Word and the Son and woman with the Spirit and the Church, or Israel as the bride of Jahweh, are no longer justified. In the words of Catholic theologian George Tavard (1973: 188), "the image of God lies in the interrelationship of man and woman. . . . Neither man nor woman is the image of God; but man and woman participate in the image only to the extent that they share in the functions and characteristics of the other."

Once labeled, partial and dualistic symbolic structures can give way to positive whole images of men and women. A search through the Old Testament uncovers Israel's statement on women that recognizes "her as an equal with man, and with him jointly responsible to God and to cohumanity" (Bird, 1974: 77). In addition, there are prophetic views that speak of lion and lamb, wild beast and helpless child living together in harmony and without fear (Isaiah, 11: 6–9), and even a reversal of prevailing sex roles so that "a woman protects a man" (Jeremiah, 31: 22). A search through the New Testament finds that almost all of Jesus' parables are paired by male and female central characters. The shepherd and the lost sheep has its counterpart in the woman and the lost coin; the Good Samaritan is paralleled by the story of Martha and Mary (Parvey, 1974: 139). Pauline injunctions to women to keep silence and cover their heads in churches are balanced by the famous passage in Paul's letter to the Galatians (3: 28): "There is neither slave nor free, Greek nor Jew, male nor female in Christ Jesus our Lord." The Galatians doctrine was allowed to continue at an other-worldly level during the years of the early Church, with the development of a celibate clergy and a growing belief in the assumption to heaven of the Virgin Mary. But in the Middle Ages a more complete image of women flourished again. Some of the powerful double monasteries were governed by women, and in the lives of certain women who later became saints there is revealed a rich panoply of human emotion encompassing courage and compassion.

Julian of Norwich, an English mystic and spiritual director, in her *Revelations of Divine Love* (1373) used a liberating language, a combination of male and female imagery, to describe Jesus: "The human mother will suckle her child with her own milk, but our beloved mother, Jesus, feeds us with himself." (quoted in McLaughlin, 1975: 238).

Men also referred to God and Christ as a mother, through giving birth to the faithful, caring for them, and suckling them. This passage from Saint Anselm of Canterbury, an eleventh-century English bishop, theologian, and monk, depicts Christ as a Mother Hen:

> Christ my mother, you gather your chickens under your wings; this dead chicken of yours puts himself under those wings. For by your gentleness the badly frightened are comforted, by your sweet smell the despairing are revived, your warmth gives life to the dead, your touch justifies sinners. Mother know again your dead son, both by the sign of your cross and the voice of his confession. Warm your chicken, give life to your dead man, justify your sinner. Let your terrified one be consoled by you; and in your whole and unceasing grace let him be refashioned by you. For from you flows consolation for sinners; to you be blessing for ages and ages. Amen.
> [quoted in McLaughlin, 1976: 44]

McLaughlin, who cites these passages, notes that this feminine imagery was common in the language of "the church at prayer." Not only was it used to characterize God and Jesus. The male clerics who used it also thereby depicted feminine aspects of themselves. As souls before God they were female because of the gender of the Latin noun, as well as Bride of Christ, which was the vocation of all Christians. But also Saint Bernard and Saint Francis further enjoined priests and prelates to be "mothers, mothers in affection and gentleness, to whom the wounded resort as to the bosom of a mother" (McLaughlin, 1975: 242).

It is natural to wonder what became of this feminine imagery. McLaughlin (1976: 50 51) suggests that the renewed emphasis on transcendence that came with the Reformation expunged many affective elements from religious practice that had been associated with the feminine. Masson (1976), however, discusses the continuation of the same Bride of Christ imagery for all believers even into the early Puritan era in America; she places the polarization of masculine and feminine elements in the nineteenth century. There is still much scholarly work to be done to sort out the facts of the matter.

For the moment, however, the significant finding is the coexistence of strong feminine and masculine elements in the imagery of God and of believers in what seems an almost timeless pattern. The early church, the medieval church, and even some branches of the Reformation give evidence of this androgynous imagery.

Powerful women figures like Joan of Arc or Catherine of Sienna, who brought Pope Gregory XI back to Rome in 1377, in addition give modern theologians and historians examples of females imbued with "masculine" strength. George Tavard (1973: 200) finds the phenomenon parallel to men of that time who partook of feminine qualities:

> The more a woman becomes God-like, the freer she is to take positions of leadership, because on the one hand she can imitate equally well the Son and the Spirit in keeping with her charisma of the moment, and, on the other, she has risen above the demands and prejudices of society. At the same time, if women may be called to male *virtues* and situations usually associated with the Son, men also raised by grace above the conditions imposed on them by society and culture, may become notable examples of classical feminine virtues and be characterized by humility, hiddenness, and devotion to others, thus achieving in their work a sort of motherhood over the Church and the world. And this has characterized many saints.

It is worth noting that a few contemporary church men and church women are once again naming God in a manner that incorporates both masculine and feminine terms. In a recent ordination of a woman to the priesthood in the Episcopal Diocese of Massachusetts, Bishop John Coburn (1977) preached a sermon about the "character of Ultimate Reality—God himself and Goddess herself":

> I deliberately use these words so that the nature of the Ultimate Reality might be considered as Ultimate Reality in itself, neither God nor Goddess, yet both.
>
> From the perspective of Ultimate Reality, these differences such as God and Goddess, are caught up, made whole, and define the One with whom we have ultimate dealings as the creator who dwells with us, within us, and empowers us to live with one another "in heaven and ultimate freedom."

McLaughlin (1976: 52) also uses the feminine naming of God as an expression of "an awesome and powerful human act" that in some way "names every human possibility":

Until recent centuries, the church at prayer had found it possible, despite a patriarchal social setting, to name God Mother and Sister as well as Brother, King, and Lover. . . . We need to recover today, not an artificially resurrected copy of fourteenth-century God-Language, . . . [instead] we need to recover the reality which that naming reflected, an experience of God within, God our Mother, God who unconditionally accepts our and her broken world, God who takes into herself and affirms by her wholeness the full potential of man and woman to be God-bearers.

Artistic and literary images.
Artistic and literary creations also reveal the major alternatives in the depiction of the sexes. Art historian Helene Roberts (1974) in reviewing classical representations of women in art identifies three major alternatives—*inside, surface,* and *mass. Inside* images that emphasize women's distinctive reproductive role are evident in the objects associated with prehistoric fertility cults. Egyptian civilization emphasized women's *surface* functions—their beauty, their adornment, their decorative nature. The Greeks combined interest in woman's inner strength, muscle, and *mass* with an interest in dynamic movement and grace, perhaps approaching most closely a contemporary androgynous ideal in which men *and* women combine *both* beauty and strength.

Among literary forms, no similar typology so neatly summarizes the partial truths and synthetic combinations that have dominated biography or the novel. Yet several critics have begun the difficult work of sorting out negative and positive representations and identifying combinations that represent a truer image. Spacks (1976*a*) suggests that it is the *story* in fiction and biography that carries the interpretive and comparative treatment of lives. It is just these stories that have recently begun to change; recent autobiographies give greater place to women's struggle for independence, particularly through work (Spacks, 1976*b*; 1977: 44).

An early identification of negative images in fiction, partial men and partial women, appeared in Leslie Fiedler's massive review *Love and Death in the American Novel* (1966). Fiedler uncovered repeated homosexual themes in the male image, a flight from women evident in their frequent absence, and a split between the "fair virgin" and the "dark lady." In a sequel, Wendy Martin (1971) reviews the skewed portrayal of women in such American classics as *The Scarlet Letter* (1850), *The Bostonians* (1886), and *Portrait of a Lady* (1881). Such works in diverse yet persistent fashion depict the difficulties that a woman's independence is likely to bring upon her. The theme continues through Kate Chopin's *Awakening* (1899), in which a young matron's gradual self-emancipation results in suicide, and Willa Cather's *My Mortal Enemy* (1925), in which a beautiful dark heroine, who though loving her husband is stifled by him and suffers damage to her own selfhood.

Martin, however, identifies some works that begin the climb out of the dualism of the dark heroine and fair virgin to develop a new and more complete image of woman. Mary McCarthy in *The Company She Keeps* (1942) contrives a narrator who sees that her problem is not loving herself enough. By continually putting her own interests second, she tries to find herself through another, through a marriage. According to Martin (1971: 345),

> The novel reveals how badly our culture needs a new mythology for women . . . [that] insufficient self-love continues to be the norm by which our culture measures adjustment for women, and self-abnegation is considered to be a form of feminine maturity.

Martin's definition of the problem leads her to retrace her steps looking for women who attempted self-actualization. She discovers Anne Bradstreet, Elizabeth Cady Stanton, Margaret Fuller, Frances Wright, and other nineteenth-century stalwarts, who, though they were not characters in novels, lived out their lives of social reform in stories that combined independent thought and social concern and brought self-liberation.

In the 1960s and early 1970s, literary critics first had to clear away the underbrush by defining negative and spoiled images of women. Mary Ellmann (1968) catalogued the variety of feminine stereotypes in literature: Formlessness, Passivity, Instability, Confinement, Piety, Materiality, Spirituality, Irrationality, Compliancy, the Shrew, and the Witch. Kate Millett (1970) showed to what humiliation authors like Henry Miller and Norman Mailer could subject their female characters. Critics are now in a position to identify the positive images of women that also emerged in nineteenth-century literature. *Literary Women* by Ellen Moers (1976) recovers the distinctive strengths of once popular female writers like Elizabeth Barrett Browning, Harriet Beecher Stowe, and Madame de Staël. Some, like Harriet Beecher Stowe and Mrs. Gaskell, document social evils and the life of the countryside. Jane Austen, George Sand, Charlotte Brontë, and George Eliot handle the workings of emotion in the person and in the family. Madame de Staël, through her invention of the character Corinne, creates an image of a distinctive feminine capacity: woman's talent as "performing heroine," whether dancer, singer, or preacher.

Moers's account gives critical and thoughtful appreciation to the positive elements in the female literary heritage that can form the basis for new images, not only for depicting women but for perceiving reality as well. By distinctive recurring metaphors (landscapes, birds, and nests as symbols of nurturing and strength; kernels and small boxes as symbols of vital energy and reproductive powers), these women writers use their own special consciousness to give positive images to future generations.

In much of contemporary fiction, however, as Elaine Showalter (1975: 459) notes, "there is not even a Dark Lady, a token, a high priestess to satisfy affirmative action requirements in the new lineup of Pynchon, Barth, Heller, Barthelme, Hawkes, Coover, Vonnegut, Elkin":

> While we have been out looking for androgyny, a new regional literature, whose region is the library, has quietly taken over, and its subjects and themes—apocalypse, war, entropy, cybernetics, baseball, computers, and rockets—are not androgynous at all.

In a follow-up review of literary criticism on women writers and women subjects (Kolodny, 1976: 420) assessed the situation as "a kind of critical stasis" where "the cataloguing of stereotypic images of women continues to dominate."

Some major exceptions to this pattern appear in the work of Doris Lessing in *Martha Quest* (1966), *A Proper Marriage* (1966), and *The Four-Gated City* (1969), and in Margaret Atwood's novel *Surfacing* (1972). Both Lessing and Atwood explore naturalistic epiphanies in what Francine du Plessix Gray (1977: 29) believes may be "a future tradition of religious quest in women's novels" providing a refuge and a sacred shelter from the patriarchal order and a source of visionary power in a desacralized world. The heroine of *Surfacing*, after a period of isolation in the wilderness, confronts herself in a mirror and realizes a new sense of self-worth that grew out of her immersion in nature: "This above all, to refuse to be a victim." No longer does she believe herself powerless (Plaskow, 1976: 334; Christ, 1976: 324). Thus Atwood affirms the association between woman and nature in such a fashion as to enhance rather than deny woman's sense of power and capacity for transcendence.

TRANSCENDENCE AND THE ANDROGYNOUS IDEAL

In all the new critical work on images of women, whether theological, literary, or psychological, there is a central underlying theme—a search for wholeness. A whole and positive image of woman would combine power, discipline, and intellectual strength with vulnerability, fecundity or fruitfulness, and a capacity for rich and complex emotions. The realization of wholeness has been variously termed transcendence, androgyny, or simply "freedom from sex-role stereotypes." However named, the principal property of such a state is its promise of equality between the sexes that would result either from enlargement of society's purposes or from greater flexibility and breadth in the personality traits of individuals.

While traditionally the Masculine principle (objective, logical, rational, changing) has been associated with males and the Feminine principle (subjective, intuitive, receptive, stable) has been linked to females, Bazin and Freeman (1974: 186) argue that "this assignment, based upon our cultural and economic heritage, should not, in fact, be made to male and female respectively" but should "offer the full spectrum of experiences and feelings covered by both principles to every human being regardless of sex."

Recently in discussing how to achieve wholeness, several authors have distinguished between different strategies. Broadly speaking, there are three possibilities: one that keeps "male" values paramount; a second that gives relatively greater importance to "female" values; and a third that seeks a balance between male and female principles. Each strategy has its critics and its supporters.

Alice S. Rossi (1969; 1976) invented the term "assimilationist" to describe the mode for achieving sex equality by keeping male values paramount in the society and expecting women to conform to them. In accepting the rules for success, women could become successful. But Rossi, like many other feminists, implicitly questioned the wisdom of this approach. The danger is that in the name of progress we shall lose touch "with those emotional and personal elements— warmth, affection, sensitivity—which make us human" (Bazin and Freeman, 1974: 198).

Two psychologists, however, have recently shown the importance of keeping such "male" values as assertiveness and initiative in a prominent place in society's value hierarchy and in the personality constellations of women. Both Block (1973) and Bem (1976) demonstrate the limitation on women's behavior that comes from an insufficient development of the property that Bakan (1966) termed *agency*. The ability to take responsibility for one's actions in unclearly defined situations, such as taking employment or being nurturant toward an animal or a baby, appears to be impaired if the person lacks initiative in an ambiguous situation.

If emphasis on female values is taken as the best strategy to achieve wholeness, some feminist critics charge that the capacity for agency in women may not be given sufficient support. Gelpi (1974), referring to Shelley, Blake, Jung, and Neumann, notes that androgyny historically has meant filling out the masculine with the feminine. Stimpson (1974: 243) also associates androgyny with this bias: "Men may incorporate feminine virtues but women must remain content with being wholly feminine." But Rossi (1969; 1976) links women's greater potential achievement with greater future emphasis on feminine values—fellowship along with creativity—or in the terms used by Bakan, Bem, and Block, *communion* along with *agency*. In the academic world she envisions the possibility of tenure decisions based not just on the established criteria of "number of publications" but on "quality of teaching," the "degree of colleagueship with students," the "extent of service to both academic institution and its surrounding community."

Ultimately nobody seems to want just a narrow "male" emphasis on rationality, strength, or assertiveness, or a narrow "female" emphasis on intuition and expressivity. Instead what most feminists want seems to come closest to what Rossi called the "hybrid" model of society in which both male and female principles hold important place. Nor does anybody seem to want that list of physical or social anomalies that Carolyn Heilbrun (1974: 143) found to be mistakenly associated with androgyny: traits that were "homosexual, bisexual, hermaphrodite, feminist, revolutionary, or, at the very least, decidedly peculiar." Rather the positive image of androgyny Heilbrun (1973: x- xi) defines as an image of human wholeness:

> Androgyny suggests a spirit of reconciliation between the sexes; it suggests, further, a full range of experience open to individuals who may, as women, be aggressive, as men, tender; it suggests a spectrum upon which human beings choose their places without regard to propriety or custom. The unbounded and fundamentally indefinable nature of androgyny is best evoked by borrowing a description of Dionysus. . . . Dionysus appears to be neither woman nor man; or, better, he presents himself as woman-in-man, or man-in-woman, the unlimited personality. . . . In the person of the god strength mingles with softness, majestic terror with coquettish glances.

Cast as an image of wholeness, as capacity for a "full range of experience," the androgynous personality becomes attractive in both men and women. The evidence from psychology is particularly striking. The women and men who are able to combine these two fundamental modalities, agency and communion, seem to be much more complex and highly developed people, able to respond effectively in a variety of situations, whereas those people with stereotyped masculine or feminine traits seem tragically limited (Block, 1973; Bem, 1976).

In the quest for a balanced society and human personality, convergence on the concept of androgyny is a significant development. However, Elaine Showalter (1975: 456, 457) concludes that its usefulness as a literary term has yet to be demonstrated. Although it has undeniable appeal "as a utopian projection of the personality," androgyny in her view is "more of an absence than a presence, a kind of feminist Snark." Ann Belford Ulanov (1976: 202), a Jungian, and therefore generally sympathetic with the concept of androgyny, also voices her caution: "We cannot get beyond sexual identity until we have gotten to it and through it to the other side."

The projection of the ideal is nevertheless useful for charting a direction. Whether that goal is realistic under present historical and social conditions must next be judged by making reference to the social conditions under which similar ideals have prevailed.

HISTORICAL AND CROSS-CULTURAL VARIATION

"The second function of mythology," Campbell (1968: 611) tells us, "is to render a cosmology, an image of the universe, and for this we all turn today, of course, not to archaic religious texts but to science." The origins of the earth, the evolution of the species, the purpose of creation are all at issue. But for the purpose of understanding symbolic portrayal of men and women, what is of particular interest is relations between the sexes as they color human interactions with nature, the supernatural, and with other persons.

According to anthropologists Martin and Voorhies (1975: 266),

> All human societies rationalize their adaptive labor divisions and social groups as being somehow reflective of the natural order of the universe. Sex and gender are invariably associated with an elaborate set of stereotyped behaviors which stress the inevitability of extant conditions in a given society.

If this is so, it should be possible to categorize societies by type of labor division and then look for characteristic ways that the relations between male and female are symbolized in each type. By this technique it should be possible to compare the emerging theme of androgyny in America with prevailing images of the sexes in societies of similar type and derive an estimate of "goodness of fit" between the symbolic portrayal of the sexes and actual social relations.

The central question to be examined here is how social conditions affect the perceived nature of man and woman. How are these conceptions reflected in culture—its images, rituals, symbols, and cosmology as they restate the roles of the sexes? For anyone who peruses the ethnographic literature it is immediately apparent that the symbolic associations between male and female and aspects of the natural, supernatural, or social world are almost infinitely varied. Male and female distinction can be found in treatment of blood (women's menstrual blood or men's blood shed in hunting and warfare), rights over land (reckoned through male or female descent), creation stories (the gender of the gods, how man and woman were formed), who may be a witch or sorcerer, who may cultivate what types of crops or use which types of tools, and so on.

Because no sustained investigation of any of these cultural elements can be undertaken here, it is necessary to focus on some sort of composite indicator of the imagery surrounding women and men in any given society. The most common such summary measure is degree of difference or similarity between the sexes, measured either by *relative status* of male and female cultural domains or by their relative degree of *segregation or overlap*. By the first measure, societies can be compared for degree of equality between the sexes. By the second measure they can be compared for the degree of segregation or integration of male and female activities. Both of these dimensions—equality of status and degree of crossover—are implicit in the concept of androgyny.

Societies also are highly varied in their structure—by type of cultural history, level of technology, size, location, and general level of complexity. It is necessary to refer to them also through some sort of composite indicator that summarizes type of social relations or division of labor. A useful summary measure is the subsistence pattern by which the society grows food and processes other resources to meet the needs of its population. The major types are hunting-and-gathering, horticultural, agricultural, and industrial. (Pastoral and fishing societies represent important variants.)

SYMBOLIC STATUS OF WOMEN BY TYPE OF SOCIETY

When different types of society are compared for the degree of equality afforded women, the relationship that emerges can be represented in the graph shown in Figure 6. Equality between the sexes appears most likely in both the simplest and most advanced societies. Women's status relative to men is lowest in those societies at an intermediate level of complexity: societies based on advanced horticulture, agriculture, or early stages of industrialization (see Figure 6 on the following page). The x, y, z lines in the figure are hypothetical in the sense that they represent what we may expect to find when all the evidence on women's status is plotted out. The graph may also be used in this theoretical mode to predict the relative status of male and female identities in the natural, supernatural, or social order of different types of society.

The curvilinear relationship drawn here is based on my analysis of data on women's roles and status in eight countries—Bangladesh, Egypt, Ghana, Mexico, Japan, France, the United States, and Poland.

Figure 6. Relative Status of Women by Type of Society and Family Structure (Theoretical).

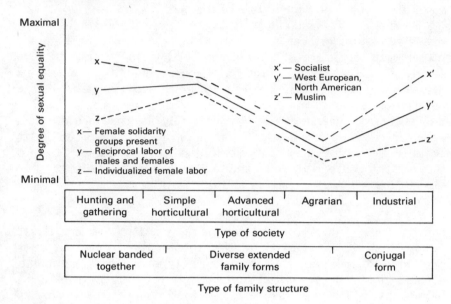

SOURCE: Giele (1977:11).

Female solidarity groups (x) are described in Sanday (1973, 1974). Reciprocal labor of males and females (y) and individualized female labor (z) appear in Johnson and Johnson (1975).

The materials described women's religious status, education, political rights, participation in the economy, and place in family life. Historical and ethnographic accounts described earlier conditions. Generally speaking, women's status seemed particularly low in societies at an *intermediate* stage of development.

Work of a number of other investigators supports the hypothesis. Ester Boserup (1970) relates ecological conditions, population balance, type of food production, and the division of labor to the status of women. Rising population pressure creates need for new food production techniques and this process pushes society from a simpler to more complex form that can extract more resources from the land. Such changes have repercussions for the division of labor and ultimately for sex roles. In hunting-and-gathering and simple horticultural societies, where the environment provides a relatively plentiful supply of food, and population is sparse, men and women tend to participate about equally in production. In peasant agriculture, the plow and large draft animals replace the hoe. Greater productivity results; larger populations can be supported. But control over production and consumption is centralized, resulting in exclusion of women from power. Men control property, pass it on to sons, and firmly allocate resources between production outside the home and consumption inside it. Women's status relative to men is low. Only in those circumstances where women can produce some goods for sale or participate in trade or village industry does their status improve (Blumberg and Winch, 1972; Blumberg, 1976). Not until the industrial period does such opportunity appear for women on a large enough scale to stimulate a rise in their relative status.

Consistent with this pattern is a phenomenon that a number of anthropologists have noted—the adverse impact of development on women. According to Leacock (1975: 605) colonial contact among native tribes of North America introduced patriarchal precepts. More recently Westerners have imposed their own model of male-female relations on native agricultural patterns where women had an important role in subsistence production. Because they have encouraged men to take control of capital and sophisticated machinery, they have left women out of the development process and subtly confined them to the home (Tinker, 1976; Bossen, 1975: 599; Buvinić, 1976).

It is just as true, however, that the status of women also rises when development proceeds somewhat farther—to the industrial stage. In a comprehensive review of women's status by major types of society, Martin and Voorhies (1975: 404) note not only the declining position of women when men take a greater role in crop cultivation such as found in peasant agriculture; but they also record the improvements in women's status that are evident with entry of women into the labor force in advanced industrial societies such as the United States and the Soviet Union. Much as Sanday (1974) showed in simpler societies that women's participation in production was a necessary (but not sufficient) prerequisite for women's power in the public domain, so women's entry into the modern labor force has given them a base from which to seek political and social power—more education, wider job opportunities, better pay, more equitable allocation of household tasks.

If, as Friedl (1975: 10) has said, rituals and symbols restate the basic social relationships of a society, then the graph that describes women's status in different societies will also fairly well summarize the nature of an important aspect of their symbolic representation of males and females as well. However, this aspect of symbolic portrayal is complemented by another—the degree of overlap in male and female imagery. This also varies by type of society.

DEGREE OF OVERLAP BETWEEN SYMBOLIC REALMS OF MALE AND FEMALE

A measure of similarity in sex roles, such as the concept of androgyny, requires not only assessment of the relative status of male and female images; but it also requires reference to the degree of overlap in the domains they inhabit. Measured by the latter criterion, the possibility for androgynous representation of the human person appears to increase steadily with the increasing differentiation of society. There is, however, great variability within societal types, particularly in the simplest societies, among the hunter-gatherers and the horticulturalists. The individual's life in the simplest society is more fully determined by sex role. With each advance in societal complexity, the individual's life is shaped by added dimensions such as age, social class, or occupation. As a result, an ever larger range of experience in the documentary world is *not* strictly colored by one's gender (Giele, 1972*b*).

Hunting-and-gathering societies.

Symbolization of sex roles in the simplest societies represents an advance beyond animals or precultural men who are able only to accept and act out their respective capacities without being able to transcend and dominate them. Relative to more advanced societies, however, these sex roles are monistic; that is, their definition is very closely tied to life crises in the reproductive cycle, such as menstruation, copulation, pregnancy, and childbirth. Among the Australian aborigines, where this type may be seen in its purest form, all the major religious rituals and ceremonies of initiation are sex-differentiated—women participating in one group or aspect of the ritual, men and boys in another. Only among old men and women (whose reproductive functions are presumably attenuated) does one find any tendency to join in rites in which both men and women participate (Berndt, 1950: 24-25; 1965: 260). The imagery of sex roles mirrors male and female reproductive functions in myth and ritual. In sum, life for the aboriginal woman is a "one-possibility thing"; there is little room for action in terms other than those dictated by gender.

Women's technology is of one kind; men's of another. Men participate in politics; women are interested but do not take active part. There seems to be only a limited part of the personality that can be thought of as similar for both men and women regardless of their sex. Where common feelings occur, they are probably in part due to a common age, as with children before they are separated into male and female groups, or old people (Friedl, 1975: 82). One would not expect, however, that women would sense any great inequality with men or feel resentment at masculine status, for it would be defined simply as different. Indeed Martin and Voorhies (1975: 190) conclude that their most accurate generalization on men and women in foraging societies is that "the worlds of the sexes are separate but equal."

Horticultural societies.

Societies based on hoe culture are socially more differentiated. Especially in those groups with advanced horticulture (permanent fields, larger surpluses), a two-class system is frequently found that distinguishes between royal and priestly castes and commoners (Lenski, 1966). The sex-role symbolism is also more complex. More dimensions enter into the imagery of sex roles than the reproductive functions alone. Brides are evaluated on the basis not only of potential reproductive success but also in terms of physical attractiveness, amount of bridewealth they can command or bring, or such other factors as their family's reputation for witchcraft (Whiting, 1963: 64). Although the notion of evaluating a bride or husband seems to be new at this stage, it makes sense in light of the differentiation of society as a whole into two classes.

The imagery suggests that one's ability to transcend or dominate the reproductive functions has grown in this type of society. An increased number of alternative standards for action crosscuts those determined by sex, making it possible for men and women to unite in common purpose, not just when they are old and have ceased to function sexually but also on the basis of common interests such as preservation of economic privilege or religious status.

The lives of women are still sharply separated from those of men, and biological functions are still an important focus of life. But one can imagine considerable pressure on sex-differentiated norms if they conflict with alternative standards such as the desire to preserve privilege. In this connection Audrey I. Richards's (1950: 248-249) observations among matrilineal tribes of the central Bantu are relevant: "Men of wealth and distinction are able to reverse the usual rules of residence." It is as though the caste set-up has the power to attenuate the consequences of sex role. Class differentiation in the society and in the image of the self thus becomes a lever that like age can be used against sex to free the individual for increasingly autonomous action relative to the environment (Friedl, 1975: 63; Martin and Voorhies, 1975: 296-297).

Agrarian societies.

With the agricultural revolution, the rise of cities, and the secure establishment of a written history, there were accompanying changes in religious symbolism and the images surrounding sex roles. Each of the great religious traditions created a dualistic cosmology in which the present world was rejected to attain some ideal state of salvation through ritual or separation from the world (Bellah, 1964).

Corresponding with this change, the imagery of sex roles was transformed by the invention of celibacy as a socially valued state. In it there was the possibility of completely transcending one's sexual nature. In addition there was an accompanying new emphasis on trying to attain some ideal of "true" manhood or womanhood. In the high Middle Ages these pure states were seen in the idealization of courtly love and the veneration of the Virgin in her role as Mother. Yet the idea of temple virgins had already appeared in classical times, as had the idealization of the Roman matron. Celibate monks and priests were known in the Eastern religions as well.

The effect of these changes was again to augment the freedom of the self in relation to the empirical sex of one's own organism. Such freedom to transcend one's own sex would have been clearest to people who lived in the cities and were associated with the rise of the universal religions and the military and official roles of developing political states. For it was precisely these institutions that in the course of their development had to sever their ties to the family-oriented society of the hinterland. But even in the countryside the emphasis on chastity increased, and there was much greater conscious effort to control sexual behavior in the service of other interests (such as protection of dowry and property rights) through early betrothal and marriage (Blumberg et al., 1970).

Yet the emotional color of relations between mothers and children and man and wife perhaps did not emerge into consciousness until physiological sex was capable of being transcended. Only then did it become fully apparent that in fact sex roles did not just entail reproductive functions but, in the human situation, carried with them complex emotional ties as well. By carrying in the mind a dual image of the transcendent celibate life and the ordinary sex role of the peasant it was perhaps possible to go on elaborating ideas of pure womanhood, motherhood, and so forth, because idealized sex role could then no longer be confused with simple biology.

Early modern society.

In Western society after the Renaissance, roughly from 1500 to the nineteenth century, there developed a new social order with multiple competing centers of commerce and learning based on the use of contract, money, and the authority of bureaucratic office. These social forms have now spread to other parts of the world through a process known as development or modernization.

Accompanying these changes in social structure was a transformation in religious and social thought. Hierarchical organization was replaced by emphasis on individual action. No longer did a person have the option of world rejection to attain the ideal; instead one sought to live for the greater glory of God in this world. A similar transformation took place in the imagery of sex roles. No longer was celibacy or the veneration of a pure virgin or mother the highest form of control over sexuality. Instead, as Morgan (1944; 1966) showed, the Puritan family expected everyone to marry, beget children, and give a great deal of attention to their training. People for the first time had before them the possibility of entering whole areas of life once denied them on the basis of class background or other ascribed status. There was an emphasis also on equality of treatment of sons and daughters.

During the early industrial period, when ideas of individualism and equality were further extended, they were experienced differently by the middle and working classes. Middle-class families experienced role segregation: wife and children were separated from the husband, who worked outside the home. In the working class, women and children were more likely to be working in the factories as well (Hareven, 1977: 103-104). The consequence was a class-related split in the image of woman, one side of which emphasized woman's role as mother and homemaker, the other side of which depicted her as productive worker (Wilson, 1976; Scott and Tilly, 1975; Hareven, 1975).

It is probably significant that articulate concern for the equal rights of women did not appear on the historical scene until this era. Even those moments of conspicuous near-equality that did surface in the salons of seventeenth- and eighteenth-century France, occurred among an elite element of society that was most conscious of the new religion and the new rationalism. It was not until the widespread acceptance of these ideas, particularly in nineteenth-century America, that a full-blown feminism was born. Such concern probably could not have appeared earlier, for the kind of consciousness of human experience that men and women share did not sufficiently develop until certain changes in social life and its symbolic representations caused them to seek common goals.

Advanced industrial society.

With rapid industrialization, the growth of science, and the spread of labor-saving technologies in the contemporary era, the traditional metaphysical basis of symbolization itself became problematic. Life is now viewed as holding infinite possibilities for which the symbols themselves are endlessly revisable. Such consciousness makes culture itself part of a self-transforming system.

Though representing biological givens that could hardly seem easily changed, the imagery of contemporary sex roles approaches an "infinite-possibility thing." Experience with bottle feeding, birth control, abortion, sterilization, operations for change of sex, and administration of sex hormones has shown the potentially problematic nature of biological givens. Experiences with nursery schools, day-care centers, romantic love, divorce, and communal families all point up the potential revisability of our present social forms that surround sex roles.

Taken together, these new and sometimes disturbing possibilities call into question any one single definition of what is appropriate male or female behavior. They also suggest an even wider domain of capacities than heretofore recognized that both men and women share. Much of the research and developing imagery on sex roles point toward the tremendous range of capacities that may be found within either sex and the considerable overlap between capacities of males and females.

The recent emergence of the androgyny theme is entirely consistent with this evolving consciousness. Like contemporary research on sex roles, it emphasizes the large area of common interests shared by men and women and further advocates that each sex be able to participate in activities formerly reserved for its opposite. It is perhaps most obviously symbolized in changing patterns of dress: since the 1930s women have increasingly adopted men's clothing such as pants, and since the 1960s men have increasingly adopted women's styles such as longer hair, brightly colored clothing, and some jewelry (Friedl, 1975: 140).

At the same time the current movement for change in sex roles is aimed at supporting a variety of individual solutions and attacking any one pattern that purports to be orthodox. In so doing, the movement exemplifies a contemporary mood that views static or pat solutions with skepticism. Instead, like the self-revising cultural spirit of this age, it seeks evolving adaptations that continually augment the capacity for autonomous behavior with respect to sex roles.

In general, increasing overlap in sex-role imagery has accompanied the increasing complexity of the society. A greater range of behaviors has become possible for each sex with each step toward modernity. This trend has resulted in increased opportunity for individuality; it has also carried with it a wider domain of shared consciousness between the sexes.

Recent androgynous trends in sex-role imagery thus appear consistent with long-term developments in social structure and are unlikely to be easily reversed. Given their solid foundation in the changing cosmology of the larger society, the logical next question is how they will be institutionalized in the actual role hierarchies and organizational structures that characterize the modern society.

TRANSLATION INTO ORGANIZATIONAL STRUCTURES

The third traditional mythological function, according to Campbell (1968: 621), is moral and social: images and symbols validate and maintain the social order. When myths change, the social order is also likely to be in flux.

Changing images of women and men now permeate contemporary America: more women participate in government, almost half of married women are employed, they have fewer children and appear to want interests outside the family—education, leisure, and liberation. With the new images of sex roles there is a need to adjust the common image of the social organizations in which men and women work—the family, the government, the firm. Sister Marie Augusta Neal (1976) says, "We are witnessing today the de-sacralization of the patriarchal family as model for business firms, industry, government, educational systems, and other organizations." Jessie Bernard (1971*b*: 152, 272–274) has called the new pattern "role-sharing"; I speak of role crossover (Giele, 1971); Saikowski (1976: 16–17) documents a new "ethic of interdependence and care" emerging in various corners of American society. All these trends are also evident in the culture-producing institutions: religion, literature, the arts, and the modern media of communications—publishing, movies, and television. Each of these institutions is experiencing pressure on its established *role hierarchies* that bring disproportionate numbers of men to the top. Each is also facing a radical critique of its *standards* for evaluating achievements that have the effect of locating worthy accomplishment primarily in the works of males.

The remedies that feminist critics suggest are based on broadening of accepted qualifications and standards to include talents and contributions formerly overlooked or undervalued. Feminists envision social organization in terms of networks rather than hierarchies (Bentley and Randall, 1974), and a community that represents the interests of all in the decision-making process. Neal (1976) uses a "circle" image rather than a "pyramid" to suggest the model of social organization that should prevail in the future. Neal argues that to curb the birthrate, women must be involved. To distribute natural resources more equitably, the Third World must also participate. The problem is "who will live, who will die, and who will decide." Feminists would uncover women's potential contributions to such pressing contemporary issues by questioning established organizational structures and role hierarchies and inviting broader participation from both men and women. This is as true in the culture-creating and -maintaining institutions as it is in commerce or government.

The strategies for accomplishing such change are complex, however. Catharine Stimpson (1977) notes that in the American stereotype the production of culture is perceived as being largely feminized. Thus any male who is an artist is perceived as being effeminate. Yet the dealers, patrons, collectors, curators, and critics, regardless of their sex, are assumed to be masculine (Wayne, 1974). Presumably a better balance would find both men and women as producers of art as well as the entrepreneurs who stimulate its production. Tuchman (1975: 191) notes that the "Friends of the Symphony" and the culture-consuming public are preponderantly women. It would seem desirable to have men better represented in these roles. But more important, several types of culture creation must be recognized; for it is not, as Tuchman says, just the author, artist, or composer who contributes to the creation of a work, but also the editor, the publisher, and the consuming public.

Whether in the church, the arts, or the media, revolutionary women and men are asking that the leading actors not be predominantly men and that the supporting cast not be preponderantly women. They ask instead for ordination of women, redefinition of the arts to include more of women's contributions, and restructuring of publishing and broadcasting to provide a forum for new social interests. Underlying their appeals are two basic premises that depart from established beliefs about the sexes: first, they assume that the invisibility of women's accomplishments in the past is related to underlying structures that have put women at a disadvantage (Kanter, 1977). Second, they assume that when institutions are restructured to draw women into leading roles, women will bring in "outsider" values, heretofore unrepresented, which when expressed will (along with the established values) better serve the community as a whole (Daly, 1973). In each field these principles emerge; they are evident in the fine details of surveys on the *roles* of women, political *actions* of women's groups to get change, and the analysis of alternative *standards* that may be institutionalized.

WOMEN IN ORGANIZED RELIGION

Although women make up slightly over half of the lay membership of churches, they have historically been barred from the clergy in the Roman Catholic, Eastern Orthodox, and Anglican churches, though they have served as members of religious orders. In the Protestant denominations that permit their ordination, women clergy have been only a tiny minority. A report from the Presbyterian Church, U.S.A., for example, lists 57 percent of the membership as women, 30 percent of the elders, and 3 percent of the clergy (Presbyterian Panel, 1975). However, the situation is changing rapidly. Few of its members are aware that 30 to 50 percent of entering seminarians are women and that changes in established practice will have to be made to accommodate their appointments to jobs when they have graduated.

In 1958, out of 158 member churches in the World Council of Churches, only 48 reported that they admitted women to the full ministry, 9 admitted women to partial or occasional ministries, and 90 did not admit them at all. By 1970, 72 of its member churches had opened full ordination to qualified women (*Women and Holy Orders*, 1966: 25–27; Hewitt and Hiatt, 1973: 81). In America, the United Methodist Church has admitted women to full ordination since 1956, as also has the United Presbyterian Church, U.S.A. Two major Lutheran groups extended full ordination to women in 1970. In June 1972 Reformed Judaism ordained its first woman rabbi, and the Union of American Hebrew Congregations expects that by 1979 one-third of all newly ordained Reform rabbis will be women (Dugan, 1976: 68). In July 1974 in Philadelphia eleven women were irregularly ordained to the Episcopal priesthood, and in September 1976 the Episcopal Church at its triennial convention voted to permit ordination of women. The Roman Catholic Church, many orthodox Christian denominations, Conservative and Orthodox Judaism, and the Missouri Synod of the Lutheran Church still do not ordain women.

Changes in women's roles in the church have come about as a result of concerted action by feminist groups and concerned clergy and lay persons. Some of the most militant manifestations have been evident in Catholic circles. Among Catholics, vigorous efforts were directed to gaining participation for women in the Vatican Council deliberations from 1962 to 1965. Women were allowed to attend but without the same status as their male counterparts. In 1963, Saint Joan's Alliance, an English Catholic group working for equal civil rights for women, formed a branch in the United States and began working for the ordination of women. In 1966, Dr. Elizabeth Farians founded the Ecumenical Task Force on Women and Religion that cooperates with the National Organization of Women. In 1970 this group protested by burning a newly issued Roman missal containing a regulation, Canon 66, restricting the role of women as lectors, and in 1971 it began petitions to Catholic bishops to permit women theologians participation in the forthcoming Synod of Rome (Farians, 1973: 8; Hole and Levine, 1971: 373, 390). At the same time different but related changes occurred among women in religious orders. Between 1966 and 1974 almost a quarter of nuns left religious life (Dowling, 1976: 34- 35). Among those remaining, modernization of dress and living arrangements removed rigid and forbidding rules that had separated sisters from the people they served.

In the estimation of Hole and Levine (1971: 373), the most radical of the Protestant feminist groups is the Unitarian-Universalist Women's Federation, formed in 1963. The federation lobbies for legislation to insure equality for women, passage of the Equal Rights Amendment, and repeal of abortion restrictions.

Surrounding the whole ordination debate has been a larger discussion on the proper place of the church in modern society and the proper role of the clergy in both the church and the world. This is essentially an argument over standards of religious action in the world. Generally it may be said that people who stand against women's ordination define the role of the church and the clergy in narrow sacramental terms. The proponents of women's ordination, on the other hand, want the church to relate to current social issues and the clergy to be able to speak meaningfully to the personal issues that concern the individual. They argue that the presence of women in the clergy will help the church relate better to those outside the church and to secular issues—population questions, families, and children. Their vision abandons hierarchy and instead envisions new models of ministry to be explored—"advocate, mother, lay person" (Russell, 1974). "Priesthood," says Kay Baxter (1966), "is not a role of domination. It is a ministry. A vocation to the priesthood is not a vocation to be in command. . . ." Mary Daly (1970: 137) says the idea of priesthood is changing; the clergy exist to serve, not to accumulate prestige and honors. In her words,

> The church of the future may be envisioned as a community based on "charismatic ministries." In order that it be transformed into a more adequately human social order there will have to be a continuing development away from symbolic roles identified with fixed states of life, toward functional roles freely assumed on the basis of personal qualifications and talents.

The movement of women in the church as in the arts, or in practical fields of endeavor, is thus one of bridging male and female worlds, leveling hierarchies, and adapting more effectively to current needs by calling on all the functions and talents of the participating community. A young woman chaplain at Wellesley College said in 1973, "On an average Sunday morning, in an average Presbyterian Church, the imagery expressed in the liturgy and the sermon is personal imagery." But because the preacher is a man the imagery is usually male, and the message contains male values articulated and accepted as the norm (Andrews, 1973). Women in organized religion now seek expression for a personal imagery that speaks to the female dimension of experience as well. Their effort does not stop with ordination. Widespread efforts are being made to root out sexist elements in liturgy and identify language and liturgical forms that express liberation. The title of a work by Sharon and Thomas Emswiler (1974), *Women and Worship: A Guide to Non-sexist Hymns, Prayers, and Liturgies*, indicates the scope of liberation efforts to reshape the entire religious culture.

Hans Kung, a noted Catholic theologian, in sixteen theses on the position of women in the church, lists major symbolic issues to be addressed. He asks that the symbol of God admit feminine as well as masculine elements, that Christology emphasize Jesus' humanity rather than his masculinity, that Mariology depict the complete woman, not just the humble handmaiden. Customs regulating marriage, education, and birth control should turn from a patriarchal to an egalitarian model that will better take into account women's potentialities. The liturgical language and corporate structure of the church should be revised to incorporate women's theological insights, to allow priests to marry, and to open the diaconate and presbyterate to women (Kung, 1976: 34-35).

SITUATION OF WOMEN IN LITERATURE AND THE ARTS

In a field such as literature it has been fairly difficult to prove that women have suffered any form of discrimination. Presumably anyone can take up a pen, and so it was for a long time thought that women writers were less numerous and less famous than men simply because they had less talent. Virginia Woolf's classic, *A Room of One's Own* (1929), showed convincingly, however, the considerable impediments to creativity that women faced in their daily lives—no money, no space, no time. More recently, Elaine Showalter (1971) has documented the double standard to which women writers have been exposed. So likely was their work to be ignored, rejected, or trivialized if they were known to be women that George Sand and George Eliot chose masculine pen names. Critics have judged women writers harshly for any deviation from ladylike subjects. Yet at the same time they have ridiculed or treated as insignificant those women writers who have dealt with delicate emotions, fine detail, or "feminine" subjects. Ultimately, women writers themselves may have presented a somewhat more constricted subject matter than male writers, not out of any failure of imagination but as a result of limited experience (Denne and Rogers, 1975). Patricia Meyer Spacks (1975: 320), in her review of the lives of women authors, finds that women's needs are identical to those of men. As she sees it, "Perhaps the balance may be different, but the substance is the same: for work and love, for independence and dependency, solitude and relationship, to enjoy community and value one's specialness." The difference is that society fails to speak to women's needs. Where their work, independence, and social ties are not supported, women writers pay a price in the blocks to their work, their guilt, and their failures of relationship.

In the visual arts the question of why there are no great women artists is also being laid to rest. Many important women artists have been overlooked or forgotten for no apparent reason. Moreover, a close analysis of the entire structure of the art world—the academies, the patrons, the dealers and galleries as well as the typical artist—reveals a predominance of men.

The story of individual accomplishments of men and women in the arts fits a pattern that by now is familiar. Women in 1970–71 received 78 percent of all the degrees in art history, yet they were only 26 percent of the nontenured and 15 percent of the tenured faculties in colleges and universities. During the same period women received three-fifths of all the degrees in studio art, yet among eighty-five art schools only one reported a woman dean (White, 1976; Suppan, 1974).

Beyond the academy, in the world of shows and dealers and foundation grants, the representation of successful artists appears again heavily weighted in favor of males. While the 1970 Census data show some 32 percent of the "writers, artists, and entertainers" to be women, Stimpson (1977: 217–218) reports that in 1970 only 15 percent of the awards by the National Endowment on the Arts to individual artists were granted to women, although by 1972, this figure had risen to 26 percent. A count of one-artist shows at the Museum of Modern Art in New York City reveals that from 1929 to April 1972 the works of only twenty-seven women were represented among a total of 293 shows, for a ratio of 9 percent (Glueck, 1974). A count of art works by men and women in the National Gallery of Art in Washington, D.C. produces a similarly dismal picture. In its collection of 2,600 paintings, only 33 paintings by twelve different women represent the work of female artists. In the graphic arts only thirty women artists represented by 400 works are to be found in a collection of 30,000 prints and drawings (White, 1976).

Is the problem that there are simply fewer women artists? Or is their work just not so "great"? In an early essay entitled "Why Are

There No Great Women Artists?," Linda Nochlin (1971) considered just these questions. Her answers to the question in that and subsequent essays are a document of the changing definition of the problem that feminist art historians have gradually evolved. At first they were inclined to accept the common opinion that women's works of art were simply fewer or less distinguished. Then their explanations dealt with the artists' family background, conflicts between the artist's role and the traditional feminine role, and ultimately with discrimination by dealers and curators (*Research News*, 1973). Nochlin discovered that many women artists had fathers who were artists. She was able to show that, because female artists were typically excluded from such important training devices as life drawing classes, the daughter of an artist was at less of a disadvantage.

Scholars systematically searching for the works of women began to uncover many more than heretofore recognized. Eleanor Tufts identified women court painters of the Renaissance who received salaries and perquisites that could compete with Holbein's—Levina Teerling of Antwerp, who served in the court of Henry VIII; the Flemish painter Catharina van Hemessen in the court of Queen Mary of Hungary; and Sofonisba Anguissola, a child prodigy, summoned by Philip II to the Spanish court where she remained twenty years (Orenstein, 1975: 508). Although the basic art history textbooks—those by Janson, Gardner, and Gombrich—mentioned not one woman artist, by 1974 Mary D. Garrard had collected 1,600 slides of 660 woman artists from the thirteenth century to the present, and by 1976 Karen Petersen and J. J. Wilson had produced a 200-page textbook on women artists from the early Middle Ages to the twentieth century, documenting needlework, quilts, and ceramics, as well as sculptures, paintings, and drawings (White, 1976; Petersen and Wilson, 1976). Much of this scholarly ferment has been helped by the growth of women's studies, by the activities of women's art groups such as the College Art Association's Committee on the Status of Women, and by the creation of new networks of cooperating artists. Some have joined together in enterprises such as Soho 20 Cooperative Gallery in New York City or in mounting special exhibitions (Harris, 1974; Orenstein, 1975: 518- 519; Harris and Nochlin, 1976).

Discovery of long-unnoticed women's art works now raises issues concerning standards of evaluation. "High" art has traditionally included painting, sculpture, drawing, and graphics, whereas tapestries, ceramics, quilts, laces, and rugs are considered "decorative arts" and "crafts" (Orenstein, 1975: 518). Given this division, especially where women are so frequently found producing the latter, it is not surprising that their work has often gone unpatronized and un-noticed. If standards are broadened, women's inventiveness and creativity can be newly appreciated. Such is the case with quilts, for example.

De Bretteville (1974: 117) describes the distinctive charac-teristics of quilts and blankets that relate to the social realities of women's lives and their biological rhythms. This genre is based on an "assemblage of fragments pieced together whenever there is time." Both in their method of creation and in their aesthetic form, they are "visually organized into many centers. . . . The assemblage of fragments, the organization of forms in a complex matrix suggests depth and intensity as an alternative to progress. . . . The quilting bee, as well as the quilt itself, is an example of an essentially non-hierarchical organization." Mainardi finds that women's quilts vary widely—in color and texture, and degree of abstraction, and in political, personal, and religious meanings that they contain. "Left in peace," Mainardi (1973: 66) says, "women succeeded on their own in building a design tradition so strong that its influence has ex-tended almost 400 years, and which must today be acknowledged as The Great American Art."

When art historians look for what women artists have been doing, they discover bold, worthy work, which either has not been defined as art or is out of fashion. Linda Nochlin (1974) recovers the art of Rosa Bonheur, whose painting *The Horse Fair* is in the Metropolitan Museum of Art. Though it depicts vigor, vitality, and energy, her work now is little known. Nochlin wonders why such works and the narrative paintings of many nineteenth-century women artists have been dropped from the rolls of art history, while the neo-Platonic symbols of Van Eyck, Dürer, or Michelangelo continue to draw enormous scholarly investment. In her view the iconography of nineteenth-century narrative-genre painting may be just as important.

Women in the nineteenth century contributed to the *democra-tization* of the arts. Because they had a great deal to do, they popularized theorem painting, painting by stencil, and reproducible needlework patterns that strongly influenced the everyday art of the era (Nochlin, 1974). Today the work of women artists carries a similar though largely implicit political message. Such group shows as "Project Womanhouse" sponsored by the Feminist Art Program of the California Institute of Arts have made an artistic statement about objects formerly thought trivial. Subjects include: dolls, pillows, clothes, intimate apparel, household appliances, bedding, and fix-tures (Orenstein, 1975: 520; Hayden and Wright, 1976: 931). "Womanhouse" demonstrates the capacity of a group of artists organized collectively to bypass the usual hierarchical dealer-gallery setup. It also dramatizes the relationship between women artists and the environments in which they live, and between designers and the ordinary people whom their designs will serve.

This new feminist principle—the interrelation between art and everyday life—is now becoming evident in architecture and urban design. Dolores Hayden (1974) uses contextual analysis to highlight the design contributions made by nineteenth-century perfectionist communities such as Oneida, the Shakers, and the North American Phalanx. These groups created a social environment, not just a single building. Hayden uses the figure in the ground, the creation in context, to criticize the usual architectural tendency that emphasizes a single ideal structure with little attention to its surroundings.

In a review of recent work in architecture and urban design Hayden and Wright (1976) consider not only the place of women in the architectural profession but also the effects of environmental design on women's roles. They fashion an exciting blend of concern for houses and women's other workplaces with attention to the nature of families, the housewife's role, and working-class women's work. They note how frequently the places where women work are designed as though women's work did not exist or were not real work. Suddenly from this feminist architectural perspective, kitchens and cooking, child care and play yards, neighborhood and community household facilities take on unprecedented significance as elements in environmental design.

The feminist impulse in art and architecture, as much as in religion, thus appears to herald a new interest in democratization and wider participation—what was referred to earlier as an emphasis on *communion.* At the same time, however, women's role as artistic *agent* is gaining in importance. More women artists are visible now. Moreover, their position appears to be strengthened by the new nonhierarchical ethos.

WOMEN IN THE COMMUNICATIONS MEDIA

As in all other major institutions of the society, most women workers in publishing and broadcasting are found in staff and support positions; a much smaller proportion are found in managerial positions. In addition, the media selectively present images of women that emphasize the emotional and traditional aspects of women's role. Both the role organization and the content of the media have come under criticism from the women's movement.

A first step has been to document discrimination against women in the publishing and communications field. In 1972 *Time* magazine reported that only about one-tenth of the most prestigious editorial and news bureau positions were held by women, although 35 percent of all American newspaper editorial personnel were women. The major television companies at that time could report only one woman network correspondent among a total of forty-three at ABC, five women out of fifty-four at NBC, and one out of fifty-six at CBS (*Time*, 1972: 53). A compilation of insiders' reports by Ethel Strainchamps (1974) revealed a pervasive pattern of women's concentration at the bottom of the production heirarchy in book, magazine, and newspaper publishing, as well as in television where they carried out anonymous clerical and research tasks.

At the same time, monitors of programing found blatant sex-role stereotyping in programs and commercials. One study found in an examination of fifty commercials that "41 percent of the sales pitches delivered by females . . . emphasized the ease, comfort, and luxury of the item; none of those delivered by males did. Conversely, 86 percent of the male-delivered commercials emphasized performance of the product, compared to only 29 percent of the females" (Chafetz, 1974: 52–53). Another study revealed that incompetent behaviors represented 20 percent of all women's actions as compared with only 9 percent of men's (Women on Words and Images, 1975: 24). Women's groups in Washington, D.C., who in 1972–73 monitored WRC-TV, found that news items were reported *by* women only 5 percent of the time and *about* women only 10 percent of the time (*Media Report to Women*, 1972–1973).

Out of consciousness of unequal treatment have come direct actions by women's groups to challenge hiring and promotion policies and stereotyped content. The 1968 challenge in Atlantic City to the sex-role concept underlying the Miss America contest was the important beginning event, although the media at that time chose to emphasize the exaggerated "bra-burner" image of women's liberation. In 1970 a sit-in at the *Ladies Home Journal* protested the lack of seriousness with which the magazine business treated the women's movement and resulted in the publication of a special issue of the magazine. In the same year women at *Newsweek* and *Time* filed charges against the magazines for sex discrimination in hiring and promotion, alleging that women were kept in research jobs and were rarely promoted to responsibilities as writers and editors; agreements were reached expressing management's good intentions (Hole and Levine, 1971: 255–262; Strainchamps, 1974: 278–281).

At the same time, legal changes gave women more leverage in protesting discrimination. In 1970 the Federal Communications Commission adopted two rules that provided that no licensee shall discriminate on the basis of sex and that every licensee shall establish a continuing positive program to assure equal opportunity in employment and practice. Such rules gave an opportunity for the Washington, D.C., women to protest license renewal for a station in their area (Stanley, 1971: 38). A 1973 decision of the Commonwealth Court of Pennsylvania (*Pittsburgh Press Company* vs. *Pittsburgh Commission on Human Relations*) ruled against sex-segregated employment ads (Kanowitz, 1973: 396–406) upholding a city ordinance against such discrimination.

All the while a positive projection of women's alternative presentation of themselves as strong and active has been gaining. Women's history collections caught public attention: the Women's History Research Center run by Laura X in Berkeley, California, and the Center for American Women and Politics at Douglass College at Rutgers University joined such older and more established centers as the Schlesinger Library on the History of Women at Radcliffe College. In 1969 KNOW, Inc., grew out of the efforts of a Pittsburgh women's group made up of members of NOW to provide modules and reprints of studies in the social sciences on changing sex roles. In 1970 Florence Howe established the Feminist Press to provide materials for women's studies courses and good books for young girls (Collins, 1974). In 1972 *Ms.* magazine set out to reach an audience of the new women and by the late 1970s could count an audience in the hundreds of thousands. Established publishers also discovered that there was a ready market for books on women (Ehrlich, 1973).

Not surprisingly, the consequences of pressure by the women's movement are now beginning to be evident. What were once "women's pages" in the newspaper now go under the heading "Family/Style" in the *New York Times*, "View" in the *Los Angeles Times*, and "Variety" in the *Minneapolis Star*. Women reporters with feminist sympathies have done a careful job of balancing reports of the women's movement against "objective" stories (Tuchman, 1976). Television has expanded the range of topics that appear in the continuing daytime serials to what Jane Wilson (1977: 24) terms "an ongoing seminar in human behavior." Models of attractive informed women are still rare, however, and when they appear it is most often as a "glossy anchorperson." The movie industry, which has also been guilty of stereotyping women (Mellen, 1973), appears about to launch a number of films that will take account of the new woman and explore more deeply the relationships in which they are involved (Wilson, 1977).

A great deal of change still remains to be accomplished. But a transformation in attitudes has already begun. It is perhaps best summarized by Betty Friedan in an assessment of Betty Ford and Rosalynn Carter during the 1976 presidential campaign. Traveling in turn with each woman, Friedan discovered they were each asked tough questions on marijuana, abortion, and the ERA, and each took firm positions in favor of women's equality. Rosalynn Carter "answers the toughest questions with a kind of warm openness." In Betty Ford's smile "is something strong and real and radiant and honest which evokes a strange new yearning from the people, especially the women." A reporter said no one would have asked such things of Pat Nixon, Jackie, or Lady Bird. Friedan (1976) reflects:

> I wonder have we created this image of a new and different First Lady, who is her own person, out of her need, or ours?
>
> Or is the Betty Ford to which the American people respond with surprising warmth no more and no less than the new American woman who is emerging out of the conflict and struggles of a decade of women's movement for us all—that unprecedented, unpredictable strong sensitive honest female humanness of a woman who is simply herself?

A NEW CONCEPTION OF HUMAN PERSONALITY

The fourth function of an adequate mythology, according to Campbell (1968: 623) is "the centering and harmonization of the individual." Expressed in psychological terms, this function refers to the integration of the self. When culture socializes the individual in a coherent fashion, through a religiously or culturally prescribed life course, the attainment of such states as integrity, generativity, wisdom, and satisfaction is presumably made easier. If the images of ideal personality are inconsistent, however, or not aligned with other cultural ideals, the task of self-integration is presumably made more difficult, if not impossible.

Especially at the present time, the ability of culture to transmit a coherent ideal image to women is in question. Of course, it may long have been true that women's attainment of self-integration had to take a somewhat different path than men's, and to the extent that the dominant culture has expressed the needs and consciousness of the dominant sexual class, women's needs and consciousness may not have been adequately expressed in the culture at large. Jean Baker Miller (1976: 22) indeed suggests that the invention of psychoanalysis was a response to the unexpressed emotional needs of men that they had largely relegated to a culture of women, and that had to be embodied in a new science to be incorporated in the official consciousness of the larger society.

Whether or not the larger culture presents a coherent image of women, or one consistent with its highest priorities, it does seem to be a clear fact that women show higher rates of mental illness than men all over the developed world. This is particularly true of depression and such indices of depression as rates of attempted suicide. Guttentag and Salasin (1977) report female rates for severe depression that are consistently 1.5 to 2 times that of men. They convincingly demonstrate that women's greater tendency to seek medical help, response bias, or hormonal events in the twenty-five-to-forty-four age group cannot adequately account for so vast and consistent a difference. Instead they argue that a combination of learned helplessness and high stress create real differences in depression between women and men. The rates are highest in low-income working women with young children, whether married, divorced, or separated. These groups are likely to be subject both to the highest stress and to the greatest sense of powerlessness—a combination that Guttentag and Salasin believe leads to depression in women.

The recent trend toward androgynous imagery of women and men needs to be viewed against this background of pathological consequences that appear to stem from a polarized and unequal representation of the sexes. Three questions are now in order. First, are emerging androgynous goals realistic, given certain incontrovertible *biological* differences that do exist between the sexes? Second, is a crisscross of personality traits between the sexes *psychologically* realistic? And third, is crossover between traditional sex roles *sociologically* realistic, given biological or psychological sex differences and pervasive socialization practices that prepare the sexes for distinct roles?

No person can yet answer these questions definitively. Only a long period of social experimentation will eventually provide needed evidence. But it can be demonstrated from a review of evolving scientific exploration that a changing perspective is emerging in the biology, psychology, and sociology of sex roles that heralds convergence on the androgynous perspective (Pleck, 1977a). At the same time these scientific shifts suggest practical steps to be taken to facilitate greater realization of equality between the sexes. In each field a paradigm shift has occurred whereby a closed system model has been replaced by an interactive one that gives a role to the influence of the environment as well as the body. The new explanatory model recognizes many more similarities in the reactions of the two sexes than had the closed system model. The shift is evident in reinterpretation of available data, construction of theories that explain similarity as well as difference, and suggestions for practical programs that will enhance convergence rather than divergence in the behavior of the two sexes.

THE NEW BIOLOGY OF SEX-RELATED CHARACTERISTICS

For biological thinking to reach its present situation, two major changes had to occur—the first in the endocrinology of sex hormones; the second in the biology of gender identity. Each had the effect of undermining reigning polarities in assignment of a particular hormone or physiological characteristic to one or the other sex exclusively.

In the field of hormone endocrinology Hall (1976), Rossi (1977), and Guttentag and Salasin (1977) have all recounted the critical shift that took place in the closed model of the endocrine system on which sex hormones presumably acted. Beginning in the 1930s this model began to undergo transformation as it was recognized that neurons, portions of the brain, and ultimately events in the social environment· had the effect of turning on or off these internal secretions. By the 1970s it could be demonstrated that a male monkey introduced into a group where he had low status in the dominance hierarchy experienced a drop in testosterone. It also became evident that androgen acted in females as well as in males and that estrogen was also found in both sexes, although in different balances. Rossi (1977: 11) describes the current intellectual situation: "To a social scientist reading the new research literature, it seems increasingly questionable that it is useful to call androgens the 'male' hormone and estrogen the 'female' hormone."

With the work of Money and Ehrhardt (1972) matters of biological gender identity also yielded to new interpretation. Some individuals with unclear or discrepant sex identity were found to be male at one level of body functioning while female at another. In other words, instances were found where genetic, hormonal, morphological, and psychological gender were not consistent with each other. This was true, for example, in those cases of androgenized females whose mother had taken a drug (diethylstilbestrol) during pregnancy that contained testosterone. The fetus, although a genetic female, had testosterone circulating through its brain at a critical stage of development and thus developed not only penislike genitalia, but a masculinized mode of behavior later in life, and in some cases a discrepant sense of sex identity. Despite a few such instances of ambiguous sex identity, Money and Ehrhardt found that in the overwhelming majority of children sex identity was fixed at a very early age (by the age of three) and was in error in only a very small minority of cases.

From a perspective outside the field of biology, what seems most significant in these developments is a shift in thought that is completely consistent with the developing imagery of androgyny. Essential components of physical sexuality—the sex hormones and the sexual dimorphism of the body—have been reconceptualized as variables that can be present in more or less degree in *both* sexes. This dramatizes the fact that there is a great range of types within each sex and considerable overlap between sexes with respect to certain traits. Moreover, the fact that environmental influences can affect the body opens up the possibility that similar social conditions impinging on both males and females may act directly on their bodies, thereby producing similar physical responses.

From emphasis on polarity to emphasis on similarity, however, the pendulum may now be about to swing back the other way. In an important recent but controversial article Alice S. Rossi (1977) has warned that the emphasis on cultural determinism and similarity between sex roles may endanger certain important sexually differentiated functions such as pregnancy, lactation, and bonding of the mother to the infant. She argues that the long evolutionary history of the human species has assured particular sensual pleasure and innate predispositions on the part of the mother caring for her infant. If this link between biology and the psychology and sociology of parenting is ignored, the parent-child bond may suffer. Rossi suggests that medical personnel seek to foster these natural maternal processes and, if the father is to be involved in the child-rearing process, should give him compensatory training to overcome his likely handicap in handling infants and toddlers easily and to become sensitive to their needs.

While some feminists will see Rossi's position as a step backward toward acceptance of the old polarities, it can also be interpreted as a step forward to institutionalize the new androgynous perspective. Rossi is not advocating a return to a hunter-gatherer society, or exclusion of women from the workplace, or segregation of fathers from child-rearing tasks. Rather, she is asking for recognition of some sex differences in innate potential so that childbearing and child rearing will not suffer in the future. In suggesting *compensatory training for males* in fields where women habitually do well, she gives a refreshing twist to the theme of equality between the sexes.

THE CHANGING PSYCHOLOGY OF SEX DIFFERENCES

Many psychologists still describe women and men in terms that assign distinct traits to one sex rather than another. But a new trend is emerging that discovers more similarity than difference in the traits thought desirable for each sex. The study by Broverman et al. (1970) on psychologists' characterizations of a normal male and a normal female has widely been interpreted to mean that there is a clear distinction between the ideal personality patterns expected of women and men. However, Stricker (1977) and Pleck (1977b) now show that these differences have been exaggerated beyond those actually shown in the findings. In fact there is a very high positive correlation (.90 or more) between the rank orders of traits described as desirable in women and those so described in men.

The similarity in ideal personality for both sexes is confirmed in another way—by reference to the nature of health and mental illness in both men and women. As in Bem's (1976) and Block's (1973) studies cited earlier, other investigators have suggested that healthy functioning for persons of either sex is heightened by a balance between assertiveness and cooperativeness, or in Bakan's (1966) terms, between agency and communion. Studies of highly creative artists and "ordinary" adults support Freud's view that the capacity for both love and work is essential to the mature and healthy person, regardless of sex. Ravenna Helson (1974: 33- 36) finds in the creative woman an internal combination of male-typed and female-typed personality functions: parts of the self are assertive, strong, and protective, and other parts are introspective, reflective, and receptive.

On the other hand, women and men who have been forced to deny aspects of the self that did not conform with the stereotyped masculine or feminine image later suffer. Psychiatrist Jean Baker Miller (1973: 377- 379) finds many of women's major personal problems come from the fact that society has not allowed them authenticity, nor the opportunity to attend directly to their own needs. Middle-aged middle-class women face a particularly high risk of illness or unhappiness in their early postparental stage. While they may want to "do" something for their own self-realization, they many times deny such needs in order to meet the demands of a husband or aging parents (Bart, 1971; Bernard, 1971a: 157; Lowenthal and Weiss, 1976: 14).

In men, by contrast, denial of intimacy and emotionality may be what is most destructive. Lynn (1974: 151) reports that males high in masculinity during adolescence were found lower in qualities of leadership, dominance, self-confidence, and self-acceptance than the feminine group. The more feminine group of male adolescents felt better about themselves as adults, perhaps because they were able to develop the sensitivity and empathy with children and women that are required of adults. Lowenthal and Weiss (1976: 11) found that widowerhood was often more traumatic for men than widowhood for women because the men were less likely to have developed intimate relations with a circle of friends and could less easily disclose themselves intimately to others.

Certner (1976) hypothesizes that men's socialization for task responsibility and women's socialization for emotional maintenance has resulted in denial of emotional qualities in men and instrumental qualities in women, with considerable resulting strain and conflict. Symptoms of illness are thus differentially distributed between the sexes. Males experience more stress diseases such as heart attack, stroke, hypertension, ulcers, alcoholism, overweight, and drug dependence. Females, on the other hand, suffer disproportionately from depression.

Similar to developments in the biological field, new discoveries in psychology thus signal a major shift in the analysis of sex differences. Maccoby and Jacklin (1974) concluded that sex differences in psychological traits are very few (limited primarily to males' greater aggression and ability in spatial relations and females' greater ability in verbal tasks). Studies of healthy psychological functioning suggest that there is a range of desirable human traits to be found in *both* sexes. Much earlier Jung had conceived of contrasexual traits embodied in every person—the anima in the male, the animus in the female (Ulanov, 1976). Erik Erikson (1950: 84-85) also conceived of similar underlying capacities or modes of action (incorporative, intrusive) that made up the behavioral repertoire of both males and females. Contemporary psychological research now interprets sex-role acquisition as internalization of a complex scheme that allows many variations much as do other forms of cognitive development or language acquisition. Thus the young child in Stage I has an undifferentiated view of sex roles; in Stage II, a polarized stereotyped conception emerges; in Stage III, transcendence of sex roles is possible because the individual adopts a symbolic or even dialectical understanding in which the person responds to "a continuous, interpenetrating and ever changing world" (Rebecca et al., 1976). Then, as in the use of language, the individual may alter surface features of behavior to respond to deeper structural requirements of the situation (Pleck, 1975).

The practical implications of these new perspectives in psychology are parallel to Rossi's recommendations for "compensatory training" in parenting. If females have greater capacity for interdependence and emotional understanding, as McClelland (1975: 81-122) and Miller (1976: 31) suggest, then added training of men in these matters would seem desirable. Precisely in this vein, Warren Farrell (1974: 16-17), advocate of "male liberation," proposes that males overcome their devaluation of behavior that they perceive as somehow feminine—for example, listening, emotional expression, and lack of interest in power—and that they adopt a more critical value toward accepted masculine traits, such as talkative domination, self-assertion, and concern with concrete tangible results. Joseph Pleck (1976: 160), a psychologist studying the male role, says "males need deeper emotional contact with other men and with children, less exclusive channeling of their emotional needs to relationships with women, and less dependence of their self-esteem on work."

Women are more likely to need help in learning to assert themselves; in such matters they too need compensatory training and support. Jean Baker Miller (1976: 40) encourages women to admit to their own desires, confront their tendency always to put the needs of others foremost, and discover ways of meeting their own needs as well. The issue is one of finding the right balance: "Women have now stated that helping in the growth of others without the equal opportunity and right to growth for themselves is a form of oppression."

THE SOCIOLOGY OF CHANGING SEX ROLES

Probably more than any other single factor the changing participation of women in the labor force has created a need to rework the sociological theory of sex roles. Over the same period men's activity rates have declined (Bell, 1975). In the major developed countries women drop out of the labor force during childbearing and for a few years thereafter and then reenter later on (Blake, 1974: 141). At the same time in the lives of men there is increasing acceptance of midlife career change, early retirement and second careers, and even time out for leaves, education, and "sabbaticals." These phenomena suggest the need for a theory that will give account of the changing social definitions of sex roles and the individual's adaptation to them at different stages of the life cycle. Such theory has to explain why sex roles are now more similar than in the past. It should also be sensitive to the changing mechanisms of early socialization and adult development that make similar performance by males and females both possible and feasible.

Answers to the question of why sex roles are now defined as more similar than in the past comes from sociological theory on social differentiation and the division of labor. Beginning with Toennies (1887; 1940), Durkheim (1893; 1960), and Weber (1947), sociologists have long described modern society as distinctive in its emphasis on achievement rather than ascriptive standards to evaluate performance. In addition, modern society has a more highly differentiated division of labor: tasks are divided into specialized roles that demand a high degree of competence in a narrow rather than broad spectrum of activities. As a result, sex, which is an ascribed status defining a broad range of tasks, should become less important as a mechanism for assigning roles in modern society and should be replaced by standards that put greater reliance on achieved characteristics such as the person's ability to perform a specific task.

In actual fact roles have become more differentiated with modernization, but with a curious result for sex roles. Between the onset of industrialization and the present time, specialization of tasks relied heavily on sex as a means of role assignment, not primarily as a result of ascriptive standards or of innate biological differences, but because family functions and productive functions were split apart by the Industrial Revolution. Primary responsibility for family functions or expressive tasks fell on women. The principal responsibility for productive functions or instrumental tasks fell on men (Parsons and Bales, 1955; Smelser, 1959; this interpretation is also consistent with a Marxist analysis; see Sacks, 1974; Zaretsky, 1976).

With the postindustrial society, family and work may once again be brought closer together with consequent convergence of sex roles. Such change will occur not by a return to the preindustrial family and economy but by further differentiation in family, economic, and state functions so that greater interpenetration occurs across institutional boundaries. The result will be a growth in what Ulla Olin (1976) has termed "the public family" and Alva Myrdal (1941, 1968; 1976) has called "the national household"—the expansion of state welfare functions to care for many aspects of life (health, child care, social security) that were formerly provided by the private family. With such change a consequent interpenetration and crossover in sex roles can also be expected to result: more women, aided by public support of family functions, will take on employment as well as family responsibility; men, assured of old-age pensions and economic supports for family health and well-being, will devote more time to leisure and family activity and somewhat less to employment.

As such trends materialize they call for a new sociological theory of sex roles that will show both males and females capable of "masculine" as well as "feminine" behavior, depending on the requirements of the social situation. A new revisionism has begun to emerge that, like the biology and psychology of sex roles, emphasizes the coexistence rather than mutual exclusiveness of sex-typed behaviors. In their analysis of family roles and work roles Parsons and Bales (1955) conceived of instrumentality and expressiveness as modes of behavior exhibited by *both* sexes. Primacy of emphasis depended on role definition; indeed in some small groups Bales reported that a leader might play both an instrumental and an expressive role. Later investigators such as Brim (1958) and Rossi (1968) noted that women took both expressive and instrumental roles in the family, thus making clear that these two types of behavior were not polar opposites on a single continuum (M. Johnson et al., 1975). More recently, in *Men and Women of the Corporation*, Rosabeth Kanter (1977) demonstrates that men as well as women will exhibit "feminine" behavior (e.g., concern with detail, emotional sensitivity to others) if their opportunities for advancement are blocked. Women, on the other hand, will display "masculine" behavior (e.g., taking initiative, seeing the big picture) if opportunities are open to them.

Now insight is needed as to the process by which individuals will learn to experience the expanded possibilities opened by more flexible and overlapping definitions of sex roles. Some clues come from the redefinition of age roles. It is possible to conceive of youth and age not as polarities but as properties of personality or behavior that coexist within one person at the same point in time (Bouwsma, 1976: 81, 86). Each represents a valuable function, youth allied with openness and change, age with maturity and wisdom. So understood, not just children but adults may continue to grow.

In the realm of sex-typed behaviors, service to others (associated with the "feminine") and pursuit of one's own goals (associated with the "masculine") are both necessary functions not only in the life of the individual but in social groups as well. What sociologists are now beginning to see is the necessity of balancing and rewarding both functions. As Arlie R. Hochschild (1975: 300) says, it is now time to "integrate the sociology of the ['head'] with the sociology of the 'heart' and somehow erase the distinction in the process." Psychologists like Barnett and Baruch (1978) identify both integration in support networks and a sense of personal competence as necessary to women's sense of well-being. Or, in the words of Jean Baker Miller (1973: 396), "the most important work in the world is the participation in the care and growth of human life," but to do this individuals must be able both to give and to take.

Work life calls for qualities that in an earlier era were "specialized out" of the workplace. These are qualities—attention to emotions, willingness to serve others—that may now be located in outsider groups such as women. Not only women themselves, but the expressive values with which they have been identified, should now be accorded a place of greater importance in corporate and public life.

In the family also, the forces of structural change appear likely to produce some changes in child-rearing that will make male and female personalities both richer and more similar in the future. Cross-cultural comparisons suggest that to the extent mothers have power, social relations in general are likely to be more egalitarian, less hierarchical, and less sex-typed than in patriarchal cultures

(Johnson, 1977; Leavitt, 1971; Tanner, 1974). As the nurturant capacities of the female personality may have in part been due to close identification with the mother, so caretaking by fathers as well as mothers should make boys more nurturant, more independent from the mother, and less compulsive about their masculinity. Girls should learn more of the direct modes of action characteristic of boys. Such changes in early socialization would then set the stage for a wider range of personality characteristics in adulthood (Chodorow, 1975; Johnson, 1977).

The capacity of each sex to perform both "male" and "female" social roles probably has to be learned and reinforced over the whole life span. It may be as Lipman-Blumen and Leavitt (1976: 30) suggest that different achievement orientations will be suitable to males and females at different stages in the life cycle. Both sexes in the long run, however, will probably be most satisfied when they can combine their social with their egoistic needs.

Erik Erikson's analysis of Ingmar Bergman's film *Wild Straw-berries* and the life cycle of its central character, Dr. Borg, gives us some glimpse of the rich crisscrossings that are possible between trust of childhood and wisdom of age, between the male and female aspects of the self. Erikson (1976) seems to be saying that only in such lacing together of the stages of life and the sexual dimorphism of human consciousness can integrity be truly realized.

Other empirical and analytic works support this interpretation. Bernice Neugarten (1976: 17) finds the experience of adulthood in middle age one of increased "interiority." Life is restructured in terms of time left to live instead of time since birth, a kind of integration of time itself on which ego stands as the moving center. Orville G. Brim (1976: 6) observes that the internal crisscross occurs with respect to sex differences as well, and reports the cross-cultural observations by David Gutmann of men and women in their middle years:

> The older men are more diffusely sensual, more sensitive to the incidental pleasures and pains, less aggressive, more affiliative, more interested in love than conquest or power, more present than future-oriented. At the same time, women are aging in the reverse direction, becoming more aggressive, less sentimental, and more domineering. While in the earlier years the husband tends to be dominant, during the aging process he becomes more dependent.

While these patterns do emerge in the experience of a number of individuals at different points in the life span, there is still uncertainty in the mind of any single individual about which course to follow. Routes to full adulthood are not yet clearly institutionalized.

The course may vary by marital status, number of children, socio-economic status, and age at which work or family responsibilities are undertaken.

It does seem clear, however, that we are entering the "century of the adult" (Graubard, 1976). In our exploration of that period in life, it will surely be important that we relate the new behavioral opportunities made possible by a longer life span to the instrumental and expressive opportunities opened by sex-role changes in work and family life. The expanding roles of men and women provide a stage where each individual can explore and integrate both "male" and "female" potentials within the self.

SUMMARY

Coming as it does after other chapters on women's changing roles in government, economy, the family, and education, this chapter tries to summarize the changes in culture that are now upon us. Culture helps people to organize their experience coherently, to anticipate change, and then to bring it about. Presently in the United States there is evidence of continuing ferment in sex roles. On the one hand, polls report considerable agreement that males are more aggressive and independent, and that females are more nurturant and caring; that the primary breadwinner responsibility is the man's, and that the child-care responsibility is the woman's. Yet other findings report widespread recognition that the sexes share certain important common traits—the capacity for deep feeling, objectivity, and rationality, and the ability to reason abstractly.

The cultural ambiguity resulting from changing sex roles is found at four different levels: (1) in the metaphysical, ideal images of male and female, (2) in the documentary and scientific understanding of the social and physical world in which the sexes now live, (3) in the institutional structures of the communications media that express either equality or hierarchy, and (4) in the psychology of the individual who selectively highlights or combines male-typed and female-typed traits.

Ideal images of male and female seem to be changing consistently in the direction of emphasizing the androgynous possibilities in personality. The process involves an identification of women's distinctive contributions, a recognition of their crucial importance to balance the male vision of reality, and finally the articulation of an encompassing ideal that both women and men should try to attain. Where once theologians found only a patriarchal God, they now find a God that is both male and female, male believers who express female qualities of sensitivity and caring, and female believers who are strong and assertive. Where once literary critics found only secondary themes in the work of women writers and artists, they now find original, creative, and distinctively feminine themes.

Our world view is not, however, yet structured to permit easy incorporation of these new images; the old cosmologies are in need of revision. New historical and cross-cultural research reveals a gradual transformation of consciousness whereby human beings now have a greater opportunity *not* to have their lives be limited by the fact of their biological gender than at any time in the past. This new cosmology emphasizes human interdependence and care more than dominance and hierarchy as the basis for human evolution and survival.

Institutions for culture transmission—the arts, religion, and the media—are the targets of feminist protest because they underrepresent women in top positions, and yet at the same time they are the vehicles for conveying new male and female images. In religion, women have historically been denied ordination to the clergy, and religious images have sanctified some of the most extreme stereotypes of sex inequality. In the arts, women's creative products have been overlooked and undervalued. In journalism and broadcasting, women are found in few managerial posts, and "women's issues" are often treated as being unimportant. Active protest by women's groups, however, has brought attention to these inequalities, and a redefinition of the standards of evaluation is now in progress. Feminist critics generally argue that women's work has been overlooked or judged inferior not because it is in fact of poor quality, but because the standards of evaluation have been too narrow.

In the last analysis, it is the individual who filters the cultural elements that are currently in a state of ferment. Psychologists who observe this process find that past stereotyping of sex roles has caused considerable suffering for both sexes. Men have had to deny their emotionality; women, their own self-direction. But research developments in biology, psychology, and sociology are presently converging on a new model of adult behavior in which both masculine and feminine aspects are present. Men who are strong and assertive may also be tender and caring. Women who are sensitive and devoted to others may also pursue their own interests.

In part, realization of this new adult ideal has been made possible by the increase in life expectancy. Life that would have been truncated by early death can now be used to explore the unrealized potentials within the self. But further change to allow the adult full expression of both "male" and "female" qualities and behaviors waits on slow and incremental changes in social structure. As more women are brought into the workplace, their self-direction and self-confidence will be strengthened. As men give more time to child rearing and child care, their own nurturant qualities will be reinforced, and they will help to form a generation in which sex differences will be attenuated.

Then the human qualities of male and female will merge in a new image of the ideal person. The society that helps such persons be born will become our image of the future.

REFERENCES FOR CHAPTER SEVEN

Andrews, Susan. 1973. "Theological and Psychological Reflections." In *God Imagery*. Chaplaincy Papers, Wellesley College, vol. 1, no. 1 (30 January).

Atwood, Margaret. 1972. *Surfacing*. New York: Simon and Schuster.

Bakan, David. 1966. *The Duality of Human Existence*. Chicago: Rand McNally.

Barnett, Rosalind C., and Baruch, Grace K. 1978. "Women in the Middle Years: A Critique of Research and Theory." *Psychology of Women Quarterly* 3, no. 2.

Bart, Pauline B. 1971. "Depression in Middle-aged Women." In *Woman in Sexist Society: Studies in Power and Powerlessness*. Edited by V. Gornick and B. K. Morgan. New York: Basic Books.

Baxter, Kay. 1966. "The Case for Ordination of Women to the Priesthood." In *Women and Holy Orders*. Report of a commission appointed by the Archbishops of Canterbury and York. London: Church Information Office.

Bazin, Nancy T., and Freeman, Alma. 1974. "The Androgynous Vision." *Women's Studies* 2: 185–215.

Bell, Carolyn Shaw. 1975. "The Next Revolution." *Social Policy* 6 (September-October): 5–11.

Bellah, Robert. 1964. "Religious Evolution." *American Sociological Review* 29 (June): 358–374.

Bem, Sandra L. 1976. "Probing the Promise of Androgyny." In *Beyond Sex-role Stereotypes: Readings toward a Psychology of Androgyny*. Edited by A. G. Kaplan and J. P. Bean. Boston: Little, Brown.

Bentley, Sally, and Randall, Claire. 1974. "The Spirit Moving: A New Approach to Theologizing." *Christianity and Crisis*, February, pp. 3–7.

Bernard, Jessie. 1971a. "The Paradox of the Happy Marriage." In *Woman in Sexist Society: Studies in Power and Powerlessness*. Edited by V. Gornick and B. K. Moran. New York: Basic Books.

———. 1971b. *Women and the Public Interest*. Chicago: Aldine.

———. 1973. "My Four Revolutions: An Autobiographical History of the ASA." *American Journal of Sociology* 78 (January): 773–791.

Berndt, Catherine H. 1950. *Women's Changing Ceremonies in Northern Australia*. Paris: Librarie Scientifique.

——. 1965. "Women and the 'Secret Life'." In *Aboriginal Man in Australia.* Edited by R. M. Berndt and C. H. Berndt. Sydney: Angus and Robertson.

Bird, Phyllis. 1974. "Images of Women in the Old Testament." In *Religion and Sexism.* Edited by R. R. Ruether. New York: Simon and Schuster.

Blake, Judith. 1974. "The Changing Status of Women in Developed Countries." *Scientific American*, September, pp. 137–147.

Block, Jeanne Humphrey. 1973. "Conceptions of Sex Role: Some Cross-cultural and Longitudinal Perspectives." *American Psychologist* 28: 512–526.

Blumberg, Rae Lesser. 1976. "Kibbutz Women: From the Fields of Revolution to the Laundries of Discontent." In *Women in the World.* Edited by L. B. Iglitzin and R. Ross. Santa Barbara, Ca.: Clio Books.

Blumberg, Rae L.; Carns, Donald; and Winch, Robert F. 1970. "High Gods, Virgin Brides, and Societal Complexity." Paper presented at the annual meeting of the American Sociological Association, Washington, D.C., August.

Blumberg, Rae L., and Winch, Robert F. 1972. "Societal Complexity and Familial Complexity: Evidence for a Curvilinear Hypothesis." *American Journal of Sociology* 77 (March): 898–920.

Bossen, Laurel. 1975. "Women in Modernizing Societies." *American Ethnologist* 2 (November): 587–601.

Boserup, Ester. 1970. *Woman's Role in Economic Development.* London: Allen and Unwin.

Bouwsma, William J. 1976 "Christian Adulthood." *Daedalus* 105 (Spring): 77–92.

Brim, Orville G., Jr. 1958. "Family Structure and Sex-Role Learning by Children." *Sociometry* 21 (March): 1–16.

——. 1976. "Theories of the Male Mid-life Crisis." *Counseling Psychologist* 6, no. 1: 2–9.

Broverman, Inge K.; Broverman, Donald M.; Clarkson, Frank E.; Rosenkrantz, Paul S.; and Vogel, Susan R. 1970. "Sex-role Stereotypes and Clinical Judgements on Mental Health." *Journal of Consulting and Clinical Psychology* 34, no. 1: 1–7.

Buvinić, Mayra. 1976. *Women and World Development: An Annotated Bibliography.* Washington, D.C.: Overseas Development Council.

Campbell, Joseph. 1968. *The Masks of God: Creative Mythology*, vol. 4. New York: Viking.

Certner, Barry. 1976. "Sex Roles and Mental Health: A Proposal for the Development of the Sex Roles Institute." Washington, D.C.: Psychiatric Institute Foundation.

Chafetz, Janet Saltzman. 1974. *Masculine/Feminine or Human?* Itasca, Il.: Peacock.

Chodorow, Nancy. 1975. "The Reproduction of Mothering." Paper presented at the annual meeting of the American Sociological Association, San Francisco.

Christ, Carol P. 1976. "Margaret Atwood: The Surfacing of Women's Spiritual Quest and Vision." *Signs* 2, no. 2 (Winter): 316–330.

Clarkson, Frank E.; Vogel, Susan R.; Broverman, Inge K.; Broverman, Donald M.; and Rosenkrantz, Paul S. 1970. "Family Size and Sex-role Stereotypes." *Science*, 23 January, pp. 390–392.

Coburn, John B. 1977. "Divinity beyond Division: An Affirmation." *Episcopal Times*, April, pp. 3, 9.

Collins, Jean. 1974. "The Feminist Press." *Change* 6 (Summer): 19–23.

Daly, Mary. 1970. "Women and the Catholic Church." In *Sisterhood Is Powerful.* Edited by R. Morgan. New York: Vintage.

——. 1973. *Beyond God the Father.* Boston: Beacon Press.

De Beauvoir, Simone. 1949; 1968. *The Second Sex.* Translated and edited by H. M. Parshley. New York: Modern Library.

De Bretteville, Sheila Levrant. 1974. "A Reexamination of Some Aspects of the Design Arts from the Perspective of a Woman Designer." *Arts in Society* 11 (Spring-Summer): 115–123.

Denne, Constance Ayers, and Rogers, Katharine M. 1975. "Women Novelists: A Distinct Group?" *Women's Studies* 3: 5–28.

Dowling, Collette. 1976. "The Nun's Story." *New York Times Magazine*, 28 November, pp. 34ff.

Dugan, George. 1976. "A Sharp Rise in Women Serving as Reform Rabbis Is Seen by 1979." *New York Times*, 12 December, p. 68.

Durkheim, Emile. 1893; 1960. *The Division of Labor in Society.* Translated by G. Simpson. New York: The Free Press.

Edmiston, Susan. 1975. "Out from Under! A Major Report on Women Today." *Redbook*, May.

Ehrlich, Carol. 1973. "The Woman Book Industry." *American Journal of Sociology* 78 (January): 1030–1044.

Ellmann, Mary. 1968. *Thinking about Women.* New York: Harcourt Brace Jovanovich.

Emswiler, Sharon Neufer, and Emswiler, Thomas Neufer. 1974. *Women and Worship: A Guide to Nonsexist Hymns, Prayers, and Liturgies.* New York: Harper and Row.

Erikson, Erik. 1950. *Childhood and Society.* New York: Norton.

——. 1976. "Reflections on Dr. Borg's Life Cycle." *Daedalus* 105 (Spring): 1–28.

Farians, Elizabeth. 1973. "The Struggle for Women's Rights in the Catholic Church." *Women's Studies Abstracts* 2 (Spring): 7–10, 89–91.

Farrell, Warren. 1974. *The Liberated Man.* New York: Random House.

Fiedler, Leslie. 1966. *Love and Death in the American Novel.* New York: Stein and Day.

Friedan, Betty. 1976. "Ford vs. Carter: The New Political Mystique." *Boston Globe*, 24 October, pp. A1, A3.

Friedl, Ernestine. 1975. *Women and Men: An Anthropologist's View.* New York: Holt, Rinehart, and Winston.

Gelpi, Barbara Charlesworth. 1974. "The Politics of Androgyny." *Women's Studies* 2: 151–160.

Giele, Janet Zollinger. 1971. "Changes in the Modern Family: Their Impact on Sex Roles." *American Journal of Orthopsychiatry* 41 (October): 757–766.

——. 1972a. "New Developments in Research on Women: An Introductory Essay." In *The Feminine Character* by Viola Klein. Urbana, Il.: University of Illinois Press.

——. 1972b. "Centuries of Womanhood: An Evolutionary Perspective on the Feminine Role." *Women's Studies* 1: 97–110.

——. 1977. "Introduction: Comparative Perspectives on Women." In *Women: Roles and Status in Eight Countries.* Edited by J. Z. Giele and A. C. Smock. New York: Wiley.

Glueck, Grace. 1974. "Making Cultural Institutions More Responsive to Social Needs." *Arts in Society* 11 (Spring-Summer): 49–54.

Goldenberg, Nancy. 1976. "A Feminist Critique of Jung." *Signs* 2 (Winter): 443–449.

Graubard, Stephen. 1976. "Preface to the Issue 'Adulthood'." *Daedalus* 105 (Spring): pp. *v–viii.*

Gray, Francine du Plessix. 1977. "Nature as the Nunnery." *New York Times Book Review,* 17 July, pp. 3, 29.

Guttentag, Marcia, and Salasin, Susan. 1977. "Women, Men, and Mental Health." In *Women and Men: Changing Roles, Relationships, and Perceptions.* Edited by L. A. Cater and A. F. Scott, with W. Martyna. New York: Praeger.

Hall, Diana Long. 1976. "Biology, Sex Hormones, and Sexism in the 1920s." In *Women and Philosophy.* Edited by C. Gould and M. Wartofsky. New York: Putnam.

Hareven, Tamara K. 1975. "Family Time and Industrial Time: Family and Work in a Planned Corporation Town, 1900–1924." *Journal of Urban History* 1 (May): 365–389.

——. 1977. "The Family and Gender Roles in Historical Perspective." In *Women and Men: Changing Roles, Relationships, and Perspectives.* Edited by L. A. Cater and A. F. Scott, with W. Martyna. New York: Praeger.

Harris, Ann Sutherland. 1974. Personal communication to Janet Zollinger Giele, 1 February.

Harris, Ann Sutherland, and Nochlin, Linda. 1976. *Women Artists, 1550–1950.* New York: Knopf for Los Angeles County Museum of Art.

Hayden, Dolores. 1974. "Social Organization and Design." *Arts in Society* 11 (Spring-Summer): 125–133.

Hayden, Dolores, and Wright, Gwendolyn. 1976. "Review Essay: Architecture and Urban Planning." *Signs* 1, no. 4 (Summer): 923–933.

Heilbrun, Carolyn G. 1973. *Toward a Recognition of Androgyny.* New York: Harper and Row.

——. 1974. "Further Notes toward a Recognition of Androgyny." *Women's Studies* 2: 143–149.

Helson, Ravenna. 1974. "Inner Reality of Women." *Arts in Society* 11 (Spring-Summer): 25–36.

Hewitt, Emily C., and Hiatt, Suzanne R. 1973. *Women Priests: Yes or No?* New York: Seabury Press.

Hochschild, Arlie Russell. 1975. "The Sociology of Feeling and Emotion: Selective Possibilities." In *Another Voice.* Edited by M. Millman and R. M. Kanter. Garden City, N.Y.: Doubleday-Anchor.

Hole, Judith, and Levine, Ellen. 1971. *Rebirth of Feminism.* New York: Quadrangle.

Inkeles, Alex, and Smith, David. 1974. *Becoming Modern: Individual Change in Six Developing Countries.* Cambridge, Ma.: Harvard University Press.

Janeway, Elizabeth. 1974. *Between Myth and Morning: Women Awakening.* New York: Morrow.

Johnson, Miriam M. 1977. "Androgyny and the Maternal Principle." *School Review* 86 (November): 50–69.

Johnson, Miriam M.; Stockard, Jean; Acker, Joan; and Naffziger, Claudeen. 1975. "Expressiveness Reevaluated." *School Review* 83 (August): 617–644.

Johnson, Orna R., and Johnson, Allen. 1975. "Male/Female Relations and the Organization of Work in a Machiguenga Community." *American Ethnologist* 2 (November): 634–648.

Kagan, Jerome. 1973. "Check One: ☐ Male ☐ Female." In *The Female Experience.* Edited by *Psychology Today.* Del Mar, Ca.: Communications/Research/Machines.

Kanowitz, Leo. 1973. *Sex Roles in Law and Society.* Albuquerque, N.M.: University of New Mexico Press.

Kanter, Rosabeth Moss. 1977. *Men and Women of the Corporation.* New York: Basic Books.

Kolodny, Annette. 1976. "Review Essay: Literary Criticism." *Signs* 2, no. 2 (Winter): 404–421.

Kung, Hans. 1976. "Feminism: A New Reformation." *New York Times Magazine,* 23 May, pp. 34–35.

Leacock, Eleanor B. 1975. "Class, Commodity, and the Status of Women." In *Women Cross-Culturally: Change and Challenge.* Edited by R. R. Leavitt. The Hague: Mouton.

Leavitt, Ruby R. 1971. "Women in Other Cultures." In *Woman in Sexist Society: Studies in Power and Powerlessness.* Edited by V. Gornick and B. K. Moran. New York: Basic Books.

Lenski, Gerhard. 1966. *Power and Privilege: A Theory of Social Stratification.* New York: McGraw-Hill.

Lewis, Michael. 1973. "There Is No Unisex in the Nursery." In *The Female Experience.* Edited by *Psychology Today.* Del Mar, Ca.: Communications/Research/Machines.

Lipmen-Blumen, Jean, and Leavitt, Harold J. 1976. "Vicarious and Direct Achievement Patterns in Adulthood." *Counseling Psychologist* 6, no. 1: 26–32.

Lowenthal, Marjorie Fiske, and Weiss, Lawrence. 1976. "Intimacy and Crises in Adulthood." *Counseling Psychologist* 6, no. 1: 10-15.

Luria, Zella. 1974. "The Second Sex 25 Years Later: A Psychologist's Evaluation." Paper presented at the Berkshire Conference of Women Historians, Radcliffe College, 27 October.

Lynn, David B. 1974. *The Father: His Role in Child Development.* Monterey, Ca.: Brooks/Cole.

McClelland, David C. 1975. *Power: The Inner Experience.* New York: Irvington.

McLaughlin, Eleanor. 1975. " 'Christ My Mother': Feminine Naming and Metaphor in Medieval Spirituality." *Nashotah Review* 15 (Fall): 228-248.

———. 1976. "Male and Female in Christian Tradition: Was There a Reformation in the Sixteenth Century?" In *Male and Female: Christian Approaches to Sexuality.* Edited by R. T. Barnhouse and U. T. Holmes, III. New York: Seabury Press.

Maccoby, Eleanor E., and Jacklin, Carol N. 1974. *The Psychology of Sex Differences.* Stanford, Ca.: Stanford University Press.

Mainardi, Patricia. 1973. "Quilts: The Great American Art." *Radical America* 7, no. 1: 36-68.

Martin, M. Kay, and Voorhies, Barbara. 1975. *Female of the Species.* New York: Columbia University Press.

Martin, Wendy. 1971. "Seduced and Abandoned in the New World: The Image of Woman in American Fiction." In *Woman in Sexist Society: Studies in Power and Powerlessness.* Edited by V. Gornick and B. K. Moran. New York: Basic Books.

Mason, Karen Oppenheim. 1973. "Studying Change in Sex-role Definitions via Attitude Data." *Proceedings of the American Statistical Association, Social Statistics Section*, pp. 138-141.

Mason, Karen Oppenheim, and Bumpass, Larry L. 1973. "Women's Sex-role Attitudes in the United States, 1970." Madison, Wi.: Working paper for the Center for Demography and Ecology, University of Wisconsin.

Mason, Karen Oppenheim; Czajka, John L.; and Arber, Sara. 1976. "Change in U.S. Women's Sex-role Attitudes, 1964-1974." *American Sociological Review* 41 (August): 573-596.

Masson, Margaret W. 1976. "The Typology of the Female as a Model for the Regenerate: Puritan Preaching, 1690-1730." *Signs* 2, no. 2 (Winter): 304-315.

Media Report to Women, vol. 1. 1972-1973. Washington, D.C.: Dr. Donna Allen.

Media Report to Women, vol. 2. 1974. Washington, D.C.: Dr. Donna Allen.

Mellen, Joan. 1973. *Women and Their Sexuality in the New Film.* New York: Dell.

Miller, Jean Baker. 1973. *Psychoanalysis and Women.* Baltimore, Md.: Penguin.

———. 1976. *Toward a New Psychology of Women.* Boston: Beacon Press.

Millett, Kate. 1970. *Sexual Politics.* Garden City, N.Y.: Doubleday.

Moers, Ellen. 1976. *Literary Women: The Great Writers*. Garden City, N.Y.: Doubleday.

Money, John, and Ehrhardt, Anke. 1972. *Man and Woman, Boy and Girl*. Baltimore, Md.: Johns Hopkins University Press.

Morgan, Edmund S. 1944; 1966. *The Puritan Family: Essays on Religion and Domestic Relations in Seventeenth-Century New England*. New York: Harper and Row.

Myrdal, Alva. 1941; 1968. *Nation and Family: The Swedish Experiment in Democratic Family and Population Policy*. Cambridge, Ma.: MIT Press.

——. 1976. Interview with Janet Zollinger Giele, 5 March.

Neal, Sister Marie Augusta. 1976. "A Sociological Perspective on the Moral Issues of Sexuality Today." In *Sexuality and Contemporary Catholicism*. Edited by F. Bockle and J.-M. Pohier. New York: Seabury Press.

Neugarten, Bernice. 1976. "Adaptation and the Life Cycle." *Counseling Psychologist* 6, no. 1: 16-21.

Nochlin, Linda. 1971. "Why Are There No Great Women Artists?" In *Woman in Sexist Society: Studies in Power and Powerlessness*. Edited by V. Gornick and B. K. Moran. New York: Basic Books.

——. 1974. "How Feminism in the Arts Can Implement Cultural Change." *Arts in Society* 11 (Spring-Summer): 81-89.

Olin, Ulla. 1976. "A Case for Women as Co-managers: The Family as a General Model of Human Social Organization." In *Women and World Development*. Edited by I. Tinker and M. B. Bramsen. Washington, D.C.: Overseas Development Council.

Orenstein, Gloria Feman. 1975. "Review Essay: Art History." *Signs* 1, no. 2 (Winter): 505-525.

Ortner, Sherry B. 1974. "Is Female to Male as Nature Is to Culture?" In *Woman, Culture, and Society*. Edited by M. Z. Rosaldo and L. Lamphere. Stanford, Ca.: Stanford University Press.

Pagels, Elaine H. 1976. "What Became of God the Mother? Conflicting Images of God in Early Christianity." *Signs* 2, no. 2 (Winter): 293-303.

Parsons, Talcott, and Bales, Robert F. 1955. *Family, Socialization, and Interaction Process*. New York: The Free Press.

Parsons, Talcott, and Shils, Edward A. 1951. *Toward a General Theory of Action*. Cambridge, Ma.: Harvard University Press.

Parvey, Constance. 1974. "The Theology and Leadership of Women in the New Testament." In *Religion and Sexism*. Edited by R. R. Ruether. New York: Simon and Schuster.

Petersen, Karen, and Wilson, J. J. 1976. *Women Artists: Recognition and Reappraisal from the Early Middle Ages to the Twentieth Century*. New York: Harper and Row.

Plaskow, Judith. 1976. "On Carol Christ on Margaret Atwood: Some Theological Reflections." *Signs* 2, no. 2 (Winter): 331-339.

Pleck, Joseph H. 1975. "Masculinity-Femininity: Current and Alternative Paradigms." *Sex Roles* 1 (June): 161-178.

———. 1976. "The Male Sex Role: Definitions, Problems, and Sources of Change." *Journal of Social Issues* 32, no. 3: 155–164.

———. 1977a. "The Psychology of Sex Roles: Traditional and New Views." In *Women and Men: Changing Roles, Relationships, and Perceptions.* Edited by L. A. Cater and A. F. Scott, with W. Martyna. New York: Praeger.

———. 1977b. "Males' Traditional Attitudes toward Women: Conceptual Issues in Research." In *The Psychology of Women: New Directions in Research.* Edited by J. Sherman and F. Denmark. New York: Psychological Dimensions.

Presbyterian Panel. 1975. "Sexism in the Church: Presbyterian Viewpoints Concerning the Role of Women in Society and in the Church." New York: United Presbyterian Church, U.S.A.

Rebecca, Meda; Hefner, Robert; and Oleshansky, Barbara. 1976. "A Model of Sex-role Transcendence." *Journal of Social Issues* 32, no. 3: 197–206.

Redbook. 1972. "How Do You Feel About Being a Woman? Results of a *Redbook* Questionnaire" (background paper). New York: Redbook.

Research News. 1973. "An Instance of Sexual Double Standard in Renaissance Art." 23 (June): 17–18.

Richards, Audrey I. 1950. "Some Types of Family Structure among the Central Bantu." In *African Systems of Kinship and Marriage.* Edited by A. R. Radcliffe-Brown and D. Forde. London: Oxford University Press.

Roberts, Helene. 1974. "The Inside, the Surface, the Mass: Some Recurring Images of Women." *Women's Studies* 2: 289–307.

Roper Organization. 1974. *The Virginia Slims American Women's Opinion Poll. Vol. 3: A Survey of the Attitudes of Women on Marriage, Divorce, the Family, and America's Changing Sexual Morality.* New York: Roper Organization.

Rossi, Alice S. 1968. "Transition to Parenthood." *Journal of Marriage and the Family* 30: 26–39.

———. 1969; 1976. "Sex Equality: The Beginnings of Ideology." *Humanist,* September-October, pp. 3–6, 16. In *Beyond Sex-role Stereotypes: Readings toward a Psychology of Androgyny.* Edited by A. G. Kaplan and J. P. Bean. Boston: Little, Brown.

———. 1977. "A Biosocial Perspective on Parenting." *Daedalus* 106 (Spring): 1–31.

Ruether, Rosemary Radford. 1974. "Misogynism and Virginal Feminism in the Fathers of the Church." In *Religion and Sexism.* Edited by R. R. Ruether. New York: Simon and Schuster.

———. 1975. *New Woman/New Earth: Sexist Ideologies and Human Liberation.* New York: Seabury Press.

Russell, Letty M. 1974. *Human Liberation in a Feminist Perspective—A Theology.* Philadelphia: Westminster Press.

Sacks, Karen. 1974. "Engels Revisited: Women, the Organization of Production, and Private Property." In *Woman, Culture, and Society.* Edited by M. Z. Rosaldo and L. Lamphere. Stanford, Ca.: Stanford University Press.

Saikowski, Charlotte. 1976. "Regaining America's Unity of Purpose." *Christian Science Monitor*, 22 April, pp. 16–17.

Sanday, Peggy R. 1973. "Toward a Theory of the Status of Women." *American Anthropologist* 75 (October): 1682–1700.

———. 1974. "Female Status in the Public Domain." In *Woman, Culture, and Society*. Edited by M. Z. Rosaldo and L. Lamphere. Stanford, Ca.: Stanford University Press.

Scott, Joan W., and Tilly, Louise A. 1975. "Women's Work and the Family in Nineteenth-century Europe." *Comparative Studies in Society and History* 17 (January): 36–64.

Shainess, Natalie. 1969. "Images of Woman: Past and Present, Overt and Obscured." *American Journal of Psychiatry* 23 (January): 77–97.

Showalter, Elaine. 1971. "Women Writers and the Double Standard." In *Woman in Sexist Society: Studies in Power and Powerlessness*. Edited by V. Gornick and B. K. Moran. New York: Basic Books.

———. 1975. "Review Essay: Literary Criticism." *Signs* 1, no. 2 (Winter): 435–460.

Smelser, Neil J. 1959. *Social Change in the Industrial Revolution*. Chicago: University of Chicago Press.

Spacks, Patricia Meyer. 1975. *The Female Imagination*. New York: Knopf.

———. 1976a. "Only Personal: Some Functions of Fiction." *Yale Review* 65 (June): 528–543.

——— 1976b. "The Art of Life." *Hudson Review* 29 (Summer): 283–292.

———. 1977. "Women's Stories, Women's Selves." *Hudson Review* 30 (Spring): 29–46.

Stanley, Nancy E. 1971. "Federal Communications Law and Women's Rights: Women in the Wasteland Fight Back." *Hastings Law Journal* 23 (November): 15–53.

Stimpson, Catharine R. 1974. "The Androgyne and the Homosexual." *Women's Studies* 2: 237–248.

———. 1977. "Sex, Gender, and American Culture." In *Women and Men: Changing Roles, Relationships, and Perceptions*. Edited by L. A. Cater and A. F. Scott, with W. Martyna. New York: Praeger.

Strainchamps, Ethel, ed. 1974. *Rooms with No View: A Woman's Guide to the Man's World of the Media*. New York: Harper and Row.

Stricker, George. 1977. "Implications of Research for Psychotherapeutic Treatment of Women." *American Psychologist* 32 (January): 14–22.

Suppan, Adolph. 1974. "Developing Careers in the Arts." *Arts in Society* 11 (Spring-Summer): 92.

Tanner, Nancy. 1974. "Matrifocality in Indonesia and Africa and among Black Americans." In *Woman, Culture, and Society*. Edited by M. Z. Rosaldo and L. Lamphere. Stanford, Ca.: Stanford University Press.

Tavard, George H. 1973. *Woman in Christian Tradition*. Notre Dame, In.: University of Notre Dame Press.

Time. 1972. "Flight from Fluff." 20 March, pp. 48–53.

Tinker, Irene. 1976. "The Adverse Impact of Development on Women." In *Women and World Development.* Edited by I. Tinker and M. B. Bramsen. Washington, D.C.: Overseas Development Council.

Toennies, Ferdinand. 1887; 1940. *Fundamental Concepts of Sociology (Gemeinschaft und Gesellschaft).* Translated and supplemented by C. P. Loomis. New York: American Book.

Tresemer, David. 1975. "Assumptions Made about Gender Roles." In *Another Voice.* Edited by M. Millman and R. M. Kanter. Garden City, N.Y.: Doubleday-Anchor.

Tuchman, Gaye. 1975. "Women and the Creation of Culture." In *Another Voice.* Edited by M. Millman and R. M. Kanter. Garden City, N.Y.: Doubleday-Anchor.

———. 1976. "Ridicule, Advocacy, and Professionalism: Newspaper Reporting about a Social Movement." Paper presented at the annual meeting of the American Sociological Association, New York City, September.

Ulanov, Ann Belford. 1976. "C. G. Jung on Male and Female." In *Male and Female: Christian Approaches to Sexuality.* Edited by R. T. Barnhouse and U. T. Holmes, III. New York: Seabury Press.

Wayne, June. 1974. "The Male Artist as Stereotypical Female." *Arts in Society* 11 (Spring-Summer): 106–113.

Weber, Max. 1947. *The Theory of Social and Economic Organization.* Translated by A. M. Henderson and T. Parsons. New York: The Free Press.

White, Barbara Ehrlich. 1976. "A 1974 Perspective: Why Women's Studies in Art and Art History?" *Art Journal* 35 (Summer): 340–344.

Whiting, Beatrice B. 1963. *Six Cultures, Studies of Child Rearing.* New York: Wiley.

Wilson, Jane. 1977. "Hollywood Flirts with the New Woman." *New York Times,* 29 May, sec. 2, pp. 1ff.

Wilson, Joan Hoff. 1976. "The Illusion of Change: Women and the American Revolution." In *The American Revolution.* Edited by A. Young. De Kalb, Il.: Northern Illinois University Press.

Women and Holy Orders. 1966. Report of a commission appointed by the Archbishops of Canterbury and York. London: Church Information Office.

Women on Words and Images. 1975. *Channeling Children: Sex Stereotyping in Prime-Time TV.* Princeton, N.J.: Women on Words and Images.

Zaretsky, Eli. 1976. *Capitalism, the Family, and Personal Life.* New York: Harper and Row.

Index

NAME INDEX

Abbott, Edith, 76, 87, 92, 131, 251
Abbott, Grace, 48, 76
Abeles, Ronald, 261, 297
Aberle, D. F., 4, 36
Abzug, Bella, 63, 198, 210
Acker, Joan, 300, 364
Addams, Jane, 76, 78
Adelman, Irma, 106, 131
Ahlum, Carol, 280, 300
Alexander, Ralph A., 131
Alexander, Shana, 77
Alland, Alexander, Jr., 6, 36
Allport, Gordon, 109, 131
Almond, Gabriel, 52, 54, 60, 81
Alper, Thelma, 259, 296
American Association for the Advancement of Science, 32, 37
American Association of University Professors (A.A.U.P.), 287
American Bar Association, 71-72, 81, 247, 297
American Civil Liberties Union (A.C.L.U.), 72
American Federation of Labor-Congress of Industrial Organizations (AFL-CIO), 49, 71, 75
American Federation of Teachers' Women's Rights Committee, 44
American Telephone and Telegraph (A.T. and T.), 69, 72, 93, 101-102
Andersen, Kristi, 54, 60, 66, 81
Andrews, Susan, 341, 360
Anguissola, Sofonisba, 343
Anselm of Canterbury, Saint, 321
Arber, Sara, 183, 365
Association of Governing Boards of Universities and Colleges, 247, 297
Astin, Helen S., 37, 249, 297
Atkinson, J. W., 301
Atwood, Margaret, 318, 325, 360
Austen, Jane, 324

Baas, Bernard M., 104, 131

Babco, Eleanor L., 304
Babcock, Barbara A., 29, 37, 224, 227, 235
Bahr, Stephen J., 154, 169, 172
Baird, Leonard L., 254, 261, 297
Bakan, David, 326, 327, 352, 360
Bakke, Alan, 287
Balch, Emily, 78
Bales, R. F., 94, 136, 229, 239, 255, 302, 355, 366
Bane, Mary Jo, 140, 179, 230, 235
Banks, Joseph A., 22, 37
Banks, Olive, 22, 37
Banks, Ruby, 221
Bardwick, Judith, 128, 131, 255, 297
Barnett, Jeanne K., 158, 182
Barnett, Rosalind C., 356, 360
Bart, Pauline B., 23, 37, 352, 360
Barth, Michael C., 235
Baruch, Grace K., 356, 360
Baruch, Rhoda, 98, 131, 297
Baxter, Kay, 340, 360
Bayer, Alan E., 249, 297
Bayh, Birch, 217
Bazin, Nancy T., 326, 360
Beard, Mary R., 142, 179
Beare, Nikki, 62
Becker, Gary, 103, 131
Beecher, Catherine, 92, 143, 179
Behrens, William W., 39
Bell, Carolyn Shaw, 89, 124, 131, 139, 140, 179, 354, 360
Bell, Daniel, 10, 18, 37
Bellah, Robert, 333, 360
Bem, Sandra L., 326, 327, 352, 360
Bengis, Ingrid, 27, 37, 113
Bennis, Warren G., 131
Bentley, Sally, 337, 360
Benus, Jacob, 135
Berelson, Bernard, 32, 37
Berger, Bennett M., 176, 179
Bergmann, Barbara R., 104, 106, 131
Berkeley, Ellen, 112, 131
Berkner, Lutz, 179
Berkov, Beth, 23, 40, 149, 150, 185
Berley, Edith Radlich, 232, 235
Bermant, Gordon, 227, 235
Bernard, Jessie, 1, 3, 23, 37, 95, 177, 179, 188, 210-212, 227,

SUBJECT INDEX